Japan in the Bluegrass

Japan in the Bluegrass

EDITED BY P.P. KARAN

THE UNIVERSITY PRESS OF KENTUCKY

Publication of this volume was made possible in part
by a grant from the National Endowment for the Humanities.

Editorial and Sales Offices: The University Press of Kentucky
663 South Limestone Street, Lexington, Kentucky 40508–4008

05 04 03 02 01   5 4 3 2 1

Library of Congress Cataloging-in-Publication Data

Karan, Pradyumna P. (Pradyumna Prasad)
  Japan in the Bluegrass / P.P. Karan.
    p. cm.
Includes bibliographical references and index.
  ISBN 0-8131-2197-3 (cloth : alk. paper)
  1. Automobile industry and trade—Kentucky. 2. Investments,
Japanese—Kentucky. 3. National characteristics, Japanese.
4. Japan—Foreign economic relations—United States. 5. United
States—Foreign economic relations—Japan. I. Title.
  HD9710.U53 K45 2001
  338.8'87292'09769—dc21   00-012374

Contents

Figures

Tables

Preface

THIS BOOK IS THE RESULT of a research project sponsored by the Japan Studies Program at the University of Kentucky, with the participation of an interdisciplinary group of scholars from Eastern Kentucky University, Northern Kentucky University, Nagoya University, and Hokuriku University, and representatives of Japanese and American businesses, state and local government agencies, the Japan/America Society of Kentucky, and investment bankers and lawyers.

The papers were originally presented at a conference at the University of Kentucky in April 1999. The conference was inaugurated by former Japanese Prime Minister Morihiro Hosokawa. It began by examining the pattern of Japanese investments in Kentucky and then moved to a discussion of social, economic, and environmental impacts of the investment on the Bluegrass region. The papers were revised and rewritten for this book.

This book presents research results of fourteen social scientists from Japan and the United States—six geographers, three political scientists, two sociologists, an economist, a planner, and an environmental scientist—who have many years of research experience in their respective disciplines. Their research findings provide a unique interdisciplinary approach exploring the impact of Japan on the Bluegrass State.

This is the first comprehensive study examining the social, cultural, economic, and environmental impacts of Japan's investment in a region by an interdisciplinary group of Japanese and American scholars. Most studies of foreign investments in the United States and abroad have focused only on economic and employment aspects at the state or national scale, ignoring the important social, cultural, and environmental impacts at regional and local levels.

Many people contributed to the success of the conference and this volume, and I would like to acknowledge the support here of Doug Slaymaker (Japan Studies), Kristin Stapleton (History), Greg Waller (English), and Larry Burmeister (Sociology), along with Julie Quinn Blyth, executive director, and Stephen D. Cecil, president, of the Japan/America Society of Kentucky. I want to thank all my colleagues in the Japan Studies Program and the Department of Geography for generously sharing their time and professional experience throughout the research project.

I acknowledge the assistance of Richard Gilbreath, director of the University of Kentucky Cartographic Laboratory, who prepared all the illustrations and maps for conference presentations. The maps for this volume were drafted by Hui Xie, a graduate student in geography, and Tony Zerhusen and Jason Litteral, both undergraduates in the Department of Geography, under the able guidance of Richard Gilbreath.

This book has benefited from several sessions with executives and workers in Japanese factories, local government officials, and residents of Kentucky communities that have Japanese firms. They were generous in providing information and answering numerous questions. In particular, I want to thank Taiji Hasegawa, president, Larry Royalty, executive vice president, and Konomi Kaji of Hitachi Automotive Products (USA); Stephen J. Hesselbrock, general manager, and Hideki Torii of Trim Masters; Kenichiro Imasu, president and CEO of Matsushita Appliance Corporation of America; Ted Ikeda, president, Rick Fields, human resources manager, and Jason Cartwright, production engineer, Matsushita Electric Motor Corporation of America; Yu Saito, executive vice president, Denyo Manufacturing Corporation; Larry Green, Bardstown city administrator; Yusitaka Mizumoto, president, Universal Fasteners; Herb Krase, vice president of administration, Toyotetsu America; Masaaki Kushida, president, and Massamichi Danjo, vice president, Y H America; Brian Deatrick of Cardinal Industrial Contracting; and Mayor Carol Walters of Harrodsburg. Responsibility for the book's contents, however, is solely with the authors.

Professor Wilford A. Bladen read the drafts of the book and offered many suggestions for improvement. Above all I thank the Japanese and American contributors for their research, writing, and dedication to the research enterprise of which this volume is a part.

Funding for the research project and field research in Kentucky communities was generously provided by the University of Kentucky College of Arts and Sciences and University of Kentucky Research and Graduate Studies.

A Note on Terms

THE TOYOTA PRODUCTION MANAGEMENT SYSTEM entails the use of *kanban* (or signboards) attached to work in progress at the assembly line. It reduces both physical and procedural wastes and increases efficiency through better management of time, space, and motions involved in the manufacturing process. When a subassembly is completed, its signboard is detached and returned to the previous workstation. Slow pace of signboards released from a workstation indicates a bottleneck at the station. It is a sign for workers to move from other stations to that one. Also, a lot of signboards accumulating at a workstation means a bottleneck forming at that station, and signals need to hasten the work. Kanban is a means to implement Just-in-Time (JIT) delivery of parts needed for automobile assembly. The suppliers deliver quality-guaranteed parts according to the kanban inventory control system, and those parts are used immediately rather than placed in stock. Under this system, suppliers have to ship their products several times a day. The parts have to arrive just in time for assembly. Kanban requires the development of a finely turned subcontracting system to meet Toyota's requirements. In addition to its own assembly line, Toyota also requires its subcontractors in Kentucky and elsewhere to use this system. The kanban system has enabled major reduction in the use of space on assembly lines, and it economizes on Japan's scarce space resource. Although developed in Japan, the kanban system is now transforming manufacturing enterprises throughout the world.

Keiretsu is a family of firms normally controlled by a large bank, with links to a common trading company and several major first-tier manufacturers spread over a range of industries.

Toyota Motor Corporation (TMC) was formed in 1982 by the merger of Toyota Motor Company and Toyota Motor Sales Company. The Toyota Group of companies comprise many firms and businesses, including wholly owned plants in many countries. In this book, the Toyota plant in Georgetown-Scott County, Kentucky, known as the Toyota Motor Manufacturing, Kentucky (TMMK) is also referred to as the Scott County plant and the Georgetown plant; Toyota North American headquarters at Erlanger, Kentucky, is called Toyota Motor Manufacturing, North America (TMMNA). In chapter 5 TMC refers to only large automobile plants in Toyota City, Japan.

Unless otherwise indicated, all employment figures in Japanese compaies in Kentucky in this book are for the year 1999 as reported in Kentucky Cabinet for Economic Development, *Announced/Reported Japanese Industrial Investment in Kentucky (At Least 10% Foreign Owned)*, 1999. The spelling of Japanese company names are also based on the above publication.

Japan and Kentucky

P.P. KARAN

UNTIL THE EARLY 1980S, Kentuckians had formed most of their impressions of Japan on painful memories of World War II. And the Japanese knew of Kentucky only as the home of a famous colonel and his chicken. Time has changed that. In the years since Toyota announced it would locate a facility in Kentucky, the cultural influences of each place have been visited on the other in significant ways.

Japan, an urban society with 126 million people living in an area 4 percent as large as the United States, was virtually closed to outsiders until 1868. Their culture, in many respects, remains somewhat baffling to Westerners. People bow instead of shake hands. They tend to see themselves as members of a group rather than as individuals. Although English is taught in schools, the average person generally does not speak it.

In Japan, of course, "chicken" and "Kentucky" still are commonly associated. KFC Corporation—Kentucky's famous chicken restaurant chain—is one of a handful of U.S. business success stories in Japan that includes Coca-Cola and IBM. Now, people in Japan are hearing Hank Williams on the radio; smoking Marlboro, Kent, and Lucky Strike cigarettes; and drinking Early Times, I.W. Harper, and Maker's Mark whiskeys.

Kentuckians, meanwhile, have become more familiar with Japanese culture, customs, and foods since the introduction to the state of Toyota and other Japanese companies. Small Japanese markets are common in several Kentucky cities, Japanese condiments line supermarket shelves, and Japanese restaurants and sushi bars serve Kentucky patrons. Increasing numbers of secondary schools and colleges in Kentucky offer courses in Japanese language and culture. Nearly three thousand Japanese live in Kentucky, and the relationship between Japan and Kentucky has come a long way since it began in earnest in the mid-1980s.

In July 1985, Toyota, following the lead of Nissan, Honda, Mazda, and Mitsubishi, announced that it was initiating a search for an appropriate site in the United States on which it would locate an assembly plant. On December 11, 1985, Kentucky's Governor Martha Layne Collins stood before an

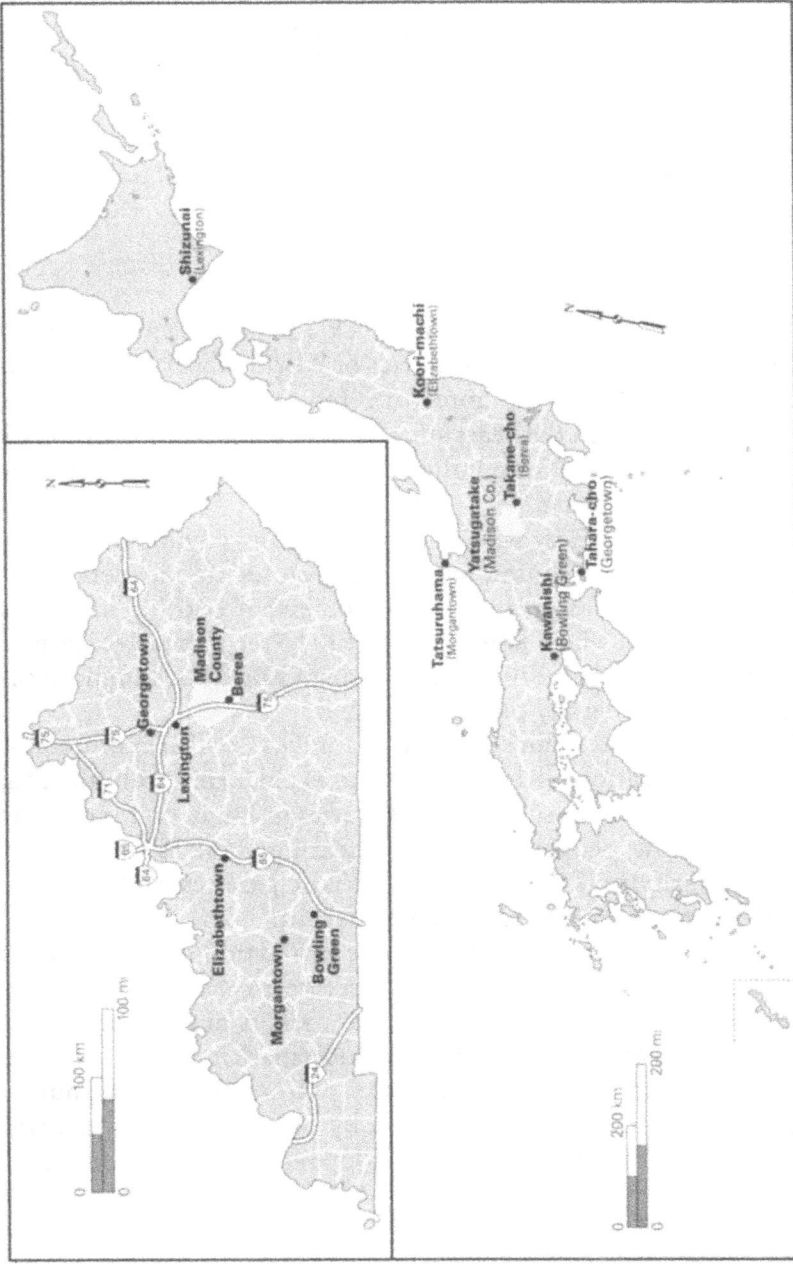

Fig. 1.1. Sister cities in Japan and Kentucky.

assemblage of top state political figures, prominent Kentucky business leaders, local politicians, and a host of reporters and news cameras to announce that Toyota Motor Corporation would build its first wholly owned assembly plant in rural Scott County, Kentucky. It was the culmination of the state's three-year effort to lure an assembly plant to Kentucky. The state had lost the Honda plant to Ohio in 1979; Nissan had located its facility in Tennessee in 1980; Mazda had formed a joint venture with Ford in Michigan in 1984; and in 1985 Mitsubishi had formed a joint venture with Chrysler in Illinois. Toyota was viewed as the state's last chance to recruit a major Japanese automaker, and Kentucky won.

Geographers Bladen and Karan discuss the pattern of Japanese investment in Kentucky within the context of Japanese investment activity in the United States in chapter 2. The major factors entering into the Japanese's decision to establish plants in Kentucky are analyzed. Most of Kentucky is a great expanse of farmland, dimpled by woodlands with flowering dogwood and crabapple trees and pocketed by small towns that are islands of manufacturing. Wide, smooth highways meet in Louisville, Lexington, Covington, and Elizabethtown and branch to all points of the Midwest and South, including auto assembly plants in other states. Along these highway spokes, small-town mayors, private citizens, and chambers of commerce have worked together to convince teams of Japanese company executives that their towns are ideal locations for factories. Of course, good location is a nice asset, as Bladen and Karan point out, but competition among states, and cities within Kentucky, is fierce. Rural Kentuckians have been forced to break out of small-town molds and jump into new roles as global traders, translators, and negotiators. Only a few years ago, attracting international trade, industry, and investment was left to state and federal governments. Not anymore. Marketing savvy and geopolitical sophistication have soaked deeply into places like Harrodsburg, Richmond, Russellville, Hopkinsville, and Bardstown. Whereas mayoral trade trips to Japan once may have been criticized as junkets, they have become almost routine. Full-time economic development professionals have been hired to run far-flung marketing campaigns and to coordinate local and state efforts.

The important roles of state and local governments in attracting foreign investment to Kentucky is discussed in chapter 3 by David Potter, a political scientist specializing in Japanese politics and policy. One thing Governor Collins omitted from her speech welcoming Toyota's decision to locate in Kentucky was that the state had to *pay* Toyota to locate in Scott County. Kentucky attracted Toyota through a hostile process (known as a bidding war) that pitted state against state in a battle fought with financial incentives. Kentucky's use of financial incentives to lure Toyota was not without precedent. In the 1980s direct state incentives emerged as a major element of formulating economic development programs in many states. The process of

The site of Toyota Motor Manufacturing, Kentucky (TMMK) near Georgetown in rural Scott County. The State of Kentucky paid more than $10 million for purchase of this land, $20 million to prepare the plant site, $10.2 million to build water and gas lines, $12.2 million for a wastewater facility, and $32 million to make highway improvements. An additional $55 million was spent by the state for training and education, as well as $7.2 million to build a training center. The money spent by the state on incentives and interest totaled more than $305 million. (Photograph by P.P. Karan)

negotiating and formulating the incentives package, due to the nature of the exercise, was generally conducted in all cases without public or legislative involvement by a few cabinet-level officials. In several states, including Kentucky, controversy centered around the size of the incentives package and when or if the state would recoup its investment. As is discussed later in this volume (chapter 7), Kentucky's incentives strategy more than recouped its investment with substantial spin-offs from Toyota. In the scholarly debate that has sought to understand Japanese foreign direct investment, comparatively little attention has been paid to a key two-part question: how do state governments negotiate with multinational corporations, and what characteristics of the bargaining environment constrain their ability to secure agreements with the multinationals that are also acceptable to their publics? Potter uses a two-level bargaining game model in international negotiations as a device for thinking about the characteristics of state government–multinational corporation negotiations.

Among other factors influencing Toyota's interest in building an automobile assembly plant in America was the trade friction and protectionist trade sentiment growing in the United States at that time. U.S. sales trends had turned in favor of Japanese small-car imports, and U.S. automakers were unable to retool existing operations due to high interest rates and a stagnant market. The "adversarial trade policy" that Japan's Ministry of International Trade and Industry (MITI) had effectively promoted for more than two decades was widely debated in the United States. The policy involved targeting industries such as automobiles, electronics, and engineering firms, which formed the major segment of the U.S. industrial base, through creation of an export manufacturing program, designed by MITI in conjunction with the Japanese industries. By allowing the private ownership of capital and property combined with state direction, Japanese industries had both state protection and promotion of capital ventures which American corporations did not enjoy. Japan was called a "capitalist development state," in which the state provided opportunities for entrepreneurship and created markets with private ownership of capital and property (Johnson 1982). In contrast, the United States has private ownership and private control. The differences allowed Japan to formulate and implement successful economic development policies to exploit weaknesses in the American political economy. The dislocation which the Japanese policies created in the United States escalated trade hostility and resulted, in part, in calls for Japan to reform its trade policies by reducing institutional barriers to American goods and to encourage domestic spending. There were calls for import restrictions on Japanese automobiles. In 1981, MITI instituted a voluntary restriction of exports to the United States to last until 1984. Japan extended its voluntary export restrictions of automobiles to 1985. As noted in *Toyota: A History of the First 50 Years,* for Toyota "setting up production facilities in the United States became a matter of the utmost urgency" to maintain its share of the American market (Toyota 1988, 329).

Kentucky, along with other state administrations, began making overtures in 1985 to the largest Japanese automobile corporation seeking to establish an assembly plant in America. Offers of tax abatements, low-interest loans, land, employee training, and other economic incentives from various states and municipalities were submitted to Toyota headquarters in Japan. By November 1985, Toyota had received offers of economic incentives from thirty-six states which considered investment by Japanese manufacturing concerns to bring the greatest investment returns. Being the last major Japanese automaker to come to America, Toyota had witnessed the dramatic escalation of the value of incentives packages awarded to other Japanese firms—from $33 million received by Nissan from Tennessee in 1980 to $83 million given to Mitsubishi by Illinois in 1985. Kentucky offered Toyota an extraordinary incentives package, the largest incentives package yet awarded to a foreign automobile corporation—a package valued at $147 million in direct state investment and $320 million when indirect costs are included. Toyota agreed to locate its first wholly owned assembly plant near Georgetown, in rural Scott County, to make an $800 million investment, to produce two hundred thousand cars per year, and to employ directly some three thousand workers.

Both Kentucky and Toyota approached the site selection process from relatively powerful bargaining positions. Possessing knowledge based on lessons drawn from the experiences of other states in their successful recruiting of Japanese firms and analyses of principal determinants used by Japanese automobile makers for site selection, Kentucky approached Toyota from a relatively strong position. Also, Toyota made a conscious decision to use the experiences of other Japanese transplants and to draw lessons from them to strengthen their American production strategy in regard to site selection and negotiating position.

Toyota's North American manufacturing headquarters in Erlanger, Kentucky, opened in 1996, and a quality and production engineering laboratory opened at the site in 1998. By May 2000 Toyota had added eighty thousand square feet to its headquarters in Erlanger to make room for added work that was done previously in Japan and Georgetown. With the $15.4 million expansion, the staff has grown to seven hundred and the total investment at Erlanger to $68 million.

The Erlanger office handles purchasing, production control, finance, and engineering for Toyota's eight North American plants, including the seventy-eight hundred–employee Georgetown plant. North American purchases through Erlanger exceed $8 billion a year from 500 companies—150 of them in Kentucky, Ohio, and Indiana. Toyota's purchases from minority-owned businesses should approach $500 million by 2002. In contrast, Ford already spends $2.5 billion a year with minority suppliers. Toyota encourages its suppliers to buy at least 5 percent of parts, materials, and services from minority-owned businesses. Other automakers, such as Ford, *require* their suppliers to meet the 5 percent minimum. The emphasis at Toyota is on sound business fundamentals—quality, price, timeliness, integrity—to keep customers.

Toyota Motor Corporation (Toyota Jidosha) is a global enterprise with headquarters in Toyota, a city with a population of 332,000, in central Aichi prefecture in central Honshu. Unryu Suganuma, a professor in the Faculty of Law at Hokuriku University, analyzes the geography of this multinational corporation (chapter 4) whose first plant was built in 1937 in Toyota City. Today it is the largest automaker in Japan and the third largest in the world with more than a dozen plants in Japan and more than thirty plants overseas in North America, South America, Asia, and Europe. The company began in 1933 as the Automobile Department of the Toyoda Automatic Loom Works and became independent of the parent firm in 1937. The company's first prototype passenger car, the Model A1, was completed in May 1935. World War II left the company in economic ruin, but with the introduction of the Toyopet Crown in 1955, passenger car production began in earnest. In the

TMMK employs nearly eight thousand, and average employee income is $61,000 (1997). Toyota's investment in Kentucky amounts to $4.5 billion. TMMK produces Camrys, Avalons, and the Sienna minivan; and builds V-5 and four-cylinder engines and powertrain parts. Annually, it produces more than 400,000 vehicles and 350,000 engines. (Photograph by P.P. Karan)

following years, new models were added in rapid succession as motorization took hold in Japan. In 1987 Toyota became the fourth automaker to surpass the sixty million mark for cumulative domestic production, following General Motors, Ford, and Chrysler of the United States.

Several other companies are affiliated with Toyota Motor Corporation. Among these are Toyota Auto Body Company (Toyota Shatai) and Toyota Tsusho. Toyota Auto Body is an automobile body manufacturer incorporated in 1945, with headquarters in the city of Kariya, Aichi prefecture. It manufactures the bodies of Toyota Motor's small cars and is developing special-purpose and multipurpose cars. Toyota Tsusho is a comprehensive trading company with headquarters in Nagoya and Tokyo. It is a core member of the Toyota group of Toyota Motor Manufacturing Corporation. It was incorporated in 1948 and has more than fifty overseas business offices and nearly a dozen overseas subsidiaries in forty-five countries. The company has diversified into telecommunications and new materials and has equity interest in a number of overseas joint ventures.

Toyota Motor Corporation's one hundred millionth domestically made vehicle rolled off the production line on October 4, 1999, at Motomachi

Plant. The milestone came slightly more than sixty-four years after the first Toyota rolled off the production line at the Toyoda Automatic Loom Works in August 1935. It comes slightly less than fourteen years after the company produced its fifty millionth vehicle built in Japan in 1986.

As Japan's top car manufacturer, Toyota has huge technological advantages, as Dr. Suganuma points out. In 1984 it became the first among domestic rivals to market an affordable sports car with a rear-engine layout. In 1998 it became the world's first automaker to mass produce a hybrid car, Prius, powered alternately by a conventional gasoline engine and a self-charging electric motor. Toyota's success in the global market comes from the production of designs and technologies that meet the demands of different regions. The hybrid Prius was entirely designed by the company's Calty Design Research in California.

Yuichiro Nishimura and Japan's leading urban geographer, Kohei Okamoto of Nogoya University, discuss the social impact of Toyota Motor Corporation's seven large plants on Toyota City in chapter 5. They discuss the influence of the Toyota production system on the local community. Since automobile manufacturing is a great assembly industry, a lot of parts suppliers are organized around the assembly plant. It is also a labor-intensive industry, and a lot of workers must be allocated efficiently around the production system. Toyota introduced the "just-in-time" system to control parts production and delivery as well as to arrange human resources in the area surrounding Toyota City.

In 1995 Toyota changed the system of day and night shifts into a sequential system (6:30 A.M. to 3:15 P.M. and 4:15 P.M. to 1:00 A.M.) to reduce production cost. Nishimura and Okamoto discuss the impact of the shift system change on the local community, where the economy and the lives of the residents are closely tied to the automobile industry.

Two Georgetown, Kentucky, residents, Janet W. Patton, a political scientist, and H. Milton Patton, a geographer and planner, discuss in chapter 6 patterns of growth and change in Georgetown since the arrival of the Toyota plant. Toyota City in Japan, like Georgetown in Kentucky, was an agricultural town long before it became an industrial city, and the municipal land areas of both cities still retain tracts of agricultural land. Like many of the people of Georgetown, Kiichiro Toyoda, founder of Toyota Motor Manufacturing Company, wished not to disturb the agricultural heritage of the area around Toyota City (then known as Koromo). Local people and leaders in both Toyota City and Georgetown welcomed the automobile production plants, viewing them as opportunities to revitalize rural economies which had become depressed. In Georgetown, Toyota's biggest impact has been to cushion the regional economy from the downturn faced by many regions in the United States in the 1980s.

In both cities the automobile industry has brought increased prosperity.

In Toyota City company housing for Toyota's employees was built near the plants. In Georgetown, most of the employees commute to work from various communities in the Bluegrass region of central Kentucky. In both towns Toyota has been an excellent corporate citizen, supporting health, education, sports, parks, and cultural activities. In Georgetown the arrival of a powerful global corporation only temporarily threw the community off balance, but several key individuals and activities, which are discussed by the Pattons, helped shape the process by which the town responded to the new challenges as the home of Toyota Motor Manufacturing, Kentucky. Fears that growth and change would destroy the way of life in Georgetown, the authors point out, have not been realized.

Internationally renowned economist Charles F. Haywood offers a rigorous analysis of the economic impact of Toyota in chapter 7. Toyota employs seventy-eight hundred persons (December 1999) at its plant in Georgetown. In 1985 the State of Kentucky offered incentives worth $147 million to lure Toyota's plant to Georgetown. Fifteen years later, the state was earning a 36.8 percent return on that investment, according to Haywood's research. Haywood looked at the cost of the incentives and the cost of borrowing $147 million. Over twenty years, Haywood points out, the state will pay about $305 million. He then compares those costs with the amount of tax revenue the state gained because of Toyota's presence in Georgetown: taxes paid by the company's employees, construction workers, suppliers, and others. From 1986 through 2005, Haywood calculates the inflows to total $1.5 billion. The use of an incentives package turned out to be a success far greater than anything that was projected in December 1985.

Yukio Yotsumoto, a Japanese sociologist, examines the social impact of Japanese businesses in small Kentucky communities in chapter 8. To gather data for the study, Yotsumoto, along with geographer Karan, visited thirty-nine Kentucky communities and conducted detailed interviews with Japanese plant managers, American and Japanese employees, and mayors or other city officials in five cities—Bardstown, Berea, Danville, Harrodsburg, and Versailles. These communities were selected for in-depth study because Japanese plants account for 20 percent or more of the employment.

Yotsumoto and Karan found that Japanese investments in these communities go beyond employment. The Japanese-owned companies are significant players in the cultural, social, and educational activities of the communities in which their businesses are located. Japanese have taken active roles as members of the small communities in Kentucky. Japanese firms lead in contributions to the United Way, Junior Achievement, the Christian Appalachian Project, the American Cancer Society, and the Pritchard Committee for Higher Education and routinely finance student and group trips to Japan as well as cultural and educational activities in public schools. They are actively involved in facilitating good understanding and cooperation between the cultures of Japan and Kentucky. When it comes to lending a helping hand, the Japanese can be very American, conducting cleanup projects and blood drives.

Miranda Schreurs, a leading American scholar of Japanese environmental politics at the University of Maryland, discusses environmental policy of Japanese corporations in Kentucky in chapter 9. Schreurs states that since most of the Japanese firms came to Kentucky after the mid-1980s, their parent firms in Japan had already made major strides in energy efficiency improvements and pollution control practices. Thus, the Japanese firms came to Kentucky with already strong environmental standards. The major problem areas may surround expectations regarding the use of toxic chemicals, for which Japanese and U.S. laws differ somewhat.

Environmental groups such as the Sierra Club have no major problems with Toyota. Sierra Club was initially concerned about what Toyota might do to the area's water supply. Only about 5 percent of Toyota's wastewater qualifies as household waste. The rest is industrial waste, which the plant pretreats before sending to the Georgetown wastewater plant that serves only Toyota. (Construction of the wastewater plant was funded by municipal bonds, all of which were bought by Toyota.) The pretreated water is reported to be so clean that not enough "food" is left for microorganisms that ordinarily clean wastewater. So Toyota, it has been reported, mixes dog food with the water to keep the microorganisms alive. Toyota regularly tests water above and below the site where the treatment plant discharges treated water into Lane's Run Creek, which feeds into Elkhorn Creek. These tests show that the stream has more natural life now than it did in the 1980s. Japanese companies in Kentucky have made major efforts to develop a reputation as environmentally friendly manufacturers.

Gary O'Dell, an environmental science scholar and geographer, assesses environmental performance of Japanese industrial facilities in Kentucky in chapter 10. O'Dell uses data on hazardous waste generation reported to the Kentucky Division of Waste Management under the provisions of the federal Resource Conservation and Recovery Act of 1976 and the federal Toxic Release Inventory established by the Emergency Planning and Community Right-to-Know Act of 1986 for this study. These programs require industrial facilities to report on materials that are potentially harmful to human health and the environment, and the programs were established prior to a significant Japanese manufacturing investment in Kentucky. Corrosive wastewater constitutes most of the exempt hazardous waste which is treated and discharged through state water permits to surface waters or to publicly owned wastewater treatment plants. O'Dell notes that Japanese firms generated 9,203 tons of managed hazardous waste and 86,030 tons of exempt waste in 1996 (out of state totals of 405,867 and 17.4 million tons respectively). About 40 percent of the waste generated by Japanese firms in Kentucky is produced by a single facility, Toyota Motor Manufacturing, Kentucky, in Georgetown. Toyota is also among the top ten in Kentucky in the quantity of toxics (1,141 tons) released primarily into the atmosphere. This quantity constitutes nearly 60 percent of the total Toxic Release Inventory for all Japanese firms in Kentucky. Most Japanese firms in Kentucky depend on off-site waste management. Toyota sent a little more than half of its toxics to off-site facilities for management, and most were recycled. Case studies of the environmental policies and practices of five Japanese plants in Kentucky are examined by O'Dell.

Geographer Stanley Brunn and sociologist James Hougland discuss attitudes about and public perception of Japanese investments in Kentucky in chapters 11 and 12, respectively. To assess public attitudes toward Japanese investment, Brunn examines editorials regarding Japanese investment in Kentucky that appeared from 1985 to 1999 in the *Lexington Herald-Leader,* the *Louisville Courier-Journal,* and the *State Journal* of Frankfort. A variety of issues related to Japanese investment, particularly building of the Toyota plant in Georgetown, are addressed in the editorials. Some express praise for the initial decision; some raise questions regarding the incentives package the state provided Toyota; and others discuss the impacts on Scott County. The *Herald-Leader* from the start has been a strong supporter of the Japanese investment and its significance to the state's economy; the *Courier-Journal's* editorials noted the scale and importance of Japanese investments in Kentucky, particularly in Georgetown.

Hougland notes that Toyota's decision to locate in Scott County in 1985 led to a combination of optimism, apprehension, and controversy. Residents of the area disagreed about the relative benefits and strains that Toyota's presence would introduce as well as the appropriateness of the incentives package used to help attract Toyota to Kentucky. On the basis of random sample surveys of Scott County residents and other central Kentucky residents conducted during the ten years following Toyota's announcement, Hougland concludes that perceptions of several positive outcomes have become increasingly prevalent, while concerns about some negative outcomes appear to be abating. While Scott County residents consistently see their community as becoming more congested and more expensive, they have become more likely to view their community as more interesting and a more exciting place to live than it was before Toyota's arrival. Support for the state's incentives package has shown consistent increases over time. The survey revealed that support for Toyota is particularly strong among those who believe that they or members of their family are benefitting from the company's presence and those who have positive views of the quality of their county. The increasing favorable perception of Toyota in central Kentucky suggests that a combination of new employment opportunities, carefully focused programs of community relations, and a commitment by Japanese corporate officials to continue investing in an area can increase the local acceptance of the new Japanese investors.

Chapter 13 explores the growing economic ties and cultural exchanges between Kentucky and Japan, Kentucky's traditional industries in Japan, and the impact of globalization on Kentucky communities. By any measure, the change has been remarkable. In 1983, two years before Toyota announced its plan to build cars in Scott County, three Japanese manufacturing plants were in Kentucky. In early 2000 Kentucky had more than one hundred Japanese-invested companies employing more than thirty-five thousand Kentuckians with a total investment of more than $7 billion. Kentucky's business climate, existing Japanese companies, available industrial sites, and financing and tax incentives continue to attract Japanese companies. For former governor Martha Layne Collins, who made more than a dozen trips to Japan while courting Toyota, there is vindication in what has happened since Toyota first located in the state. As the study by Charles F. Haywood in chapter 7 points out, Toyota's economic impact has far exceeded original expectations.

The social and cultural bond between residents of the Bluegrass region and the Japanese people continues to grow. Japanese executives who return home to Japan find many reminders of the state they left behind. Kentucky's name appears more frequently in advertising and marketing efforts in Japan. At Toyota dealerships in Japan, the Kentucky flag, signs saying "Kentucky U.S.A.," and baskets representing Kentucky crafts are used to sell the Camry made at the Scott County plant. It is unfortunate that sales have been sluggish due to the continued economic recession in Japan. The image of Kentucky is very good in Japan. All of this might be just a beginning. Then again, it could be an indication of how two extremely different places have gained an appreciation for each other.

REFERENCES

Butters, Jamie. 1999. Japanese Take Kentucky Personally. *Lexington Herald-Leader Business Monday,* 3 May,10–11.
Johnson, Chalmers. 1982. *MITI and the Japanese Economic Miracle: The Growth of Industrial Policy, 1925–1975.* Stanford: Stanford Univ. Press.
Tompkins, Wayne. 1999. Kentucky Likes Japanese Presence. *Louisville Courier-Journal Business Section.* 3 April, 1–2.
Toyota Motor Corporation. 1988. *Toyota: A History of the First 50 Years.* Tokyo: Dai Nippon Printing Co., Ltd.

Part I

Japan in the Cultural and Economic Landscape of Kentucky

2

Japanese Investment in Kentucky

P.P. KARAN AND W.A. BLADEN

JAPANESE FOREIGN DIRECT INVESTMENT—the setting up of Japanese-owned manufacturing plants—has seen steady rise in Kentucky as well as throughout the southeast United States since the early 1980s. As Japanese firms began to invest overseas following the yen revaluation (*endaka*) in 1985–1986, the number of Japanese companies operating in Kentucky grew rapidly. This wave slowed down considerably in the mid-1990s after the burst of the Japanese bubble economy, slow economic recovery, weak corporate profits, and continued liquidity problems in the Japanese banking system.

Two major analytical approaches explain what motivates foreign direct investment and help elucidate the large capital inflows into the United States during the 1980s. The first is based on classical investment theory, in which movement of capital is explained in terms of changes in real interest rate differentials between countries. Foreign investors weigh incremental expected returns against the marginal cost of capital. They are motivated by the desire to earn the highest rates of return for any given level of risk. Foreign investors also attempt to hedge against interest rate and exchange rate fluctuations by diversifying asset holdings (Graham and Krugman 1989; Hufbauer 1975).

The second approach is based on the theory of the firm, in which investment is explained in terms of the strategic behavior of the firm. A firm or multinational corporation expands its activities overseas (a) to maintain profitability when faced with competition due to rising production costs, rising wages, and adverse changes in foreign currency exchange rates; (b) to increase or maintain market share in the foreign country; (c) to retain access in an overseas market, especially in terms of trade restrictions (Barrell and Pain 1999); (d) to maintain control over an advantage specific to the firm, such as marketing, management, and/or technology, or comparative advantage in producing in a foreign market; and (e) to improve the firm's ability to meet the overseas market's needs (Hymer 1976; Dunning and Rugman 1985). The strategic decisions of the multinational corporation hinge on factors which are both internal and external to the firm.

Hymer (1976) articulated the widely accepted notion that a firm whose operations cross national boundaries faces extra costs of managing geographically widespread operations including those dealing with different languages, cultures, technical standards, and customer preferences. To overcome these extra costs, the firm must possess internal firm-specific advantages which largely take the form of economies of scale or of superior product technology. A number of works have attempted to pin down the firm-specific advantages that drive foreign direct investment. Aharoni (1966) noted the importance of imperfect information about markets as a determinant of foreign direct investment flows; Vernon (1966; 1974) pointed out the linkage between the product cycle in technology and the shift from exports to direct investment among multinational firms; Kindleberger (1969) noted the role of firm-specific advantages other than technology, such as organizational and marketing skills. Caves (1971) has noted that advantages possessed by multinational enterprises include a number of intangible assets such as organizational and marketing skills and product and process technologies. Buckley and Casson (1976) have suggested existence of some "internalization" advantages for the firm's foreign direct investment activity. These advantages are associated with a firm exploiting a market opportunity through internal operations rather than through the sale of rights to the firm's intangible assets to other firms. Dunning (1988) has pointed out that the advantages of internalization must interact with both firm-specific advantages and locational advantages to explain foreign direct investment.

Since the seminal work of Hymer, the general consensus is that a firm's corporate strategy is a more important factor in explaining foreign direct investment than the classical investment theory. Most scholars studying foreign direct investment tend to focus on industrial-organization motivations to explain the expansion of multinational enterprises. Recent work by Frankel (1992) suggests that the difference between U.S. and Japanese capital costs narrowed during the 1980s, indicating that cost-of-capital differences are not as significant an explanation of Japanese foreign direct investment.

The fast growth in foreign direct investment from Japan rapidly built a significant presence in the United States. The foreign direct investment represented a fundamental shift in the strategies of many Japanese multinational corporations to replace exports, at least partially, with the sales of overseas affiliates, and is attributable to a number of factors. Primary among these were the desire of Japanese firms to overcome mounting threat of protectionism in the major American market and to position themselves as "insiders." This is reflected in the fact that most Japanese investments in the United States are trade-replacing in nature, concentrated in such industries as automobiles and electronics. Japanese strategies in the United States were geared to serving the local market with a small percentage of the sales exported to other countries, although that proportion is rising as Japanese affiliates expand. Recent evidence points to the fact that Japanese multinational firms are building up networks of suppliers to serve their American affiliates. Trends thus indicate rising local content by Japanese affiliates located in the United States, although this is often achieved through sourcing from locally based Japanese suppliers.

A substantial concentration of Japanese manufacturing plants, most of them related to the automobile industry, emerged in Kentucky by the late 1980s. The issue of Japanese investment has been high on the economic agenda since the late 1970s as the state government began to make energetic attempts to encourage Japanese firms to set up manufacturing plants in Kentucky. At the national level the political edge sharpened markedly in the early 1980s as the Japanese trade surplus continued to grow and as United States–Japan trading friction intensified. In the case of trade, the issues were a mixture of high level of import penetration of the American market by Japanese firms and the structural impediments which inhibited imports into Japan and closed some parts of the Japanese market to foreign firms (Mann 1989).

Aside from the broader national dimension, Japanese direct investment is seen by the Kentucky state government as being potentially the most dynamic and influential source of international investment. In 1999, 109 Japanese firms in the state employed approximately thirty-five thousand workers. There is no doubt that the Japanese presence in Kentucky has grown rapidly. Japanese firms continue to be courted assiduously by the state government, at the highest level, down to county and city levels. For example, Kentucky governors and the staff of the Commerce Cabinet make annual trips to Japan to attract Japanese businesses to Kentucky.

Japanese investment in Kentucky is both an economic and a political phenomenon. Its geographical form is the outcome of a complex interaction between economic and political forces, both internal and external. The goals in this chapter are to set Japanese investment in Kentucky into its broader context, to examine the geographical location of the Japanese foreign direct investment in the United States and in Kentucky, and to explore some of the underlying mechanisms and causes.

Growth of Japanese Investment in the United States

For twenty-five years following the end of the second World War (until 1971), Japan's foreign direct investment was limited. Japan's major priority during this period was reconstruction of its domestic manufacturing base, which was destroyed by the ravages of war. The Japanese successfully achieved this and by 1963 had regained the country's pre-war share of international trade.

After 1965 Japanese exports were increasingly directed toward the United States and comprised a narrow range of consumer durables such as automobiles, television sets, and radios. Soon Japanese exports to the United States began to greatly exceed U.S. exports to Japan (Cohen 1985). By 1971 Japan had built up a $3.2 billion trade surplus with the United States. In response the United States introduced restrictions on a number of Japanese imports and allowed the exchange value to slide from 360 yen to 300 yen to the dollar. In Japan this event is known as the "Nixon Shokku." It was a shock to the Japanese because the 360-yen-to-the-dollar exchange rate had existed since 1949 (Allen 1981). Japan's reaction to the U.S. policy was to divert some of the export trade to western Europe (with whom Japan also soon built up a huge trade surplus) and to start investment in manufacturing in the United States to circumvent the effects of the import restrictions and the stronger yen. The objective was to maintain its share of the U.S. market, which Japan considered vital (Marsh 1983).

Japan ranked seventh as an investor in the United States in 1980. As the trend in Japanese investment in the United States continued to be steeply upwards in the 1980s, Japan ranked second as a foreign direct investor in 1989 and 1995. The sharp appreciation of the Japanese yen since 1985, especially after the Plaza Agreement in September 1985, and the continuation of high yen (i.e., 263 yen/dollar in February 1985 to 152 yen/dollar in August 1986 to approximately 104 yen/dollar in the early 1990s) created new and changed economic conditions which prompted Japanese firms to increase production in the United States (Bagchi-Sen 1995). In addition, since the 1970s major Japanese corporations increasingly adopted globalization strategies to

Table 2.1. Largest source countries of foreign direct investment in the United States, 1980–1995 (rank order by percentage share of total foreign direct investment)

Country	1980	1989	1995
Netherlands	23.1 (1)	15.1 (3)	12.1 (3)
United Kingdom	17.0 (2)	29.7 (1)	23.6 (1)
Canada	14.6 (3)	7.9 (4)	NA
West Germany	9.2 (4)	7.0 (5)	NA
Netherlands Antilles	8.0 (5)	2.6 (8)	12.1 (3)
Switzerland	6.1 (6)	4.8 (6)	NA
Japan	5.7 (7)	17.4 (2)	19.4 (2)
France	4.5 (8)	4.1 (7)	NA

Source: U.S. Department of Commerce, Bureau of Economic Analysis. *Foreign Direct Investment in the United States, 1997 Benchmark Survey.* Washington, D.C., 1999.

expand overseas production. Small and medium sized corporations also have sought to internationalize their activities as part of their survival strategies. In addition, Japanese have invested heavily in research and development facilities in the United States to develop and customize products for the American market and provide technical support for manufacturing (Florida and Kenny 1994).

The United States has been the destination for nearly half of total Japanese investment since 1986. It also accounted for nearly 64 percent of manufacturing investment between 1986 and 1989. Investment in transport equipment was a major focus. Japanese automobile makers made massive investments in the United States while they agreed to voluntarily restrain exports to the United States since 1981. Five of the Japanese automobile companies had already started production in 1989, and by early 1990 more than two million units of automobiles were produced by Japanese plants in the United States. To overcome foreseeable competition, Japanese firms have made sizable investments in such related fields as design, sales, and financial service and have started exporting cars made in the United States. To increase use of locally procured parts, automakers are producing engines in the United States and have made investments in companies that make auto parts.

REGIONAL PATTERN OF JAPANESE INVESTMENTS IN THE UNITED STATES

Japanese-owned corporations exercise control over a relatively small share of the U.S. aggregate employment, sales, and investments in manufacturing, and their economic impact on the national economy is small. Yet, for certain industries and regions of the country, such as the Bluegrass region of Kentucky, the potential impact is considerable. The locational choices of Japanese investors within the United States reveal a preference for three regions: (1) the country's traditional manufacturing heartland, comprising the northeast United States and upper Midwest, which in 1987 accounted for 41.8 percent of all workers employed by Japanese manufacturing plants in the United States; (2) the Far West and Southwest with 32.1 percent of the workers, mainly in California; and (3) the Southeast with 23.4 percent of the workers (McKnight 1988). Until 1980 the majority of Japanese investment was located mainly in California, which had nearly 38 percent of the Japanese-employed manufacturing workforce in the United States.

Since 1980 there has been a gradual shift of geographic investment from the Far West and Southwest to the Midwest and South, although California continues to be a major locational choice. Illinois, Michigan, Indiana, and Ohio in the Midwest and Tennessee and Kentucky in the South have recorded impressive gains. The growth of Japanese investment to the Midwest and South can be partly explained by Japanese investment in automobile produc-

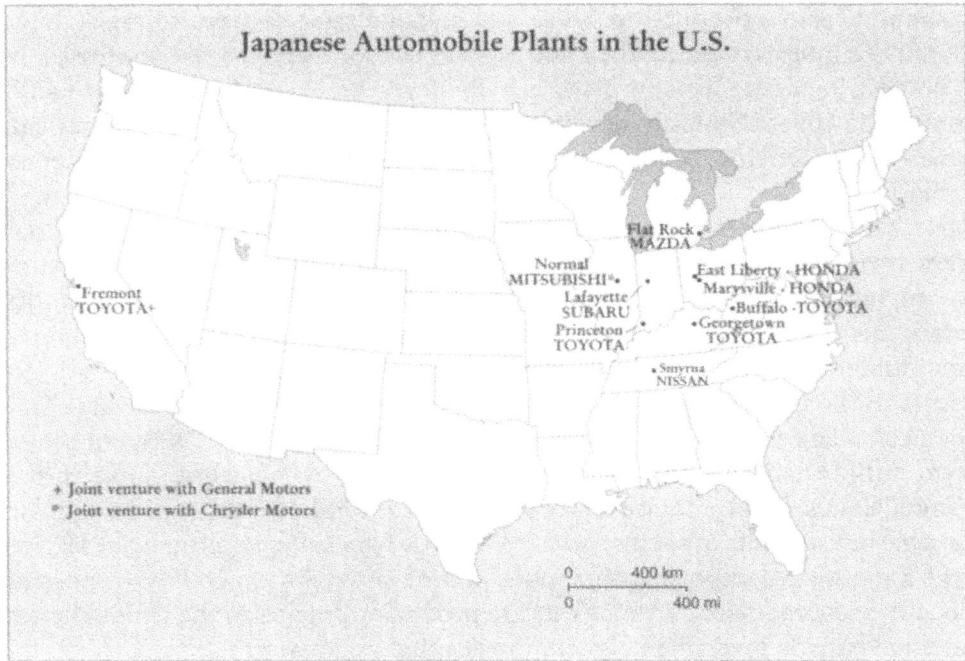

Fig. 2.1. Japanese automobile plants in the United States.

tion. The American automobile industry is geographically concentrated in Michigan, Illinois, and Ohio in the Midwest and Georgia, Tennessee, and Kentucky in the South (Rubenstein 1986). Japanese automakers have followed the regional locational strategy of the major American automobile manufacturers (fig. 2.1). The geographic concentration of Japanese investments in the South and Midwest reflects a location close to the population and market in order to minimize the distribution costs of their product to the consumer.

Japanese investments in the South have grown steadily (table 2.2). Georgia was the first state to start recruiting Japanese companies in the early 1970s under Governor Jimmy Carter. Atlanta became a focus of Japanese business in the South in late 1970. An active role played by Governor Lamar Alexander of Tennessee led to the establishment of the Nissan plant at Smyrna. Kentucky spent more than $125 million, including $55 million in worker-training grants, to persuade Toyota to build an auto plant in Georgetown. With tax incentives the total bill has been estimated at $350 million (War Between the States 1988).

It is interesting to examine the relationship between the location of Japanese foreign direct investment in the United States and the economic characteristics of the recipient states. Since new plant and plant expansion activities

Table 2.2. Manufacturing employment in Japanese-owned plants in southern states, 1991–1997 (in thousands)

States	1991	1995	1997
Alabama	5.9	7.3	7.4
Arkansas	3.2	4.4	4.0
Florida	1.6	4.3	3.6
Georgia	13.0	18.4	19.4
Kentucky	17.2	22.3	29.4
Louisiana	—	0.9	1.1
Mississippi	1.3	1.7	1.4
North Carolina	9.5	13.9	13.1
South Carolina	8.5	12.4	10.5
Tennessee	14.6	25.5	25.0
Virginia	4.5	5.6	7.5
West Virginia	—	1.2	1.3

Source: U.S. Department of Commerce, Bureau of Economic Analysis. *Foreign Direct Investment in the United States, 1997 Benchmark Survey.* Washington, D.C., 1999; and *Foreign Direct Investment in the United States: Establishment Data for Manufacturing, 1991.* Washington, D.C., 1994.

create new jobs, it is interesting to see if foreign direct investment in new plants and plant expansions occurs most often in states in which unemployment problems are relatively severe or in which government policies toward potential investors are relatively favorable. A detailed empirical analysis of data by Ray (1991) revealed, contrary to popular belief, that differences in the relative tax burden across states did not influence new foreign direct investment activity and that state incentives programs to encourage businesses to invest in a state generally did not have a significant impact on new plant and plant expansion resulting from foreign direct investment activity. High state unemployment rates tended to discourage foreign direct investment activity. High unionization rates among employees by state tended to discourage foreign direct investment. Data indicates that the United Kingdom and European Union have tended to locate investments in states with relatively high employment shares in the petroleum and automobile industries. Japan has concentrated foreign direct investment activity in states with high auto-industry employment, and Canada has concentrated direct investment activity in states with high steel-industry employment shares. Since each of these major industries experienced high unemployment in the 1980s, it can be said that each of the major countries and suppliers of foreign direct investment activity in the United States invested in states plagued with serious structural unemployment problems. In this context, foreign direct investment helped alleviate some of the social and economic hardship associated with persistent unemployment.

PATTERN OF JAPANESE INVESTMENTS IN KENTUCKY

The Japanese investment in Kentucky came in two waves. The first wave arrived with the biggest Japanese automaker, Toyota, when it decided to build its plant in Georgetown in 1985. The first giant wave engendered a much more broadly based second wave: small Japanese companies arriving to supply parts and components to the big auto companies. This second surge of investment started to roll across Kentucky beginning in 1987 as smaller Japanese companies searched for towns and cities located along major transportation arteries with easy access not only to the Toyota plant in Georgetown but also to other Japanese automakers like Nissan (Smyrna, Tennessee), Honda (Marysville, Ohio), Mazda (Flat Rock, Michigan), Mitsubishi (Bloomington, Illinois), and Isuzu (Lafayette, Indiana). Tiny communities and modest cities that grew up beside the wide highways of Kentucky—towns that still have V-J Day parades and an all-American appearance—began to coax successfully Japanese companies to build factories and hire workers in their neighborhoods. Since the late 1980s small Kentucky towns have been winning new factories and jobs, and the influx of Japanese companies is improving local economies.

Today Japanese manufacturing plants in Kentucky are in small or medium sized towns close to interstate highways 64, 65, and 75 and adjacent to the Bluegrass Parkway and other major highways in the state (fig. 2.2). Among these towns are Ashland, Bardstown, Berea, Bowling Green, Danville, Edmonton, Elizabethtown, Erlanger, Flemingsburg, Florence, Frankfort, Franklin, Georgetown, Glasgow, Harrodsburg, Hopkinsville, Lawrenceburg, Lebanon, Leitchfield, Lexington, London, Louisville, Maysville, Morgantown, Munfordville, Nicholasville, Paris, Richmond, Russellville, Scottsville, Shelbyville, Somerset, Sonora, Springfield, Stanford, Versailles, Walton, Williamsburg, and Winchester (table 2.3). Three of Kentucky's largest cities, Louisville, Lexington, and Bowling Green, have a number of small Japanese auto-related plants that employ fewer than one hundred workers each.

Most of the parent companies of Japanese firms investing in Kentucky are based in Japan's Keihin Industrial Region, which extends along Tokyo Bay and nearby inland areas with major concentrations in Tokyo, Kawasaki, and Yokohama and covers parts of Tokyo, Kanagawa, Saitama, and Ibaraki prefectures (fig. 2.3). This region ranks first in Japan in the value of goods produced. The Hanshin Industrial Region, which extends along Osaka Bay, is the home of more than a dozen major Japanese firms investing in Kentucky. Chukyo Industrial Region, which is centered on the city of Nagoya in Aichi prefecture, is the home base for more than thirty Japanese companies operating in Kentucky, including the Toyota Motor Corporation. The Tokai Industrial Region, located along the Pacific coast in Shizuoka prefecture, is the home base for Fuji Kiko, Fuji Univance, and Miyama Kogyo, whose affiliates operate plants in Hopkinsville, Winchester, and Louisville. Three companies

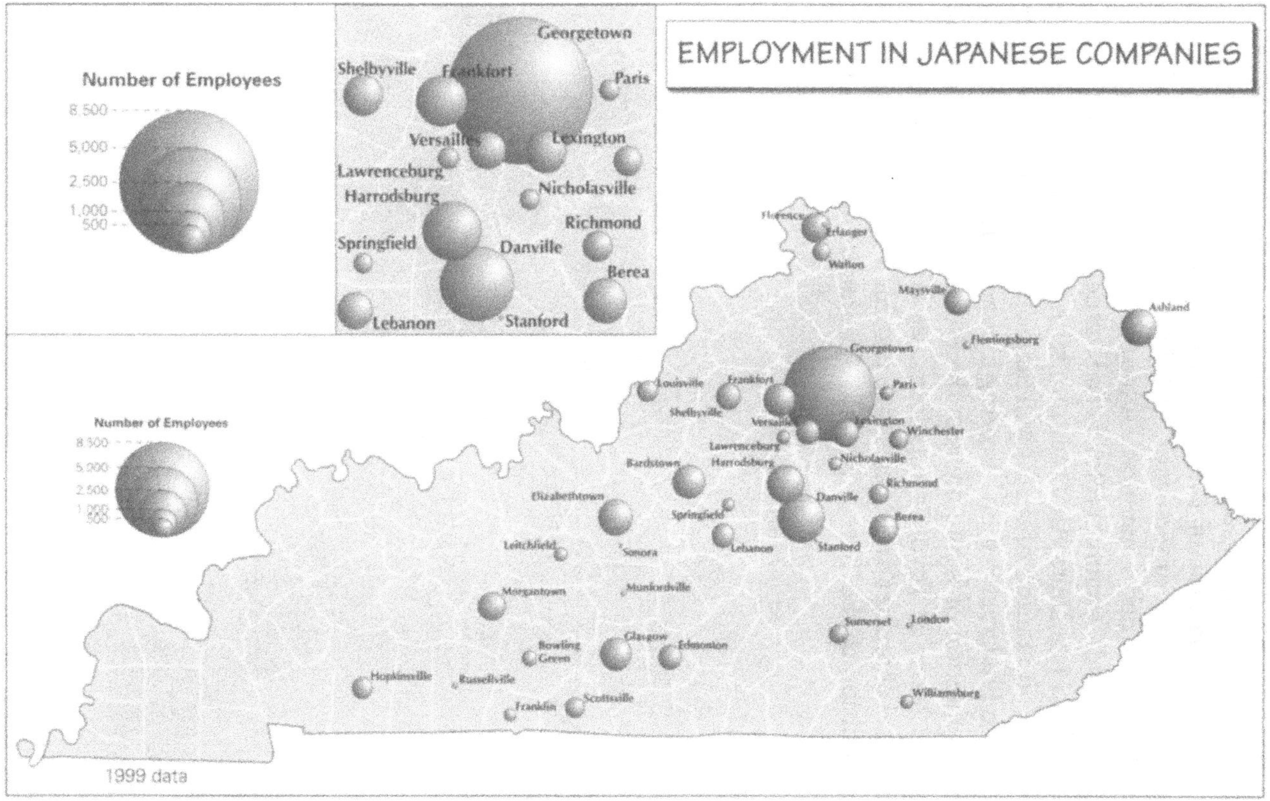

EMPLOYMENT IN JAPANESE COMPANIES

Number of Employees

8.500
5.000
2.500
1.000
500

1999 data

Fig. 2.2. Employment in Japanese companies, 1999.

located in the Setouchi Industrial Region, along the Inland Sea with principal industrial centers of Hiroshima and Okayama, have affiliates operating plants in Shelbyville and Flemingsburg (table 2.4).

Toyota, the largest of the Japanese firms in Kentucky, is located in Georgetown, near the intersection of I-75 and I-64 with excellent connections to Louisville and Cincinnati, Ohio. Lexington has a regional airport, but Louisville and Cincinnati (Northern Kentucky) are international airports, and Cincinnati is a Delta Air Lines hub with worldwide connections. More than half the population of the United States lives within a five hundred-mile radius of the Bluegrass region, creating a huge market potential. More than half the population of Kentucky is in the Bluegrass region, providing a large labor pool. Most of Toyota's suppliers also have Bluegrass locations. The region's rural character and open space provide a number of amenities.

In addition to the Toyota Motor Manufacturing plant, which employs

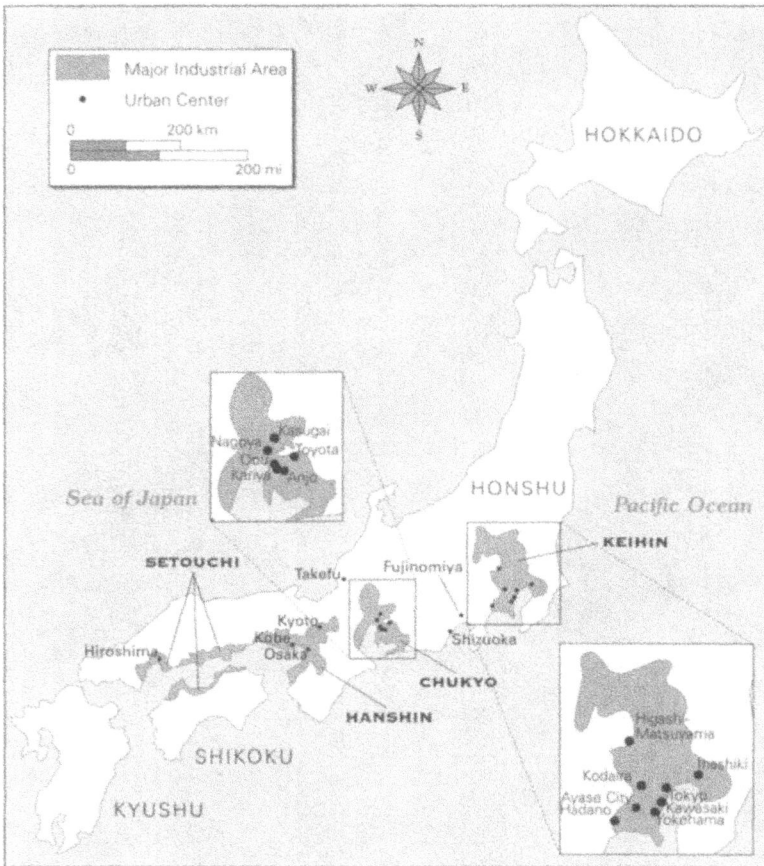

Fig. 2.3. Headquarters of Japanese firms investing in Kentucky.

Table 2.3. Employment in Japanese plants in Kentucky cities, 1999

City	Employment in Japanese Plants	Population, 1980	Population, 1998	Percent emp. in Japanese firms in each city
Ashland	1,600	27,064	22,402	7.0
Bardstown	1,402	6,401	7,879	17.8
Berea	1,073	8,600	10,341	10.4
Bowling Green	361	40,450	44,822	0.8
Danville	2,601	12,942	16,470	15.8
Edmonton	824	1,448	1,559	52.9
Elizabethtown	1,562	15,380	19,905	7.8
Erlanger	50	14,466	16,901	0.3
Flemingsburg	102	3,043	3,333	3.1
Florence	1,102	15,586	19,501	5.7
Frankfort	1,320	25,973	26,418	5.0
Franklin	250	7,738	8,109	3.1
Georgetown	8,525	10,972	14,365	59.3
Glasgow	1,328	12,958	14,062	9.4
Harrodsburg	1,720	7,265	7,862	21.9
Hopkinsville	630	29,386	32,045	2.0
Lawrenceburg	298	5,116	7,949	3.7
Lebanon	765	6,590	5,754	13.3
Leitchfield	282	4,533	5,459	5.2
Lexington	958	204,165	241,749	0.4
London	60	4,002	7,045	0.9
Louisville	616	298,694	255,045	0.2
Maysville	915	7,983	8,479	11.3
Morgantown	1,000	2,000	2,515	39.8
Munfordville	47	1,783	1,640	2.9
Nicholasville	270	10,400	17,099	1.6
Paris	275	7,935	8,898	3.1
Richmond	540	21,705	27,644	2.0
Russellville	60	7,520	7,869	0.8
Scottsville	560	4,278	4,736	11.8
Shelbyville	915	5,329	6,849	13.4
Somerset	530	10,829	12,618	4.2
Sonora	30		290	10.3
Springfield	262	3,179	2,930	8.9
Stanford	18	2,764	2,989	0.6
Versailles	767	6,427	8,233	9.3
Walton	469	1,651	2,027	23.0
Williamsburg	284	5,560	6,008	4.7
Winchester	521	15,216	15,937	3.3
Total	34,937	877,331	925,736	

Source: Population Estimates, 1998, Kentucky Population Research. University of Louisville; Population, 1980, Kentucky Cabinet for Economic Development, Frankfort, Kentucky; Employment data from Kentucky Cabinet for Economic Development, Frankfort, Kentucky.

seventy-eight hundred workers, six other Japanese-owned plants located near Georgetown from 1986 to 1998. These are Louisville Forge and Gear Works LLC, Toyota Tsusho, Vuteq Corporation, and A R K, all subsidiaries of Japanese firms based in Aichi prefecture, and Trinity Industrial Corporation and International Crankshaft, subsidiaries of firms in Tokyo. The companies manufacture steel forgings, automotive steel, automotive windows, paint finishing systems, and automotive crankshafts. The parent company of Louisville Forge and Gear Works is Aichi Steel Works, which has headquarters in Tokai, south of Nagoya. A member of the Toyota group, Aichi Steel was established in 1934 as the steel manufacturing department of Toyoda Automatic Loom Works. The company produces and sells special steel materials and forged steel products. A R K and Toyota Tsusho America are affiliates of Toyota Tsusho Corporation, a comprehensive trading company that is a core member of the Toyota group. International Crankshaft is part of the Sumitomo group, which comprises some eighty firms. Toyota's just-in-time production system and the need for close technical cooperation between companies have led to tendencies toward spatial clustering of plants in the Bluegrass region.

AK Steel Corporation, with head office in Tokyo, manufactures steels and coils in Ashland and employs sixteen hundred workers. The company was established in 1989. AK Steel's parent company is Kawasaki Steel Corporation, with headquarters in Tokyo and Kobe. It ranks among the top five in Japanese crude steel production and has thirteen overseas subsidiaries, including Aramco Steel Company.

Bardstown, thirty miles from Louisville, attracted eight Japanese plants between 1986 and 1996. The plants employ approximately fourteen hundred workers. The largest company, Intertec Systems LLC (with Japanese head office in Aichi prefecture) employs 425 persons in the manufacture of polyurethane auto instrument panels. Jideco of Bardstown and Trim Masters employ 300 each in automotive parts industries (windshield wiper motors and automatic speed control devices, and door trim panels). Trim Masters has its Japanese headquarters in Aichi prefecture, and Jideco in Kanagawa prefecture. Other Japanese plants in the city are F E T Engineering of Aichi, which makes automotive interior molds; AMB of Kanagawa, which makes blower motors; Mabex Universal Corporation of Aichi, producer of protective foam; and Sumitok Magnetics Company of Osaka, which manufactures ceramic magnets. A nonautomotive-related Japanese plant in Bardstown is Inoac Packaging Group of Aichi, which manufactures heavy-wall plastic bottles for the cosmetic industry. Bardstown, with a rich history and local distilleries that produce 60 percent of the world's supply of bourbon whiskey, is an example of a town that has been successful in securing Japanese plants.

Berea, located on I-75 in Madison County (which extends into the foothills of Appalachia), has four Japanese manufacturing plants. Tokico of Kawasaki, the largest plant in Berea, makes auto shock absorbers, struts, and caliper brakes and employs 564 persons. Tokico, incorporated in 1949, is the industry's largest producer of shock absorbers and gasoline flowmeters. The company also sells suspension systems to U.S. automobile makers. KI Corporation, based in Kanagawa, manufactures components for shock absorbers and employs 312 workers. Matsushita Electric Motor Corporation makes small electric motors and employs 160 persons. Kentucky Steel Center, affiliate of a Japanese-based firm in Osaka, is engaged in steel processing. It was established in Berea in 1996.

Bowling Green has three Japanese plants: Bando Manufacturing with the parent company in Tokyo, NHK-Associated Spring Suspension with parent company in Yokohama, and TWN Fastener of Hadano (a city in western Kanagawa prefecture) employ more than 360 workers. They manufacture power transmission belts for industrial machines and automobiles, coil springs for automotive suspensions, and drywall fasteners for the building industry. NHK-Associated Spring Suspension is operated by NHK Spring of Japan and Associated Spring Company of Connecticut. NHK Spring Company is one of the world's largest spring manufacturers. The company has nine branches and twenty-seven affiliated companies in Japan. In the overseas market it has manufacturing bases in seven countries. Eighty percent of its production is related to the automotive industry, and it realizes annual sales of more than $1 billion.

Danville is another focus of Japanese plants in the Bluegrass region. The largest Japanese plant in Danville is Matsushita, a home appliance manufac-

Jideco of Bardstown (Kentucky), established in 1986, employs three hundred workers. Its Japanese parent company is Jidosha Denki Company (JIDECO) of Yokohama. Jideco makes windshield wiper motors and automatic speed control devices for automobiles. (Photograph by P.P. Karan)

Table 2.4. Major Japanese firms operating plants in Kentucky, 1999

City	Japanese parent company and product	Location in Kentucky
Anjo, Aichi	Central Motor Wheel Company wheels	Paris
Ayase, Kanagawa	Toshin Company, auto parts stamping	Stanford
Fujinomiya, Shizuoka	Miyama Kogyo Company, stamping/assembly	Louisville
Hadano, Kanagawa	Topura Company, drywall fasteners	Bowling Green
Higashi Matsuyama Saitama	Yamamoto F B Engineering, auto brake	Louisville
Hiroshima	Toyo Seat, seat for autos	Flemingsburg
Inashiki, Ibaraki	Jonan Industries Company, plastic inj. molding	Winchester
Kanagawa-Ken	Shimoda, wiring harness for wiper motors	Bardstown
Kawasaki	Tokico Ltd., auto shock absorbers	Berea
Kodaira City, Tokyo	Toyo Denyo Company, auto welding equipment	Walton
Kariya, Aichi	Aisin Seiki Company, diecastings for autos	London
Kyoto	Takara Shuzo Company, packaged beverages, distilled products, and distillers dried grain	Frankfort
Nagoya	Aichi Kikai, transmission gears	Richmond
	Aichi Steel Works Ltd., steel forgings	Georgetown
	Chukyo Yushi, industrial mold release agents and thermosensitive paper additives	Elizabethtown
	Chuo Springs, automotive cable controls	Glasgow
	Far East Tooling Co., Ltd.,	
	Automotive interior molds	Bardstown
	Electro formed tooling	Lebanon
	Gomunoinaki Co., Ltd., rubber auto parts	Winchester
	Howa Kasei, automotive armrests	Springfield
	Inoac Corporation.	
	Plastic bottles for cosmetics industry	Bardstown
	Polyurethane auto instrument panel	Bardstown
	Maruyasu Industries, auto gasline and brake line tubing assemblies	Lebanon
	Toyota Tsusho	
	Recycle steel, automotive steel	Georgetown
	Auto seat/door trim	Harrodsburg/Georgetown
Nishi Kasugai-gun, Aichi	Toyoda Gosei, plastic auto parts	Lebanon
Niwa-gun, Aichi	Nakagawa Sangyo Company, auto muffler parts	Sonora
	Yamazaki Mazak Corporation, machine tools	Florence
Obu City, Aichi	Aisan Industrial Company, auto engine parts	Franklin
	Tokai Kogyo Company, auto trim	Maysville
Okayama	Katayama Kogyo Company, window frames and flexible stainless steel mesh joints for auto industry	Shelbyville

Table 2.4. Continued

City	Japanese parent company and product	Location in Kentucky
Osaka	Daikin Clutch, automotive/truck after market	Florence
	Itochu Corporation, steel wire tire cord	Danville
	Kyeoi Steel Ltd., fabricated steel	Louisville
	Matsushita Appliance Corporation, vacuum cleaners	Danville
	Nissho Iwai Corporation, drywall fasteners	Bowling Green
	Sumikin Bussan Corporation, steel processing	Berea
	Sumitomo Electric Industries	
	Magnet wire	Edmonton
	Automotive electric wiring harness	Scottsville/Morgantown
	Sumitomo Special Metals, ceramic magnets	Bardstown
	Wako Electronics Co., Ltd., appliance thermostats	Louisville
	Yuasa Battery Company, storage batteries	Richmond
Shizuoka	Fuji Kiko	
	Steering columns	Hopkinsville
	Automotive seat mechanisms	Walton
	Fuji Univance Corporation, auto and RV parts	Winchester
Takefu, Fukui	Matsushita Electric Motor Company, small electric motors	Berea
Tokyo	Akebono Brake, brake parts	Munfordville/Elizabethtown
	AMAK Brake, auto disc pads	Glasgow
	Asahi Glass Co., Ltd., automotive glass	Elizabethtown
	Asahi Tec, wheels	Somerset
	Bando Chemical, power transmission belts	Bowling Green
	Bridgestone Corporation, auto air springs	Williamsburg
	Calsonic Group, blower motors	Bardstown
	Clarion Co., Ltd., automotive radio equipment	Walton
	Denyo Co., Ltd., generators	Danville
	Fujikura Ltd., wiring harness	Shelbyville
	Hayes Lemmerz Intl. Inc., wheels	Somerset
	Hitachi Ltd., auto electric devices, alternator and starter motors	Harrodsburg
	Ichikoh Industries, Ltd., rear- and side-view auto mirrors	Shelbyville
	Itochi Corporation, steel parts, processing	Louisville
	Jidosha Kiki, brake parts	Russellville
	Kawasaki Steel Corporation, steel sheets, coils	Ashland
	Kokoku Intech Company, rubber components for auto, medical, and business machine industries	Richmond
	Kokoku Wire, automotive cable controls	Glasgow
	Mitsubishi Corporation	
	Steel wire tire cord	Danville
	Plastic acrylic sheets	Florence
	Mitsubishi Electric Corporation, electronic auto products	Maysville
	Mitsubishi Heavy Industries	Hopkinsville
	Horizontal and vertical machining centers and lathes	

Table 2.4. Continued

City	Japanese parent company and product	Location in Kentucky
Tokyo (continued)	Mitsubishi Rayon Co., Ltd., plastic acrylic sheets	Florence
	Mitsubishi Steel Manufacturing, torsion bars	Hopkinsville
	Mitsui & Company, animal feed additives	Louisville
	Neturen, spring wires for autos	Florence
	Nippon Glass, laminated and tempered glass parts	Versailles
	Nippon Zeon Company, synthetic elastomers	Louisville
	Obara Corporation, welding equipment	Erlanger
	Sumitomo Corporation	
	Crankshafts and steel forgings	Georgetown
	Cranes and excavators	Lexington
	Tachi-S Company	
	Auto and truck seat covers	Glasgow
	Auto seat covers	Maysville
	Tokyo Rope Manufacturing Company, steel wire tire cord	Danville
	Topy Industries, Ltd., auto wheels	Frankfort
	Toyo Radiator Company	
	Copper and brass radiators for off-road industrial equipment	Hopkinsville
	Heat exchangers for autos	Hopkinsville
	Trinity Industrial Corporation, paint finishing systems	Georgetown
	Yokohama Hydex, and	
	Yokohama Rubber Company	Versailles
	Automotive air conditioning and power steering hoses	
	Y K K Corporation, automatic attaching machines, metal buttons, snap fasteners, hooks and eyes	Lawrenceburg
Toyota, Aichi	Araco Corporation	
	Trim for car seats	Leitchfield
	Seat for autos	Nicholasville
	Door trim panels	Bardstown
	Chubu Industries Co., Inc., automotive windows	Georgetown
	Fuji Seiko, carbide cutting tools	Lexington
	Kito Machine Industry Co., Ltd., welding equipment	Lexington
	Toyo Seisakusho, tape for auto industry	Lexington
	Toyoda Iron Works, auto stamping	Somerset
	Toyota Motor Corporation, automobiles and auto engines	Georgetown
	Toyotomi Kiko Ltd., automotive body panels	Springfield
Yokohama	Jideco Group, blower motors	Bardstown
	Jidosha Denki Company	Bardstown
	Windshield wiper motors and speed control devices	
	Keiaisha Manufacturing, components for shock absorbers	Berea
	NHK Spring, coil springs for auto suspension	Bowling Green
	Ohi Seisakusho	
	Auto components	Winchester
	Auto door hinges, seat support hardware, hood and door latches	Frankfort

Source: Kentucky Cabinet for Economic Development, Frankfort, Kentucky.

FET Engineering, located in Bardstown, makes automotive interior molds. Established in 1988, it is wholly owned by Far East Tooling of Nagoya, Japan. (Photograph by P.P. Karan)

turer. It employs 2,000 workers making vacuum cleaners and microwave ovens. Matsushita is Danville's largest employer and one of the largest manufacturers of home appliances in America. Most Matsushita products are shipped overseas. A T R Wire and Cable makes steel wire tire cord and bead wire and employs 564 people. A T R Wire and Cable is a joint venture of Osaka-based Itochu Corporation (C. Itoh and Company until 1992) and Tokyo-based Mitsubishi Corporation and Tokyo Rope Manufacturing Company (Tokyo Seiko), which produces various types of wire ropes, wires, and steel cords. Production of steel cords for auto tire is the main business of the company, which was incorporated in 1887 and established in its present form in 1946. Another Japanese company, Denyo Manufacturing Corporation of Tokyo, established a plant to manufacture generators in Danville in 1994.

Two Osaka-based Japanese firms in Edmonton, Sumitomo Electric Wiring Systems and S P D Magnet Wire Company, manufacture wiring products and magnetic wire for the automotive and cycle industries. Both Sumitomo Electric Wiring Systems and S P D Magnet Wire Company are affiliates of Sumitomo Electric Industries, with headquarters in Osaka and Tokyo. Established in 1897 and with annual sales of nearly $6 billion, it is one of the major enterprises in the Sumitomo group.

Two Tokyo-based companies, A P Technoglass Corporation and Ambrake Corporation, manufacture automotive glass and brakes in Elizabethtown and employ more than 1,500 workers. Ambrake Corporation is a joint venture

Kentucky Steel Center, located in an industrial park in Berea, Kentucky, was established in 1996. The plant processes steel and is wholly owned by Sumikin Bussan Corporation of Osaka, Japan. (Photograph by P.P. Karan)

between Akebono Brake Industry of Japan and Delco Division of General Motors. A third, smaller company, Cytech Products, a joint venture of Tomen Corporation and Chukyo Yushi, makes industrial mold-release agents and thermosensitive paper.

Obara Corporation, a Tokyo-based firm, manufactures welding equipment in Erlanger, and Toyo Seat, a Hiroshima-based firm, makes auto seats in Flemingsburg. Four Japanese-owned plants in Florence employ more than 1,100 workers. IT Spring Wire and Airtech Acrylics LLC, subsidiaries of Tokyo-based firms, manufacture spring wire for autos and plastic acrylic sheets. Meritor Automotive, an affiliate of an Osaka-based firm, specializes in automotive business, and Yamazaki Mazak Corporation, an Aichi prefecture firm, makes machine tools. Yamazaki Mazak, the world's third largest machine tool company, began producing in Kentucky in 1979.

Frankfort has three Japanese plants from Kyoto, Tokyo, and Kanagawa. Leestown Company, an affiliate of Takara Shuzo Company, makes packaged beverages and distilled products. Takara Shuzo, incorporated in 1825, is a distiller of alcoholic beverages such as *sake,* with annual sales of more than $1 billion. It is the largest domestic producer of *mira* (a sweetened cooking wine) and *shochu* (a distilled drink made from rice or sweet potatoes). Since 1970 it has been developing new fermented products, including pharmaceuticals. Tokyo-based Topy Corporation manufactures auto wheels, and Kanagawa-based Ohi Automotive makes auto door hinges, seat support hardware, and hood and door latches. These Japanese firms employ more than 1,300 workers. Topy is a world leader in the production of wheels for cars, trucks, buses, and off-road vehicles and undercarriage components for construction and earth-moving machinery.

Franklin Precision, an affiliate of Aisan Industries in Obu City in western Aichi prefecture, manufactures auto engine parts in Franklin. ACK Controls (an affiliate of Nagoya-based Chuo Springs) and AMAK Brake and Technotrim (affiliates of Tokyo-based firms) have plants in Glasgow that make auto cable controls, disc pads, and seat covers. Together these three companies employ more than 1,300 workers.

Harrodsburg, Kentucky's oldest city, attracted its first Japanese plant, Hitachi, in 1985. At the time, strong anti-Japanese sentiments lingered from the destruction of a National Guard unit from Harrodsburg in the Bataan death march, which left widows, children, and parents with bitter feelings. More than half a century later, Hitachi has proved to be a good resident, employing 950 workers. Trim Masters, a joint venture of Johnson Controls, Toyota Tsusho, and ARACO Corporation, came to Harrodsburg in 1988, bringing 700 more jobs. Hitachi manufactures autoelectric devices, and Trim Masters makes auto seats and doors, seat covers, and trim.

Hopkinsville has four Japanese plants, three from Tokyo, M H I Machine Tool (an affiliate of Mitsubishi Heavy Industries), Meritor Suspension Systems (a joint venture of Rockwell International and Mitsubishi Steel), and CoPar (an affiliate of Toyo Radiator Company), and one from Shizuoka, Douglas Autotech Corporation (an affiliate of Fuji Kiko). M H I Machine Tool specializes in vertical and horizontal machining centers; the other com-

Hitachi Automotive Products (USA) was established in 1985 in Harrodsburg, Kentucky. The plant employs 950 persons and is owned by Hitachi Ltd. of Tokyo. It produces automobile electric devices, alternators, and starter motors. The pond and rock garden in front of the plant suggests Japanese landscape. (Photograph by P.P. Karan)

panies manufacture steering columns, torsion bars, and copper and brass radiators. These companies employ more than 600 workers.

A subsidiary of Tokyo-based firm Y K K Corporation, Universal Fasteners employs nearly 300 people and makes automatic attaching machines, metal buttons, snap fasteners, hooks, and eyes in Lawrenceburg. Three Aichi-based firms, Curtis-Maruyasu, TG (USA) Corporation, and F E T Engineering, manufacture automotive gas line and brake line, plastic parts, and electroformed tooling equipment in Lebanon. Curtis-Maruyasu is a Japanese-American venture which makes auto gas and brake lines and employs 20 workers in a small town where unemployment was about 12 percent. In Leitchfield, Inoac Packaging Group and Trim Masters manufacture plastic bottles and trim for car seats.

Tokyo-based Link-Belt Construction Equipment Company, an affiliate of Sumitomo group, employs more than 900 persons in Lexington in the excavating equipment business. Two other Japanese companies in Lexington, Tokyo-based Toyo Seisakusho and Accuromm (a joint venture of Fuji Seiko and Toyota Tsusho) make tape and carbide cutting tools for the auto industry. About 950 workers are employed in Japanese firms in Lexington. In nearby Nicholasville, Trim Masters makes seating for automotive interiors. To the south in London, Aisin Automotive Casting, an affiliate of Aisin Seiki of Kariya, makes aluminum die castings for automobiles and employs about 60 persons. Aisin Seiki is Japan's leading manufacturer and seller of automotive components. Incorporated in 1949, it is a member of the Toyota group with eight overseas offices and twelve subsidiaries and affiliates and annual sales of more than $4 billion.

Two major Japanese firms making synthetic elastomers and thermostats in Louisville are Tokyo-based Zeon Chemicals (affiliate of Nippon Zeon Company) and Osaka-based Wako Electronics. Together these two plants employ about 420 persons. In addition, six smaller Japanese-owned plants employ fewer than 50 persons each. They make brake parts, fabricated steel, stamping and assembly equipment, and bioproducts.

Maysville has two Tokyo-based plants, Mitsubishi Electric and Technotrim (a joint venture of Johnson Controls and Tachi-S Company), manufacturing electronic auto products and seat covers. There is also Green Tokai, an affiliate of Tokai Kogyo Company, that makes auto trim products and is based in Obu City (Aichi prefecture). Japanese companies provide employment for nearly 950 persons in Maysville. Osaka-based Sumitomo Electric Wiring Systems employs more than 1,000 persons in Morgantown. Tokyo-based Akebono plant makes brake parts in Munfordville. Akebono Bureki Kogyo is one of Japan's leading manufacturers of brake mechanisms for automobiles, railway cars, and industrial machinery. Incorporated in 1936, its major stockholders are Japanese automakers and Bosch of Germany.

Central Manufacturing Company in Paris, a Japanese firm based in Anjo (a satellite city of Nagoya), manufactures aluminum wheels and related products and employs about 300 workers. It is a joint venture operated by Kelsey-Hayes Company, Chuo Seiki Company, and Toyoda America.

In Richmond, Yuasa-Exide of Osaka employs 300 workers. Auto Parts Technology, an affiliate of Aichi Kikai of Nagoya, and Kokoku Rubber of Tokyo each employ 120 persons. They manufacture batteries, transmission gears, and rubber components for auto, medical, and business machinery. Established in 1943, Aichi Kikai is a principal manufacturer of automobile engines and transmissions with annual sales of more than $2 billion.

J S Technos Corporation, a joint venture of Japanese companies based in Tokyo and Hiroshima, makes brake parts in Russellville. Osaka-based Sumitomo Electric Wiring Systems manufactures plastic connectors and electric wiring harnesses for automobiles in Scottsville. Shelbyville has three Japanese firms: Ichikoh Manufacturing, an affiliate of Ichikoh Industries; Alcoa Fujikura from Tokyo; and Katayama America, an affiliate of Katayama Kogyo Company of Okayama. These three plants manufacture rearview and sideview auto mirrors, wiring harness, and window frames and provide employment for nearly 900 persons.

Somerset has two Japanese plants—Toyotetsu (an affiliate of Toyota-based Toyoda Iron Works) and Tokyo-based Hayes Lemmerz—specializing in auto stampings and aluminum wheels and employing more than 500 persons. Hayes Lemmerz is a joint venture of Hayes Lemmerz, Asahi Tec, and Tomen Corporation. N S U Corporation (an affiliate of Nakagawa Sangyo Company based in Nawa-gun) makes muffler components in Sonora (Hardin County). Automotive armrests are made by an Aichi-based plant in Springfield. Auto parts stamping equipment is made in Stanford by a subsidiary of Toshin Company of Ayase, Kanagawa.

Versailles is the site for two Tokyo-based companies, Y H America and United L-N Glass. Y H America, owned by Yokohama Hydex Company and Yokohama Rubber Company, manufactures air conditioning and power steering hose, fittings and hose assemblies, and sealant and primer for automobiles. United L-N Glass, which makes laminated and tempered glass parts for automobiles, is a joint venture formed by Libby-Owens-Ford Glass and Nippon Sheet Glass of Japan. The Versailles plant combines the best of both companies in technology and marketing expertise.

Three Japanese firms, Tokyo-based Waltex, an affiliate of Toyo Denyo; Clarion Manufacturing, an affiliate of Clarion Company; and Shizuoka-based Dynamec (a joint venture of Bertrand Faure and Fuji Kiko), make auto welding equipment, audio equipment, and auto seat mechanisms in Walton (Boone County). These three plants employ about 470 workers. Firestone Products, owned by Bridgestone Corporation of Tokyo, manufactures auto air springs in Williamsburg and employs about 285 persons.

Winchester has five Japanese plants. The largest is Ohi America, owned by Ohi Seisakusho of Yokohama and Nissho Iwai of Tokyo. Ohi America makes auto components and employs nearly 235 persons. The other companies are Itochu Steel of Tokyo; Ainak Industries, an affiliate of Gomunoinake Company of Nagoya; Wintech of Ibaraki; and Fuji Univance of Shizuoka. They make a variety of products for the automobile industry such as rubber parts, plastic moldings, and recreational vehicle parts.

A majority of the Japanese plants located in Kentucky are suppliers of parts not only for Toyota of Kentucky but also for other domestic and Japanese automakers in the United States. For example, the major customers of Y H America in Versailles include Mitsubishi Climate Control, AutoAlliance International, Calsonic North America (California), Calsonic Climate Control (United Kingdom), Calsonic Climate Control (Spain), Cami Automotive, Honda of America, Isuzu Motors America, Mazda North America, Nissan Forklift Corporation, Subaru-Isuzu Automotive, Toyoda TRW Automotive, Zexel U.S.A., Libby-Owens-Ford, Toyota of Canada, Toyota of Kentucky, Toyota of Indiana, United L-N Glass, Vuteq of Kentucky, Vuteq of Illinois, Guide Corporation, North America Lighting, Stanley Electric, and Textron.

Kentucky's position provides Japanese companies a central location within easy reach of major automobile manufacturing plants and industrial centers in the United States and Canada. Since many of the small communities where Japanese plants are located are in less-developed areas of the state, Japanese investments have played a big role in the local economies. In turn, the politically and socially conservative people in these small communities have provided a stable and hard-working labor force with high "work ethics" in the words of a Japanese plant manager.

The importance of agglomeration economies has also played a significant role in decisions to locate Japanese firms in Kentucky (Head, Reis, and Swenson 1995). Japanese investors prefer to situate their plants in areas with concentrations of previous Japanese investments in the same industry and, in the case of auto-related firms, where the previous investments were made by group affiliates. In conjunction with factors such as labor and incentives, agglomeration benefits have driven locational choice.

Japanese Presence in Kentucky

Most Kentuckians and many Japanese perceive that Kentucky has several advantages in attracting Japanese businesses to the state. A survey of Japanese executives in Kentucky was conducted in March/April 1999 to find out why their companies chose to locate in Kentucky. A number of factors were mentioned: work ethics and reliability of the labor force in the smaller towns and communities where most of the Japanese plants are located, cost and availability of transportation, cooperation of local and state business and political leaders, availability of technical and vocational training programs for employees, and the geographic and climatic similarities between Japan and Kentucky.

It is clear that locational decisions by Japanese firms are made primarily on economic factors such as access to transportation and availability of labor force. When these criteria are met, Japanese businesses prefer to locate in smaller cities on the periphery of major metropolitan areas in Kentucky. Absence of labor unions in the peripheral communities is a major consideration in locational decision making for Japanese firms. The Japanese management style and the American union style are often viewed as incompatible (Gordon 1985), but in many places labor unions and Japanese management have learned to work together. Japanese managers in Kentucky have attempted to develop a feeling of company loyalty among workers to create a family-like atmosphere in the plant. Labor recruited from rural areas in Kentucky tend to respond better to this approach than workers from large metropolitan areas.

Efforts to unionize Toyota's Georgetown plant have not succeeded. The United Auto Workers (UAW) targeted the plant in 1985 when Toyota announced the location. The UAW opened an office in Georgetown in April 1989 but closed it in the early 1990s. Attempts to organize the union at the plant have been extremely difficult. For one thing, many employees—who earn as much as $60,000 a year with overtime—are strongly opposed to the union. Most workers appreciate the high wages and direct access to management. No local union has ever been formed at a foreign-owned auto plant in the United States. Workers at the Toyota-run plant in Fremont, California, are represented by the UAW, but that plant is half-owned by General Motors, which brought the union with it. Most Daimler Chrysler plants in the United States were organized before Daimler-Benz acquired Chrysler in 1998. In February 2000 an effort to organize an Alabama Mercedes plant faded.

In Japan, factories in peripheral areas surrounding major industrial regions have recruited workers from rural areas. The same preference for rural workers has been demonstrated in Kentucky. People from rural Kentucky are responsive to Japan's personal style of business. Our interviews with workers in Japanese plants and Japanese managers indicate that both the Japanese and rural Kentuckians feels comfortable with the traditional style in labor management as well as in business relationships.

Cooperation from state and local governments was often cited in the interviews as a major factor in the decision to locate in Kentucky. Many county and city officials in Kentucky, it appears from our interviews, have done excellent jobs in recent years in attracting Japanese plants to their communities. Japanese executives in Kentucky have also made major efforts to establish good relations with the communities through their support of local activities by generous grants. Other things being equal, incentives packages have made the difference in the final locational decision in many cases.

The important role played by the Kentucky office in Tokyo, which opened in April 1983, is also significant in attracting Japanese investments to the state. Jiro Hashimoto, who had been with Sumitomo Corporation, a major trading house, for twenty years, became the chief representative of Kentucky's Tokyo office. "My most difficult task was to give Kentucky a new image as an industrial state for Japanese investors, rather than as the home of Kentucky Fried Chicken and bourbon whiskey," remarked Hashimoto in an interview with *the Daily Yomiuri* (Tokyo). The telephone rarely rang for a while after the office was opened. At that time, twenty-one U.S. states already had representative offices in Japan. What should a latecomer do after all other state offices had supposedly finished or nearly finished inducing Japanese investments? Taking a hint from a map of automobile manufacturing companies in the United States, the Kentucky office in Tokyo decided to target auto parts suppliers to take advantage of the presence of major Japanese automakers in Kentucky's neighboring states—Honda Motor in Ohio and Nissan Motor in Tennessee. Hashimoto spent one and a half years "seeding"—visiting companies and relevant government offices—before Japan's top auto wheel producer, Topy Industries, decided to invest in Kentucky and established a plant in Frankfort in 1986.

In May 1984, one year after the opening of the Tokyo office, the Kentucky representative contacted Toyota for the first time and scheduled a meeting between Toyota executives and Kentucky state officials visiting Japan. At that time there was widespread belief that the largest automaker in Japan would not build a wholly owned plant in the United States because it had agreed with General Motors in the preceding year to set up an equally owned venture in California. Nonetheless, thirty-two locations, including those in Kentucky, Georgia, Indiana, Kansas, Missouri, and Tennessee, fiercely competed with one another to entice Toyota. In December 1985, the automotive giant decided to set up Toyota Motor Manufacturing, Kentucky, wholly owned by the Toyota group, in Georgetown. Hashimoto's experience at a leading trading company does not let him miss chances to lure Japanese investment to Kentucky.

Almost all the effort of the Kentucky office in Tokyo is spent inducing Japanese investment in Kentucky. The Kentucky office highlights the Bluegrass State's geographical advantage of being located at the center of the thirty-one-state distribution area that has 70 percent of the U.S. market, the state's good transportation network, a high-quality workforce, and various business incentives. Timing, clear goal setting, and efforts to win battles with other states are three major factors contributing to the success of Kentucky's office in Tokyo.

During the interviews many Japanese pointed out cultural and geographical similarities between Japan and Kentucky as an element in their attraction to the Bluegrass State. Regional and place identities are strong among people of both Japan and Kentucky. Few states are so vivid regionally as Kentucky, and this is evident remarkably in the common idiom (Karan 1973; Karan and Mather 1977). Most Kentuckians identify strongly with their home county. Likewise the Japanese closely identify themselves with their home region or prefecture (Mather, Karan, and Iijima 1998). In Tokyo and other large cities of Japan, people coming from other prefectures or regions have established social associations or clubs where members from the specific area meet regularly in an effort to maintain identity and bond with others from their home place.

In Japan, Bluegrass country music is a *shumi,* a hobby or "taste" like calligraphy or tea ceremony, that goes a long way toward defining lifestyle and circle of friends. At a Country Gold Music Festival held in Kumamoto in September 1998 at an outdoor venue overlooking scenic Mount Aso, an active volcano in the lonesome heart of the southern Japanese island of Kyushu, we noticed people coming from all over Japan—from Hokkaido to Okinawa. Many fans made a weekend of the event. They tossed back *mizuwari* (Scotch and water) and exchanged *meishi* (name cards) documenting membership in Bluegrass music clubs like Chuck Wagon Family in Kyoto, Deep River in Tokyo, and Cattle Call in Okayama. In most Japanese cities, Bluegrass bands, such as Turquoise at the Chuck Wagon in Fukuoka, are popular. Stephen Foster's famous ballad "My Old Kentucky Home" is enormously popular in Japan—so much so that the home in Bardstown said to have inspired the song has become a popular stop for Japanese tour groups in the United States. There are other links. The Marlboro man, long banished from American television, is riding high on late-night airwaves in Japan. Breaking broncos and kicking up dust that disappears in the cigarette smoke, the cowboy brings the message, "Smoking is cool." The Bluegrass music, songs, and cigarettes reflect similarities in likeness for cultural icons between Japan and Kentucky. Geographically and culturally, Japan and Kentucky—or "Kentakky" in *katakana,* the Japanese alphabet for words borrowed from other languages—have found they have much in common.

Kentuckians have come to realize that Japan is essential to the state's economy. It would be interesting to speculate where Kentucky would be if the 109 manufacturing plants accounting for more than thirty-five thousand jobs and nearly $7 billion in direct investment had not located in Kentucky. It is expected that investment by Japanese firms will continue as Japan's best companies transfer production abroad in response to the ever-growing pull of the global marketplace (Hirsh and Henry 1997). The overregulated Japanese marketplace no longer works best for Japanese multinational companies.

REFERENCES

Aharoni, Yair. 1966. *The Foreign Investment Decision Process*. Boston: Harvard University Graduate School of Business Administration.

Allen, G.C. 1981. *The Japanese Economy*. London: Weidenfeld and Nicolson.

Bagchi-Sen, S. 1995. Foreign Direct Investment in the U.S. Manufacturing Industries: Sources and Specific Variations. *Geografiska Annaler* Series A, 77B(1):17–29.

Barrell, Ray, and Nigen Pain. 1999. Trade Restraints and Japanese Direct Investment Flows. *European Economic Review* 43(1):29–45.

Buckley, Peter J., and Mark C. Casson. 1976. *The Future of Multinational Enterprise*. London: Macmillan.

Caves, Richard E. 1971. International Corporations: The Industrial Economics of Foreign Investment. *Economica* 38(141):1–27.

Cohen, Stephen D. 1985. *Uneasy Partnership: Competition and Conflict in U.S.-Japanese Trade Relations*. Cambridge, Mass.: Balinger.

Dunning, John H. 1988. The Eclectic Paradigm of International Production: A Restatement and Some Possible Extensions. *Journal of International Business Studies* 19(1):1–31.

Dunning, John H., and Alan M. Rugman. 1985. The Influence of Hymer's Dissertation on the Theory of Foreign Direct Investment, in Honor of Stephen H. Hymer: The First Quarter Century of the Theory of Foreign Direct Investment. *The American Economic Review*, May, 228–32.

Florida, Richard, and Martin Kenny. 1994. The Globalization of Japanese R & D: The Economic Geography of Japanese R & D Investments in the United States. *Economic Geography* 70:344–69.

Frankel, Jeffrey A. 1992. Japanese Finance: A Survey. In Paul R. Krugman, ed. *The United States and Japan: Trade and Investment in the 1990s*. Cambridge, Mass.: National Bureau of Economic Research.

Gordon, Andrew. 1985. *The Evolution of Labor Relations in Japan*. Cambridge, Mass.: Harvard Univ. Press.

Graham, Edward M., and Paul R. Krugman. 1989. *Foreign Direct Investment in the United States*. Washington, D.C.: Institute for International Economics.

Head, Keith, John Reis, and Deborah Swenson. 1995. Agglomeration Benefits and Locational Choice: Evidence from Japanese Manufacturing Investments in the United States. *Journal of International Economics* 38:223–47.

Hirsh, Michael, and E. Keith Henry. 1997. The Unraveling of Japan Inc.: Multinationals as Agents of Change. *Foreign Affairs* 76 (March/April): 110–16.

Hufbauer, Gary C. 1975. The Multinational Corporation and Direct Investment. In *International Trade and Finance: Frontiers of Research*, editor, Peter B. Kenen. Cambridge: Cambridge Univ. Press.

Hymer, Stephen H. 1976. *International Operations of National Firms*. Cambridge, Mass.: MIT Press.

Karan, P.P., ed., 1973. *Kentucky: A Regional Geography*. Dubuque, Iowa: Kendall/ Hunt Publishing Company.

Karan, P.P., and Cotton Mather, eds., 1977. *Atlas of Kentucky*. Lexington: Univ. Press of Kentucky.

Kindleberger, Charles P. 1969. *American Business Abroad: Six Lectures on Foreign Direct Investment*. New Haven, Conn.: Yale Univ. Press.

Mann, Catherine L. 1989. Determinants of Japanese Direct Investment in U.S. Manufacturing Industries. Board of Governors of the Federal Reserve System, International Finance Discussion Paper #362.

Marsh, F. 1983. *Japanese Overseas Investment: The new Challenge*. London: The Economist Intelligence Unit Limited.

Mather, Cotton, P.P. Karan, and Shigeru Iijima. 1998. *Japanese Landscapes: Where Land and Culture Merge*. Lexington: Univ. Press of Kentucky.

McKnight, S. 1988. *Japan's Expanding US Manufacturing Presence: 1987 Update*. Washington, D.C.: Japan Economic Institute.

Ray, Edward John. 1991. A Profile of Recent Foreign Investment in the United States. *Annals of the American Association of Political and Social Scientists*, July: 50–65.

Rubenstein, J.M. 1986. Changing Distribution of the American Automobile Industry. *Geographical Review* 76(3):288–300.

Vernon, Raymond. 1966. International Investment and International Trade in the Product Cycle. *Quarterly Journal of Economics* 83(1):190–207.

Vernon, Raymond. 1974. The Location of Economic Activity. In John H. Dunning, ed. *Economic Analysis and the Multinational Enterprise*. London: George Allen & Unwin.

"War Between the States." 1988. *Newsweek*, 30 May, 44.

Part II

Toyota in Kentucky and Japan

3

State and Local Government Negotiation with Japanese Multinational Corporations

DAVID M. POTTER

SINCE THE 1980S, FOREIGN DIRECT INVESTMENT (FDI) in American states has been a concern of academics, policy makers, and businesspeople. Since the mid-1980s the inflow of Japanese direct investment, especially automobiles, into the Midwest and South has engendered a corresponding public and academic debate as to its effects. In the academic discussions that have sought to understand that investment, comparatively little attention has been paid to a key question: how do state governments negotiate with multinational corporations (MNCs), and what characteristics of the bargaining environment constrain their ability to secure agreements with MNCs that are also acceptable to their publics? In this chapter, Robert Putnam's model of the two-level bargaining game in international negotiations is used as a device for thinking about the characteristics of state government–MNC negotiations.

This research is significant for three reasons. First, most of the research has focused on negotiations between states, or alternatively, governments such as the European Union that can be seen as variants of states (Putnam 1988; Evans, Putnam, and Jacobsen 1993; Schoppa 1997). This study extends Putnam's two-level framework from state-state negotiations to negotiations between subnational governments and MNCs. It is clear both from the perspective of interdependence theory and from practical international politics that subnational governments increasingly play roles in international relations. In countries like the United States, subnational governments may have significant room to formulate what may be considered independent, if not autonomous, foreign political and economic policies. In recent years, they have engaged in foreign economic policies that include official visits to foreign countries, transnational agreements, and the establishment of more or less permanent economic representation overseas (Grubel 1993; Fry 1998).

Fry (1998, 5) notes that "state governments now operate almost as many permanent offices overseas as the U.S. government operates embassies." Considering structural factors that might enhance or inhibit their abilities to negotiate in the international arena deserves attention.

Second, MNCs and their impact on the international economy and specific societies have engendered an enormous academic and policy-oriented literature. Again, from the perspective of interdependence theory and practical politics, the behavior of MNCs in their negotiations with governments merits research in its own right. This study combines both of these research agendas by examining the characteristics of the negotiation process between American state governments and foreign MNCs over siting of manufacturing facilities. The structural characteristics of the negotiating process outlined below are applicable to any state government entering into negotiations with any major MNC.

Finally, the chapter is significant because it attempts to expand our understanding of the political dynamics of Japanese and other FDI in Kentucky.

Toyota Motor Manufacturing, North America (TMMNA) in Erlanger, Kentucky, provides centralized support for Toyota's U.S. and Canadian manufacturing activities. A new $15 million production engineering/quality laboratory has been completed. Toyota's U.S. investments total $9.2 billion; it employed 164,865 with direct payroll of $1.4 billion in 1998. Auto parts purchases by TMMNA totaled $8.3 billion ($6.6 billion for U.S. production and $1.7 billion for exports to Japan). Other purchases of goods and services amounted to $2 billion. Toyota produced 791,091 vehicles in the United States in 1998; more than 30,000 vehicles were exported (8,145 to Japan, the rest to other countries). There were 1,470 Toyota dealerships in the United States in 1998. (Photograph courtesy of Toyota Motor Manufacturing, North America)

To date, the literature on Japanese FDI in industrialized nations,[1] including the United States, has focused on economic motives and impacts (Dunning 1986; Strange 1993; Han 1994; Mason and Encarnation 1994; Sachwald 1995; Hollerman and Myers 1996; Belderbos 1997); management practices (Trevor 1983; Kissler 1996; Besser 1996); and general social, political, and economic issues of industrial recruitment in American communities (Gelsanliter 1990; Yanarella and Green 1990; Sherman 1994; Chapman Elhance, and Wenum 1995; Kim 1995). Studies that take up negotiations between state governments and MNCs tend to be descriptive (Gersanliter 1990; Sherman 1994; Chapman, Elhance, and Wenum 1995; Kim 1995). In this regard, Yanarella and Green's edited volume (1990) stands out as an exception, but its authors have tended to be varied in their research and conclusions. This chapter focuses on the issue of state-MNC negotiation as a way to account for the various issues in this diverse literature.

The research for this study draws from the Kentucky state government's experience negotiating with Toyota Motor Corporation to establish its Georgetown plant, a headquarters for Toyota Motor Manufacturing, North America in Erlanger (fig. 3.1), and proposed construction of a parts distribution center for Toyota Motor Sales in Hebron, but it also draws from the lessons of other negotiations between state governments and MNCs. FDI by the automotive industry has been chosen for two reasons. First, automotive investment is large scale, involving significant costs to the investor as well as to the state inviting that investment. Because of the perceived benefits to state economies and economic development policies from automotive investment,[2] state government officials are willing to engage in serious negotiations with corporations. MNCs, for their part, have incentives to bargain for concessions that will alleviate their costs. Second, because the results of those negotiations are likely to have a variety of impacts on state and local economies and communities, they tend to have high profiles. As a result, a great deal of journalistic and scholarly literature has been produced on this topic, which allows the researcher to reach accurate conclusions about the negotiating process.

THE MODEL

The core of Putnam's (1988) framework consists of the argument that negotiators of international agreements must negotiate on two levels simultaneously.[3] On what he called Level 1, negotiators from each state bargain with each other across the table. On what he called Level 2, Level 1 negotiators must then bargain with key agencies and constituencies within their own governments and societies to secure ratification of the agreement made at Level 1. Ratification may consist of a formal vote on a Level 1 agreement by

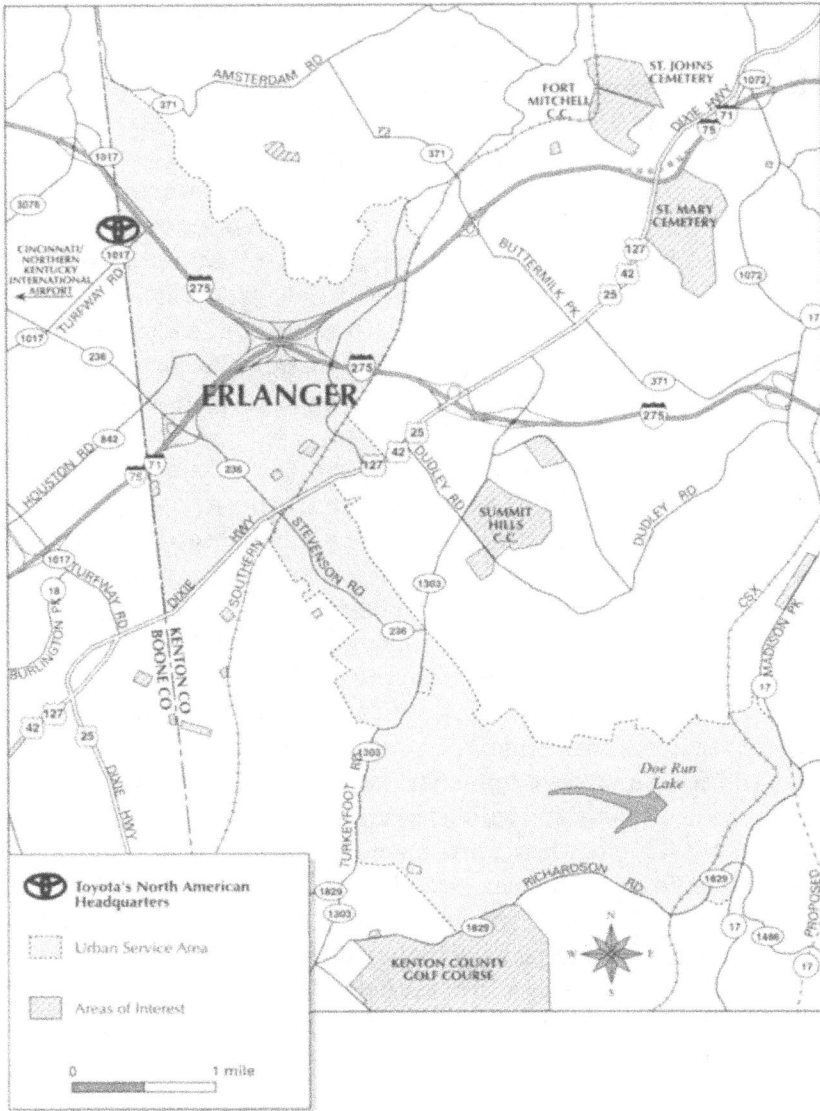

Fig. 3.1: Erlanger: Toyota's North American headquarters.

a legislature or executive body or may consist of a de facto acceptance or veto by key constituencies not formally part of a formal ratification process.

Based on this understanding, Putnam introduces the idea of win set: "the set of all possible Level I agreements that would 'win'—that is gain the necessary majority among constituents—when simply voted up or down" by Level 2 actors (p. 437). Level 1 agreements are tentative until ratified: Putnam observes that "the only formal constraint on the ratification process is that since the identical agreement must be ratified by both sides, a preliminary Level I agreement cannot be amended at Level II without reopening the Level I negotiations" (p. 437). The Level 2 win set thus determines the success of international agreements.

This is significant because the sizes of win sets affect the ability of Level 1 negotiators to effect an agreement. The larger the range of acceptable outcomes, the greater the possibility for agreement. Yet, Putnam argues that Level 2 coalitions and their preferences, as well as Level 2 institutions, affect the size of the win set. In general, the more intransigent are Level 2 preferences for no agreement or a substantially modified one, and the more Level 2 institutions' ratification roles are formalized, the smaller that side's Level 1 win set. Homogeneity v. heterogeneity of preferences among Level 2 ratifiers, differences in constituencies' participation rates, and the ability of Level 1 negotiators to make side payments are also factors. This is a significant feature in this chapter because the organizational structures that link each side's Level 1 and Level 2 actors differ. I argue that difference greatly affects the scope of win sets.

Putnam's model, despite its utility in analyzing links between domestic and international politics, focuses on endogenous factors.[4] Because its focus is on state-state negotiations, it ignores structural characteristics of the international system. This paper must inevitably deal with structural characteristics of the political system (largely the United States, for our purposes here) in which state governments operate when they conduct negotiations with outside actors such as MNCs. At the risk of inelegance, this paper adds an additional level of analysis, Level 3, to encompass those environmental characteristics that condition state government–MNC negotiations.

Level 3: Structural Characteristics of State Government–MNC Negotiations

In the case at hand, the primary objective of state-MNC negotiations is to agree on a site for the MNC's facility. Other issues are negotiated as well, but these are usually consequences of the main negotiations over a suitable site. These negotiations have a number of important features.

First, the bargaining game discussed here takes place in an environment characterized by severe competition in an anarchic system. A large number of states engage in competitive bidding in which there is little or no incentive to cooperate or coordinate decision making. Given the economic transnationalism that lies behind the North American Free Trade Agreement (NAFTA), if anything, states in Canada and Mexico add to the number of potential competitors.[5] Moreover, in an industry like automobiles or machine tools, the number of major corporate players is limited. In such an environment, states perceive their efforts to bring in a large multinational, the Toyota case is a good example, as a zero-sum competition.

The anarchic environment is abetted, even created, by the lack of suprastate organization that could promote cooperation or coordination of state investment policies. The federal government has largely left FDI policies, except in certain cases involving national security, to the states themselves. That is not to say, however, that the federal government is irrelevant in state economic development issues, and specifically it does not mean that it is irrelevant in fostering a climate, conducive or not, in which states attempt to attract FDI. There is general agreement in the literature from the 1980s on Japanese direct investment in the United States that the threat of protectionist policies at the federal level was an important pull factor inducing Japanese firms to invest in the United States. Simply, the federal government does nothing deliberate to affect specific MNC decisions to locate in particular states. The impact of federal nonpolicy is highlighted if we look at national government decisions concerning FDI across the industrial democracies. First, there is a range of host government policies concerning FDI (Bailey, Harte, and Sugden 1996), and host governments with unitary systems have attempted to guide FDI into particular regions in accordance with national priorities (Han 1994).

In such an environment, MNCs will be able to choose among states when deciding on a location. Indeed, they have fifty states from which to choose, more if we add the impact of NAFTA. Nissan Motors reportedly considered thirty-four states in its initial search for a site for the plant it eventually built in Smyrna, Tennessee; a Nissan supplier considered nineteen before it decided to locate in that state (Kim 1995, 54).

State constitutions represent another potential environmental obstacle to state attempts to recruit outside investment. A number of constitutions, Kentucky's included, place strict limits on levels and types of state debt and other schemes that can be used to promote private sector investment (Green 1990).

This environment affects how the states' Level 1 actors approach their MNC counterparts and in turn how those counterparts enter negotiations. First, the state government acts as supplicant, asking the MNC to locate a facility within its borders instead of in some other state. State governments, of course, have no power to coerce MNCs into investing in their states. In the typical case the MNC announces its intention to establish a plant or other facility in the host country, and in turn state government executives respond with invitations to look at the state, begin preparations on incentives packages, and so on. Former governor Martha Layne Collins's trip to Japan to plead Kentucky's case before Toyota is not exceptional. Former Tennessee governor Lamar Alexander and former Ohio governor James Rhodes had made similar trips to court Japanese automobile manufacturers (Gelsanliter 1990; Kim 1995).

Second, states are immobile, while their MNC counterparts are not. States cannot move to adjust to changing economic realities; MNCs can and do.[6] Significantly, MNC decisions on a single facility, while potentially very important to the state, are but one of many decisions about facilities around the world. While states may be focused on one automotive or other operation, MNCs tend to see things in terms of a broader global corporate strategy. In 1995, for example, a year before Toyota announced it would establish its North American operations subsidiary in Erlanger, its chairman announced the company's plans to establish manufacturing plants in China, Vietnam, Mexico, and other countries. The driving force behind this international expansion was the recognition of a prolonged slump in demand in Japan's domestic market (*Gurobaruka wo Sekkyoku Suishin* 1995).

Third, state governments have a limited range of incentives they can offer MNCs. The literature on MNC site selection, moreover, demonstrates that state incentives packages tend to be homogeneous (see, for example, Yanarella and Green 1995; Kim 1995; Chapman, Elhance, and Wenum 1995). At most, the literature suggests that states may lose FDI by having too negative policies (Hollerman 1981). Furthermore, many issues that affect site selection—geography, climate, labor force, and proximity to markets and transportation arteries—are either beyond state government control or difficult to adjust to suit MNC needs in the short run.

Finally, it is not at all clear that even these homogeneous, often limited financial incentives have much impact on inducing MNCs to choose one state over another. Chernotsky (1983, 48) found that financial incentives ranked low in German and Japanese companies' decisions to locate in Charlotte, North Carolina. Interviews (Potter 1999) and other literature (Yanarella and Green 1990; Han 1994; Kim 1995) essentially confirm this. Dunning (1986) found that in Britain grant incentives to induce Japanese MNCs to locate in certain areas were not viewed by the companies as serious considerations when deciding on sites but were more important to them once they had made the decision to locate.

We can clearly see the effects of this environmental configuration in the pattern of negotiations that led to Kentucky's initial agreement with Toyota for the Georgetown plant. Following the latter's July 1985 announcement that it planned to open new plants in the United States and Canada, officials from seventeen states appealed to the company to locate within their borders:

nearly every Midwest and Southern state was represented (*Toyota Koujou Zehi* 1985). Every Canadian state applied for the future Ontario plant as well. Claiming that such a process would avoid suspicion of favoritism or unfairness, Toyota announced in August that it would follow a process of "open bidding" (*koukai nyusatsu*) from prospective states and municipalities to decide on its plant sites. In a questionnaire it sent to each prospective government, it asked if land, electricity, water, roads, and incentives packages would be available *(Koukai Nyuusatsu de Kettei* 1985). In the initial stages of negotiation, therefore, prospective Level 1 state negotiators had every reason to stake out as large win sets as possible. That former governor Collins was willing to invest as much as the state eventually did to secure an agreement, much criticized for being the largest incentives package paid to a MNC at the time, becomes understandable if we consider the Level 3 constraints and the subsequent structuring of opening negotiations they afforded Toyota.

RATIFICATION: LEVEL 2 ABILITY ON EACH SIDE TO MODIFY LEVEL 1 AGREEMENTS

A structural asymmetry of accountability exists between Level 1 and Level 2 players in state-MNC negotiations. The ratification of the agreement with Toyota concerning its Georgetown plant is instructive in this regard. Governors, who because of the entrepreneurial nature of game initiation tend to be the key Level 1 negotiators, are elected officials whose careers depend on pleasing their coalition constituencies. Moreover, governors must answer to their state legislatures, whose members are in turn responsible to their constituents, to local governments, and sometimes to the courts. Finally, local governments (if they weren't already in the race) must be persuaded to accept the new industrial site.

Moreover, Level 1 and Level 2 parties in the states tend to have different views of the benefits of FDI. Level 1 executives tend to see foreign investment solely in terms of economic benefits: employment, economic and technological development, etc. Level 2 ratifiers in the site communities tend to see not only the economic benefits but also social disadvantages: increased traffic and pollution, transformation of small-town lifestyle, and so on.

Local governments can also impede ratification because they have powers over local zoning ordinances and local corporate taxes, and, of course, they must represent those people in the state most likely to be directly affected by the introduction of a major industrial site (Gelsanliter 1990; Sherman 1994).

Furthermore, barriers to entry during the ratification phase are low, which makes it easy for opponents of Level 1 agreements to slow down, if not stop, ratification. The Georgetown case is instructive: national actors (i.e., Ralph

Nader and the National Building Construction Trades Union) involved themselves in, respectively, a suit before the state Supreme Court to prevent the state from using public moneys for the incentives package and negotiations to alter the conditions of construction contracting. Yanarella and Reid (1990) argue that local opposition to the Georgetown plant site failed because it was neither politically nor organizationally united. In this case, we may say that structural characteristics blunted the opposition's efforts. Yet Yanarella and Green take it for granted—and this is the key point—that plant site opponents would participate.

Japanese corporate Level 1 negotiators, on the other hand, face different relations with their Level 2 ratifiers. Internally, corporations are not democratic and are under no obligation to report their actions to the public. They are certainly not legally accountable to their own publics nor to those of the states in which they wish to locate. Barriers to entry of actors outside the industry group, therefore, are high. *Keiretsu* stakeholders, such as allied banks, labor unions, supplier firms, affiliated corporations, and stockholders, may be important Level 2 ratifiers, but the keiretsu structure and especially enterprise unionism largely internalize the relationship between levels. Given their tendency to view credit decisions involving keiretsu partners from the long-term perspective, banks are not likely to seriously challenge a manufacturer's decision to locate overseas. This would have been especially true during the bubble economy era of the late 1980s when huge capital surpluses and the hollowing out of Japanese industry made it particularly attractive for banks to lend for overseas projects.

Of course, many Japanese suppliers will tend to follow their main manufacturer. For them, relocation rather than opposition to the MNC's move overseas is their main choice. Kim (1995) points out that the Nissan supplier mentioned above moved to the Smyrna area to locate near other firms within the industry group. For others, however, the relocation of a main manufacturer overseas means loss of a customer. In the mid-1980s, for example, Toyota had to worry about the impact of potential American suppliers if its Japanese subcontractors were to move en masse into the United States. Given the economic frictions between the two countries at the time, Toyota decided to establish tie-ups with American suppliers and correspondingly limit the number of subcontractors it would take with it to Kentucky. (*Toyota, Taibei Shinshutsu Chousei ni Nayamu* 1985.)[7] Unlike the situation facing Kentucky negotiators, opposition to Toyota's win set from local business would be internalized.

Similarly, enterprise unions are unlikely to publicly oppose management decisions to relocate abroad. In the Toyota case, the union was notably quiet about the decision to locate in Kentucky, with the president of the All-Toyota Labor Federation publicly on record that the move was unavoidable and that the federation would negotiate simply to maintain employment levels within the Toyota group (*Bei-shinshutsu de Roudou Jouken Hyoujunka* 1985). This is in contrast to the vocal effort the National Building Construction Trades Union, which was organized with national level help, mounted to alter the deal (see Gelsanliter 1990). In sum, a major Japanese corporation is in a position to internalize potential Level 2 opposition to a move in ways no American state government can match. In particular, while this is not likely to be directly relevant to a specific negotiation with a particular state, it certainly means that MNC Level 1 negotiators are free of Level 2 ratifiers who can force no agreement.

It is possible for interlevel negotiations across the table to occur in a two-level bargaining game, a situation referred to as reverberation (Putnam 1988, 454–56; Schoppa 1997, 32–34). Level 1 negotiators attempt to expand their counterpart's win set by persuasion or threats targeted at the counterpart's Level 2 constituents. Honda's efforts to sell the local community on its Marysville site and Toyota's use of a senior American executive to negotiate with sympathetic Georgetown officials (Gersanliter 1990) are examples of this kind of tactic. Since 1986 Toyota's efforts to portray itself as a positive contributor to the commonwealth's economic and social life can be understood as a continual use of a reverberation strategy. It strikes me that this is critical for the MNC in its negotiations with state governments because it proposes to move into the state's jurisdiction. As a result, it has an incentive to assist the state's efforts to win ratification from local communities. More important to the MNC, because of its site decision, in future negotiations the state's Level 2 ratifiers will become the MNC's Level 2 ratifiers as well.

The bargaining stakes change when site location negotiations become an iterative game. Assuming a satisfactory first investment, a MNC may be inclined to invest capital in a new facility in the state again. Essentially, this reduces the competition from other states and correspondingly expands the MNC's win set. Consequently, a state should have less incentive to provide special benefits to a MNC to induce it to invest. The MNC in turn should perceive advantages, such as reduction of transaction costs, that offset the potential state concessions. For example, Toyota's siting of its North American headquarters in Erlanger in 1996 followed the establishment of the Georgetown plant by a decade.

This hypothesis is largely confirmed in the Erlanger and Hebron cases. Partly, the decision on subsequent sites is conditioned by the initial agreement. In Toyota's case, northern Kentucky is a likely spot for headquarters and parts distribution facilities because it is close to sister facilities in Indiana, West Virginia, and Kentucky. So, however, is southern Ohio, which would be somewhat closer to the Ontario, Canada, plant. Toyota appears to have decided that northern Kentucky was its preferred site early on, before it entered into negotiations with state and county officials. As observed in the discussion of state Level 1 bargaining resources, representatives from both the Economic Development Cabinet (EDC) and Toyota characterized the state incentives package for the Erlanger deal as "icing on the cake," and which, the EDC was at some pains to explain, did not involve direct cash transfers to the company (Boyer 1996; Carfagno 1996). On the other hand, Toyota was careful not to commit to the Erlanger site until it had agreed with the EDC on an incentives package. One respondent interviewed for this paper indicated that had the incentives package been unacceptable to Toyota, it would have seriously considered sites out of state. Similarly, Ohio and Kentucky were publicly in competition for the Hebron site in the months before the December 17, 1998, announcement that Hebron had been chosen.[8]

A significant feature of iterative investment bargaining games, exemplified by Toyota's negotiations over the Erlanger and Hebron sites, is that the Level 1 actors change. The governor acted as Kentucky's Level 1 negotiator in the initial negotiations for the Georgetown site in 1985. Local governments served initially as Level 2 ratifiers, then as Level 1 negotiators in the series of collateral negotiations that ensued once ratification had been secured. In the negotiations for the Erlanger and Hebron sites, negotiations followed the jurisdictional pattern seen in the Georgetown case. The EDC was involved in the early stages when Toyota requested financial incentives. But site decisions and local incentives fall under local jurisdiction. In the Erlanger case, Toyota ended up bargaining with Boone County and the City of Erlanger, both of which claimed jurisdiction over the site, and the Tri-County Economic Development Corporation (TriEd). One respondent referred to the latter organization as a "facilitator" in negotiations between municipalities and outside investors, a definition which sidesteps neat placement in Putnam's framework. Distinguishing Level 1 from Level 2 in the latter phase is not as straightforward as a nation state–centric model of negotiation would suggest.

The Erlanger site presented its own difficulties since it straddles a county line. Because the property, formerly owned by Cincinnati Bell Telephone, lies predominantly in Boone County, Toyota entered into negotiations with Boone County for incentives and other arrangements. Kenton County, in which the remainder of property lies, can be seen as a Level 2 ratifier. As it turned out, however, the building Toyota proposed to use is located mostly in Kenton County, within the city limits of Erlanger. As such, the city could expect to impose its gross receipts tax on Toyota earnings posted at that facility: the tax would have been high because all of Toyota's North American receipts would have been posted there. In the final phases of the negotiations, therefore, the City of Erlanger became a Level 1 player in the bargaining over tax structure and levels, while contenting itself with the role of Level 2 ratifier of the whole deal. (It is the author's impression that the City of Erlanger was not opposed to the Toyota decision in principle.)

The change in the bargaining game can also be noted in the quiescence of potential Level 2 ratifiers in the Erlanger and Hebron siting cases. There is a progression from high opposition to the Georgetown plant following a high profile negotiation between governor and Toyota, to lower profile state-TriEd-county negotiations with Toyota over its Erlanger site, followed again by low profile negotiations over the Hebron parts plant site. The latter two engendered almost no public opposition. In part, scope of Level 2 participation was less than in the Georgetown case. Because the negotiations over the Erlanger site involved location of a national headquarters in an existing facility, issues the National Building Construction Trades Union had cited in its campaign during the ratification of the Georgetown plant did not arise. In any event, it did not send national representatives to northern Kentucky.[9]

Similarly, no local environmental opposition organized. This may be due to three factors. First, northern Kentucky already has a fair number of manufacturing firms in the region. Second, both the Erlanger and Hebron sites were already zoned for commercial use. A significant difference in the ratification processes of the two Toyota decisions probably lies in this distinction. Toyota in 1986 proposed to establish a major manufacturing facility in a largely rural county, with significant local impacts. In 1996, it proposed to take over an existing building complex in a northern Kentucky industrial park to establish its North American subsidiary's headquarters. The appreciable social and environmental impact of substituting Toyota for Cincinnati Bell at that site would be difficult to determine.[10] Area staked out by organized interests as environmentally sensitive or of significant historical value was not involved. Finally, significant local interests in the form of the TriEd and county government (Boone, at least in the headquarters decision; Kenton and Erlanger effectively became Level 2 ratifiers because of the zoning mix-up) were incorporated into Level 1 bargaining. In sum, concocting overlapping win sets between local authorities and the corporation was eased by the absence of any local constituency committed to no-agreement (i.e., the status quo before Toyota announced its decision).

CONCLUSION

We should be aware that an iterative game changes the dynamics of MNC-government negotiations, but certain characteristics persist. Municipalities are no more mobile than state governments. The possibility that Toyota might locate its North American headquarters in a nearby state was publicly bruited during all three negotiations. Toyota's preliminary structuring work—in particular it used TriEd offices to assist in the location of suitable sites in northern Kentucky without divulging its identity in the early stages of its site search—means that it will enter a negotiation with a local government with an information advantage. Moreover, there is no reason to believe that the structural asymmetry of accountability between government and MNCs does not affect win sets. The fact that there has been little or no public opposition to Toyota's direct investments in northern Kentucky does not preclude the possibility that there could have been. While Toyota might have taken such opposition into account in expanding its win set to include fewer incentives or to meet demands for local or union participation in construction contracts (which it did in the Georgetown case), it would not be legally obliged to factor in Level 2 opposition in ways that local governments would.

Finally, how local governments negotiate and the kinds of incentives packages they can offer does not seem to be a significant factor for Japanese MNCs. One respondent who had observed the negotiations over the Erlanger site noted that incentives packages were fairly low on Toyota's list of location criteria. A bigger factor cited by local officials was the Greater Cincinnati/ Northern Kentucky International Airport. While Toyota did receive economic incentives, including a reduced gross receipts tax from the City of Erlanger, no one suggests that such enticements alone will sway a MNC in favor of one community over another.

NOTES

1. Not surprisingly, the Japanese literature on this topic has tended to focus on economic issues as they affect Japanese MNCs and the Japanese economy (see, for example, Morita 1992; Minamoto 1992) and on FDI in Asia (Horaguchi 1992).

2. See, for example, University of Michigan 1998. This is the case not only in the United States but worldwide. See Bennett and Sharpe 1985; Jenkins 1987; Doner 1991. Even in this literature, however, the focus has of necessity been on the negotiations between national governments and MNCs.

3. Putnam allowed for the possibility that subnational or private sector negotiations might have this dual character as well, which point is explored in this paper, but he chose to concentrate his analysis on international negotiations.

4. In subsequent research, some attempt has been made to consider environmental factors. See Evans, Jacobsen, and Putnam 1993.

5. A startling example of the impact of NAFTA on interstate competition can be found in an anecdote cited by Fry (1998): In 1995, a delegation from the Mexican state of Baja California Norte went to South Korea to try to persuade a major corporation from that country to locate a television parts plant in the Tijuana area. The delegation was accompanied by the California secretary of trade and commerce, who supported the proposal. The California government calculated that it was better to have a large maquiladora operation just across the border, with attendant economic spillover benefits, than to have the same plant locate to another state in the Midwest or South.

6. Thomas (1997) argues that capital mobility is the factor that most significantly impairs host governments when they negotiate with MNCs.

7. A 1990 interview conducted at a die cast metal manufacturer in northern Japan tends to confirm this view of the "internationalization" of small and medium-sized businesses in Japan. The company had recently set up a manufacturing operation in Rizal, the Philippines. When queried as to the company's decision to locate there, the president responded that "we didn't decide to locate there, it was decided for us" when the company's major customer, Mitsui, had established a facility in the province.

8. Respondents from the Kentucky side, perhaps somewhat wishfully, observed that the company did not seriously consider possible sites in Cincinnati. Toyota's willingness to stay in state, according to respondents on both sides of the negotiations, is due to Toyota's desire to maintain a relationship with the commonwealth.

9. One interview respondent did note that Toyota has worked with that union since 1986 when contracting for new construction.

10. A typical example of the attention paid to the latter decision was a report in a local newspaper that the City of Erlanger was interested in attracting a Japanese restaurant to the area.

REFERENCES

Asian Auto Makers Find a Back Door to the U.S. Market. 1985. *Business Week,* 9 December, 52–53.

Bailey, David, George Harte, and Roger Sugden. 1996. *Transnationals and Governments: Recent Policies in Japan, France, Germany, the United States, and Britain.* London and New York: Routledge.

Bei-shinshutsu de Roudou Jouken Hyoujunka. 1985. *Chuubu Nihon Keizai Shinbun.* 17 December, 3.

Belderbos, Rene.1997. *Strategic Trade and Multinational Enterprises: Essays on Trade and Investment by Japanese Electronics Firms.* Amsterdam: Thesis Publishers, 1994. Oxford: Clarendon Press.

Bennett, Douglas, and Kenneth Sharpe. 1985. *Transnational Corporations Versus the State: The Political Economy of the Mexican Auto Industry.* Princeton: Princeton Univ. Press.

Besser, Terry. 1996. *Team Toyota: Transplanting the Toyota Culture to the Camry Plant in Kentucky.* Albany, New York: State Univ. of New York Press.

Boyer, Mike. 1996. Execs See Boone Co. as N. America "Profit Center." *Cincinnati Enquirer.* 2 February, 1.

Carfagno, Jacalyn. 1996. State Lands Toyota Headquarters with $13.25 Million in Incentives. *Lexington Herald-Leader.* 2 February, 1.

Chapman, Margaret, Arun Elhance, and John Wenum. 1995. *Mitsubishi Motors in Illinois: Global Strategies, Local Impacts.* Westport, Conn.: Quorum Books.

Chernotsky, H.I. 1983. Selecting U.S. Sites: A Case Study of German and Japanese Firms. *Management International Review* (23:2) 45–55.

Doner, Richard. 1991. *Driving a Bargain.* Berkeley and Los Angeles: Univ. of California Press.

Dunning, John H. 1986. *Japanese Participation in British Industry.* London: Croom Helm.

Evans, Peter, Harold K. Jacobson, and Robert Putnam, eds. 1993. *Double-Edged Diplomacy: International Bargaining and Domestic Politics.* Berkeley and Los Angeles: Univ. of California Press.

Fry, Earl H. 1998. *The Expanding Role of State and Local Governments in U.S. Foreign Affairs.* New York: Council on Foreign Relations Press.

Gelsanliter, David. 1990. *Jump Start: Japan Comes to the Heartland.* New York: Farrar, Strauss, and Giroux.

Grady, Dennis O. 1987. State Economic Development Incentives: Why Do States Compete? *State and Local Government Review* (19:3) Fall, 86–94.

Gray, Grattan. 1987. Oh What a Feeling. *Canadian Business,* February, 82–88.

Green, William. 1990 Constitutional Dimensions of State Industrial Recruitment. In Yanarella, Ernest, and William Green, eds. (53–86) *the Politics of Industrial Recruitment.* New York, Westport, Conn., and London: Greenwood Press.

Grubel, Ruth. 1993 Government Efforts to Promote International Trade: State Trade Offices in Japan. In Robert P. McGowan and Edward J. Ottensmayer, eds. (41–53) *Economic Development Strategies for State and Local Governments.* Chicago: Nelson-Hall.

Gurobaruka wo Sekkyoku Suishin. 1995 *Chubu Nihon Keizai Shinbun,* 3 January, 1.

Han, Man-Hee. 1994. *Japanese Multinationals in the Changing Context of Regional Policy.* Aldershot: Avebury Press.

Hollerman, Leon. 1981. Japanese Direct Investment in California. *Asian Survey* (21:10) 1080–1095.

Hollerman, Leon, and Ramon Myers, eds. 1996 *The Effects of Japanese Investment on the World Economy: A Six-Country Study, 1970–1996.* Stanford, California: Hoover Institute Press.

Horaguchi Haruo. 1992. *Nihon Kigyou no Kaigai Chokusetsu Toushi: Ajia no Shinshutsu to Tettai.* Tokyo: Tokyo Daigaku Shuppankai.

Jenkins, Rhys. 1987. *Transnational Corporations and the Latin American Automobile Industry.* Pittsburgh: Pittsburgh Univ. Press.

Kim, Choong Soon. 1995. *Japanese Industry in the American South.* New York and London: Routledge.

Kissler, Leo. 1996. *Toyotismus in Europa.* Frankfurt and New York: Campus Verlag.

Koukai Nyuusatsu de Sentaku. 1985 *Chuubu Nihon Keizai Shinbun,* 15 August, 15.

Mason, Mark, and Dennis Encarnation, eds. 1994. *Does Ownership Matter? Japanese Multinationals in Europe.* Oxford: Clarendon Press.

Minamoto, Masayuki. 1992. *Kaigai Chokusetsu Toushi to Nihon Keizai: Toushi Masatsu wo Koete.* Tokyo: Yukikaku.

Morita, Kazuo. 1992. *Kigyou no Kaigai Shinshutsu: Chuukei, Chuushoukigyou no Kaigai Toushi.* Tokyo: Doubunkan.

Putnam, Robert. 1988. Diplomacy and Domestic Politics: The Logic of Two-Level Games. *International Organization* (42:3) Summer, 427–60.

Sachwald, Frederique, ed. 1995. *Japanese Firms in Europe.* Luxembourg: Harwood Academic Publishers.

Schoppa, Leonard. 1997. *Bargaining with Japan: What American Pressure Can and Cannot Do.* New York: Columbia Univ. Press.

Schoppa, Leonard. 1993. Two-Level Games and Bargaining Outcomes: Why Gaiatsu

Succeeds in Japan in Some Cases but Not Others. *International Organization* (47:3) 353–86.

Sherman, Joe. 1994. *In the Rings of Saturn*. New York and Oxford: Oxford Univ. Press.

Strange, Robert. 1993. *Japanese Manufacturing Investment in Europe: Its Impact on the UK Economy*. London and New York: Routledge.

Thomas, Kenneth P. 1997. *Capital Beyond Borders: States and Firms in the Auto Industry, 1960–1994*. New York and London: St. Martin's.

Toyota, Taibei Shinshutsu Chousei ni Nayamu. 1985. *Nihon Keizai Shinbun*. 31 October, 8.

Toyota Koujou Zehi Waga Chi he. 1985. *Nihon Keizai Shinbun*. 4 August, 4.

Toyota Motor Corporation. 1996. *Annual Report 1996*. Toyota City: Toyota Motor Corporation.

Trevor, Malcolm. 1983. *Japan's Reluctant Multinationals: Japanese Management at Home and Abroad*. London: Frances Pinter.

University of Michigan Transportation Research Institute, Office for the Study of Automotive Transportation, and the Institute of Labor and Industrial Relations. 1998. *The Contribution of the International Auto Sector to the U.S. Economy: Executive Summary*. Ann Arbor: University of Michigan.

Yanarella, Ernest, and Herbert Reid. 1990. Problems of coalition building in Japanese Auto Alley: Public Opposition to the Georgetown/Toyota Plant. In Yanarella, Ernest, and William Green, eds. (153–174) *the Politics of Industrial Recruitment*. New York, Westport, Conn., and London: Greenwood Press.

Yanarella, Ernest, and William Green, eds. 1990. *The Politics of Industrial Recruitment*. New York, Westport, Conn., and London: Greenwood Press.

4

The Geography of Toyota Motor Manufacturing Corporation

Unryu Suganuma

The world automobile industry is in transition. In the European and North American continents, the merger of Germany's Daimler-Benz and American Chrysler on May 6, 1998, created the world's fifth largest car maker (*The Economist* 9 May 1998). In Asia, the currency crisis and many consecutive years of economic recession in Japan, as well as the banking crisis, have had an impact on the auto industry. In March 2000 Daimler-Chrysler offered to take over 34 percent of shares of Mitsubishi Motor Corporation, effectively bringing the firm under the umbrella of one of the world's leading automakers. Renault SA of France has already acquired a 36.8 percent stake in Nissan Motor Company. Ford Motor Company has acquired a 33.4 percent stake in Mazda Motor Corporation, and Fuji Heavy Industries has agreed to let General Motors (GM) Corporation take a 20 percent stake. After Mitsubishi Motor Corporation joins Daimler-Chrysler group, the only Japanese automakers without foreign capital investment will be Honda Motor Company and the Toyota group.

Toyota Motor Corporation (TMC) remains profitable even with the Japanese economy in its worst shape since World War II. TMC had the highest profit margin of any Japanese company for the fiscal year ending in March 1998 (*Nihon Keizai Shimbun* 27 June 1998). Moreover, the World Investment Report by the United Nations Conference on Trade and Development ranks TMC as seventh in overseas assets among one hundred multinational corporations (*Sankei Shimbun* 11 November 1998). In fact, TMC seems to be the only Japanese multinational corporation to enjoy its vibrant status in production and sales (fig. 4.1) and ranks third among the major world automakers (fig. 4.2).

Why is Toyota doing so well? The answer to this question provides the context for a geographic analysis of the company. Throughout the evolution

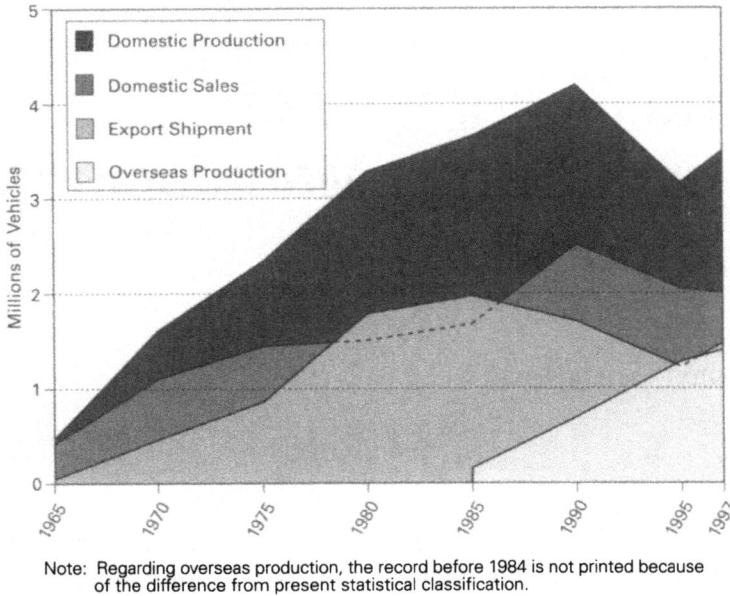

Fig. 4.1: Toyota: Domestic and overseas production, domestic sales and export, 1965–1997. (*Source:* Toyota Motor Corporation, 1998)

of Toyota, from a tiny family business to a multinational corporation, many members of the Toyoda[1] clan have contributed to the development of the long-term geostrategic vision of the company. TMC has overcome numerous problems, including the Japanese-U.S. economic conflict and trade problems, and geo-economic considerations have led Toyota to develop a global expansion strategy. In the twenty-first century, it appears that Toyota will continue to remain the top automaker in the world.

EVOLUTION OF A JAPANESE MULTINATIONAL CORPORATION

Toyota Motor Company was established in 1937, and Toyota Motor Sales Company was established in 1950. These two companies merged in 1982 to form the Toyota Motor Corporation (TMC). To consider the legacy of Toyota, two persons must be noted: one is Kiichiro Toyoda (hereafter Kiichiro), the founder of TMC, and the other is Sakichi Toyoda (hereafter Sakichi), Kiichiro's father, who provided the ideology behind TMC, or Toyotaism. Toyota's history started during Sakichi's era. Sakichi was born during the Japanese era of modernization when the Meiji government came to power (1868). Because a number of the leaders of the new Meiji government dedicated themselves to the enormous task of transforming Japan into a modern nation and catching

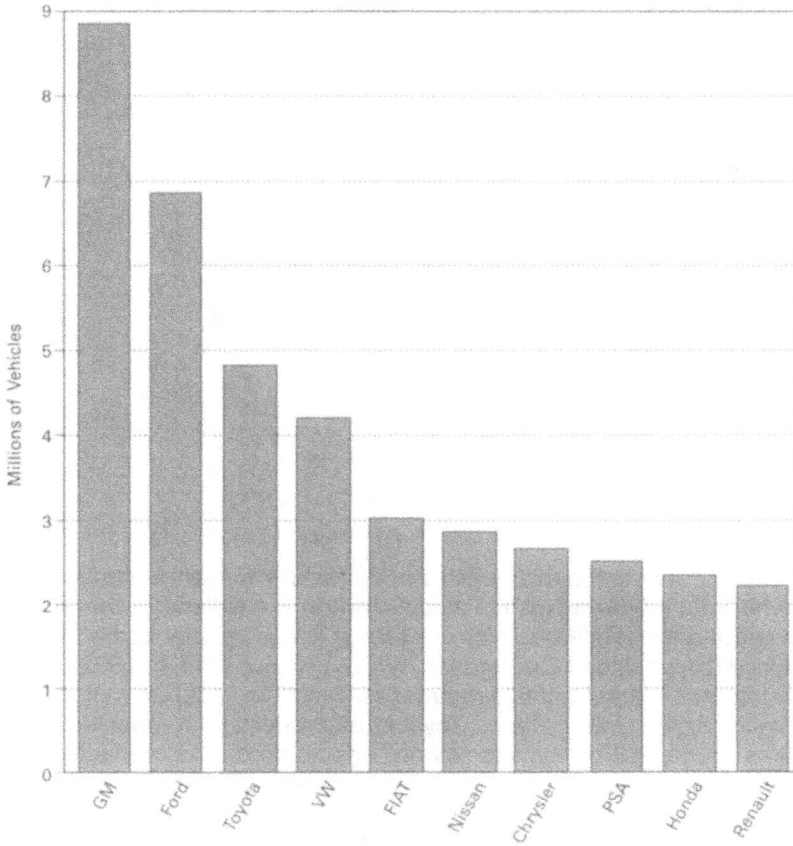

Note: The figure excludes recent mergers, such as Daimler-Benz and Chrysler as well as others.

Fig. 4.2. Production of major world automobile manufacturers, 1998. (*Source:* Toyota Motor Corporation, 1999)

up with the West, the timing could not have been better for ambitious entrepreneurs, including inventors and investors. Both the rapid influence of industrial products from Europe and the United States and the open door policy to the West allowed many individual entrepreneurs to realize that modernization of the national industries was critically important. Sakichi was one of those people in Japan. He had a great business talent with considerable visionary power with respect to invention; he developed many useful devices during his life. At age twenty-three (1890), he developed his first invention, a hand loom, or manually operated loom, which was ignored by the small-scale Japanese textile business community. In April 1895, Sakichi was recognized as one of the ten most influential inventors in the nation over the previous one hundred years by the Japanese Patent Office. Since J. Kay, L. Pole, and

Toyota City, situated in the middle of Aichi prefecture in east-central Japan, lies in a region where the Mikawa Heights slope down to the flatland of the Mikawa Plain. Formed around the fertile basin of the Yahagi River, the city is the birthplace and namesake of Toyota Motor Corporation. With a population of 348,532, Toyota City is first and foremost an automotive metropolis. Toyota is to Japan much like its sister city Detroit is to the United States. Toyota has production companies in more than twenty-five countries. Foreign subsidiaries ensure production and supply are in line with regional demand and stimulate employment and parts procurement to promote local economic development. (Photograph by P.P. Karan)

J. Wyatt in 1733 and R. Arkwright in 1769 had already contributed their inventions of similar machines to the British textile industry, Japanese enterprise was evidently one hundred years behind the European countries.

Despite this, however, Sakichi changed the history of the world textile industry. With suggestions from his friends, he went into the weaving business. In 1889, along with his partners, Sakichi opened a textile mill fitted with steam-powered looms, which increased productivity fourfold and reduced costs by more than 50 percent (Toyota Motor Corporation 1988). At the same time, Mitsui and Company expressed an interest in marketing Sakichi's steam-powered looms. But Sakichi dissolved his previous business, Toyoda Shokai, and established Toyoda's Loom Works (1907) with capital of ¥1 million. With capital of more than ¥1 million, Toyoda's Loom Works was considered a large-scale enterprise, having the same capital as Mitsui Company. In 1918, Sakichi formed Toyoda Spinning and Weaving Company with capital of ¥5 million. Even today, Toyoda Spinning and Weaving continues to flourish as one of the fifteen core corporations in the TMC group.

Disturbed by the number of Western machines used in his mills, Sakichi asserted, "By using Japanese brains and arms, I will make a great Japanese product which is better than those of the West" (*Toyota Jidosha Kogyo Kabushiki Kaisha Shashi Henshu Iinkai* 1968, 3). Eventually, in 1926, Sakichi invented an automatic loom with the highest international standards. However, he paid a price in order to concentrate on the invention of the power loom and later described the tough time: "Apart from food and clothes, I also needed money for my research and my projects. It seems like serious inventors always end up being poor and being cut off from others; sometimes they even get persecuted. It is as if an inventor has to have his fill of hardship before he can fulfill his ambitions" (Toyota Motor Corporation 1988, 26).

Platt Brothers from the United Kingdom, then the world's largest maker of spinning and weaving machinery, approached Sakichi with an offer to purchase the patent rights. Three years after Sakichi's invention of the automatic loom, Kiichiro, his son, went to England to negotiate with Platt Brothers. Both sides reached an agreement with a price of £100,000, which ultimately became the research fund of TMC (*Toyota Jidosha Hanbai Kabushiki Kaisha Shashi Henshu Iinkai* 1971). Sakichi died in 1930, a year after he sold the patent rights to the Europeans. He never saw the first Toyota automobile.

As an inventor, Sakichi was interested in technology. When Sakichi traveled to the United States in 1910, he witnessed the power of western technology, in particular the automobile. Sakichi entrusted his dream of making an automobile to Kiichiro. After the Kanto earthquake in 1923, Japan imported a number of buses from overseas for the rescue mission. Sakichi told Kiichiro, "human beings must at least accomplish an undertaking. I spent my life inventing a spinning machine. Son! For the sake of society, you have to accomplish one thing. How about making an automobile" (*Toyota Jidosha Kogyo Kabushiki Kaisha* 1959, 10). Kiichiro had inherited his father's dream and had been inspired by his father's achievements in the textile industry. Funded by the £100,000 from his father's invention, he immediately began researching small gasoline-powered engines. Kiichiro believed that the Japanese automobile industry someday would be the best in the world, just as Sakichi had invented a world-class automatic spinning machine (*Aichi Toyota Jidosha Kabushiki Kaisha Shashi Henshushitsu* 1970).

Those working under Sakichi also helped fulfill his conviction by applying his basic doctrine regarding management after his death. Kiichiro later codified these ideas. On the sixth anniversary of Sakichi's death (1936), Kiichiro declared them the principles of Toyota. Toyotaism contains the following five principles.

1. Contribute to the development and welfare of the country by working together, regardless of position (i.e., both management and labor), faithfully in one's duties.

2. Be the vanguard of the times through endless creativity, inquisitiveness, and pursuit of improvement.
3. Be practical, and avoid frivolity.
4. Be kind and generous; strive to create a warm, homelike (i.e., family) atmosphere.
5. Be reverent to Shintoism and Buddhism, and show gratitude for things great and small in thought and deed (*Toyota Jidosha Kogyo Kabushiki Kaisha* 1979, 29; Toyota Motor Corporation 1988, 38).

The fundamental management style of both TMC and its suppliers, as well as affiliates, is currently based on these five principles, which have been handed down to the present generation, serving as guidelines for policies and activities. By examining Toyotaism, one can conclude that these principles reflect Japan's national policies during the Meiji era, such as "wealthy nation, strong army" and "industry development."

The first principle of Toyotaism emphasizes the solidarity relationship between management and labor by creating a single power in the industry. To create successful business eventually led to dedication to the nation. To achieve a successful business and to keep stability in the group, Toyotaism stresses that management-labor relations should be harmonious, one of the fundamental cultural elements in Japanese society (Sato 1988). In fact, the ideas of cooperation and harmony are heavily colored by the elements of Confucianism (Benedict 1946).

Regarding the second principle of Toyotaism, the creative and research mind for the future generation of automobile has been another theme behind Toyota's business. Today, slogans such as "good product and good idea" (*Toyota Jidosha Kogyo Kabushiki Kaisha* 1979, 182), "high quality and high performance" (Ibid., 495), and "building low-priced, high-quality vehicles" (Toyota Motor Corporation 1988, 67) reflect the second principle of Toyotaism.

The harmony principle also mirrors both the third and fourth principles for the individual spirit at work. Therefore, one should keep splendor. At the same time, one has to have a life of simplicity and fortitude. Since Toyota originated as a family business, the family atmosphere has remained essential for successful management. At work, one should highlight a family atmosphere with a warmhearted and friendly spirit. This family cooperation and harmony atmosphere is the most important theme for the successful business of Toyota. Even the catch phrase of the current Toyota pamphlet emphasizes the word harmony by stating, "Harmony between people, society, and the environment" with a subtitle "Our goal is to be 'the good corporate citizen' in the international community (Toyota Motor Corporation 1998d, 1)."

Similar to the ideas of "cooperation" and "harmony," religion—Shintoism and Buddhism—is another crucial essence of Toyotaism (covered by the fifth principle). In other words, to gain the cooperation of the workforce, Toyota has used the strategy of unifying people into a single group by codifying religious beliefs.

Based on Toyotaism, Kiichiro began the process of making an automobile. When Kiichiro traveled to England by way of the United States to conclude negotiations with Platt Brothers, Japan did not have a single automobile. The first automobile appeared on Japanese soil when Mr. Thompson, an American who lived in Yokohama, imported a locomobile-steam automobile from the United States in April 1900. Until Shintaro Yoshida completed Japan's first gasoline-powered automobile, whose engine was brought from the United States in 1907, the Japanese automobile industry did not exist (*Toyota Jidosha Kogyo Kabushiki Kaisha Shashi Henshu Iinkai* 1968). In fact, many Japanese pioneers were hampered by the fact that the parts and machinery industries were not developed sufficiently and remained family enterprises. After his stimulating travel across the United States, Kiichiro was determined to make automobiles in Japan, and he changed the history of the industry.

Unlike Sakichi, Kiichiro studied mechanical engineering at Tokyo Imperial University and received the finest technical education. His knowledge of engineering directly contributed to the success of his automobile business. Kiichiro believed that advanced technical knowledge was useful only if one first mastered the practical technology of the shop floor, an attitude he inherited from his father (*Toyota Jidosha Hanbai Kabushiki Kaisha Shashi Henshu Iinkai* 1971). He struggled to master the technologies required for auto manufacture and visited companies selling auto parts and machine tool makers. Fortunately for Kiichiro, the expansion of GM and Ford in Japan during the end of the 1920s provided a great knowledge resource, providing him the know-how for setting up an auto assembly plant and other necessary information to make automobiles. Despite the establishment of technical ties with overseas makers and adoption of Western technology, conditions were not conducive to fostering the Japanese automobile industry into the future. Instead, Kiichiro believed that it was necessary to promote the development of basic technology to produce an automobile that was suitable for conditions in Japan.

Kiichiro's dream gradually became a reality as Toyoda Automatic Loom Works completed its first Model A1 passenger car in 1935. Two years later, Toyota Motor Company was established with a capital of ¥12 million. Risaburo Toyoda (hereafter Risaburo), the adopted son of Sakichi, became president, and Kiichiro was appointed executive vice president.

Initially, Toyota Motor Company consisted of seven departments: Administration, Sales, Manufacturing, Engineering, Technical, Total Vehicle Engineering Administration, and Research. During the 1930s, because of good infrastructure and other convenient factors in the urban cities of Japan, Toyota Motor Company selected three office locations, namely, Tokyo, Osaka, and Nagoya (Toyota Motor Corporation 1988). From the early days, the leader-

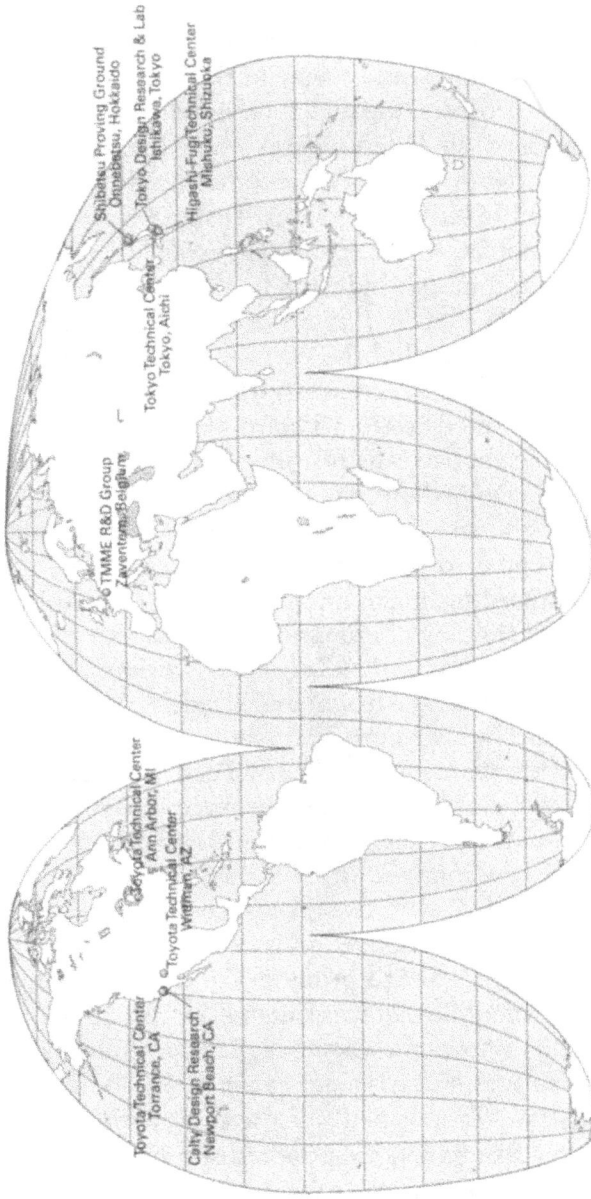

Fig. 4.3. Toyota research and development centers in the world. (*Source*: Toyota Motor Corporation, Tokyo)

Shibetsu Proving Ground
Onnebetsu, Hokkaido

Tokyo Design Research & Lab
Ishikawa, Tokyo

Higashi-Fuji Technical Center
Mishuku, Shizuoka

Tokyo Technical Center
Tokyo, Aichi

TMME R&D Group
Zaventem, Belgium

Toyota Technical Center
Ann Arbor, MI

Toyota Technical Center
Wittman, AZ

Toyota Technical Center
Torrance, CA

Calty Design Research
Newport Beach, CA

ship in Toyota emphasized research and development. At present Toyota's research and development facilities are spread across the world in Asia, Europe, and North America (fig. 4.3). Kiichiro headed the Research Department and advocated a policy of "building low-priced, high-quality vehicles." He frequently stated, "If we don't build passenger cars, we will not be able to develop any meaningful technology (Toyota Motor Corporation. 1988, 74)." Under the guidance of Kiichiro, the prototype Model AA passenger car began to be produced for the general public. The Model AA was renamed the Kokusan Toyota Go, meaning "the domestically produced Toyota," and became the first automobile to use the Toyota name. The name Kokusan Toyota Go symbolizes the realization of Sakichi's dream.

In short, Toyota originated from a family business and has evolved into one of the major multinational corporations in the world. It is important to note the link between the Toyota philosophy developed by Sakichi and the successful business philosophy of TMC developed by Kiichiro. The linkage led the successful family business of the Toyoda family to become an international corporation. It is not an exaggeration to note that the Toyoda family is one of Japanese revolutionaries who changed the landscape of not only the automobile industry but also the national economy. Furthermore, it is not an exaggeration to state that Toyota has contributed to transforming the world landscape through the automobile.

THREE STAGES OF CORPORATE GROWTH

When Japan was defeated in World War II on August 15, 1945, it was a day for new beginnings for the Japanese automobile industry. Kiichiro stated, "Catch up with America in three years. Otherwise the Japanese auto industry will never stand on its own" (Ohno 1984, 200). During Kiichiro's lifetime, he had tirelessly tried to make the best automobile in Japan. Toyota developed into a global corporation in three stages (fig. 4.4). The first stage emphasized a strategy of crossing national space. The second stage stressed a strategy of

Fig. 4.4. The three-stage development strategy of Toyota.

crossing continental space and included two phases: expansion overseas–1 (concentration on exports) and expansion overseas–2 (establishment of production plants). The third stage highlighted globalization strategy. Toyota had no ambitious plan in the early stage (until 1950) to market its automobiles in Japan, as well as worldwide. Rather, Toyota was forced to search for its own survival route through various factors, such as the Japanese-U.S. economic conflict, the appreciation of Japanese currency, and the wave of globalization.

The First Stage: A Cross-Nation-Space Strategy

The first stage of corporate growth was to expand the cross-nation-space strategy by marketing products in Japan and in other nations around the world. In other words, Toyota would blanket entire nations with its product. After the first automobile was produced by Toyota Motor Company, the leadership of the company began to target its network in the city of Nagoya in Aichi prefecture. By creating a number of auto suppliers and affiliates, the company formed a Toyota village that eventually became today's Toyota City. In 1938, the first production plant (or Honsha Plant) was established. Toyota did not build another production plant immediately. During the next twenty years, leaders of Toyota concentrated on building its suppliers and affiliates around the Honsha Plant in Aichi prefecture. Not until 1959 did Toyota Motor Company decide to create a second production plant in Toyota City (table 4.1). By adding firms and expanding space around Toyota City, the fundamental base of the Toyota network, or *keiretsu,* was formed. Just as a spider spins a web, Toyota spun its first stage of corporate growth strategy off its web of many small firms that smoothly kept up the production plant. By 1989, some forty years after the establishment of the first production plant, Toyota had created eleven additional production plants around Toyota City (table 4.1 and fig. 4.5). Toyota dealerships were established in all prefectures of Japan (fig. 4.6).

Three major points characterized the strategy of the first stage. First, the network of auto suppliers was created. In order to make a high quality automobile, it was indispensable to have auto suppliers to support Toyota's production. Second, several affiliates were built. It was necessary to provide housing and entertainment facilities for Toyota's employees and their families. As the philosophies of Toyotaism indicate, the family atmosphere of the Toyota employee is one of the crucial factors for the success of Toyota's business. Third, by webbing Toyota dealers, the company built a channel of distribution for its automobile all over Japan. As figure 4.6 indicates, most dealers are concentrated in three urban prefectures, Nagoya, Tokyo, and Osaka, rather than in other regions, such as Okinawa and Iwate prefectures. While the

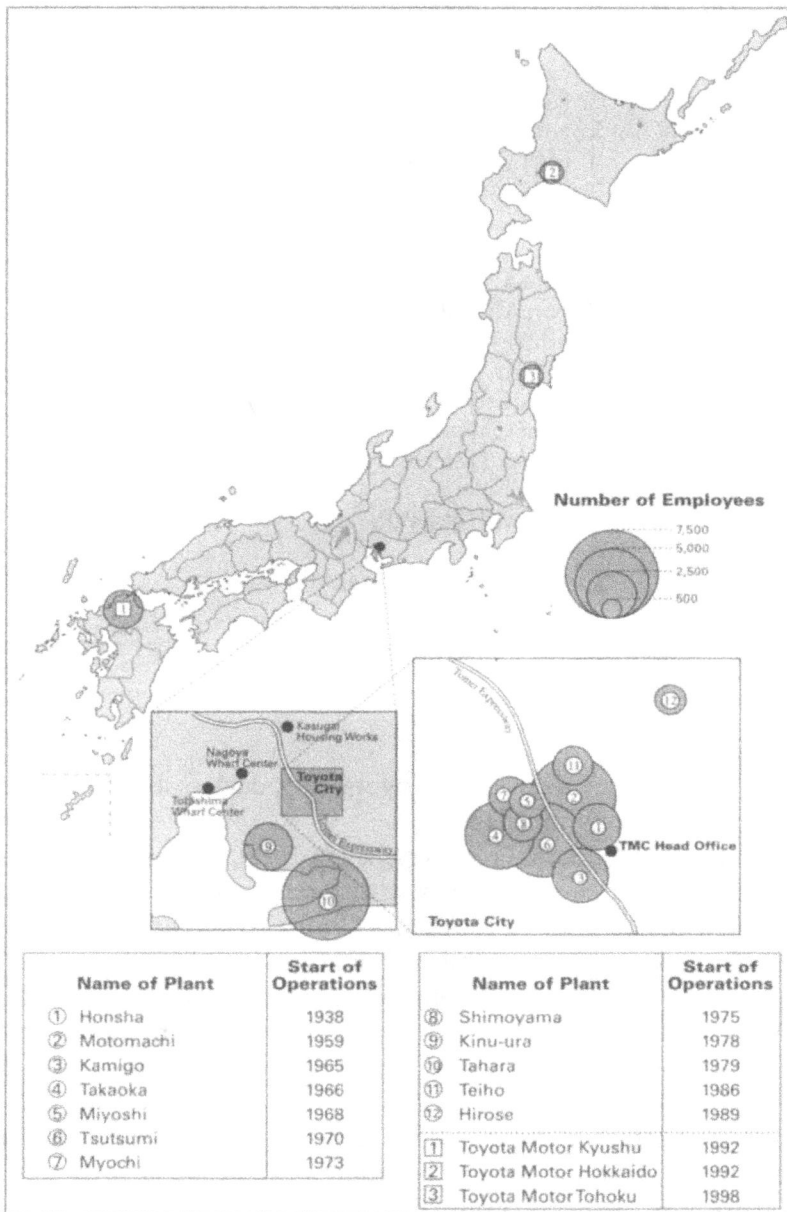

Number of Employees

- 7,500
- 5,000
- 2,500
- 500

Kasugai Housing Works
Nagoya Wharf Center
Toyota City
Tobishima Wharf Center

Toyota City
TMC Head Office

Name of Plant	Start of Operations		Name of Plant	Start of Operations
① Honsha	1938		⑧ Shimoyama	1975
② Motomachi	1959		⑨ Kinu-ura	1978
③ Kamigo	1965		⑩ Tahara	1979
④ Takaoka	1966		⑪ Teiho	1986
⑤ Miyoshi	1968		⑫ Hirose	1989
⑥ Tsutsumi	1970		1 Toyota Motor Kyushu	1992
⑦ Myochi	1973		2 Toyota Motor Hokkaido	1992
			3 Toyota Motor Tohoku	1998

Fig. 4.5. Toyota: Employment in manufacturing plants in Japan, 1999. Toyota's Georgetown plant resembles the Tsutsumi plant in Toyota City in layout and equipment. (*Source:* Toyota Motor Corporation, Tokyo)

Table 4.1. Toyota facilities in Japan and operation years

Name of plant	Location of plant	Year
Honsha Plant	Toyota City, Aichi Prefecture	1938
Motomachi Plant	Toyota City, Aichi Prefecture	1959
Kamigo Plant	Toyota City, Aichi Prefecture	1965
Takaoka Plant	Toyota City, Aichi Prefecture	1966
Miyoshi Plant	Toyota City, Aichi Prefecture	1968
Tsutsumi Plant	Toyota City, Aichi Prefecture	1970
Myochi Plant	Toyota City, Aichi Prefecture	1973
Shimoyama Plant	Toyota City, Aichi Prefecture	1975
Kinu-ura Plant	Southwest Toyota City, Aichi Prefecture	1978
Tahara Plant	Southern Toyota City, Aichi Prefecture	1979
Teiho Plant	Toyota City, Aichi Prefecture	1986
Hirose Plant	Toyota City, Aichi Prefecture	1989
Toyota Motor Kyushu, Inc.	Fukuoka Prefecture	1992
Toyota Motor Hokkaido, Inc.	Southern Hokkaido	1992
Toyota Motor Tohoku Co., Ltd.	Tohoku Region, Miyagi Prefecture	1998

Source: (Toyota 1999b, 4).

production plants are centralized in Toyota City, dealers are concentrated in large urban cities throughout Japan.

As the second production plant opened in 1959, the leadership of Toyota turned its cross-nation-space strategy to different countries on different continents worldwide. During the 1950s and 1960s, Toyota adopted nation-specific strategies to export automobiles after successfully networking in Japan with targeted nations. To target foreign consumers and to gain market share, Toyota Motor Sales (TMS) set up its export department to pioneer overseas markets. As an independent sales company, TMS was created in April 1950 and was capitalized with ¥80 million.

The first substantial export order for the company came in February 1952 from Brazil, an order for one hundred Model FXL large trucks. Brazil was a market with great potential; Toyota did not miss this opportunity. In November 1955, TMS sent its first staff to Sao Paulo to set up an overseas station to conduct various marketing activities, including a market survey and appointment of distributors. Since Brazil is a developing country with poor economic infrastructure (e.g., poor roads), TMS decided to market the four-wheel-drive (4WD) Land Cruiser, which was mounted with a powerful engine and had a rugged chassis, making it both powerful and able to withstand poor roads. Moreover, there were only two other vehicles—the Ameri-

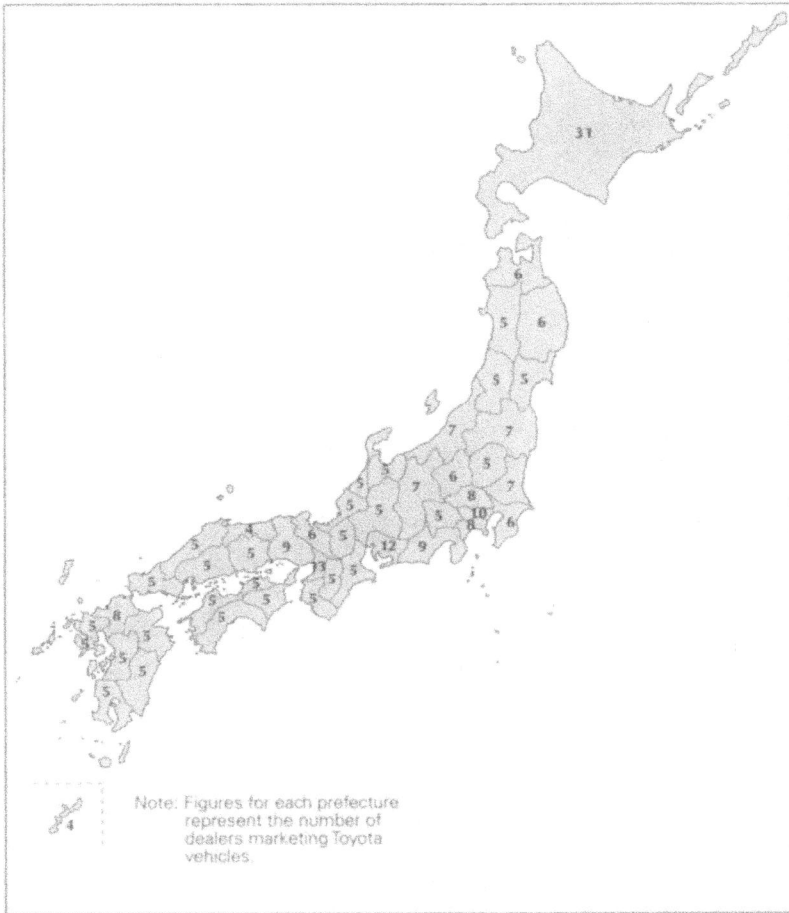

Fig. 4.6. Toyota dealers marketing in Japan, 1999. Toyota has the most elaborate dealer network in Japan. The company has tried to replicate the best parts of that system in the United States—giving the dealers technical assistance, recruiting black dealers, and paying special attention to women. Recognizing that in the United States two thirds of new car purchases are made or influenced by women, Toyota views women as deserving of particular attention. (*Source:* Toyota Motor Corporation, Tokyo)

Table 4.2. Toyota's overseas production companies (year of operation and employees)

Region	Location	Name of overseas production company; location of city	Year	Employees
Latin America	Brazil	Toyota do Brasil S.S., Industria e Cornercio; Sao Paulo	1959	716
Africa	South Africa	Toyota South Africa Motors (Pty.) Ltd.; Kwazulu-Natal	1962	8261
Oceania	Australia	Toyota Motor Corporation Australia Ltd.; Jafarabad, Chaittagong	1963	4426
Asia	Thailand	Toyota Motor Thailand Co., Ltd.; Samut Prakan	1964	4249
Europe	Portugal	Salvador Caetono I.M.V.T., S.A.; Ovar	1968	1984
Asia	Malaysia	Assembly Services Sdn. Bhd.; Selangor, Darul Ehsan	1968	984
Asia	Indonesia	P. T. Toyota-Astra Motor; Sunter II, Jakarta	1970	6001
North America	U.S.A.	TABC, Inc.; Long Beach, CA	1971	492
Asia	Thailand	Thai Hino Industry Co., Ltd.; Samut Prakan	1972	659
Africa	Kenya	Associated Vehicle Assemblers Ltd.; Mombasa	1977	364
Latin America	Ecuador	Manufacturas Armadurias y Repuestos; Chia Cundinamarca	1979	400
Asia	Thailand	Toyota Auto Body Thailand Co., Ltd.; Samut Prakan	1979	111
Latin America	Venezuela	Toyota de Venezuela Compania Anonima; Cumana, State of Sucre	1981	930
Asia	Bangladesh	Aftab Automobiles, Ltd.; Chittagong	1982	88
North America	U.S.A.	New United Motor Manufacturing, Inc. (NUMMI); Fremont, Calif.	1984	4619
North America	Canada	Canadian Autoparts Toyota, Inc. (CAPTIN); Delta, B.C.	1985	188
Asia	Taiwan	Kuozui Motors, Ltd.; Chung Li City	1986	2462
North America	Canada	Toyota Motor Manufacturing Canada, Inc.; Cambridge, Ontario	1988	2095
North America	U.S.A.	Toyota Motor Manufacturing, Kentucky, Inc. (TMMK)	1988	7696
Asia	Philippines	Toyota Motor Philippines Corporation; Pranaque, Metro Manila	1989	1671
Asia	Thailand	Siam Toyota Manufacturing Co., Ltd.; Chonburi	1989	708
Asia	China	Shenyang Jimbei Passenger Vehicle Manufacturing Co., Ltd.; Shenyang	1991	6445
Latin America	Colombia	Sociedad de Fabricacion de Automotores S.A.; Cundinamarca	1991	1098
Europe	U.K.	Toyota Motor Manufacturing (UK) Ltd.; Derbyshire and Flintshire	1992	2905

Region	Location	Name of overseas production company; location of city	Year	Employees
Asia	Malaysia	T & K Autoparts Sdn. Bhd.; Selangor, Darul Ehsan	1992	104
Asia	Philippines	Toyota Autoparts Philippines, Inc.; Rosa, Laguna	1992	422
North America	U.S.A.	Bodine Aluminum, Inc.; St. Louis, Mo.	1993	759
Asia	Pakistan	Indus Motor Company Ltd.; Bin Qasim, Karachi	1993	419
Middle East	Turkey	Toyotasa Toyota-Sabanci Automotive Industry & Trade, Inc.; Sakarya	1994	612
Asia	Vietnam	Toyota Motor Vietnam Co., Ltd.; Vinh Phuc Province	1996	260
Asia	China	Tianjin Jinfeng Auto Parts Co., Ltd.; Tianjin City	1997	1128
Latin America	Argentina	Toyota Argentina S.A.; Zarate Provincia de Buenos Aires	1997	590
Asia	China	Tianjin Toyota Motor Engine Co., Ltd.; Tianjin City	1998	1478
North America	U.S.A.	Toyota Motor Manufacturing, Indiana, Inc.; Princeton, Ind.	1998	330
North America	U.S.A.	Toyota Motor Manufacturing, West Virginia, Inc.; Buffalo, W.Va.	1998	89
Asia	China	Toyota Fenjin Auto Parts Co., Ltd.; Tianjin City	1998	157
Asia	China	Tianjin Toyota Forging Co., Ltd.; Tianjin City	1999	58
Asia	China	Sichuan Toyota Motor Co., Ltd.; Sichuan Province	1999	1150
Asia	India	Toyota Kirloskar Motor Ltd.	1999	1000
Europe	France	Toyota Motor Manufacturing France S.A.S. (planning)	2001	115

Source: The number of employees is based on (Toyota 1999a, 4–5), and other data are based on (Toyota 1999b, 6–7).

can Jeep and the British Land Rover—in competition; it was a golden opportunity for Toyota to set foot in the Brazilian market. In 1959, Toyota created the first overseas production companies in Brazil (table 4.2).

The expansion strategy of Toyota did not stop with Brazil, but reached to other countries in Latin America. (The leaders of Toyota began to use the cross-nation-space strategy to build the cross-continent-space strategy.) From the mid-1950s, TMS carried out aggressive sales activities centered on the Land Cruiser in other Latin American countries: El Salvador in 1953, Colombia in 1956, Costa Rica in 1957, Venezuela in 1962, and Puerto Rico in 1965. Eventually, Toyota moved its Latin American headquarters from Brazil to Colombia.

Toyota also employed its cross-nation-space strategy in other countries on other continents. In Southeast Asia, Toyota made its first exports as early as the end of the 1940s. However, the full scale of the export of automobiles to Thailand began during the period of the 1950s and 1960s. In the Middle East, Toyota presented its SA passenger model, Toyota's first postwar export automobile, to the king of Egypt in 1947. In the beginning, Toyota hesitated to export any products to Europe, one of the world's most sophisticated markets. Finally, during a visit to Tokyo by Walther Krohn, president of Erla Auto Import A/S, Toyota was persuaded to ship a sample right-hand-drive Crown to Denmark in December 1962. Toyota's entry into Africa started in April 1957, when twelve Crowns and Land Cruisers were exported to Ethiopia (table 4.3). With the first-stage strategy nearly completed, the first phase of the second-stage strategy was executed.

The Second Stage: Expansion Overseas–1
(Concentration on Exports)

After successfully entering a particular country's market, Toyota began to use its second tactic—the cross-continent-space strategy. Once representative countries on the Latin American continent accepted its products, leaders of Toyota began to market across the continent (table 4.3). Almost at the same time as the expansion in Latin America, Toyota sought to develop its market by crossing into the North American continent, in particular the United States. Due to the weather conditions, Toyota's automobiles in Canada were not selling in large quantities. In the end, Toyota overcame many difficulties and began to export the New Corona to Canada in 1967 and the Corolla in 1968.

However, there was disagreement and opposition within the Toyota Motor Company. In the final analysis, leaders of Toyota felt that if Toyota approached exporting to the United States with the determination of Sakichi and the dedication of Kiichiro, the day would come when not only automatic looms but also automobiles could be exported by Toyota and compete at an international level (Toyota Motor Corporation 1988). For marketing to the United States, Toyota adopted three geographical divisions—western, central, and eastern regions. Because of geographical proximity between the western coast of the American mainland and Japan, California was targeted by Toyota at first. In addition, the existence of large port cities in the West Coast region of the United States became a crucial factor for leaders of TMC in deciding to export Toyota products. In August 1957, two Toyota Crown sample cars left Yokohama Port and were shipped to Los Angeles. These cars became the first Japanese passenger cars to be exported to the American mainland.

Two months later, in October 1957, a Toyota subsidiary—Toyota Motor Sales, U.S.A (TMS, USA)—was founded. The corporation was initially capitalized at $1 million, with Toyota Motor Company and TMS each investing half of the capital (fig. 4.7). TMS, USA's office was located on a large boulevard in Beverly Hills, with an initial staff of thirteen, comprised of eleven Japanese sent from Japan, one Japanese hired locally, and one second-generation Japanese-American. Thereafter, TMS, USA began organizing its dealerships by establishing Hollywood Toyota Motor in California and started negotiating franchise contracts. By the end of 1960, there were eighty-five dealerships in the United States, including Hawaii. Moreover, six months after

Table 4.3 Toyota Exports from Japan by region (in thousands of vehicles)

	North America	Latin America	Europe	Africa	Asia	Oceania	Middle East	Total
1988	947.8	61.1	429.8	84.2	106.4	74.9	111.5	1815.7
1989	814	51.2	441.5	46.8	107	95.9	112.8	1669.1
1990	780.2	60.1	446.6	47.9	123.6	84.1	134.6	1677.1
1991	768.2	79.4	436	52.4	135.6	76.1	155.9	1703.6
1992	684.3	99.9	406.8	54.4	154.9	82.1	215.8	1698.2
1993	603	96.6	347.6	39.8	186.6	83.8	181.6	1539
1994	653.5	89.2	334.9	37	153.5	91.4	144.8	1504.5
1995	454.4	110.9	263.3	51	148.3	76.7	97.8	1202.4
1996	456.3	86.2	304.8	50.6	172.4	82.1	124.2	1276.7
1997	526.5	119.6	401.4	54	152.3	93.6	146.8	1494.3
1998	584.3	110.3	369.7	56.2	66	104.2	172	1462.8
Total	7272.5	964.5	4182.4	574.3	1506.6	944.9	1597.8	17043

Source: (Toyota Motor Corporation 1999b, 21).

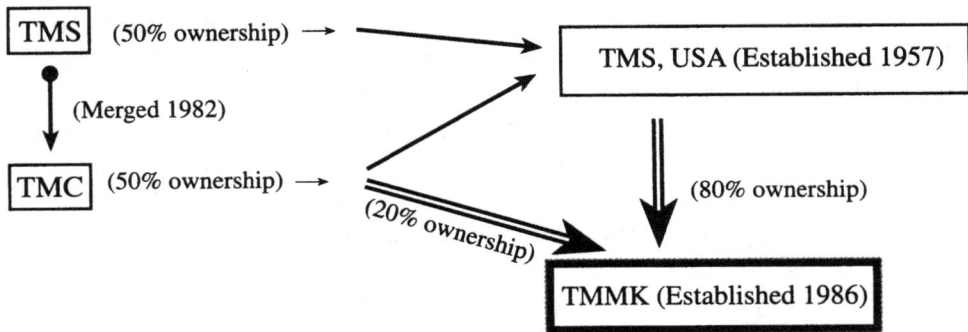

Fig. 4.7. Establishment of TMMK.

founding TMS, USA, Toyota established Toyota Motor Distributors as a directly operated distributor serving the West Coast region. All Toyota overseas corporations had Japanese citizens as president and executive vice president.

Export of the Crown by Toyota did not go smoothly. The design of the Crown was not suited for American highways. The car tended to vibrate badly at speeds of more than 60 miles per hour and overheated when driven over mountains and on long, straight desert stretches, such as those between Los Angeles and Las Vegas. Toyota exported the Tiara models to replace the earlier Crown, but many problems also existed with these cars. The setback in the United States taught Toyota a valuable lesson: it was vital to conduct repeated tests under local conditions. Toyota learned that motor vehicles which are not competitive in every aspect of a particular market, including performance, price, and brand name, have no chance at all of being accepted. Toyota made the most of this lesson by striving to develop eminently international products. The first result of the effort was the Model RT-40 New Corona (*Toyota Jidosha Kabushiki Kaisha* 1988). This model successfully expanded in the United States during the 1960s. The leading slogan for advertisement of the New Corona was "Get Your Hands on a Toyota and You'll Never Let Go." This later became "Toyota: We're Quality Oriented" (Toyota Motor Corporation 1988).

Once Toyota successfully got its foothold in the U.S. market by penetrating the west region, Toyota unfolded its strategy in the central region. During this period, TMS, USA moved to put into order a sales network that would cover the entire country and make use of leading local businesses as distributors. Especially for the fourteen midwestern states, a stronghold of the Big Three automakers, it was decided to appoint a private distributor. Among many candidates, TMS, USA focused on the distributor for British Leyland. Mid-Southern Toyota Distributors was established in Chicago in January 1966. By 1967 the total number of dealers increased to 716 from 200 in 1964.

After triumphant expansion in the west and central regions selling the New Corona, TMS, USA decided to extend its marketing to the East Coast region, in particular the New York region, in the 1970s. Backed by political influence resulting from Toyota's contribution of a lot of money to local politicians during their election years, TMS, USA set up distributors in Baltimore and Boston, in addition to New York. By the 1970s, TMS, USA had grown from its original West Coast operational base into a business that covered the entire United States.

Approaching the 1970s, two major developments occurred in the world economy: one was the oil crisis, and the other was the breakdown of the Bretton Woods system (e.g., the appreciation of Japanese currency). The oil shocks of the 1970s provided an opportunity for Toyota to take a respectable market share in the United States. Reasonably priced Japanese automobiles, such as Toyotas, enjoyed brisk sales. By 1973, Toyota was able to consolidate its system for annual sales of three hundred thousand units in the United States (*Toyota Jidosha Kabushiki Kaisha* 1988). On the other hand, the appreciation of the Japanese yen forced Toyota to take a new direction when competing with American subcompacts. The company changed the emphasis of its product line from high-grade small cars to sporty cars, such as the Celica, and to multiuse pickup trucks. American consumers responded extremely favorably to the pickup trucks of Toyota when they were introduced in the West Coast region. Thereafter distribution expanded to the northern and central regions, then stretched out to the eastern parts of the United States. Because the pickup trucks had increasing potential as vehicles for recreational use, driving comfort was enhanced by adding air conditioning and power steering. In other words, the trucks became almost like passenger cars fitted with rear decks (Maema 1988). Furthermore, the appreciation of the Japanese yen also brought the second phase of overseas expansion strategy—the local assembly plan to market Toyota automobiles in the country.

*The Second Stage: Expansion Overseas–2
(Establishment of Production Plants)*

After the oil crisis, the Japanese economy commenced its recovery in 1979. With the further appreciation of Japanese currency, exports of Japanese automobiles to the United States grew quickly, but a series of price increases caused by the yen's appreciation resulted in a considerable loss in their price competitiveness. In addition, the Japanese-U.S. economic conflict, especially over automobiles, was gradually worsening (table 4.3). In the end, to decrease exports from Japanese companies, Japan's automakers, including Toyota, were forced to consider seriously the need for local production. This led Toyota to enter its second phase of the second-stage strategy: setting up local assembly plants.

This new phase also forced Toyota to reorganize its structure. In January 1982, Toyota Motor Company and Toyota Motor Sales decided to merge to form the Toyota Motor Corporation (TMC). Eiji Toyoda (hereafter Eiji), the cousin of Kiichiro and president of Toyota Motor Company, and Shoichiro Toyoda (hereafter Shoichiro), the eldest son of Kiichiro and president of Toyota Motor Sales, issued a joint statement: "To cope with the turbulent 1980s and to progress further along the path we have taken thus far, a need has emerged to integrate our production and sales functions, which are in fact two sides of the same coin, so that they can augment each other more comprehensively and organically" (Toyota Motor Corporation 1988, 314). Eiji was named as chairman and Shoichiro as president of the new Toyota Motor Corporation (TMC). As Eiji stated, "We must win the struggle to survive in a changing world. . . . Let us return to our original organization, let us grasp our capabilities to their fullest, and let us make the effort needed to carve ourselves a new future" (Ibid., 315). By integrating the functions of both companies and restructuring the new organization, the merger led Toyota to develop its international operations and to make decisions more quickly. The new corporation was reorganized into eight groups: Head Office, Purchasing, Domestic Sales, Overseas Affairs, Engineering and Production Engineering, Logistics Control, Production, and Offices.

When the voluntary restrictions (i.e., Japanese companies restricted their exports voluntarily) on Japanese automobile exports to the United States were initiated in 1981, it was imperative for Toyota to set up production facilities in the United States. Leaders in Toyota realized that Toyota's dealers in the United States would suffer, and many customers would be lost if the company failed to maintain a punctual and stable supply of products to the American market (*Toyota Jidosha Kabushiki Kaisha* 1988). After the failure of a joint-production venture with Ford, Toyota successfully made a joint venture deal with GM when Chairman Roger B. Smith of GM met Chairman Eiji of Toyota in March 1982. For Toyota, joint production with GM would reduce the risk related to local production and would let Toyota accumulate experience in local production in the United States. GM and Toyota reached an agreement on an annual production volume of two hundred thousand units of a passenger car based on the FF Sprinter. The closed GM plant in Fremont, California, was chosen as the production site (Kawahara 1995). The agreement between GM and Toyota comprised the following main points.

1. The objective is to establish a joint venture company to produce a small passenger car, and it is not intended to establish any other form of cooperative relationship.
2. The equity ratio for ownership of the new company will be 50 percent Toyota and 50 percent GM.

3. The board of directors of the new company will be made up of equal numbers of representatives from each of the partners, and the company's president, who will be the chief executive officer, will be selected by Toyota.

4. Production will be carried out at the Fremont Plant, previously operated by GM, and the small passenger car produced will be a new front-wheel-drive model.

5. Production will begin as early as possible in the 1985 model year, and annual production will be approximately two hundred thousand cars.

6. The joint venture will be terminated not later than twelve years after the start of production (Toyota Motor Corporation 1988).

Recently, the Toyota-GM joint venture just renewed the contract for another five years. According to interviews with leaders of the Toyota Group by the author (November 9, 1998), Toyota will continue to cooperate with GM even though there is no new additional agreement.

While accumulating local production experience with GM, Toyota announced in 1985 that it would establish plants on the North American continent. A number of site proposals from local governments were submitted to Toyota. After all factors, such as the procurement of parts, the convenience of transportation, land prices, electricity supplies, labor resources, and tax incentives and other preferential treatment from local governments, were reviewed, Toyota eventually selected two sites—Georgetown, Kentucky, in the United States and Cambridge, Ontario, in Canada.

When Toyota creates local production plants in industrial countries, usually a small community, like Georgetown, Kentucky, or Cambridge, Ontario, is the most favorable type of place targeted. However, when Toyota decides to build production plants in the developing countries, the type of place targeted is the urban city, such as Shenyang or Tianjin in China (table 4.2). One of the major reasons for Toyota to locate in large cities in the developing countries is that cities in these nations have relatively good infrastructure facilities. Toyota also focused exclusively on port cities in developing countries to build production plants. Toyota's manufacturing facilities are spread over all continents (fig. 4.8).

Toyota has taken advantage of small American communities without strong labor unions. In the case of the production plant in Kentucky, the good infrastructure impressed the leaders of Toyota. Certainly, geographical location of the Bluegrass and its physical environmental conditions (similar to Toyota City) were critical decision factors for leaders of Toyota. Tax incentives and local government supports were also major factors. For example, the Kentucky state government offered to establish a Japanese school for the children of Japanese employees at the Kentucky plant.

With more than two hundred reporters present, along with Governor

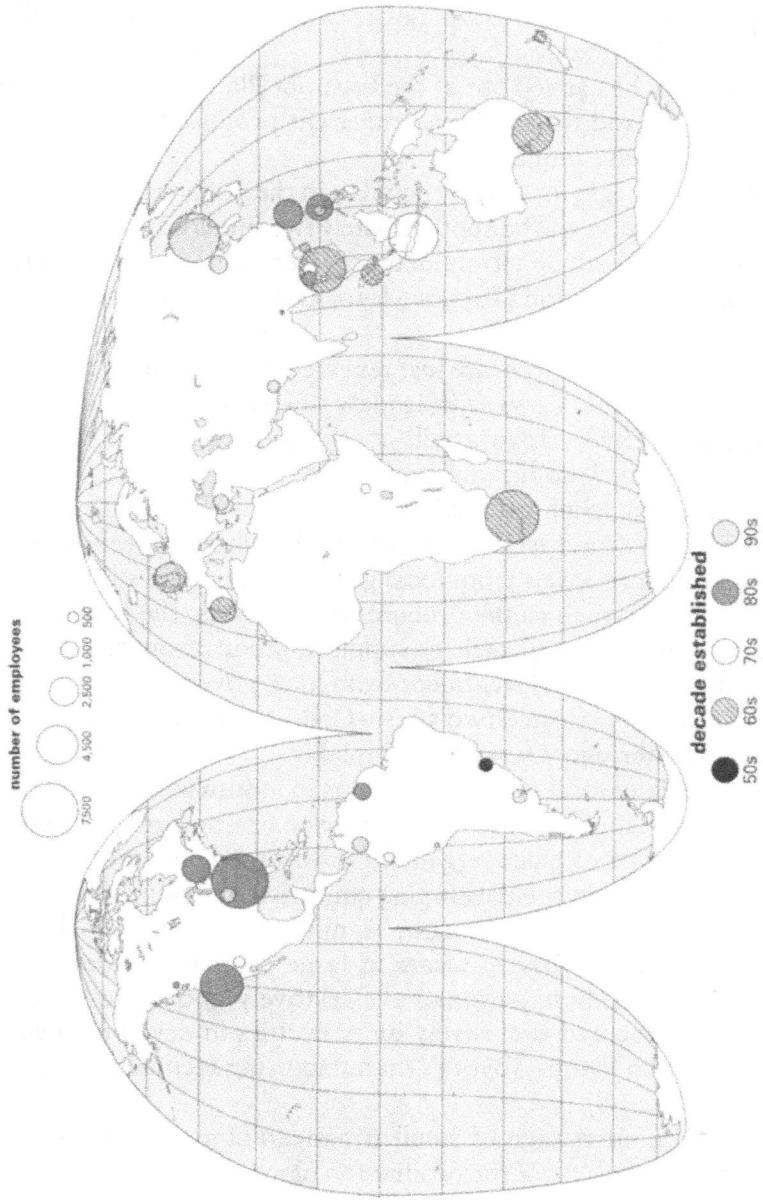

number of employees

7500 4,500 2,500 1,000 500

decade established

50s 60s 70s 80s 90s

Fig. 4.8. Toyota: Employment in manufacturing plants around the world, 1999. (*Source:* Toyota Motor Corporation, Tokyo)

Martha Layne Collins and other state officials, at a press conference in Kentucky, President Shoichiro stated, "We view today's official announcement of our plant site selection as one of the highlights in our company's history, which began in 1935 with the production of the first trial Toyota passenger car. In fact, choosing the site for our American plant was one of the most difficult decisions we have ever had to make at Toyota. After considering all of the factors involved, however, we decided that Kentucky is the best location for our American plant . . ." (Toyota Motor Corporation 1988, 338).

In January 1986, Toyota established Toyota Motor Manufacturing, Kentucky (TMMK) in the United States and Toyota Motor Manufacturing, Canada (TMMC). After studying local tax systems and future operating methods, Toyota decided to establish TMMK as 80 percent owned by TMS, USA and 20 percent owned by Toyota; TMS, USA's share constituted a reinvestment in the United States of profits it had earned there (fig. 4.7). Once again, a Japanese, Kaneyoshi Kusunoki, executive vice president from Toyota, was appointed president of both TMMK and TMMC.

There is no doubt that the experience with GM was particularly helpful as Toyota established its first North American plants. For instance, in developing an information system for the new plants, Toyota modified the daily order system formulated for the joint venture with GM so that it could include information support for TMMK and TMMC. Thus, both plants take further advantage of producing cars locally. It was not coincidental that the establishment of the assembly plant in Canada occurred at the successful conclusion of the North America Free Trade Agreement (NAFTA) between Canada and the United States.

The Third Stage: Globalization Strategy

In June 1995 TMC announced its New Global Business Plan, which focuses on efforts to further localize (overseas) and to increase imports of automobiles produced overseas (in Japan). These twin pillars have been the canon of Toyota's global business strategy since the mid-1990s (Toyota Motor Corporation 1998e). In the case of further localization, Toyota's worldwide localization activities have continued for years (table 4.4). For example, North American production amounted to more than 962,000 units in 1998, versus 783,000 units in 1996. Production at TMMK in 1998 was 474,588 units, up from 390,000 units in 1996. TMMK began to produce the new Sienna minivan in August 1997 (Toyota Motor Corporation 1998e and 1999b), and overall production capacity of TMMK was raised to 477,527 units a year in 1999.

In the case of increased imports and sales of vehicles produced overseas in Japan, Toyota established the DUO (Dealer User Onward, cooperation between dealer and user to move sales) sales channel in 1992 to market

Table 4.4 Toyota overseas production by region (in thousands of vehicles)

	North America	Latin America	Europe	Africa	Asia	Oceania	Middle East	Total
1988	74.2	5	2	73.7	34.3	55.1	0	244.4
1989	252	5	2.9	83.3	73.3	53.9	1.2	471.6
1990	382.3	5.1	7.1	83.8	135.9	59	4.5	677.7
1991	369.2	6.8	9.7	84.3	147.5	49.4	3.1	669.9
1992	489.8	3.1	11.7	67.9	140.7	49.3	2	764.5
1993	532.8	2.6	49.5	81.1	161.9	58.7	2.1	888.7
1994	581.3	3.7	93.5	76.7	222.7	68.5	4.8	1,051
1995	729.9	3.7	95.5	87.7	259	54.1	23.3	1,253
1996	783	3.2	124.4	85.1	255.1	67.6	27.7	1,346
1997	838.3	3.8	108.8	91.2	246.7	77.6	23.8	1,390.1
1998	962.8	15.3	175.7	74.1	124.8	100.4	14.4	1,467.6
Total	5995.6	57.3	680.8	888.9	1,801.9	693.6	106.9	10,2228

Source: (Toyota Motor Corporation 1999b, 19).

Volkswagen (VW) and Audi cars in Japan. Sales of VW and Audi through DUO outlets in 1997 were 34,000 units, versus 32,000 units in 1996. By 1998 these sales reached 39,000 units throughout 141 outlets in Japan. Sales in 1997 of the Toyota Cavalier recorded 9,000 units, and sales of the TMMK-produced Avalon passenger car reached 5,000 units (Toyota Motor Corporation 1998e). Furthermore, Toyota has published a Supplier's Guide for overseas suppliers. The Supplier's Guide is a handbook aimed at providing first-time suppliers a greater understanding of Toyota's purchasing activities, and it outlines how to sell to Toyota. For current suppliers, it aims at providing a greater understanding of Toyota's thinking concerning purchasing and its purchasing system. Since November 1997, Toyota has provided an Internet service, which makes overseas supplier requests for auto parts easier. In 1998, Toyota built a $2.5 billion New Supplier Center, where suppliers can exhibit their products in Toyota City. For instance, by strengthening its global business strategy, TMMK exported 23,000 units of 5S engines to Japan in 1997 and 66,000 units of parts for the Camry to Australia in 1997 (Toyota Motor Corporation 1998a).

By March 1998 Toyota had thirty-four overseas subsidiaries and affiliates, as well as more than 150 distributors overseas in five continents, and twenty-five countries and districts have Toyota manufacturing operations (Toyota Motor Corporation 1998b). As a result, Toyota has successfully entered the foreign market in different countries of the five continents. The purpose of the fourth stage—global business strategy—for Toyota is to create a deep-rooted network of the local community overseas. Toyota has actively played the role of a good corporate citizen around the world by donating millions of dollars for social and cultural activities, such as nature conservation, preservation of local culture, exchange student programs, traffic safety campaigns, and social welfare, within local communities (Toyota Motor Corporation 1998d). Contributing $1 million to build a local community center in Kentucky and offering to establish a twenty-year program in which TMMK would contribute $400,000 each year to schools in Scott County are good examples (Toyota Motor Corporation 1988). As former president Hiroshi Okuda of TMC states, "We will also increase our share by introducing new technologies, like our hybrid [electric-and-gasoline-powered] car. The company that can identify what technologies are needed, introduce them quickly, and commercialize them will succeed. The company that cannot do that will be absorbed. I think that will be what the automotive industry will be like in the 21st century." Okuda responded to the question of how the company can best use its cash reserves by noting, "Of course, we'll use some of that money domestically for research and development. But most will go to foreign investment. We will build factories overseas. And after that, we will invest some money in telecommunications and housing business" (*Business Week* 15 June 1998, 58).

The global business strategy has been a major tactic for Toyota to keep consumers driving its products from generation to generation. To launch slogans, such as "For People, For Society, For the Earth" and "Enriching Society Through Car Making," worldwide shows that Toyota has strenuously tried to be a part of local communities (Toyota Motor Corporation 1998d). Once again, Toyota has brought principles of Toyotaism to its companies overseas (Ogawa 1994). The emphasis of the "family" as a member of the local community is a primary strategy for Toyota in the 1990s. By undressing the image of Japanese cars overseas, Toyota's strategy has created a mirror of new indigenous products, which are managed, designed, assembled, and driven by the local people. This strategy certainly will work if local people feel comfortable with the products. Toyota automobiles will be driven by local people for generations to come.

In short, all of the above strategies created by Toyota can be characterized as follows: first, Toyota started to target the international market by focusing on the national (i.e., micro) level and then to the global (i.e., macro) level. After creating a number of footholds all over the five continents, it began to be a part of local communities by donating millions of dollars. These four stages gradually provided opportunities for Toyota to increase local production as well as reduce the tension created by the trade conflict with the United States. Because of globalization and a successful conclusion of NAFTA, Toyota has benefited greatly. As a member of the local community, Toyota has played a wise strategy overseas, which ultimately let Toyota bring Toyotaism to its companies overseas.

Second, according to local conditions, especially weather and economic infrastructures, Toyota provided products which fit local people's needs. A certain model car favored in one country does not necessarily sell in another country. When Toyota confronted a problem of an unknown field, such as local production in the 1980s, it implemented a strategy of forming a joint venture with GM to develop learning local production experience within a limited period and with limited cooperation. The experience of the joint venture with GM was a crucial factor enabling Toyota to set up its own manufacturing companies overseas, such as in Kentucky. Even though Toyota learned the know-how of running the manufacturing operation locally, it has never planned to have a full-scale cooperation (e.g., the merger between Daimler-Benz of Germany and Chrysler of the United States). When a reporter asked if Toyota will change its strategy to joint investment (with someone) overseas in the future, former president Okuda of Toyota stated, "I think Toyota will want to do this on its own. We don't really join with partners. It's difficult for us to join various cultures and customs (*Business Week* 15 June 1998, 58)." Without the merger, Toyota will continue to emphasize its keiretsu system in the group (Maema 1998).

Third, when Toyota created a new manufacturing operation overseas, Toyota headquarters usually dispatched an officer from Japan to take the chief executive officer position in the foreign country. Despite Toyota's efforts to be "a good corporate citizen around the world," the corporate culture of Toyota has never disappeared. Just as in Toyota in Japan, minority groups have not been promoted to the chief executive officer positions. In Japan, in hiring minorities, especially females, the TMC has the worst record of any company overseas. No female has worked in an executive position since the establishment of TMC. Former Singapore Prime Minster Lee Kuan Yew once stated that he can give the names of many Singaporean CEOs who work at American and European companies in Singapore, but he cannot name a single Singaporean CEO who works for a Japanese company in Singapore (The Annenberg/CPB Collection 1992, vol. 7). In other words, no local people are allowed to take the CEO position of a Japanese company, including Toyota.

Fourth, Toyota has often changed the new model of its automobile by creating the "C" model strategy. "C" model means that many automobiles made by Toyota, in particular passenger cars, are given names that start with the English character "C," and most of them are unknown overseas. For instance, according to the 1997 passenger car registrations by model in Japan, there are more than thirty types of automobiles: Aristo, Avalon, Caldina, Camry, Carib, Carina, Cavalier, Celica, Celsior, Century, Chaster, Corolla, Corolla II, Corona (or Carina II), Corsa, Comfort, Cresta, Crown, Curren, Cynos, Ipsum, Mark II (or Cressida), MR2, Prius, Raum, Scepter, Sera, Soarer, Sprinter, Sprinter Carib, Starlet, Supra, Tercel, Vista, and Windom (or Lexus). Interestingly, about 18 type "C" models dominate these passenger cars. According to Toyota, the "C" model strategy is purely coincidental to when Corolla became the "hot" product around the world. Therefore, leaders in Toyota believe the "C" model auspicious; it will bring "fortune" to their business (interview by the author with the head of the public relations department of Toyota in Tokyo on November 9, 1998; hereafter interview on November 9, 1998). Toyota probably has the most models of passenger cars in the world, but only some fifteen types of these models are well known overseas. Among these, Corolla, Camry, Tercel, Starlet, Lexus, Celica, and Corona have been popular in the export market (fig. 4.9). By 1997 more than ninety passenger car models were produced by Japanese automakers in Japan. Among all models in Japan, Corolla was the number one passenger car for the twenty-nine consecutive years from 1969 to 1997 (Toyota Motor Corporation 1998a).

Fifth, the selection of "place" by Toyota during its three stages of growth can be summarized as follows. During the first stage, Toyota mainly concentrated on developing Toyota City as well as Tokyo and Osaka. When the company began exporting overseas in the 1950s, Toyota targeted port cities, including those in the United States. During the second stage of the expansion overseas, leaders of TMC decided to locate assembly plants in large cities in developing countries, such as Tianjin in China. However, when Toyota built production plants in the industrial countries, small communities, such as Georgetown, Kentucky, were selected.

THE KEIRETSU STRUCTURE OF THE TOYOTA GROUP

Keiretsu, vertical affiliates, have been a well-known characteristic of Japanese business culture. Toyota has one of the most complicated keiretsu, which involves thousands of companies worldwide. Hiromi Shioji analyzed the Toyota system in *Gendai Nihon no Kigyo Gurupu* [The Business Group in Today's Japan] edited by Kazuichi Sakamoto and Masahiro Shimotani (pp. 51–75) in the 1980s. At the dawn of the twenty-first century, Toyota has expanded its network greatly. The keiretsu system (fig. 4.10) comprises mainly three groups: the companies of the TMC group (circle A), the enterprises that provide auto parts to suppliers (circle B), and corporations that involve the sales, rental, and leasing businesses, real estate, and research institutions in Japan, as well as manufacturers and subsidiaries overseas (circle C). Compa-

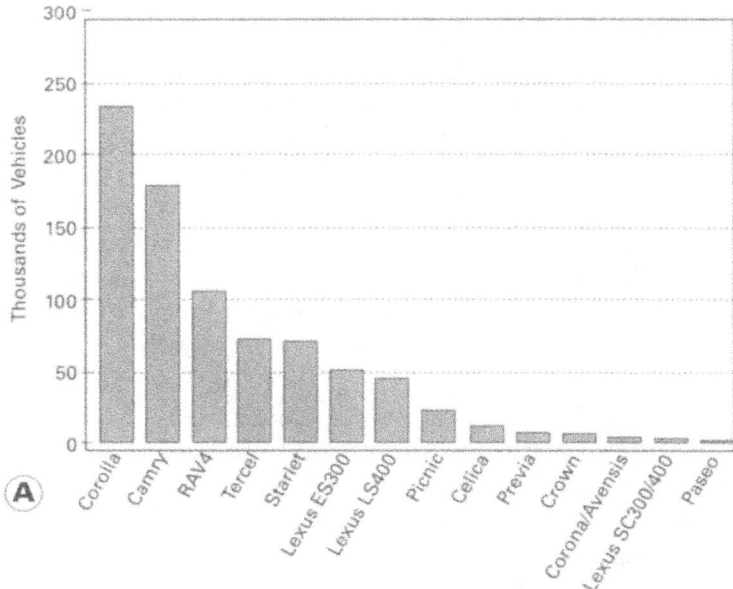

Note: Passenger cars only (including commercial vehicles of the same name).
Less than 1,000 of the following models were exported: MR2, Supra, Yaris,
Lexus IS200, and Century.

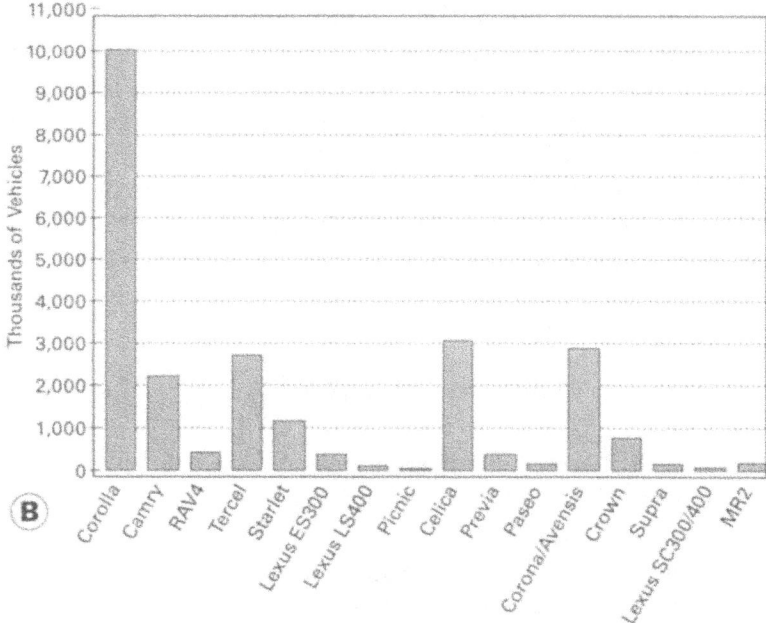

Note: Passenger cars only (including commercial vehicles of the same name).
Less than 1,000 of the following models have been exported: Supra, Yaris,
Lexus IS200, and Century.

Fig. 4.9. Toyota: Exports.
A. Exports in 1998. **B.** Total exports of various makes, 1999. (*Source:* Toyota Motor Corporation, Tokyo)

nies in the D, E, and G zones are created by three interwoven circles—A, B, and C.

Circle A in figure 4.10 contains about fifteen companies. Needless to say, TMC is the "heart" of circle A (i.e., the TMC Group) as well as of the entire Toyota keiretsu system. The other fourteen corporations in circle A serve as "internal organs" (i.e., the major driving forces) inside the Toyota system. They are:

1. TMC
2. Toyoda Automatic Loom Works
3. Aichi Steel Works
4. Toyoda Machine Works
5. Toyota Auto Body Company
6. Toyota Tsusho Corporation
7. Aisin Seiki Company
8. Denso Corporation
9. Toyoda Boshoku Corporation
10. Towa Real Estate Company
11. Toyota Central Research and Development Laboratories
12. Kanto Auto Works
13. Toyoda Gosei Company
14. Hino Motors
15. Daihatsu Motor Company

Along with TMC, circle A has ¥824.16 billion capital with 159,035 employees (Toyota Motor Corporation 1998c).

The members of circle B in figure 4.10 are suppliers who provide mainly auto parts and components. Two supplier organizations, Kyohokai and Eihokai, are involved with Toyota in this circle. The former primarily provides auto parts and components, and the latter mainly supplies molds, gauges, jigs, and contractors for plant facilities. These suppliers serve as the "food" of the whole Toyota keiretsu system. To receive inside information regarding Toyota (e.g., the future plans or changing management style), many companies have joined these two organizations. Circle B involves about three thousand companies that have business with Toyota amounting to more than ¥1 billion annually (interview on November 9, 1998). Many books, including those published by Toyota, give only a fraction of the number of suppliers. For example, *Outline of Toyota* (1998) states that about 320 companies in both Kyohokai and Eihokai support Toyota.

Since the expansion of TMC in the 1990s, the number of companies in circle C in figure 4.10 has increased dramatically. As of the writing of this paper, at least three hundred affiliates and subsidiaries, which TMC directly or indirectly provides capital, exist worldwide. Because of rapid expansion

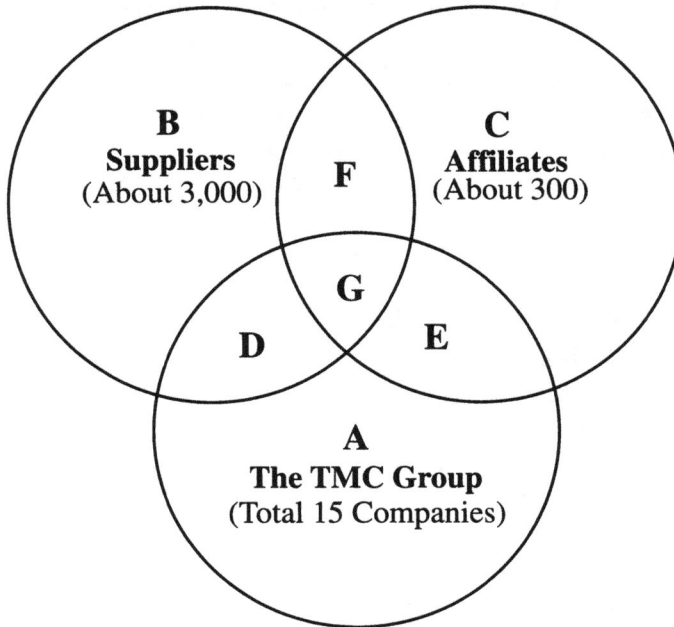

Fig. 4.10. Toyota *keiretsu* system.

worldwide, the leaders of Toyota (interview on November 9, 1998) in the Tokyo headquarters have lost count of the number of subsidiaries and affiliates. These affiliates in circle C primarily work as the "blood" of the entire system. The corporations in this circle have the complicated duty of ensuring that the Toyota system runs smoothly. These corporations include domestic plants; dealers and rental and leasing agents; prefabricated housing manufacturers and real estate companies; newspapers; insurance firms; overland and marine transports; research institutions; and overseas manufacturing operations, subsidiaries, and affiliates. In the keiretsu system, the formation of most overseas corporations is complicated.

The interwoven zones of the three circles represent one of most complicated keiretsu systems of the Japanese enterprises. Four overlapping areas (D, E, F, and G) in figure 4.10 indicate the mysteriousness of Toyota's keiretsu structure. According to the analysis by Hiromi Shioji, the numbers of companies in areas D, E, and G were estimated at one, two, and nine respectively (Shioji 1987, 58). Since 1987 Toyota has not increased the "core" group in circle A by a single corporation; Shioji's analysis is relatively valid today. The problem is zone F, which is the overlap of circles B and C. Area F in figure 4.10 had twenty-seven companies in the 1980s, but the exact numbers of companies in circles B and C are not known.

In short, the Toyota keiretsu system reflects a mysterious picture of a Japanese corporation system. It is unlikely that Toyota will desert this system in the next century. However, the wave of economic globalization has pushed Toyota to face reality in the international arena where the keiretsu structure normally does not exist. Further study of the keiretsu (or quasi-keiretsu) system overseas is needed.

THE FUTURE

There is an increasing tendency for automakers to develop their own production technology to meet their needs and to fit the particular conditions in Japan more precisely. With its own production system, Toyota has done what every automaker wishes to do. As a survivor, Toyota has developed two major pillars, or theories, of production: just-in-time and *jidoka* (fig. 4.11).

Just-in-time refers to a production methodology whereby the parts needed for assembly arrive beside the production line at precisely the right time and in the right quantity. This method of production is long-standing in Toyota's history. In fact, when TMC was started, Kiichiro instructed his employees to forget the commonly held notion that warehouses are essential in a plant. Kiichiro clarified that just-in-time does not mean simply that it is important to do something on time. Rather, this term refers to the need to be precise in terms of quantity as well. This is because excess creates waste (Toyota Motor Corporation 1988). Based on this system, TMC does not permit anything in

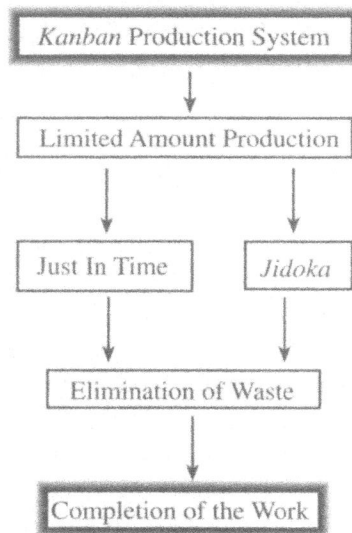

Fig. 4.11. Toyota *kanban* system.

excess of one day. Moreover, supply of parts is allowed to sit idly beside a line because warehouse stock is a physical and financial burden to management.

The second pillar is jidoka, which means "self-working." Toyota differentiates between self-working and self-moving automation machines. Self-working automation allows an operator to stop the machine when a problem occurs during the production process (e.g., defective parts). As a result, jidoka results in a reduction in personnel and a dramatic increase in productivity (Ohno 1984). The idea of a self-working automation machine is rooted in the invention of automatic looms by Sakichi. Indeed, the automatic looms had a device that enabled the machine to judge good and bad. Thus, no defective goods were produced. Although it is impossible to eliminate all defective auto parts during production, Toyota's process enables it to reduce the problem. In short, the purpose of jidoka is to build quality into each process of the production line (*Toyota Jidosha Kabushiki Kaisha* 1988).

The traditional view of the automobile assembly line is that upstream sections should supply downstream sections. Raw materials are made into parts, parts are assembled into units, and these units flow to the final assembly line. Thus, parts progress from upstream to downstream sections, and the automobile is assembled. Toyota has changed this process by turning the production flow backward. This enables the downstream sections to go to the upstream sections to pick up the right items at the right time and in the right quantities. As a result, the upstream sections should produce only as much as is requested. As a method of coordinating a great number of sections, it would be necessary only to indicate clearly what quantity of which item would be required. By transferring information between processes using various-sized cards, the well-known production system of Toyota—the *kanban* (signboard) system—was formed (*Toyota Jidosha Kabushiki Kaisha* 1988; Monden 1991). By circulating the signboard among the various sections, production volume may be controlled. For instance, the board displays various code numbers and letters to inform floor employees of how line operations are proceeding and when and where problems have occurred. Cards are suspended above the production lines and may be pulled to stop the line if complications arise. As a result, it was clear to the person in charge of each process that there was a keen need to adjust the production speed of the process and that the layout of the production processes had to be improved.

In short, under these two main concepts of production, leaders of Toyota believed that auto parts could be supplied from a preceding process to the subsequent process in the same way that items were supplied by a supermarket to customers. In other words, auto parts by the suppliers should be at the right time and in the required amounts—resulting in an elimination of inefficient production. Rather than sending parts on to the next stage as soon as they were completed, the employee at the later process would go to the preceding process when he or she needed the parts and pick up only the number

Employees exercise before the start of the workday at this small automobile parts factory in northern Tokyo. Numerous such factories exist in Japan. The motor vehicle industry assembles various processed materials and parts; depending on classification, several thousand parts of various kinds are required to assemble a vehicle. (Photograph by P.P. Karan)

required. In turn, at the earlier process, only enough parts would be produced to replenish what the later process had used (Ogawa 1994).

It is important to note that the production system has not been the only method used by Toyota to survive in the automobile industry. In fact, some people have considered the automobile a "bad" product that pollutes the environment, and an "unsafe" product that is dangerous for children (Maema 1998). To respond to these calls, Toyota has focused on safety and environment measures as well as dedicating itself to local communities. By developing new technologies, including VICS (Vehicle Information and Communication System), AHS (Advanced Cruise-Assist Highway Systems), and the Hybrid System, Toyota has demonstrated a concern for producing safe and clean products. This has eliminated a stereotypical image of the automobile that pollutes the environment (Toyota Motor Corporation 1998d). Both an Internet site and almost all pamphlets produced by Toyota detail facts about safety and environmental issues (Ibid., 1988, 1998a, 1998c, and 1998e). Improving plant safety and ergonomics is not only important but also saves money and boosts morale, which in turn make union organizing harder. The

Toyota plants are scattered among the rice fields on the outskirts of Toyota City, Japan. Generally Toyota plants in industrially advanced countries are located in small towns and plants in developing countries are located in large metropolitan centers. (Photograph by P.P. Karan)

small group of union activists at Toyota's Georgetown plant cites safety as a primary concern.

At plants in Asia and Europe, workers tend to be about the same size, weight, and strength. But American factories hire a much more diverse group of employees, which presents extra challenges in designing work stations for repetitive tasks. For example, at the Georgetown plant, the diverse workforce means work processes must accommodate workers who range in height from five feet to six-and-a-half feet. In 1998, Toyota's incident rating (number of times employees require medical attention per one hundred workers per year) at Georgetown jumped 14 percent to 25.7 percent, just above the industrial average of 25 percent. Since then, the plant has re-examined and refocused its efforts on improving safety. The aim is to bring the incident rating down to 9.9 percent by 2003. At Georgetown, Toyota's system for handling worker injuries is similar to those stipulated in the United Auto Workers contract. Toyota pays workers 65 percent of their basic pay during initial disability, compared with 60 percent under the United Auto Workers contract. Those who cannot return to the assembly line can take a worker's compensation buyout or accept other work within the plant. At the Kentucky plant, those workers are guaranteed their manufacturing wage rate for one year and a percentage of that rate for the second year.

Given the fact that Toyota builds and paints thousands of cars each day at various plants around the world, it is not surprising that it produces pollutants. Paint that misses the vehicle, called over spray, is a potential air pollutant. For example, Toyota's Georgetown plant produces eighty thousand pounds of "paint sludge" each week. The over spray is collected by water in large vats, then distilled to sludge. Since 1992, most of the sludge is dried and recycled into products such as low-density asphalt and decorative landscaping blocks. This is part of Toyota's continuing effort to develop a reputation as an environmentally friendly manufacturer.

In Japan, Toyota is attempting to revamp its corporate image through a $126 million theme park at Tokyo's waterfront. Toyota's park, which is called Mega Web, is designed to attract younger car buyers at a time when a stubborn recession has been sending auto sales plunging. Tokyo's waterfront is vibrant and a big hit with the young Japanese, and the raging success of Tokyo Disneyland has shown how effective amusement parks can be at attracting children and young couples. Mega Web is part of a futuristic waterfront amusement complex called Palette Town, which has a concert hall, adventure rides, and a giant Ferris wheel. The park includes exhibits of Toyota's models from the 1950s. Visitors can also design a car on computers, play with clay models, and take jaunts in a tiny electric car that showcases an automated driving system. While Mega Web may attract young buyers, Toyota still must come up with models that appeal to them.

Toyota faces additional challenges. As the earth has limited natural resources, in particular petroleum, the gasoline-powered automobile eventually will become problematic. Despite the creation of the hybrid automobile, Toyota must face the reality that the earth has only limited petroleum. The issue will be the crucial problem for Toyota in the twenty-first century when the natural resource depletes. Probably, current leaders of Toyota are thinking about the next strategy to deal with the issue because this issue is imperative to determine the fate of the automobile industry during this millennium. Everyone is looking forward to seeing what kind of strategies Toyota will develop, and what kind of automobile Toyota will contribute to human society. As a survivor, Toyota has conquered many problems so far and probably will continue to survive in the twenty-first century.

NOTES

The author wishes to thank Dr. P.P. Karan for his suggestions and comments on this paper. Also he thanks Kristen Smith and Jeanette Jeneault for reviewing earlier drafts, as well as Keiko Aoki, Akihiro Kawakami, Yukiko Nakazato, Masahide Ohno, and Kentaro Someya for their support of original sources.

1. Many people may wonder why the founder name of TMC is Toyoda, not Toyota. In Japanese, Toyoda and Toyota share the same Chinese charac-

ters. When the leaders of TMC decided on a trademark, they selected Toyota because its spelling in *katakana* uses eight strokes, a felicitous number suggestive of increasing prosperity. The trademark also symbolized the company's plan to change from a family business into a well-known corporation (Toyota Jidosha Kabushiki Kaisha 1979, 77). However, some firms in the TMC group still use the word Toyoda.

REFERENCES

Aichi Toyota Jidosha Kabushiki Kaisha Shashi Henshushitsu. 1970. *Aichi Toyota Nijugonen shi* (The 25-Year History of Aichi Toyota). Nagoya: Toyota Jidosha Kabushiki Kaisha.

The Annenberg/CPB collection. 1992. *The Pacific Century.* Produced by the Pacific Basic Institute in Association with KCTS/Seattle, videocassettes, 10 vols.

Benedict, Ruth. 1946. *The Chrysanthemum and the Sword: Patterns of Japanese Culture.* Boston: Houghton Mifflin Company.

Kawahara, Akira. 1995. *Kyoryoku no Honshitsu* (The Major Competition). Tokyo: Daiyamondo Sha.

Maema, Takanori. 1998. *Toyota vs. Bentsu* (Toyota vs. Daimler-Benz). Tokyo: Kodansha.

Mercedes Goes to Motown. 1998. *Business Week,* 9 May.

Monden, Yasuhiro. 1991. *Shin Toyota Shisutemu* (The New Toyota system). Tokyo: Kodansha.

A New Kind of Car Company. 1998. *Economist.* 9 May.

Nihon Keizai Shimbun. 1998. *Keijoeki, Toyota Shui* (Toyota at the Top, Recurrent Profit). 27 June.

Nissan Seeking Loan from Development Bank to Write Off High-Interest Debt. 1998. *New York Times,* 12 November.

Ohno, Taiichi. 1984. How the TOYOTA Production System Was Created. In *The Anatomy of Japanese Business,* edited by Kazuo Sato and Yosuo Hoshino. New York: M.E. Sharpe, Inc.

Ogawa, Eiji. 1994. *Toyota Seisan Houshiki no Kenkyu* (Studies of Toyota's Production System). Tokyo: Nihon Keizai Shimbun Sha.

Sankei Shimbun. 1998. Toyota ga Nanai (Toyota Ranks at the Number Seven). 11 November.

Sato, Yoshinobu. 1988. *Toyota Gurupu no Senryaku to Jisho Bunseki* (The Analysis of the Toyota Group's Strategies). Tokyo: Hakutou Shobo.

Shioji, Hiromi. 1987. Keiretsu Buhin Meka no Seisan Shihon Renkan: Toyota Jidosha no Kesu (The Relations of Capital Production in Keiretsu Maker: The Case Study of Toyota). In *Gendai Nihon no Kigyo Gurupu* (The Business Group in Today's Japan), edited by Kazuichi Sakamoto and Masahiro Shimotani. Tokyo: Toyo Keizai Shinposha.

Toyota Jidosha Kabushiki Kaisha. 1988. *Sozo Kagiri naku: Toyota Jidosha Gojunen Shi* (The Unlimited Creativity: The 50-Years History of TMC). Aichi: Toyota Jidosha Kabushiki Kaisha.

Toyota Jidosha Hanbai Kabushiki Kaisha Shashi Henshu Iinkai. 1971. *Motarizeshon to Tomoni* (With Motorization). Nagoya: Toyota Jidosha Hanbai Kabushiki Kaisha.

Toyota Jidosha Kogyo Kabushiki Kaisha. 1959. *Toyota Jidosha Nijunen Shi* (The Twenty-Year History of Toyota). Aichi: Toyota Jidosha Kogyo Kogyo Kabushiki Kaisha.

———. 1979. *Toyota no Ayumi* (A History of Toyota).

Toyota Jidosha Kogyo Kabushiki Kaisha Shashi Henshu Iinkai. 1968. *Toyota Jidosha Sanjunen Shi* (The 30-Year History of Toyota Motor Corporation). Nagoya: Toyota Jidosha Kogyo Kabushiki Kaisha.

Toyota Motor Corporation. 1999a. *Corporate Directory.* Tokyo: Toyota Motor Corporation.

———. 1999b. *Toyota and the World, 1999.* Tokyo: Toyota Motor Corporation.

———. 1999c. *Toyota no Gaikyo, 1999* (Outline of Toyota, 1999). Tokyo: Toyota Motor Corporation.

———. 1998a. *The Automobile Industry Toyota and the World 1998.* Aichi: Toyota Motor Corporation.

———. 1998b. *Corporate Directory.* Aichi: Toyota Motor Corporation.

———. 1998c. *Outline of Toyota.* Aichi: Toyota Motor Corporation.

———. 1998d. *Toyota.* Tokyo: Toyota Motor Corporation.

———. 1998e. *Toyota Announces 1997 Progress Report on Its New Global Business Plan.*

———. 1988. *Toyota: A History of the First 50 Years.*

Toyota's Okuda on Catching Up with Ford. 1998. *Business Week,* 15 June.

5

Yesterday and Today

Changes in Workers' Lives in Toyota City, Japan

YUICHIRO NISHIMURA AND KOHEI OKAMOTO

TOYOTA CITY, JAPAN, is the headquarters of Toyota Motor Corporation (TMC). TMC has seven large plants in Toyota City, where about twenty-four thousand people work on assembly lines. About four hundred factories of affiliated companies and subcontractors are scattered throughout the city. About half of the employed persons in the city work for automobile-related industries, and including the employees of related businesses and their families, it is said that around 70 percent of the total population of the city (348,532 in 1997) is involved with TMC to a greater or lesser extent. Thus, Toyota City is a typical company town (fig. 5.1).

In a company town, the company has strong and direct relationships with the region in various ways. The rise and decline of a company's financial strength affects the regional economy, while the influx and efflux of workers affect regional society. Huge plants alter the landscape, and industrial wastes degrade the environment. We can understand the regional structure of a company town by looking at these aspects. Many geographical studies have examined Japanese company towns, and some have dealt with the relationship of TMC and Toyota City. For example, Miyakawa (1980) described the economic and political influences of TMC on the local community, and Iseki, Abe, and Miyamachi (1987) analyzed the role of TMC in local environmental management.

The influence of automotive industries on the region is more complex, however, due to their production system. Since automobile manufacturing is a great assembly industry, many parts suppliers must be organized around an assembly plant. It is also a labor-intensive industry requiring many workers to be allocated efficiently at production spots. An efficient method to control parts production and delivery as well as to arrange human resources is the

Fig. 5.1. Toyota City.

just-in-time (JIT) system introduced by TMC. This study sheds light on the influence of the production system on the local community.

This chapter first describes the history of TMC reorganizing the region to meet its production system needs. Then, it focuses on the change of working hours in 1995 and examines the influence of the Toyota production system on local communities.

CONCENTRATION OF FACTORIES AND SUBCONTRACTORS

TMC began as the Automobile Department of the Toyoda Automatic Loom Works, which was located in Kariya City (southwest of the area that is now Toyota City), and became independent in 1937. At that time, Toyota City was a leading sericultural town named Koromo. (After the opening of Japan to the world in the 1860s, silk exports increased and the area developed as a center of the sericultural industry.) However, in 1930, the market for raw silk collapsed, which damaged the Koromo region. The town invited the automotive industries to revive the regional economy. Kiichiro Toyoda, who is the founder of TMC, decided to locate a factory in Koromo for several reasons. One reason was that Koromo Town offered inexpensive land subsidized by the town, which was a favorable condition for factory construction. Another reason was the abundant workforce available from the agricultural sector (Toyota Motor Manufacturing 1967).

In 1938 the first Toyota automobile plant, now called Head Plant, was founded in Koromo Town. World War II left the company in economic ruin, but with the introduction of the Toyopet Crown in 1955, passenger car production began in earnest. In 1951, Koromo Town merged with neighboring small villages to form a city. Then, the changing of the name of the city Koromo to Toyota became an issue. As a consequence of the conflict between the old *Gemeinschaft,* or native group, and the newcomers aiming to transform the traditional local community into an industrial society, the name of the city was changed to Toyota City when the second plant, Motomachi Plant, was established in 1959. In the following years, as motorization took hold during the period of high economic growth in Japan, large automobile plants were constructed in succession in and around Toyota City (fig. 5.2).

The plants built in the late 1960s and early 1970s are concentrated around the border between Toyota City and neighboring Miyoshi Town (fig. 5.2). These plants assemble passenger cars and produce major parts for the engine and chassis. Such spatial concentration allowed TMC to deliver major parts rapidly. In those days, TMC extended production scale and pursued efficient production simultaneously.

Until the 1950s there were few subcontractors in Toyota City. Before World War II, TMC made many parts in-house, and after the war they began

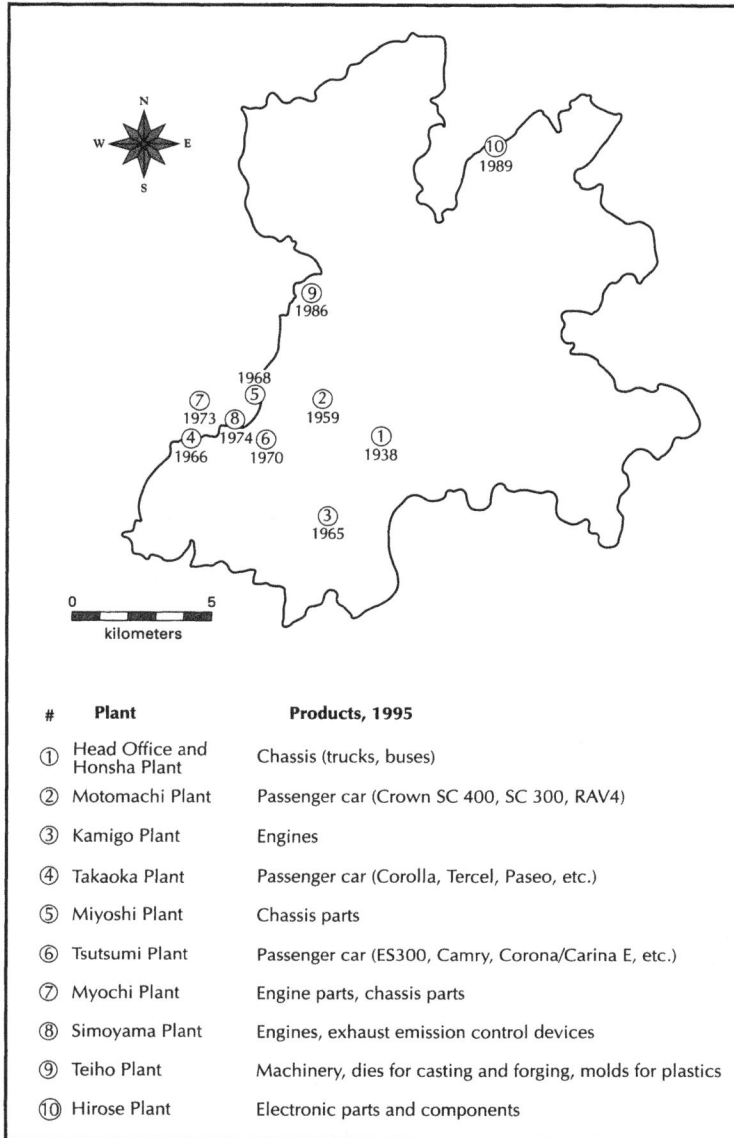

Fig. 5.2. TMC plants (and year established) in and around Toyota City. (*Source:* Toyota Motor Corporation, Toyota City)

#	Plant	Products, 1995
①	Head Office and Honsha Plant	Chassis (trucks, buses)
②	Motomachi Plant	Passenger car (Crown SC 400, SC 300, RAV4)
③	Kamigo Plant	Engines
④	Takaoka Plant	Passenger car (Corolla, Tercel, Paseo, etc.)
⑤	Miyoshi Plant	Chassis parts
⑥	Tsutsumi Plant	Passenger car (ES300, Camry, Corona/Carina E, etc.)
⑦	Myochi Plant	Engine parts, chassis parts
⑧	Simoyama Plant	Engines, exhaust emission control devices
⑨	Teiho Plant	Machinery, dies for casting and forging, molds for plastics
⑩	Hirose Plant	Electronic parts and components

Toyota's Takaoka Plant in the southwestern part of Toyota City, Japan, lies in the midst of rice fields. The plant started operations in 1966 and has plastic molding, stamping, body, painting, and assembly shops. It produces Prius, Corolla, Sprinter, Tercel, and Paseo passenger cars. (Photograph by Yuichiro Nishimura)

dealing with subcontractors in other cities such as Kariya and Nagoya. As the mass production system started in the 1960s, TMC relocated suppliers close to TMC plants to supply mechanical parts efficiently. That established the localization of subcontractors within Toyota City. In 1965, TMC developed an extremely effective method of streamlining manufacturing operations—*kanban*, or the Just-in-Time (JIT) system of inventory control for subcontractors. The technique obliges suppliers to deliver parts exactly when they are needed—no sooner and no later. The concentration of subcontractors was accelerated by the introduction of JIT methods, although it is controversial whether JIT necessarily produces concentration of factories (Mair 1992).

A lot of factories related to automobile industries are distributed throughout the city (fig. 5.3). Most large factories are located around TMC plants in the southwest of the city. They connect very closely to TMC plants through the JIT production system. In the late 1960s, these subcontractors were required to deliver their parts several times per day only during the daytime. Since 1975, however, they have started to deliver the parts not only during the day but also at night. The frequency of parts delivery has also increased

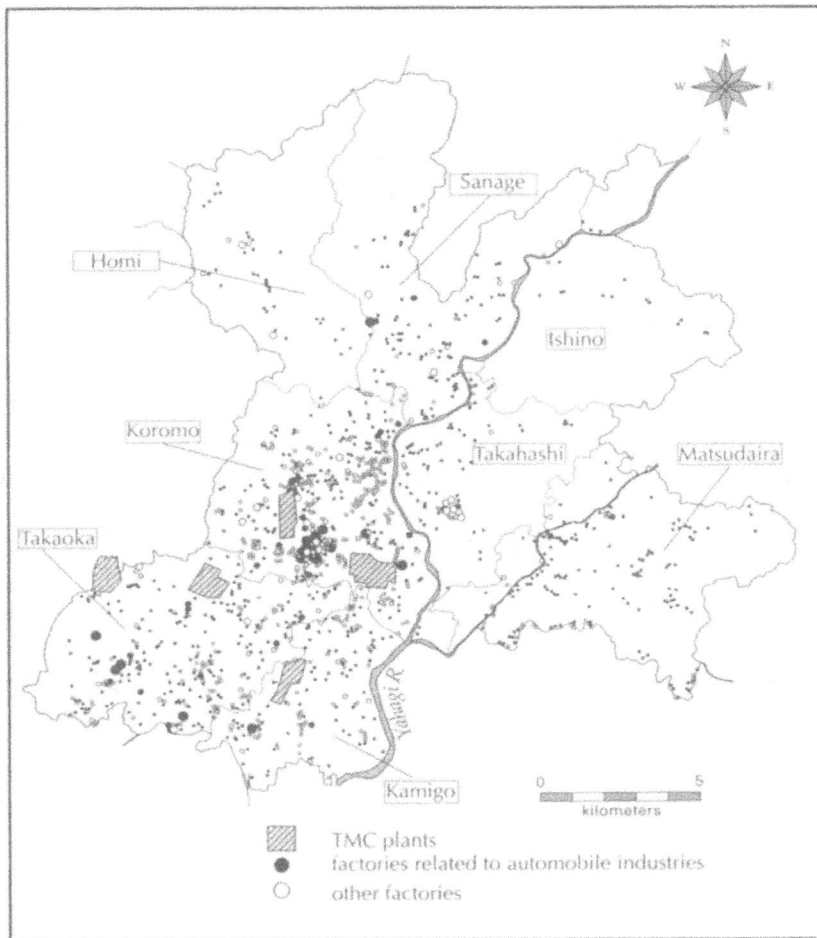

Fig. 5.3. Factories in Toyota City in 1982. (*Source:* Toyota City Office, 1982)

(Azumi 1982). Thus, the activities of subcontractors have been affected spatially as well as temporally by the Toyota mode of production. The municipal government adopted an urban plan suitable for an Automobile Industrial City and reinforced road construction, which allowed rapid parts delivery between factories as well as smooth commuting for workers. Improvement of public transport services was disregarded.

URBANIZATION OF TOYOTA CITY
AND LIFE COURSES OF TOYOTA WORKERS

The expansion of automobile production after 1960 required a large number of assembly line workers, resulting in an increase in the number of employees in Toyota City (fig. 5.4). Before 1959, automobile production did not even reach one hundred thousand units, but after 1960, automobile production and the number of workers increased dramatically. Until the 1980s, both production and the number of employees continued to grow, though the growth in both categories slowed in the mid-1970s due to the impact of the oil crisis.

TMC employees during the expansion era can be divided into two categories. The first category is workers from local farms. Many sons of farmers worked for a plant, and took care of their farms on weekends (Matsui 1958). The second category is the new migrants from different areas of Japan. In the latter half of the 1960s, more than eight thousand people flowed into Toyota City every year. These newcomers came mainly from Chubu (central Japan) and Kyushu (fig. 5.5).

In the postwar period of high economic growth, Japan experienced a massive inland migration from rural areas to urban areas, and many migrants moved to the industrial areas around Tokyo, Osaka, and Nagoya (Okamoto 1997). Few workers came to Toyota City from Hokkaido and Tohoku because the majority of migrants from these locales were destined for the industrial areas around Tokyo. As TMC developed its mass production system in the 1960s, not only TMC personnel but also the staff of Toyota City, including the mayor and municipal assembly members, visited bordering rural areas to recruit middle-school and high-school graduates to augment the workforce in Toyota City.

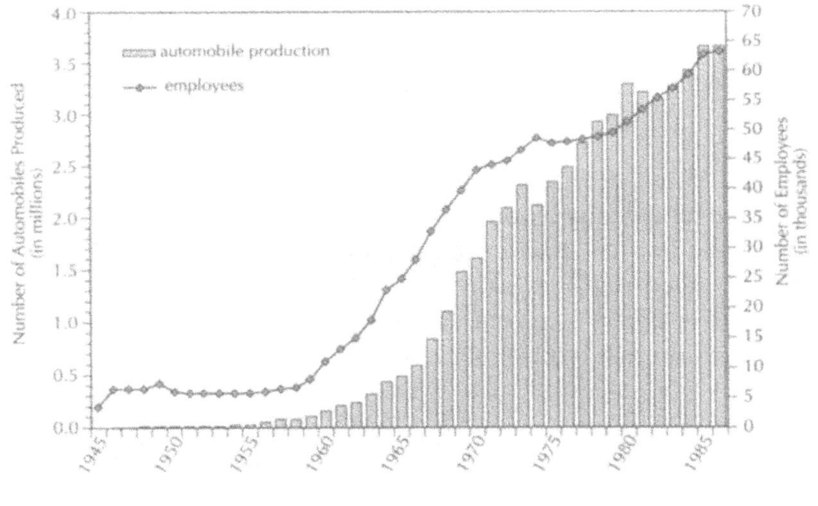

Fig. 5.4. Automobile production by TMC and number of TMC employees, 1945–1986. (*Source:* Toyota Motor Corporation, Toyota City)

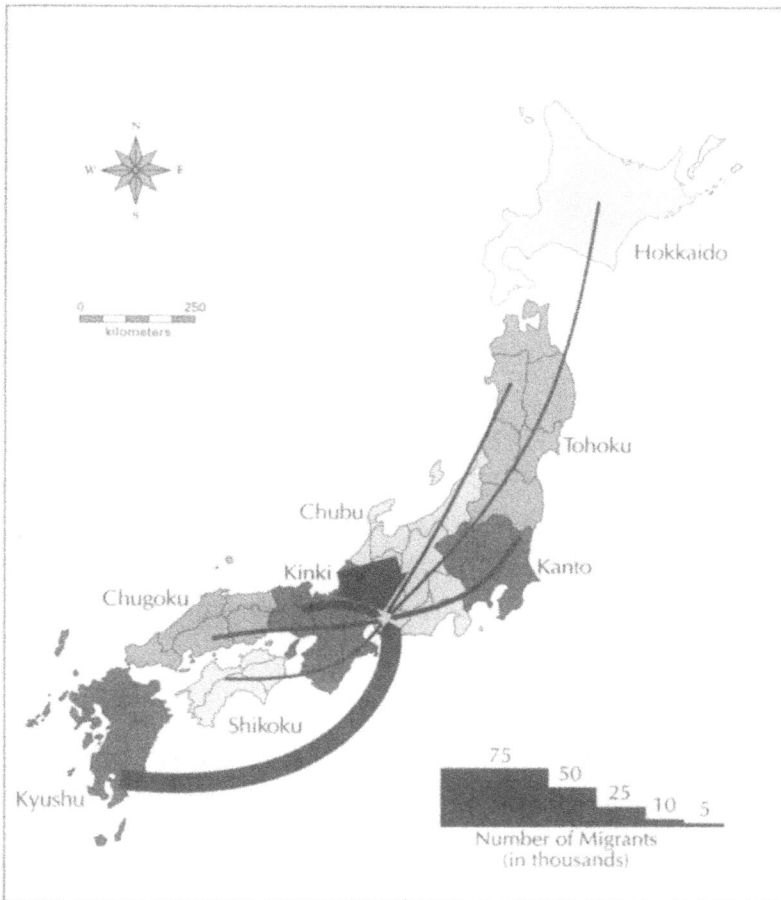

Fig. 5.5. Flow of migrants to Toyota City from other regions of Japan, 1960–1969. (*Source:* Toyota City Office, 1996)

The influx of migrants brought rapid population growth and dramatic change to the employment structure of Toyota City. The population of the city nearly doubled from 104,529 to 197,193 during the 1960s, although the annexation of neighboring towns contributed to the population increase. During the same decade, the ratio of employed persons in secondary industries increased from 35 percent to more than 60 percent, while the percentage in the primary sector dropped sharply from 43 percent to 12 percent (fig. 5.6).

Most of the migrant workers were single males. After settling in Toyota City, they married, had children, and hoped to move from their cramped quarters to larger houses. In 1964, TMC started a housing loan fund to encourage employees to buy their own homes. In 1969, the Toyota Housing

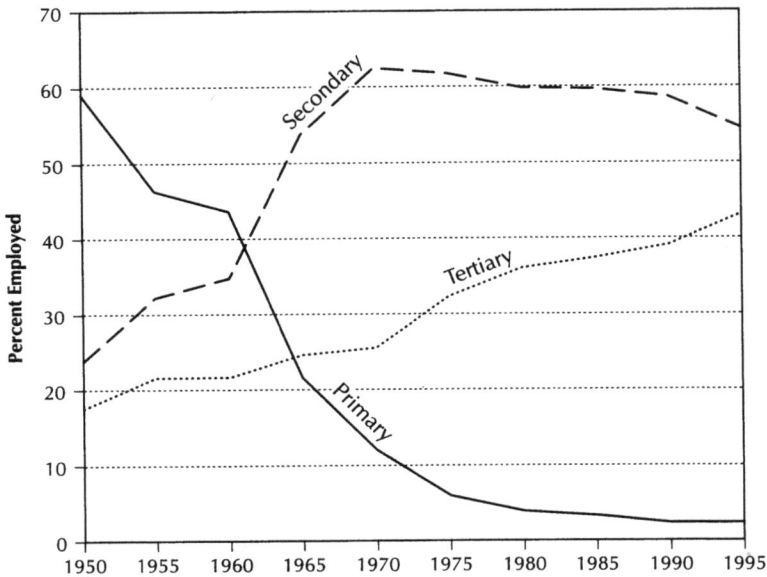

Fig. 5.6. Employment in three major economic sectors in Toyota City, 1950–1995. (*Source:* Population Census of Japan, 1950–1995)

Corporation, a housing company, was established as one of the Toyota Group corporations. It began construction of housing complexes within Toyota City to provide affordable houses for TMC employees.

The development of plants, subcontractors' factories, and housing for employees brought rapid urbanization to Toyota City. The Densely Inhabited District (DID) expanded between 1960 and 1980 (fig. 5.7). The thick line indicates the DID in 1960, which corresponds to the urban core of old Koromo Town. In the 1960s, TMC started to build company houses and dormitories around Head Plant, and the DID consequently expanded to the south. After that, Toyota Housing Corporation developed housing complexes around existing urbanized areas, which brought a further extension of the DID.

TMC plants are concentrated in the southwestern part of the city. There are many dormitories for bachelors and company-owned houses in this area. Unmarried and newly wed employees live here close to their workplace. After they purchase their own homes, they commute relatively long distances by cars, which they assembled themselves and purchased from their employer. Actually, many TMC workers buy their own homes when they are around the age of thirty (Fujita, 1988a). Even an employee coming from a poor rural region can have a house and Toyota car at a young age—and this is the ideal life course TMC has promoted for its employees since the 1960s. However, we should recognize that not all employees of the company attain such a life

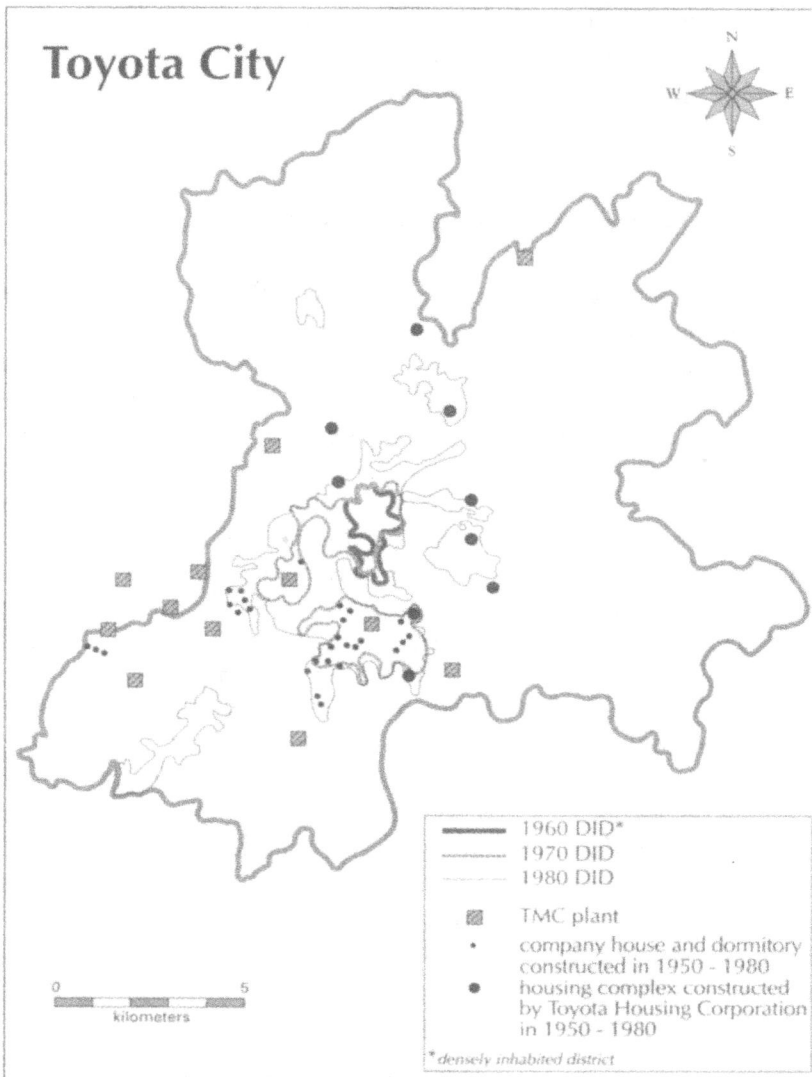

Fig. 5.7. Toyota City: Expansion of DID and housing construction by TMC. DID (Densely Inhabited District) is defined as an area that is composed of a group of contiguously enumerated districts, each of which has a population density of 4,000 persons or more per square kilometer, and whose total population is 5,000 or more. (*Source:* Population Census of Japan, 1960, 1970, 1980; Toyota Motor Corporation, and Sato ,1987)

course. Many workers leave TMC and find new jobs at small subcontractors in Toyota City or the commercial and service sectors in the Nagoya metropolitan area (Fujita 1988a). The decision to resign is often the result of working both day shift and night shift at TMC plants.

The Day and Night Shifts in Assembly Plants

In 1962 TMC introduced the night shift at assembly plants. TMC expected a great surge in demand for the automobile in the near future because Japan had entered a period of high economic growth in the 1960s. Since that time, many employees work a day shift and a night shift. In this working-time management, one group of employees works a day shift one week and works a night shift the next week (fig. 5.8). Another group works in the reverse order to balance the number of employees of both shifts. This style of shift allocation is common in the Japanese automobile industry.

The day and night shift plan is very important to JIT. JIT is a production system without stock; that is, a company produces only the amount expected for demand. That means a company has to be able to quickly adjust the amount of production, and flexible utilization of labor force is indispensable. Actually, TMC has used temporary workers at times to adjust the labor force, but they have mainly utilized their own human resources.

TMC had three strategies, at different time-scale levels, for the flexible use of human resources. The first was the temporal change of shift system. As a rule, each plant makes different types of cars. If the demand of a certain type of car decreases greatly, the plant that produces this type of car discontinues day and night shifts, and temporarily uses only the day shift. Surplus workers are transferred to a plant producing high-demand cars. Since plants are concentrated in and around Toyota City, workers can easily change their workplace. The second strategy is working on weekends, usually daytime on Saturdays. It can be called the production adjustment at week level. The third strategy is the adjustment at day level. There are two to four hours between a day shift and a night shift (fig. 5.8). These periods are used for overtime work. In the high-economic-growth period in Japan, overtime work was normal, and Toyota assembly workers were accustomed to working overtime. TMC has realized the flexible use of human resources through combining these three strategies.

Almost all laborers who worked at night, overtime, and on weekends were male. Fujita (1988b) reported that the long shifts and irregular working hours at the time made it difficult for workers to have lives outside their work. Activities at home and in the local community were limited. This labor management system requires the wives of employees to stay home to allow husbands to concentrate on their work. Wives have to manage all the housework and child care (Kimoto 1995).

Day and Night Shift

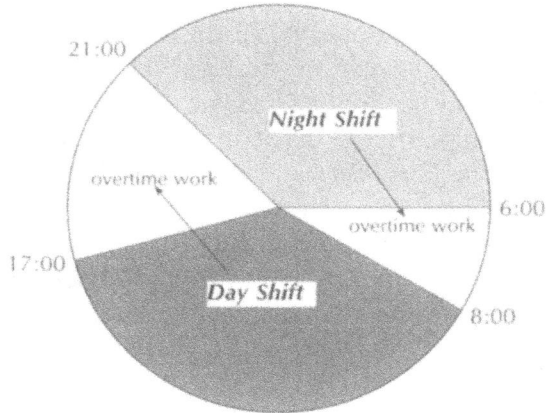

	Mon	Tue	Wed	Thu	Fri	Sat	Sun	Mon	Tue	Wed	Thu	Fri	Sat	Sun
A group	D	D	D	D	D	off	off	N	N	N	N	N	off	off
B group	N	N	N	N	N	off	off	D	D	D	D	D	off	off

D: day shift, N: night shift

Sequential Shift

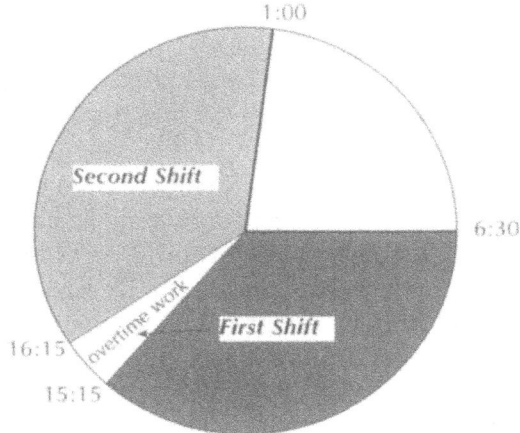

	Mon	Tue	Wed	Thu	Fri	Sat	Sun	Mon	Tue	Wed	Thu	Fri	Sat	Sun
A group	1	1	1	1	1	off	off	1	1	1	1	1	off	off
B group	2	2	2	2	2	off	off	2	2	2	2	2	off	off

1: first shift, 2: second shift

Fig. 5.8. Change from day and night shifts to sequential shift.

The 1990s Recession and the Reaction by TMC

Since 1990 TMC has faced upheaval of the business environment and has had to change the TMC production strategy. On a global scale, TMC faces the difficult condition of the appreciated yen. Automobiles made by TMC in Japan weaken the competitive position of TMC in world markets. In addition, the increase of the Japanese trade surplus has been severely criticized in the United States. To increase profit margins without being susceptible to the influence of foreign exchange fluctuations, TMC accelerated the transplantation of manufacturing to the United States and Europe. TMC intended to cope with the saturation of global automobile markets through these transplants. One goal in the "2005 years vision" of TMC is the local production of automobiles tailored to each country. TMC changed its corporate strategy in Japan from export oriented to domestic oriented.

On the domestic scale, production was restructured spatially. The work ethic of the younger generation has changed. They tend to avoid heavy work or physical labor. These changes led the firm to relocate domestic plants. Toyota City is located in the Nagoya metropolitan area and is close to the neighboring metropolitan areas of Tokyo and Osaka. Young workers are attracted to the commercial and service sectors in these metropolitan areas. Therefore, it has become difficult for TMC to attract assembly line workers. TMC decided to build new plants in the outer regions of Japan, such as Kyushu and Hokkaido, where the new plants could employ high school graduates.

In 1992, Toyota Motor Kyushu Corporation (TMKC) started operation of a plant at Miyata Town, Fukuoka prefecture, Kyushu Island. At one time, Miyata Town was a coal-mining town. For more than twenty years, since mining declined in the 1960s, Miyata Town had been advocating that TMC build a plant there. In 1989, TMC decided to build an automobile assembling plant in Miyata Town. TMC selected Miyata Town as the plant location due to the presence of a nearby interchange on the Kyushu expressway. Subcontractors followed TMC and also built factories around Miyata Town. Subcontractor factories numbered only about thirty to forty, however (Endo, 1997). TMKC operates the JIT production system without a concentration of subcontractors. A lot of parts are delivered via expressway or shipping from distant suppliers.

The Change of the Shift System

In May 1995, TMC changed the day and night shift system into a sequential shift system. Under this new working-time management plan, the first shift is from 6:30 A.M. to 3:15 P.M. and the second shift is from 4:15 P.M. to 1:00 A.M.; the two shifts are consecutive rather than separated by a long interval (fig.

5.8). Workers alternate two periods every week in the same way as with the day and night shift system. About twenty-five thousand workers in twelve plants in and around Toyota City adopted this change. So it was expected that this change of the shift system would influence the daily lives of not only the Toyota employees but also the other citizens.

Why did TMC change the shift system? There were two reasons. The first reason was cost reduction. The high currency exchange rate for Japanese yen in the 1980s had weakened the competitive position of the Japanese automotive industry in world markets. Management tried to reduce labor expense in order to decrease production costs. In the old day and night shift plan, workers had received three kinds of extra wages: allowance for working a night shift, allowance for working overtime, and allowance for working alternating day shift and night shift. These allowances sometimes added up to a quarter of the entire monthly income of a worker. By changing the day and night shift system into a sequential shift system, TMC reduced some of these allowances, including about half of the allowance for working a night shift and almost all of the allowance for working overtime because overtime work was largely eliminated by the new shift system. While the domestic demand for automobiles has dropped since the collapse of the bubble economy at the beginning of 1990s, local production in plants located overseas is increasing, especially in the United States. Under these circumstances, overtime work is not as necessary. TMC expected labor expenses to decrease by ¥3 billion a year due to the change of the shift system (Nihon Keizai Shimbun May 8, 1995).

The second reason for the change in the shift system was to improve working conditions. Young people today tend to dislike working in factories. TMC faced occasional worker shortages because young people easily gave up these jobs. The night shift work and overtime work placed great burdens on workers. TMC had to attract workers by improving working conditions. In the new shift system, the hours after the first shift and the hours before the second shift are available for leisure or volunteer activities.

The first reason, cost reduction, was more important to TMC, but TMC stressed the second reason in announcements. An increase of leisure time for employees was an official aim of the change. TMC enlarged the parking lots around the plants by three thousand spaces because the workers on the first shift and second shift would use the parking lots at the same time during the short interval between shifts. This cost around ¥3 billion, which would be recovered within a couple of years (Yomiuri Shimbun April 22, 1995).

THE IMPACT OF THE SHIFT SYSTEM CHANGE ON THE COMMUNITY

The new shift system affects the community in various ways. First, there is an influence on TMC subcontractors. According to newspaper articles, the three affiliate body manufacturers of Toyota—Shatai, Arako, and Toyoda Auto Loom Works—introduced sequential shifts simultaneously with the change by TMC. Moreover, about 40 percent of the eighty main suppliers in the Nagoya metropolitan area had already adopted sequential shifts or introduced the system by May 1995. Consequently, about nine thousand people working in these companies changed their working hours (Asahi Shimbun May 2, 1995).

To learn the effect on subcontractors in more detail, we conducted a questionnaire survey in 1999 and received answers from forty-six companies. According to this survey, the reaction to the change was diverse among subcontractors, and it seemed to depend on various aspects of their business practices such as transactions with other companies, utilization of the labor force, and parts supply method. For example, one subcontractor, a bolts and nuts maker, changed the working hours of two shifts from 8:00 A.M.–5:00 P.M./5 P.M.–6:00 A.M. to 7:00 A.M.–4:00 P.M./4:00 P.M.–1:00 A.M. in response to the shift system change by TMC. This company is located near the Motomachi Plant and has a close transaction relationship with TMC. It needed to synchronize its production schedule with that of TMC.

Some subcontractors used a three-shift system (twenty-four-hour production) and supplied parts not only to TMC but to other automobile manufacturers like Honda, Mitsubishi, and Matsuda. They did not alter their shift system, because they needed to maintain three shifts to adjust to the production schedules of different customers. Other subcontractors worked only a day shift prior to the shift system change at TMC. They responded that it was impossible to operate the night shift because they hired many female workers. Although a lot of subcontractors hired women, these women could not work at night because until recently the Japanese Labor Standards Law prohibited night work by women.

Two of the surveyed subcontractors changed their parts delivery schedules for TMC, though they did not change their production schedules. They stopped night delivery because TMC discontinued nighttime production activities. Thus, production schedules and distribution schedules are not necessarily linked in subcontractors. Some suppliers located far from Toyota City have depots near TMC plants. By using these depots, they can produce and deliver the parts independent from the change in the shift system at TMC.

Next, we turn our attention to local businesses other than subcontractors. A convenience store chain, Family Mart, has changed part of its delivery system. This chain has forty-five stores in the Toyota region, and food commodities like lunch boxes and rice balls are distributed to each store three times a day, from a distribution center in Okazaki City near Toyota City. Family Mart changed the departure time of the midnight delivery from the center to one hour earlier to meet the demand of workers finishing the second shift. The change of delivery time included the change of production time in the food factory of the chain. As another example, a chain of *sento*, or bathhouses, also changed their hours of operation. The closing time shifted from midnight to 3 A.M. (Yomiuri Shimbun May 15, 1995).

Few commercial businesses took measures to meet the new situation, however. According to a questionnaire survey by the Chamber of Commerce and Industry of Toyota City conducted two months after of the shift system change, only eight of twenty-eight restaurants around the main plants made some adaptations. Six restaurants changed their business hours, and two restaurants changed their menus for the first shift workers whose finishing time was poorly timed for either lunch or dinner (Toyota Chamber of Commerce and Industry 1995).

Traffic congestion during morning and evening rush hours has eased. Actually, traffic on main roads has decreased by 30 percent from 7 A.M. to 8 A.M. On the other hand, traffic has increased around 4 P.M. Since this hour corresponds to the time children return home from school, some countermeasures were considered for safe traffic. Schoolteachers checked which streets the children used and guided them to safer streets. TMC advised their workers not to drive on roads without sidewalks. Police changed the signal cycle of about 198 traffic lights, or about 37 percent of all traffic lights in Toyota City. As a result, most potential problems were avoided.

CHANGES OF THE DAILY LIVES OF TOYOTA WORKERS AND THEIR FAMILIES

The influence on citizens other than Toyota workers is indirect, while the change on the daily lives of Toyota workers and their families is very direct. To examine such influences, the Toyota City Research Institution of Transportation Planning conducted a panel survey. Data on daily life were taken from an activity diary survey of the households of Toyota workers as well as the other households. In this survey, the space-time budgets for both husbands and wives were scrutinized in detail. (For a survey method, see Okamoto 1997.) This panel consisted of two time surveys. The first survey was done during two weeks of April 1995, just before the change, and the second survey was done during two weeks in October in the same year, or five months after the change. (For survey results in detail, see Nishimura 1998.)

Here we will focus on data from sixty-one households in which husbands worked a day shift, a night shift, the first shift, the second shift and in which the daily activity data on all these shifts were completed. Figure 5.9 shows the aggregate daily paths of husbands on a day before the change and on a day after the change; the chart shows the aggregate daily routine of wives on a day before the change for comparison purposes. In the top dia-

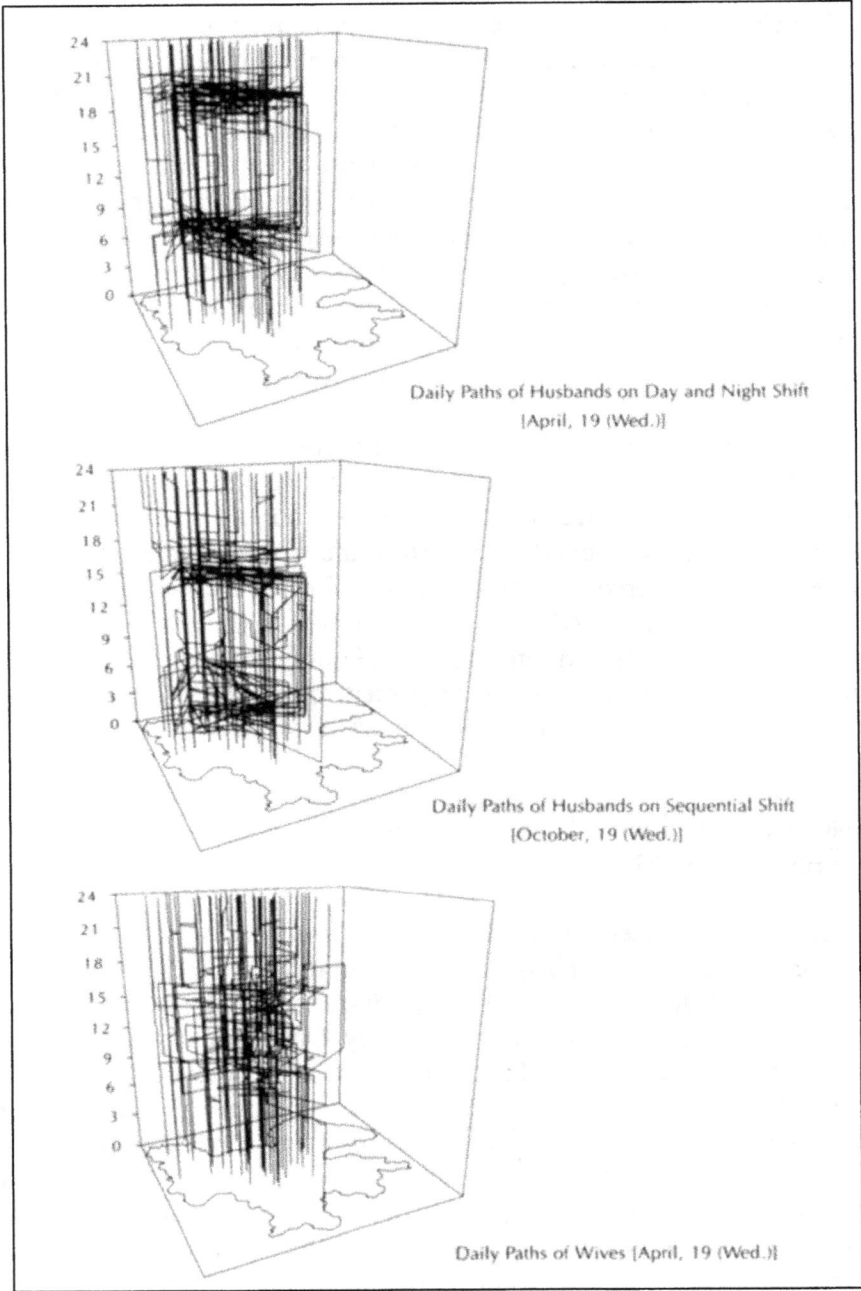

Fig. 5.9. Aggregated daily paths of TMC workers and their wives (*Source:* Nishimura, 1998)

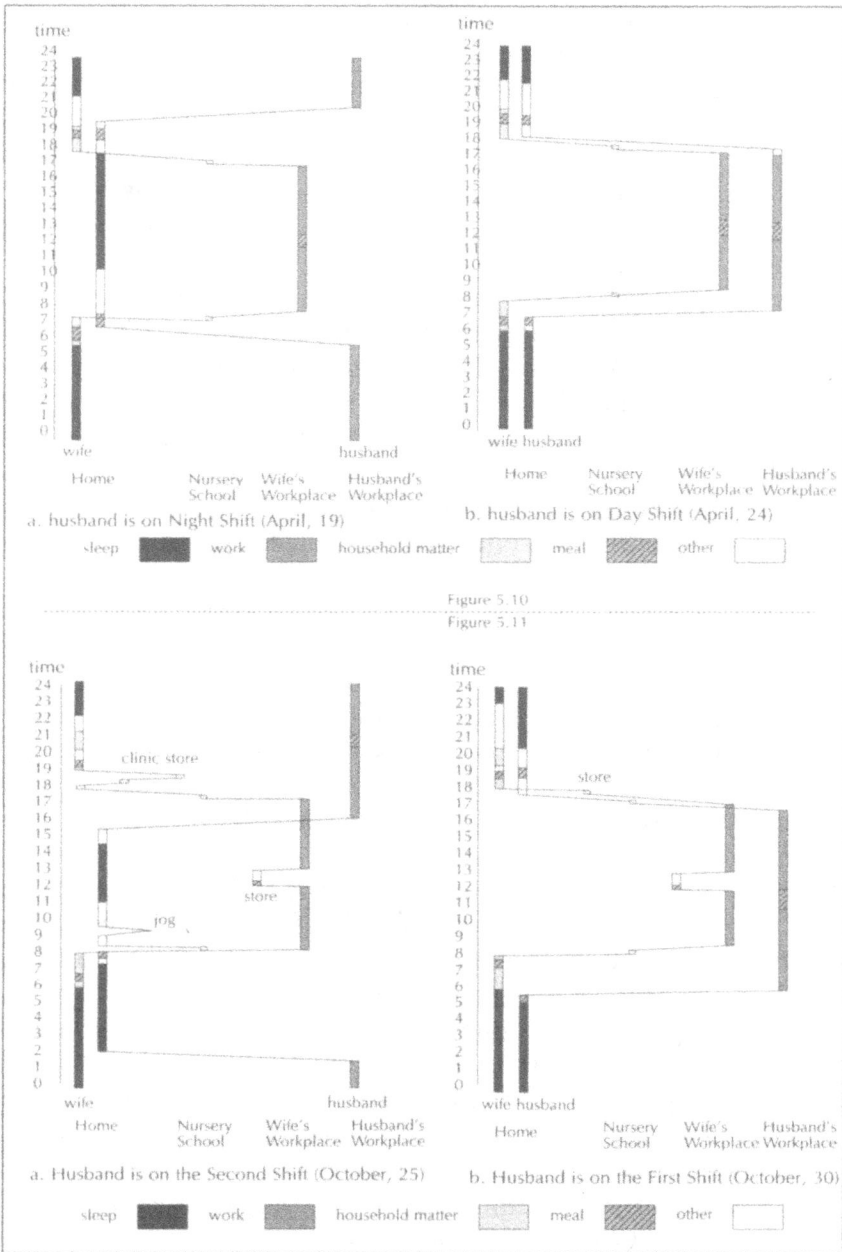

time

a. husband is on Night Shift (April, 19)

b. husband is on Day Shift (April, 24)

Figure 5.10

Figure 5.11

a. Husband is on the Second Shift (October, 25)

b. Husband is on the First Shift (October, 30)

Fig. 5.10. Daily paths of one household on the day and night shift.(*Source:* Nishimura, 1998)
Fig. 5.11. Daily paths of one household on the sequential shift. (*Source:* Nishimura, 1998)

gram, between 6 A.M. and 8 A.M., day shift workers leave home and gather at several plants, while, at the same time, night shift workers return home from the plants. Between 6 P.M. and 9 P.M., the reverse phenomena occur. In the sequential shift system, the pattern is basically the same, but the commuting times are different, and the pattern of daily paths is a bit more complicated, which means that outdoor activities other than commuting by husbands increased slightly. The aggregate routine of wives is rather complicated. Each wife has her own activity pattern.

Figure 5.10 illustrates the patterns of one family and charts the daily paths of wife and husband before the shift change. Figure 5.10a shows a day when the husband works a day shift, and figure 5.10b shows a day when the husband works a night shift. In this family, the wife works full time. During the day shift, the time-space paths of wife and husband are parallel. During the night shift, the paths are inverse to each other. The wife stays at home at night and the husband stays at home during the daytime, but they have breakfast and supper together with both shifts. The wife escorts the child to and from the day nursery.

Figure 5.11 shows the same family's daily life after the shift change. Figure 5.11a is one of the days of the week when the husband works the first shift. Figure 5.11b is a day when the husband works the second shift. The path of the husband deviates from the path of the wife. So they can hardly engage in co-activities such as having a meal together. This is true especially when the husband works the second shift. On the other hand, the husband can pick up the child after first shift work and can take the child to the nursery before the second shift.

From this example we can surmise that the change of the shift system produced two important influences on family life. One influence pertains to the co-activity of the family members. The other is the influence on the sharing of household chores by the wife and husband.

Table 5.1 indicates how long the wife and husband spend awake together at the same location. The length of time they spend awake together is extremely short when the husband works the second shift. Since the husband returns home at midnight and sleeps late into the morning, the husband can hardly see his children. Table 5.2 shows the ratio of husbands who eat with any other members of their families. In modern society, each member of the family performs his or her life activities in the daytime, so dinner is an important event for family cohesiveness. Before the change, many husbands ate with the family even when working the night shift. But after the change, it became impossible for husbands to have dinner with the family when working the second shift. The husband had to have dinner alone in his home or eat out.

The share of household chores performed by husbands has increased (fig. 5.12). When working the second shift, husbands have to leave home so early in the morning that many husbands began preparing breakfast by them-

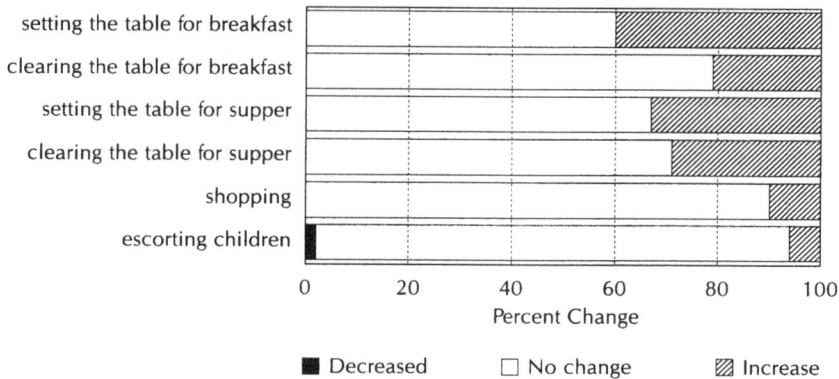

Fig. 5.12. Changes of husband's share of household activities. (*Source:* Based on field survey)

selves; for this reason, the ratio of husbands setting the table for breakfast, in particular, has increased. But many wives still prepare breakfast for their husbands. Some wives set the table for meals six times a day. Nevertheless, the change of the shift system led to the change of gender role traditions and led

Table 5.1. Length of awake time couples spend at the same place in a day

Husbands	Average time
Day shift	3 hours 56 minutes
Night shift	3 hours 12 minutes
First shift	4 hours 27 minutes
Second shift	1 hour 49 minutes
Other than Toyota workers	4 hours 24 minutes

Source: Based on field survey.

Table 5.2. Percentage of husbands who eat with other members of the family

Husbands	Breakfast	Supper
Day shift	52.2	65.2
Night shift	24.0	78.0
First shift	18.1	81.9
Second shift	45.4	0.0
Other than Toyota workers	63.4	54.2

Source: Based on field survey.

husbands to become independent. In the two-income family of figures 5.10 and 5.11, the husband shared the child care activity of escorting their child to and from day nursery after the shift system change, though the wife performed this responsibility before the change. The husband took his child to the nursery on the day that he worked the second shift (fig. 5.11b) and took him home on the day that he worked the first shift (fig. 5.11a). But husbands cannot do both on the same day and cannot do either for successive weeks because their off hours change every other week.

BUILDING THE NEW TIME-SPACE

At the beginning of the twenty-first century, global environmental problems are a focus of attention. Successful development of technology to reduce carbon dioxide emissions could be a matter of life or death for automobile companies in the near future. In 1998 TMC began to sell a model of hybrid electric vehicles, the Prius, in Japan. Development of an environmentally friendly car surely is a part of the answer to the environmental problem, but the realization of sustainable transport requires us to reconsider the relationship between the automobile and society. TMC has recently focused on the research and development of an Intelligent Transport System (ITS). ITS includes a variety of technologies to advance both automobiles and infrastructure. ITS is expected to become a $500 billion business in Japan in the future.

This technological development is imposing another change in the way of life in Toyota City. As part of the research and development of ITS, TMC started in Toyota City in May 1999 a social experiment of the "shared personal commuter EV [electric vehicle] system," called Crayon. This is a commuter system of electric vehicles shared among several people. The participants in the system reserve two-seater electric vehicles via the Internet and pay a nominal charge for each ride with an IC (integrated-circuit) personal identification card. Almost all TMC workers commute by car. The experiment of the EV car share program is being implemented with the cooperation of three hundred TMC workers.

Men have predominated in the automobile assembly workplace since the period of high economic growth in Japan, but the labor force shortage of the late 1980s caused TMC to consider employing women on the assembly line. The Labor Standards Law and Equal Employment Opportunity Law were revised in April 1999 and made it possible for women to work at night. Under this revised law, TMC has started to introduce women onto the assembly lines. Two changes of working environment made it possible for women to enter TMC plants: the introduction of the new shift system and the improvement of assembly lines. The shift system change in 1995 reduced physical fatigue because night work and overtime work were decreased by the

Shared commuter system (Crayon) in Toyota City. Increased use of motor vehicles has prompted Toyota to promote effective use of a variety of transportation means, including ride sharing. (Photograph by Yuichiro Nishimura)

sequential shift. Physical fatigue was also reduced by improvements on the assembly lines. Here, "improvement" means not full automation but reconsideration of the way duties between machines and workers are divided and assigning the exhausting work to robots. The latest type of assembly line was introduced at the Tsutsumi Plant in Toyota City and the Miyata Plant in Kyushu. On the new line, physical labor was reduced, enabling women and the elderly to work in the plant (Fujita 1997). These plants are trying to raise the percentage of female workers. In the U.S. plants of Toyota, such as the plant in Georgetown, Kentucky, many female workers are on the assembly lines. TMC might be able to put the experience in its U.S. plants to use in the development of female employment in its domestic plants.

In Toyota City, many facilities used by citizens, such as Toyota co-op and Toyota hospital, are TMC establishments for corporate welfare (Fujita and Hill 1995). These facilities are dispersed throughout the city. Until the early 1980s, construction of public facilities was not centralized, though each facility was well equipped on the basis of abundant revenue. Toyota City did not have an urban core because of the influence of the "automobile society."

In the city center of Toyota, around the Toyota Railway station, renewal plans create a "new face" for the city. The redevelopment project on the station's west exit (seen here) was completed in 1988, and a similar plan for the east exit was finished in 1995. The area around the station has a new, youthful image. (Photograph by Yuichiro Nishimura)

The new era has led Toyota City to turn to the concept of city planning. The city government feared that a city without a core would retain the image of an old industrial city, which cannot attract young people. So they started a redevelopment program for the city center in 1983. First, a department store and a multiuse commercial building were built around the Toyota railway terminal, and these buildings were connected to each other by a pedestrian deck. Then, some public facilities, such as a new library, a concert hall, and a Japanese-style garden, were constructed intensively in this area. A parking lot guidance system using ITS technology was introduced to reduce traffic congestion. The city center has become more attractive to citizens and is easier to access by car.

The redevelopment program aims to create a new landscape worthy of the Mother City of a Japanese leading company. TMC and the city government are trying to grow out of an old industrial city to become the center of new technology based on the automobile industry. Their new initiatives are transforming both the production structure and the urban structure, and that will make a new time-space of citizens' daily lives.

REFERENCES

Azumi, Norio. 1982. Aichi-ken ni okeru jidosha-buhin no hokan kino to sono henka (Storage Function of Automobile Parts and its Change in Aichi-ken: Especially During the Recent Low-Growth Period). *Annals of the Japan Association of Economic Geographers,* 28–2, 79–92.

Endo, Koichi. 1997. Gurobaru-ka no moto deno kigyo to shakai (1)(2)(3) (Firm and Region in the Globalization [1][2][3]). *Keizai-hyoron, Osaka-city Univ.,* 47–1:21–45(1), 47–4:27–57(2), 48–1:59–79(3).

Fujita, Eishi. 1997. Jidosha sangyo to jinji, romu-kanri, seisan-saisei no henbo (Transformations of Automobile Industry, Labor Control and Production System). *Annual of the Association of Japan Labor Sociologist,* 3–35.

———. 1988a. A kigyo syudan no rodo-ryoku juyo to rodo sijo no kozo (An Industrial Group and Labor Market Structure). Fujita, Eishi. and Hikari Nohara.(eds.). *Jidosha sangyo to rodosha (Automobile Industry and Workers).* Horitsu Bunkasha, Kyoto.

———. 1988b. A jido-sha ni okeru rodo-sha seikatsu to rodo-sha zo (Workers Life and Actualities of Workers in a Motor Corporation). Fujita, Eishi, and Hikari Nohara. (eds.). *Jidosha sangyo to rodosha (Automobile Industry and Workers).* Horitsu Bunkasha, Kyoto:361.

Fujita, Kuniko, and Richard Child Hill. 1995. *Toyota City Industrial Organization and the Local State in Japan, Japanese Cities in the World Economy.* Temple Univ. Press.:175–200.

Iseki, Hirotaro, Kazutoshi Abe, and Yoshihiro Miyamachi. 1987. The Role of Private Enterprises in Environmental Preservation: A Case Study of Toyota Motor Co., Ltd. UN Center for Regional Development (ed.). *Environmental Manage-*

ment for Local and Regional Development. Part I: The Japanese Experience: 453–69.

Kimoto, Kimiko. 1995. *Kazoku jenda kigyo-shakai (Family, Gender and Corporate Society).* Minelva syobo.

Mair, Andrew. 1992. Just-in-Time Manufacturing and the Spatial Structure of the Automobile Industry: Lessons from Japan *Tijdschaft voor Econ. en Soc. Geografie.* 83–2:82–93.

Matsui, Sadao. 1958. Toyota-jidosha kojo syuhen chiiki no nogyo (Agriculture in the Region Around the Factories of Toyota Motor Manufacturing). *Chirigaku Hokoku, Aichi-Kyoiku-Univ.* 27–37.

Miyakawa, Yasuo. 1980. Evolution of Industrial System and Industrial Community. *Science Reports, Seventh Series, Geography, Tohoku University.* 30(1):21–64.

Nishimura, Yuichiro. 1998. Jidosha-seizo-jujisha no seikatsu no jikukan henka (The Time-space Tranformation of Automobile Manufacturing Workers : an Analysis Based on the Concepts of Production Project and Family Project). *Jinbun Chiri (The Human Geography),* 50–3:232–55.

Okamoto, Kohei. 1997, Suburbanization of Tokyo and the Daily Lives of Suburban People. Karan, P.P. and Stapleton, Kristin. eds. *The Japanese city.* Lexington: University Press of Kentucky, 79–105.

Sato, Keiji. 1987. Shigaichi keisei katei to kyoju kankyo (Urbanization and Residential Environment). Tsumaru, Taisuke, Kyoko Kubota, and Hiroichi Endo (eds.). *Toyota to kigyo-shakai (Toyota and Local Communities).*

Toyota Chamber of Commerce and Industry Dept. of Food Services. 1995. *Ganbare Toyota no insyokuten -Toyota shin kinmu taisei eikyo kekka hokoku syo (Report on Effects of New Shift System).*

Toyota Motor Manufacturing. 1967. *Toyota jido-sha 20 nenshi (Twenty Years of Toyota Motor Manufacturing).* Toyota City.

Toyota City office. 1982. *Toyota-shi to jidosha sangyo (Toyota City and Automobile Industry).*

———. 1996. *Watashitachi no machi to jidosha sangyo (Our City and Automobile Industry).*

6

Dynamics of Growth and Change in Georgetown, Kentucky

JANET W. PATTON AND H. MILTON PATTON

GEORGETOWN, KENTUCKY, developed at the site of Royal Spring, which was discovered in 1774 by surveyors from Fincastle County, Virginia. The first permanent settlement of Georgetown occurred in 1785, when Rev. Elijah Craig led a party of Virginia Baptists to Royal Spring. Georgetown was incorporated December 16, 1790, and it became the Scott County seat on June 22, 1792. Scott, the state's eleventh county, was formed out of part of Woodford County. It is named after Revolutionary War General Charles Scott, who became Kentucky's fourth governor. Georgetown College was chartered in January 1892 as the first Baptist college west of the Allegheny mountains. By 1890 Scott County's population reached eighteen thousand. For the next seventy years, the county's population was either stable or declining. Adjacent Lexington-Fayette County, the regional trading center and home to the state university and thoroughbred farms, provided the social center for those who harked back to ancestral landed gentry.

The first regional post–World War II industrial development began in Georgetown in 1946 when Elroy Mallard relocated a pencil factory from central Tennessee. The payment of wages changed the conditions of employment in an economy of tenant farmers. Sons of tenant farmers remember as children sitting around the cracker barrels at the local stores hearing farmers talk about how hard it was to find good help. Mysterious fires were known to break out in places that paid money for work, putting such places out of business.

IBM decided to build its Selectric Typewriter plant in Lexington, on state land north of the mental institution, in 1958. That act established a contemporary industrial base in the Bluegrass. The dominant product endured until it was supplanted by computers thirty years later. Ownership ultimately passed to Lexmark, makers of computer printers. Fewer than ten miles from the plant, Georgetown was a generation away.

In the 1970s, while the economy and population showed signs of decline, completion of north-south Interstate 75 and east-west Interstate 64, which cross just south of Georgetown, made a quiet but ultimately profound change in the accessibility and character of the community. I-75 parallels the main line of the Southern Railroad from Detroit to Miami, and I-64 runs from Norfolk, Virginia, to St. Louis, Missouri, and westward. Georgetown found itself at major crossroads in an interstate-dominated economy. In this chapter, the growth and change in Georgetown-Scott County since the 1985 arrival of a major Japanese corporation are analyzed.

SELECTION OF THE GEORGETOWN SITE: "IT WAS JUST A FEELING"

Early in 1985 quiet rumors circulated that General Motors' Saturn plant site selection team ranked a Georgetown site number two. The site was a large farm just north of Georgetown which had been purchased for $1,200 per acre by an investor a few years before when farmers shunned the property as being overpriced.

In late fall, rumors suddenly spread through the community that Toyota might soon announce the location of a plant in Georgetown. Excitement, shock, fear, and anticipation were felt throughout the community. News stories in major national papers heightened the speculation. When a farmer's wife was reported as the final holdout in site negotiations, it was front page news in the *Los Angeles Times*. Many citizens had links with "inside sources" to negotiations confirming that an announcement was eminent. Characteristic of Kentucky, negotiations were directed by its governor, Martha Layne Collins. Scott County and Georgetown were informed at the very last stage of the process and had little or no input during the site selection process.

On December 11, 1985, the large ballroom of the Hyatt Regency Lexington filled with press from around the world. Governor Collins, Senator Wendell Ford, and Dr. Shoichiro Toyoda, president of Toyota Motor Corporation (TMC), announced Georgetown-Scott County as the site for the first Toyota manufacturing plant in America, soon to be one of the largest auto plants in North America. The excitement of the moment filled the ballroom with the euphoria of witnessing an international event and then emptied it as reporters scrambled for the phones.

Journalists and academics quickly fell to analyzing the decision and applying favored theories about location, state incentives wars, politics, and speculative impacts. The Kentucky incentives package, the largest ever granted by any state, drew much criticism. A source privy to internal site team discussion suggests that after all basic requirements for the plant, such as transportation networks, access to markets, and a greenfield site, were satisfied, the location was selected on behavioral grounds by Chairman Eiji Toyoda. As a career marketing executive, he had led Toyota into the American market. He once drove a new model on a test run from Chicago to Miami, stopping in the Bluegrass and liking what he saw.

As the Hyatt ballroom emptied, a small knot of reporters gathered around the managing director of Toyota, who served as head of the site selection team. Fluent in English, son of a Japanese diplomat, and engaging in manner, he fielded all questions with comfort for forty-five minutes. He reflected an open style, sensitivity, perspective, and set of goals that have held consistent for fifteen years. His comments reflected understatement, while Toyota has consistently over-performed. Among the questions and answers were: *Q: Why did you select Kentucky? A: It was just a feeling. Q: This is a hard-nosed business decision? A: Yes, but with all things being equal, it was just a feeling. It is an area similar to the area in which we operate in Japan. Q: Did you pick a state that doesn't have a Japanese plant in order to influence import policies? A: No, we seek to serve the people with the best possible product, and it is the people who select their representatives. Q: Were you concerned about Georgetown and its people? A: Yes, because the plant is so large and the town is so small. It was a concern, but just a concern. We will respect their way of life and community. Q: Why are you building a U.S. plant? A: We have wanted to establish ourselves as part of the U.S. auto industry for twenty-five years. First, we developed marketing experience. When we felt comfortable about doing business here, we developed a joint plant with GM to produce cars and learned about manufacturing here. When we felt comfortable with that, we decided it was time to build a plant. Q: When was the decision on location made? A: It was made in New York on Sunday (December 8th) in a meeting with Chairman Toyoda and President Toyoda.* (He implied that other sites were still in the running at that time, among the thirty states submitting proposals and twenty-two states visited.)

The announcement of the new plant promised twenty-five hundred new jobs. Direct TMMK employment eventually reached seventy-eight hundred (1999), more than tripling employment projections of the original announcement.

Invitations to the groundbreaking were sent to every official in Georgetown-Scott County, including the most minor members of its numerous boards and commissions. It was a rainy winter day in a muddy pasture on the 1,600-acre site. A local official tried to apologize to Chairman Toyoda for the weather. "No," he replied with a smile, "the gods are crying tears of joy, raining down on us, melding our two peoples together." For some, that observation marked the beginning of a cultural evolution. It would not be long before the community and a new generation of workers learned that the word "quality" was more than an advertising slogan and that "continual improvement" was very close to a religion. Ultimately, the successful melding, or hybridization, of the two cultures in the Georgetown Camry plant established the future direction of Toyota's worldwide operations, an international demonstration in the global economy. Toyota announced at the ground-breaking a $1 million gift to the community. It was to be for a community center, Georgetown's number one priority

Toyota's arrival was a landmark for not only Georgetown, but also Toyota. It was not a routine location decision but the achievement of a long-term goal for a company that nearly failed after World War II. The chairman was the grandson of the founder, an inventor and loom manufacturer in the Meiji era. The company began building automobiles in the 1930s and in recent decades emphasized marketing. In Japan, Nissan was considered to be the better car, while Toyota was considered to be built on advertising. The chairman would soon be replaced by his cousin, a doctorate in automotive engineering, who had been focusing on production technology surpassing the U.S. industry. The Georgetown plant would be a test of hybridization focusing on quality and efficiency. It would quickly achieve the highest plant efficiency award in the American industry, and within ten years, it would produce America's top selling vehicle, known for quality.

Dr. Fujio Cho managed the plant during its formative years and working constantly to combine effectively both cultures into a production system that achieved highest quality. He lived in Georgetown, joined Rotary, and was seen frequently on the shop floor, personally working on production problems and safety. His son attended local Georgetown College. Cho left Georgetown to become a director of Toyota Motor Corporation. He was appointed president of Toyota Motor Corporation in April 1999. His departure from Georgetown caused sadness among many residents who revered his humane and sensitive approach and style. Most had never known a high executive in common work shirt with a common desk among many in the same room, or the passion he displayed in personally seeking solutions to such problems as an employee's severed finger. Veteran auto workers knew that such things were generally ignored in American auto plants with blame placed on the worker. In this case, modifications were made to Toyota's presses throughout the world, twenty-four-hour standby ambulances were located at the plant, and special arrangements were made for immediate helicopter evacuation to the nearest specialty hospital.

COMMUNITY RESPONSE AND LOCAL PLANNING

"Shock" is the best descriptor for community reaction to the site location announcement. National press and land speculators immediately descended on Main Street, respectively interviewing anyone they could find and promising lucrative options to anyone who would sell. While the business community was ecstatic, local elected leadership, having only recently been informed, were confused, dispirited, or outright angry for what others had brought on them without consultation or warning.

National opposition groups, who had been organizing since the announcement, used the groundbreaking to dramatize their concerns. Opposition focused on several issues. Labor groups challenged the use of nonunion construction workers; critics of the incentives package, such as Ralph Nadar, denounced corporate giveaway; environmental and preservation groups worried about pollution and quality-of-life issues; and a legacy of anti-Japanese World War II sentiment surfaced from time to time. Some governors in the National Governor's Conference considered declaration of a truce, proposing a moratorium on incentives package warfare among the states.

Among those filing lawsuits challenging the incentives package and permitting process were Jerry Hammond, secretary-treasurer of the Kentucky Building Trades Council, and Lucky McClintock, president of the central division of the Building Trades Council and a Scott County resident. The lawsuits were designed to slow construction and force Toyota and Ohbayashi, the construction contractor, to negotiate a labor contract. The suits, reinforced by demonstrations and adverse publicity, accomplished their objective. By December 1986, Ohbayashi accepted union workers and Hammond withdrew his suits and the threat of a protest demonstration in Washington, D.C., on Pearl Harbor Day. Other suits ended in June 1987, when the constitutionality of the economic incentives package was affirmed by the Kentucky Supreme Court with a vote of four to three (Gelsanliter 1990, Hoyman 1997).

In the fury of the interstate bidding war for Toyota, local government impact had been finessed or ignored. State economic development staff had focused on what they knew best, interstate highways, major rail line, land availability, and available workers. Only after the fact did the state modestly fund the Toyota Impact Center, staffed by the part-time planning director for Georgetown-Scott County. The state also assigned a local government expert from its Department of Local Government to coordinate state programs on behalf of the community and give advice as needed. A resident of Scott County, Bob Leonard performed a critical role in bridging change for local governments during the next five years.

While shock gave way to fear of being overrun, several key individuals and activities began to shape a process by which the community would respond to the new challenges and seek to guide the change to achieve local community goals. Through negotiation, local government was able to implement several decisive actions, which enhanced the community's ability to promote its own interests. The state assumed the responsibility for building permits and other regulatory processes for the Toyota plant that required little local input. However, matters of land use, utility location, local tax policies, annexation, and local government management and services were clearly the realm of local government. While Governor Collins was and is highly popular in Scott County, even she was not in a position to direct these matters. One local issue after another during the next year made the governor's staff and Toyota managers uncomfortable.

One example is the provision of a new publicly funded sewer plant to serve the Toyota plant, which had been specified in the incentives package. The five members of the County Board of Adjustment met for their usual monthly meeting in January 1986, about six weeks after the announcement. The typical agenda was to approve variances such as church locations and enforce ordinances such as locating barns at least forty feet from adjacent property lines. Other requested variances were typically decided by counting the number of neighbors who appeared to protest. At the end of the January meeting, the director and engineer for the Georgetown Municipal Water and Sewer District stood to ask for location approval for the sewer treatment plant for the Toyota site. He was asked for his application. He explained that he met with Toyota "officials" in Frankfort in November and told them that the location on Lanes Run adjacent to the plant was appropriate because it met the standard of being a "blue line stream" on the topographic map. The board inquired how this location related to any existing community plan. The response was dumbfounded silence. The board asked him to complete a proper application like everyone else was required to do and return in February.

At the next meeting of the board, the five members, probing a variety of environmental and locational issues, concluded that the application and presentation were inadequate. The process proceeded in like manner for more than four months, with growing audiences and experts brought before the board in formal hearings. The search for the highest expert knowledge was the heart of the process. State economic development staff and the biggest lobbyists in the state had become frustrated with the process. They were looking for ways to circumvent the board's authority but did not put any personal pressure on the members. At nearly every meeting, additional safeguards were added, increasing the cost of the facility by $2 million. In the midst of the hearings, a wealthy landowner through whose land wastewater would flow legally challenged the Water and Sewer District and the state permitting process. Their technical and legal experts added to the testimony and intensified statewide press coverage.

Finally, board members were satisfied that they had drawn out the highest state of the art in facility design and that the scientific community could add nothing more. The board knew there was a better location alternative from a community land use perspective, but it was too late to change it. Before an overflow audience and without prior consultation, a member of the board moved to approve, with conditions assuring that its operational performance would not materially damage the environment. There was a unanimous vote of approval. That night, the board could have as easily voted unanimously in the negative. In effect, the board retained for the community the power to close the plant immediately if a violation of the conditions occurred.

Legal counsel for the Board of Adjustment was newly appointed City Attorney Charlie Perkins. The hearings were his testing ground in administrative process, citizen participation, and local policy development. As attorney for the City of Georgetown, the City-County Planning Commission, the Board of Adjustment, and the Housing Authority, Perkins guided processes with patience, skill, and careful respect for the requirements of the administrative process for the next thirteen years. Some credit him, and his fortuitous appointment one month before Toyota's announcement, with the positive outcomes in the community during the ensuing years. The Board of Adjustment hearings established the standards and practices for planning and policy development for both city and county at the outset of the change process.

During the same period (late 1980s) the county became increasingly concerned with its financial situation. Scott County Judge Executive Charlie Sutton was among the critics of the state incentives plan. With the termination of federal revenue sharing, the county was nearly bankrupt. Efforts to impose a payroll tax in 1985 had been defeated. Early in 1986, however, the Scott County Fiscal Court moved quickly to impose a payroll tax of 1 percent that it would levy on the construction workers as well as employees of the new plant when it became operational. The action was met with hostility and threats by the state. Tension with the city heightened when the county refused to consider sharing the new revenue with the city, which had been levying a 1 percent payroll and net profit tax since the 1970s.

The issue of annexation was a major concern to the city. Annexation was not included in the incentives package, and it was believed that Toyota was opposed to annexation. Annexation would add to Toyota's tax liability for both its occupational and net profits, on top of what had been added by the new county tax. Generally, tension existed between the two governments and between each government and Toyota. When Tom Prather was appointed mayor of Georgetown in October 1986, he initiated a process of regular consultation with Alex Warren, a Toyota vice president. As a result of this working relationship, which has continued through the years, Toyota announced in April 1987 that it would seek annexation and the City of Georgetown undertook a number of key actions to upgrade its police and fire protection. Both services were enlarged and professionalized, and new facilities were established. The new generation of city officials realized the need for far greater professionalization in public administration (Hoyman 1997).

While annexation of Toyota into Georgetown was important for revenue generation, it was equally important for coherent urban land use development (fig. 6.1). Urban services, especially water and sewer, and annexation were soon tied together in all urban development extensions. Arrival of Toyota heightened the need to further strengthen planning and land use regulation practices in a locale that already had a strong tradition of a joint city-county planning commission. Essentially, a strong discipline was imposed for all new developments, adjacency, consistency with the comprehensive plan, urban services, and annexation. Outside the urban area, a strict five-acre minimum was required. During the 1991 mandatory review of the comprehensive plan, great effort went into the refinement of these basic requirements.

While government officials worried about finances, increased traffic was the number one concern of citizens. Older residents still fondly remembered playing baseball or driving tractors on Main Street in the middle of Georgetown. As part of the initial package with Toyota, the state upgraded exit ramps to I-75 and a four-lane access road to and around the plant site connected at each end to I-75. From suggestions submitted by schoolchildren, the access road was named Cherry Blossom Way. Soon afterward, the state added additional lanes to I-75 south to Lexington and twelve miles to the north. However, despite assurances by the state that the community would not be forgotten, the state did not come up with funds for the bypass around Georgetown that had been on the county's transportation plan since 1979. The county refused to share in the cost, so Georgetown paid for the local share of the first quadrant of the bypass (Hoyman 1997). Georgetown opened the second quadrant of the bypass in 1998, with plans to eventually construct a bypass around the urban services area with routine state funding. There also has been substantial widening and upgrade of Kentucky 25, the old north-south Dixie Highway. Traffic can be heavy between shifts, but overall it is less than the typical metropolitan area at rush hour. With continuing upgrades and improved policies and new and rebuilt infrastructure in roadways, water, sewer, schools, parks, and public buildings, Georgetown-Scott County is in an enviable position for any community its size.

SOCIAL AND POLITICAL SETTING OF GEORGETOWN-SCOTT COUNTY IN 1985

Georgetown-Scott County began the 1980s in recession, economically and psychologically. High interest rates in the 1970s and declining markets had depressed the traditional agricultural economy. Clarke Equipment, which moved to Scott County in the early 1970s, held promise, but within ten years, the company padlocked the gates of its huge, modern forklift plant and moved production to Korea. Heads were low on Main Street, and a peculiarly mean-spirited 1981 mayoral election marked the tenor of the times. National inflation and low tobacco prices had settled in to begin a decline of the agriculturally

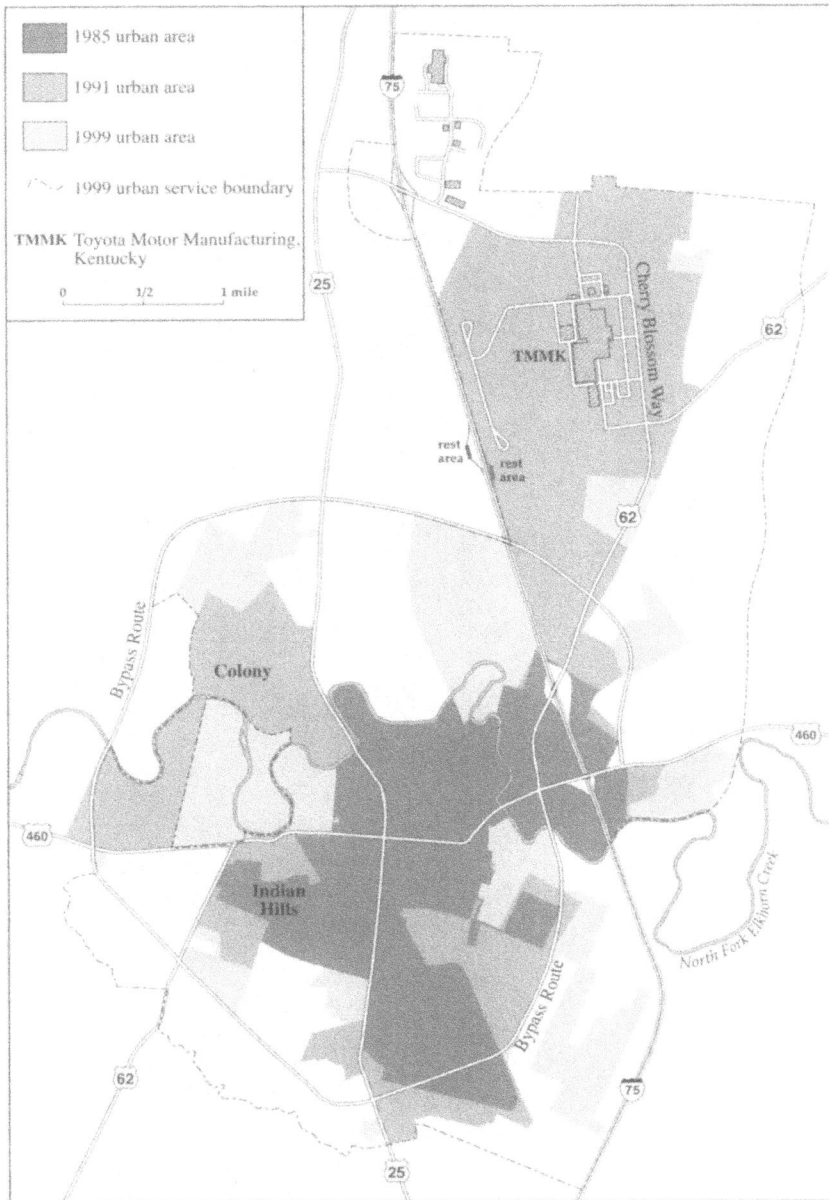

Fig. 6.1. Growth of Georgetown, 1985–1999. Until Toyota and its parts suppliers arrived and began creating a new middle class, Georgetown and Scott County had extremes of wealth (represented by old-money horse owners and some of the most individualistic tobacco farmers) and poverty (seen in unpainted houses with ice-boxes on their porches and abandoned cars in their yards), and little in between. A number of new subdivisions have now developed on the outskirts. And, around the courthouse, utility wires have come down, sidewalks have been bricked, and alumi-num sidings removed to reveal the original facade underneath. (*Source:* Georgetown/Scott County Planning Commission and field survey, 1999)

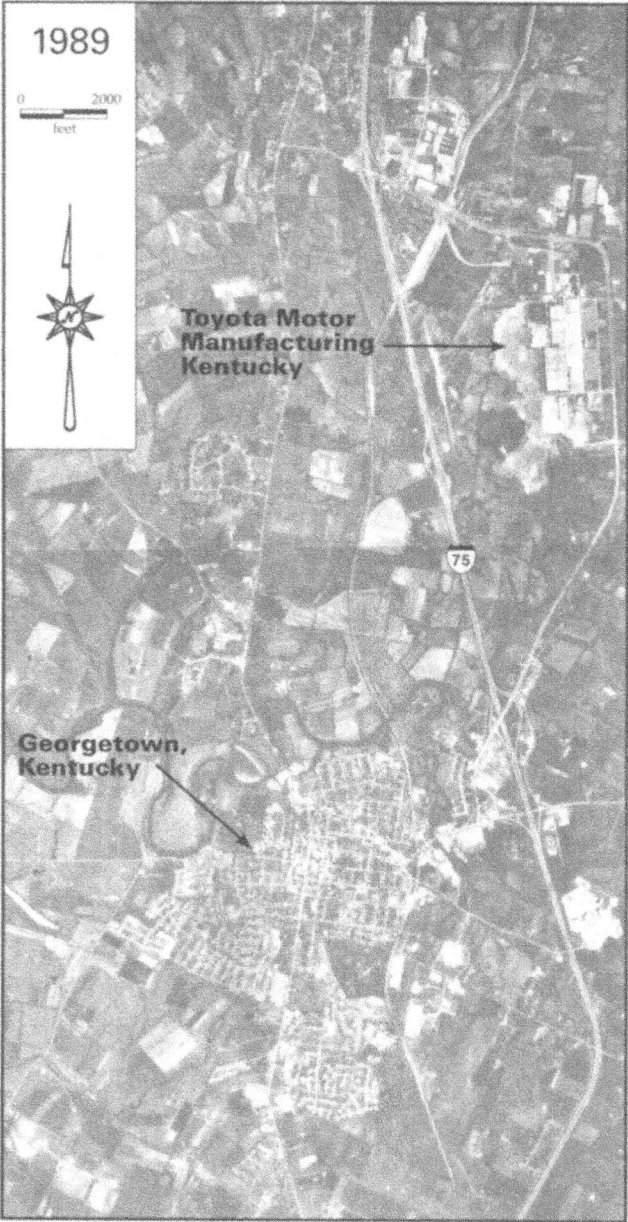

Aerial view of Georgetown and the Toyota Plant, Scott County, Kentucky, in 1989 during initial Camry production. (Photograph courtesy of Georgetown-Scott County Joint Planning Commission)

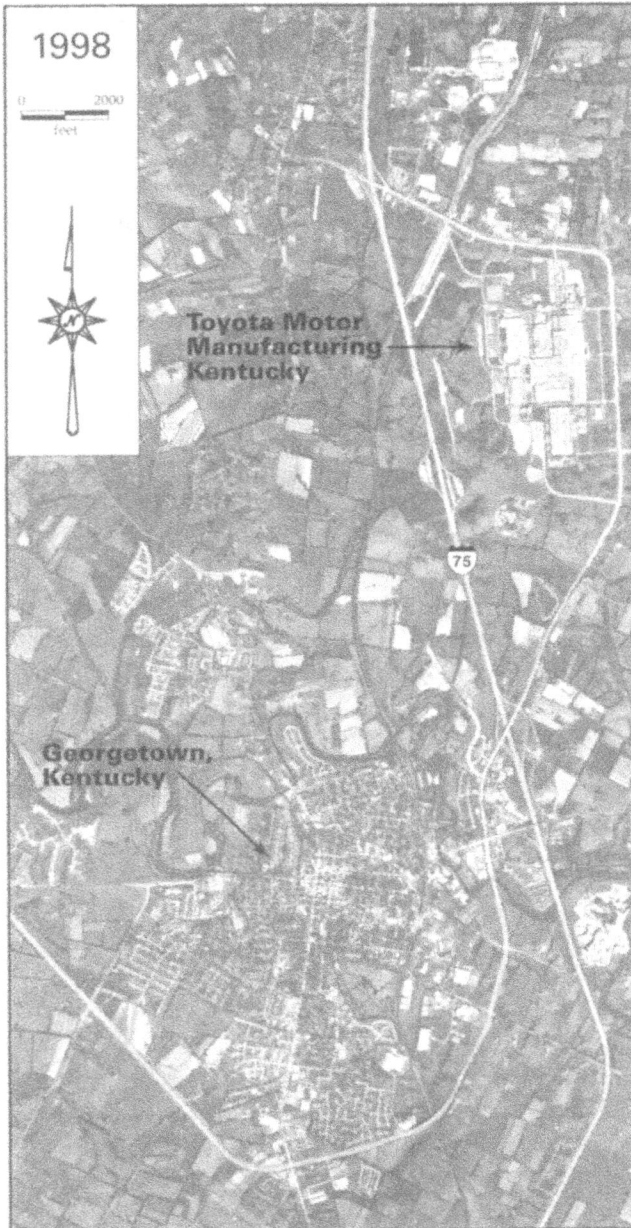

Aerial view of Georgetown and the Toyota Plant in 1998 after the development of additional facilities that produce Camry, Avalon, and the Sienna van. The urban area has grown only moderately since the arrival of Toyota because most workers do not live in Georgetown but prefer to commute from their homes in adjacent counties. The town's business district retains much of its distinctive character. Most of the city's commercial development is moving toward the eastern edge, close to the huge plant. Several restaurants, car dealerships, and an outlet mall have sprung up. (Photograph courtesy of Georgetown-Scott County Joint Planning Commission)

based economy. Scott County's unemployment rate had reached 7 percent by 1985 and continued to rise through the Toyota plant's construction period to 9.9 percent in 1988.

The population of Scott County in 1980 was 21,813, with approximately 11,000 people living in Georgetown (fig. 6.2). While there had been little net population growth from 1960 to 1985, there were some changes in the community. The arrival of IBM in Lexington provided new employment opportunities for area high school and college graduates in the late 1950s and early 1960s. Suburban Indian Hills and Indian Acres subdivisions on the south edge of town were largely built by and populated with IBM families using IBM earnings. Pensions and severance pay beginning in the late 1980s provided considerable passive income. Johnson Controls and Hoover (now merged and producing seats for Toyota) established production plants in Georgetown during this period.

During the 1960s and 1970s, the growth of state government caused an increase in the number of professional employees residing in Georgetown. Georgetown—located only twenty miles west of the state capitol, Frankfort, and within easy reach of the more urban Lexington—was a logical residence choice for these professionals. By the 1970s, a small but constant trickle of newcomers moved to Scott County seeking to have it both ways—urban employment and small-town or country living. Small clusters of intellectuals, writers, and artists began to be identifiable on the hill farms and woods north

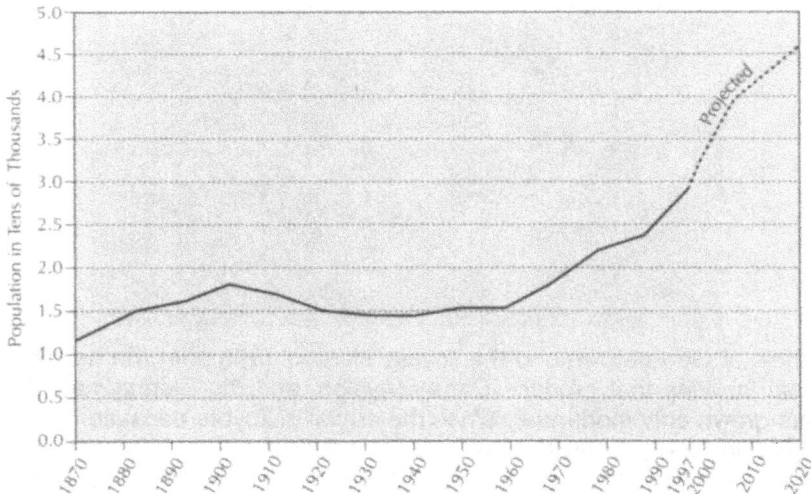

Fig. 6.2. Scott County: Population growth.

of Georgetown. In the mid-1970s the first large influx of "outsiders" arrived from Michigan. They were executives and engineers employed by Clarke Equipment Company's newly built forklift plant.

The community, however, continued to think of itself as traditional small-town southern America. And politics in 1985 resembled traditional rural southern politics. More than 95 percent of the county's registered voters were Democrats, and any competition for local elections happened within the Democratic primary. Personalities and factions tended to dominate.

City government, with a mayor-council form of government, had a mayor elected at large for a four-year term and eight council members elected at large for two-year terms. The three-way divisive mayor's race in 1981 resulted in the election of the weakest candidate. City government was of lowest visibility during the next four years, including the fall of 1985 when the state negotiated for Toyota. Sam Pollack, a well-liked retired state Department of Education administrator, was elected mayor that fall and looked to the part-time office as a good way to remain active in retirement. At the center of national attention and faced with previously unimagined challenges and problems, Pollack took office three weeks after the Toyota announcement. He had considerable wisdom and encouragement but resigned within six months due to a heart attack he had during a trip to Washington, D.C. It was the duty of the eight City Council members to select a new mayor from their own ranks. Three aspired to the position. Tom Prather, a relatively young, well-educated third-generation auto dealer and grandson of a former mayor, was elected by a one-vote margin. Selection of this articulate spokesman passed leadership to a new generation with a more contemporary style.

Scott County was governed in 1985 by a county judge executive and three commissioners who constituted the fiscal court. Charles Sutton was in his third four-year term as county judge executive when Toyota announced its decision to locate the plant in Georgetown-Scott County. At the time, the fiscal court was perceived as representing rural interests, often deadlocked, and seeing its role as protecting the status quo. Judge Executive Charles Sutton was uncomfortable about the implications of rapid growth for Scott County but was successful in passing the new 1 percent payroll tax and initiating land purchases for a new water supply reservoir. In 1988, Sutton resigned to take a law enforcement position with state government under a new governor. After a one-year interim, George Lusby was elected county judge executive in 1989. A former school principal, a veteran City Council member, and a resident of the city who was also widely supported in the county, Judge Lusby played a key role in forging cooperative governmental policy initiatives during the next ten years.

Historical preservation and environment were values deeply embedded in the community. Historians in the community and at Georgetown College had long been active with informed publications and encouragement of preservation. Many newcomers had selected Georgetown-Scott County as a place to live because its agricultural small-town landscape and environment pleasantly reflected a good place to live. A book on the fifty "Safe Places to Live" in 1972 listed Georgetown as "the" place in Kentucky. It was considered a good place to live, and few if any wanted fundamental change. Social and cultural activities were dominated by the professional class and landed aristocracy, but there was little conspicuous display of wealth and little evidence of a power elite that dominated or controlled. There was no country club and were no cultural amenities other than the few offered by Georgetown College.

While the schools had integrated following the U.S. Supreme Court ruling and the city and county schools had merged in the 1970s, vestiges of traditional southern racial segregation remained, especially in housing patterns and social interaction. The minority population had dwindled to less than 10 percent. It wasn't until the early 1980s that the community, using community block grants, began to provide comparable public services, such as adequate water and sewer service, to its principal black neighborhood. As farmers continued their eternal search for "good labor" to house tobacco and undertake other unappealing chores, a new Mexican minority began to arrive in the late 1980s to assume these tasks. The Japanese and Spanish languages were introduced simultaneously to a community unused to any direct foreign influence.

Georgetown-Scott County in 1999

Nearly fourteen years later, small-town life continues, moved to a larger scale with higher stakes. Growth and change are apparent as the nineteenth-century small town settles into the twenty-first century. Eight thousand more people currently live in Scott County, with many more commuting daily from across the region to work. Slightly more than half of the county's residents (15,714) live in Georgetown—92.6 percent are white, 6.7 percent are African American, and .7 percent are of other ethnicity. The 1998 civilian labor force was 16,219 with 11,686 in manufacturing (7,800 of these at Toyota) and the rest employed in retail trade, services, government, transportation and utilities, construction, and finance, insurance, and real estate. Service and construction jobs, thus, have grown significantly along with manufacturing.

Economic data highlight the significant improvement in the economic well being of community residents. Unemployment decreased from a high of 9.9 percent in January 1988 to 2.2 percent, the fifth lowest rate in the state, in December 1998 (fig. 6.3). Personal income, at $21,887 in 1998, is the tenth highest in the commonwealth.

Not all Scott County residents have enjoyed the new prosperity, how-

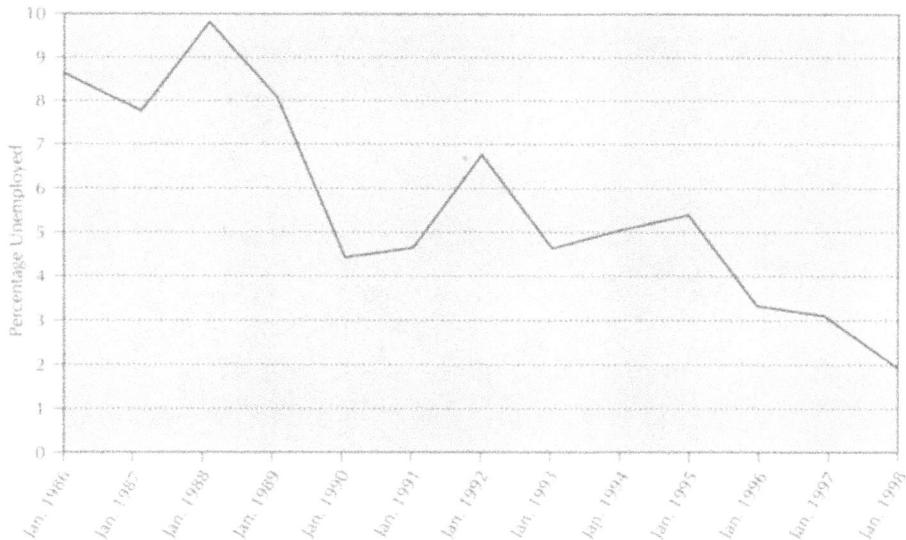

Fig. 6.3. Scott County: Unemployment pattern, 1986–1998.

ever, despite the fact that the community has been open to inclusiveness. While there has been a major decrease in the number of Kentucky Temporary Assistance Program recipients as a result of welfare reform and the growing economy, the numbers of persons receiving food stamps, SSI, and Medicaid stayed constant during the 1990s. One local nonprofit agency, Scott United Ministry, a community-wide ecumenical outreach service, has seen its budget and clientele increase fivefold since 1991. It has provided services to an estimated 10 percent to 12 percent of the population during this period. Much of the geography and sociology just five miles north of Georgetown resembles Appalachian topography, geography, and sociology.

Part of the "contract" between Toyota and Kentucky was an emphasis on hiring Kentucky workers. State employment offices played a major role in the hiring process, and Toyota's commitment was fulfilled. Ninety-five percent of employees are Kentuckians from all parts of the state. Kentuckians are known to be place-bound so when Toyota hired a worker, he or she might not make an immediate move to Scott County. There was a six-month probation period; retaining home ties was important; the employee's house might be in a distressed area with depressed prices; and the job of the spouse was important. It took time for long commutes, long hours, hard work, and economic security to result in moving families and loyalties. Anticipated growth of Scott County was dampened by this factor as well as a national change in land development tax laws in 1986 and a euphoric early local housing construction approach which assumed that most buyers would be upper income

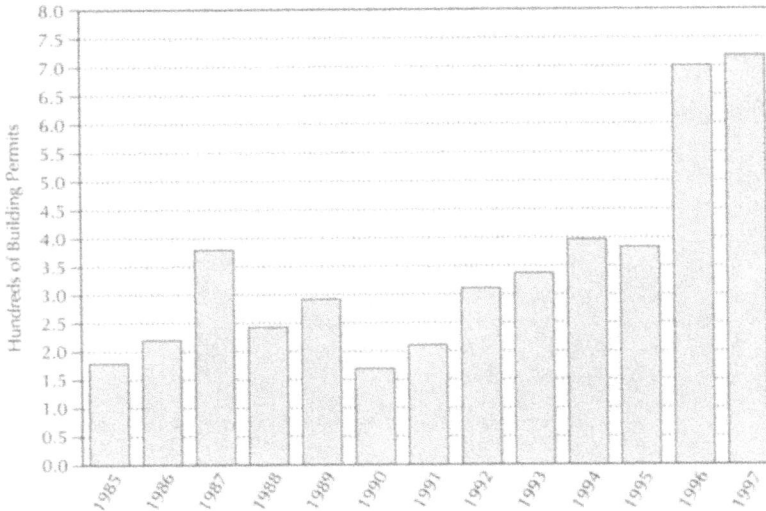

Fig. 6.4. Scott County: Building permits, 1985–1997.

executives. In 1999, about 21 percent (1,638 of 7,800) of Toyota workers lived in Scott County.

There has been a dramatic increase in housing and commercial construction during the last fifteen years. The number of building permits has increased from 178 for construction valued at $7.6 million in 1985 to 914 for construction valued at $86.2 million in 1998, an increase of more than tenfold (fig. 6.4). In a comparable period, the assessed value of real estate and personal property has increased from $440,701,570 to $3,978,104,552, also a tenfold increase.

By the late 1990s a full range of housing was being constructed in Georgetown and Scott County. Upon Toyota's arrival, and five years beyond, there was no true housing industry. Home construction and development was done by small companies, building three to five houses per year. While several large Lexington builders had been engaged in the market from time to time in previous decades, their profile was small through the late 1980s. Immediate over-building in the high priced market that followed the Toyota announcement resulted in bankruptcies of a number of hopeful amateurs. Nearly all the early outside land speculators had fallen away by 1988. Three locally based small companies developed a few new subdivisions.

By the early 1990s the Georgetown-Scott County housing market began to mature as an integral part of the Lexington metropolitan market. Three large developers and merchant builders, Ball, Barlow, and Cutter, arrived in Georgetown. Each created its own development. Independent builders had

Housing development along U.S. Highway 62, adjacent to the TMMK plant in Georgetown-Scott County. Both single-family homes and duplexes are offered for rent or sale. (Photograph by P.P. Karan)

grown from a few to many, dependent on local subdivisions and related independently purchased lots. At the end of the 1990s, appraisers began to equate historical factors that go beyond Scott County's isolated rural borders, to recognize Georgetown's integration in a regional market. A fifteen-mile radius (versus a county boundary) includes downtown Lexington and some distance south and nearly reaches Frankfort. The distinction makes a significant difference in banking practices, market reach, and a variety of community perspectives. All of this is augmented by the Georgetown-Scott County Comprehensive Plan of 1991, whose emphasis was quality of life, environmental preservation, and retention of small-town virtues.

Through the years, Scott County had had the smallest retail take of all 120 Kentucky counties due to its proximity to Lexington. The number of local "mom and pops" and multigenerational family businesses had been declining for several decades. Increased commercialization came late to Georgetown, but now Wal-Mart, Kmart, Winn-Dixie, Kroger, an outlet center, and a variety of strip stores and fast food chains have created a substantial increase in available shopping choices. At the time of this writing, a Wal-Mart megamart is on the horizon. It will be the third generation of progressively larger stores in the period, each leaving vacant structures and parking lots in its wake. The number of motels located at the interchanges has increased dramatically. The two historic banks have been purchased by larger ones, a new bank has been created, and two additional banks have entered the market with branch offices. Branch bank facilities have proliferated.

Scott County remains dry, prohibiting all sales of alcohol. A referendum vote to make parts of Georgetown wet was defeated in 1997. The dry status of the city and county is blamed for the lack of quality restaurants, although there are several home-cooking establishments and many chain restaurants.

Public education data indicate a significant increase (fig. 6.5). With an increase from 4,098 pupils in 1984–1985 to 5,359 in 1997–1998, school enrollment is up 30 percent. To accommodate this increase, three new schools—two elementary schools and one high school—have been built, and most facilities have undergone major renovation and upgrades. An additional elementary school is being planned. The county school board had delayed building a new high school in the 1970s. As the number of temporary classrooms mushroomed around the existing high school, the school board could no longer delay action. It proposed in 1993 a $20 million comprehensive high school to be built on a new site. Voters rejected a bond issue to fund the school, sending school planners back to the drawing board. The credibility of the proposed plan and program was questioned in the community, because the school board operated independently in formulating the plan, ignoring the local government cooperative processes. A modification of plans and location of the facility on land already owned by the school system (incorporating the existing junior high school) reduced the cost. Toyota made a voluntary

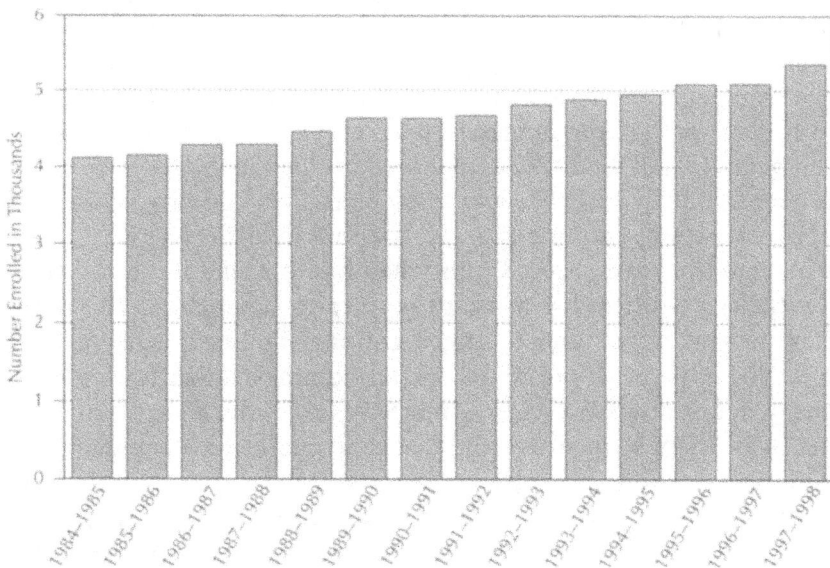

Fig. 6.5. Scott County: School enrollment, 1984–1998.

up-front payment of ten years of its in-lieu-of-taxes contribution, and a change in state law permitted a larger bonded indebtedness. As part of the Toyota incentives package and use of public bonds, Toyota does not have an obligation to pay property taxes for the first twenty years. Following common national practices in such economic development bonding, Toyota voluntarily agreed to pay the equivalent of its share of school taxes. By agreeing to pay ten years of those property tax obligations in advance, the school board was able to move forward in the construction of a $14 million high school without voter approval of a bond initiative.

Political life demonstrates both continuity and change. The possibility of fiscal court deadlock and the pattern of recent planning commission appointments led to a petition drive and successful referendum vote in 1997 to change county government. With the 1998 election, Scott County Fiscal Court changed from three commissioners nominated by district and elected at-large to a seven-magistrate board elected by district. With the county judge executive presiding, the eight-member fiscal court now more broadly reflects and represents both city and rural populations.

The 1993 defeat of Mayor Prather by Warren Powers, a three-term former mayor who had served in the 1970s and 1980s, represented a resurgence of traditional politics. Powers's strength was knowing how to respond to citizens' complaints in a timely way. Powers's five years in office did not reflect recognition of the changes accompanying the presence of Toyota. The succeeding mayor, retired school principal Everette Varney, moved quickly to support new community initiatives, especially in the areas of environment, education, and international programs.

As a result of economic growth, tax revenue has increased dramatically (fig. 6.6). In 1985, $531,079 of payroll tax and $94,005 net profit tax was paid to Georgetown; in 1996–1997, $6,797,501 in payroll tax and $485,028 in net profit tax was paid to the city and county. City and county budgets have grown significantly since the arrival of Toyota. Scott County's 1985 budget was $2 million; the county spent $13.5 million in 1997–1998. Georgetown's 1985 budget was $3 million, and 1998 expenditures were $11 million. Starting fiscal year 1999, Georgetown reported cash assets of $6,619,603. The county reported $9,235,391. This is a significant improvement over the fiscal constraints of the early 1980s.

New public wealth from the local tax system established through city annexation and county-imposed payroll tax in the early years after the decision to locate the Toyota plant in Scott County has resulted in fulfilling long-established goals for additional public services and facilities (fig. 6.7). The election of a new mayor and the modification of the county fiscal court in late 1998 gave opportunity for the implementation of a long-held agenda. Among the active implementation items in early 1999 were

- construction of an expanded senior citizen center;
- institutionalization of the Elkhorn Creek and open space preservation efforts, with implementation of a trail system throughout the urban area and riparian reforestation within the urban area, providing a system longer than in any other Kentucky community;
- imminent groundbreaking for a $5 million jointly funded indoor swimming facility (a dream of two generations of competitive and recreational swimmers);
- recent groundbreaking for a new, state-of-the-art Scott County Public Library with a newly imposed county-wide tax;
- further development of Scott County as a state leader in alternative agriculture and a new grading, processing, and marketing center, in part learned from the experience of sister city Tahara-cho, Japan;
- creation of a major reservoir and naturally protected small watershed in northern Scott County, providing further local security from regional drought;
- actions leading to a permanent Japanese garden of regional importance and activities such as the first-in-America exhibit of Kazan Watanabe art, which will provide increased visibility for the community; and
- expansion and extension of a new general aviation airport established only a few years ago as a joint facility with Lexington's Blue Grass Airport.

City water and sewer are administered not directly by the city but by a special district, the Georgetown Municipal Water and Sewer District, whose members are appointed by the city. Rates have risen moderately, but the district quickly imposed a $700 tap-on fee for every new house and facility. The Water and Sewer District announced a $200 increase in that fee and a modest reduction in water rates for other users. Two new sewer plants—one for use by Toyota and the other, funded by bonds, for community use—have been constructed. In earlier years, the district relied on federal grants. Historically, the water source relied on Royal Spring, an underground stream that emerges in the middle of Georgetown. With development in the community and impingement on the aquifer by north Fayette County, dependency on Royal Springs for city water has become problematic. The district now supplements its supply with water from the north branch of Elkhorn Creek and by purchase from Frankfort through a new pipeline from the Kentucky River. Kentucky American Water System, based in Lexington, supplies Toyota.

Equalized Assessment

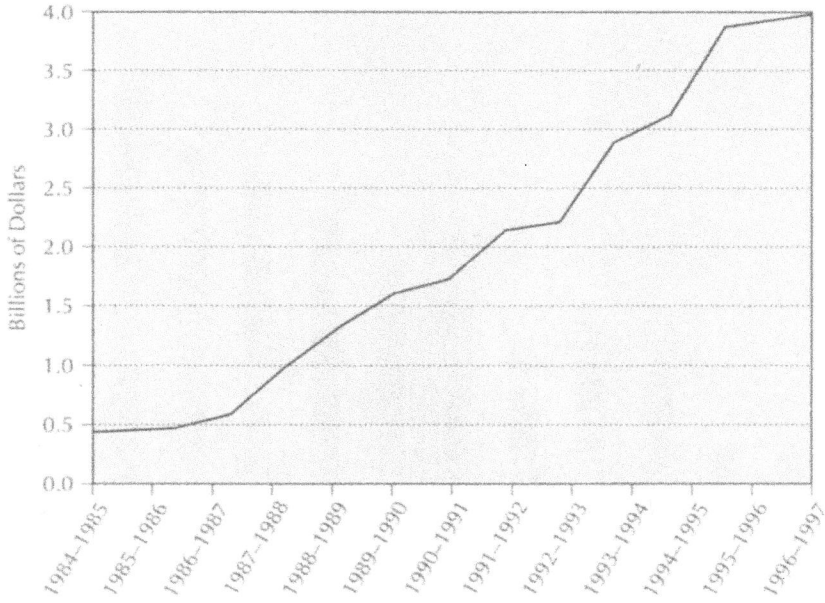

State Tax Paid

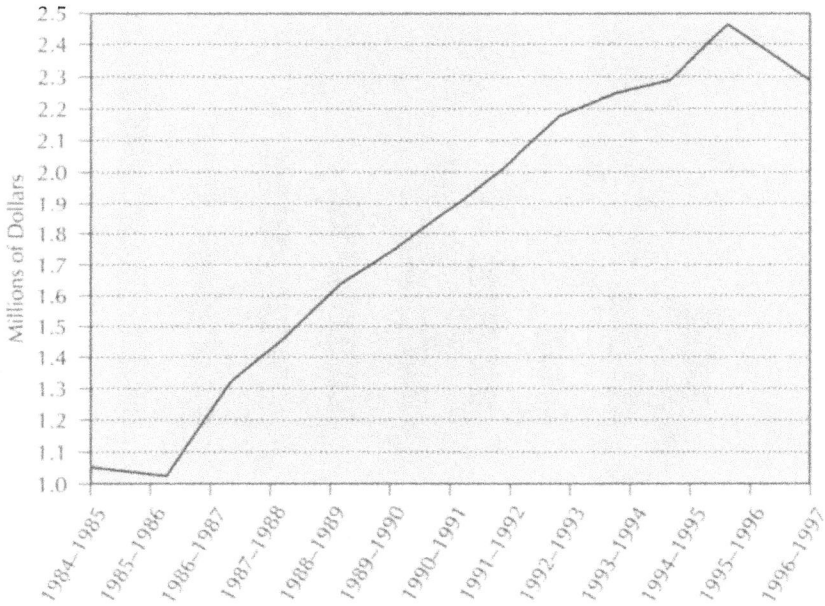

6.6. Scott County: Real estate and personal property assessments and state tax paid, 1984–1985 to 1996–1997.

Georgetown

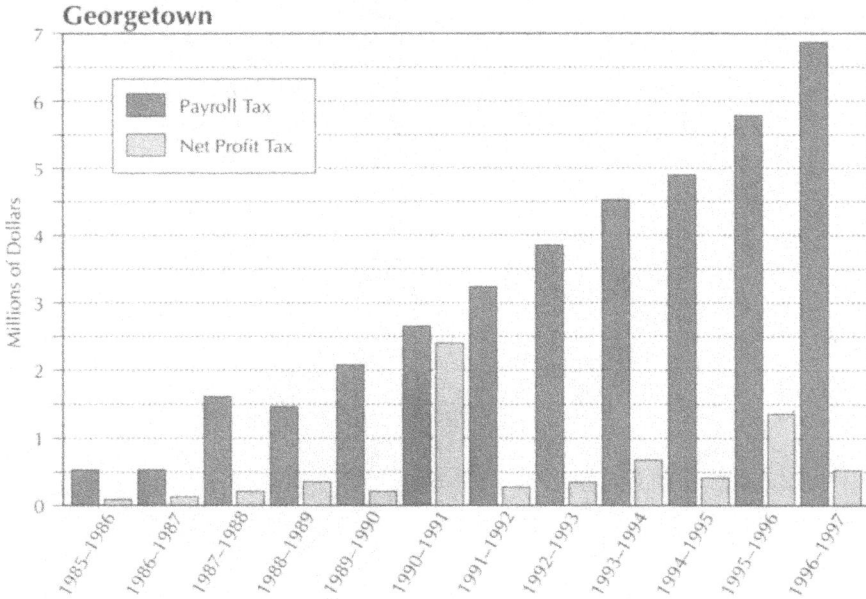

Scott County

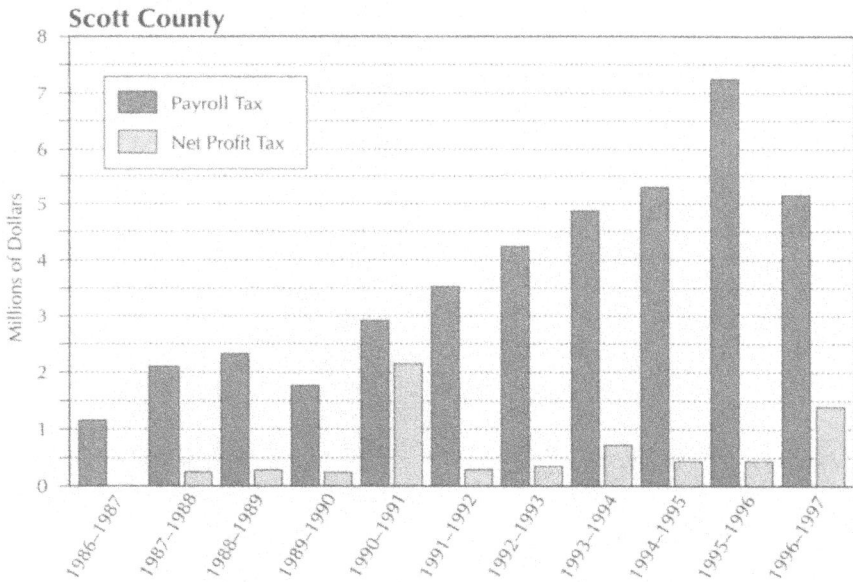

Note: 1986–1987 Net Profit Tax is not significant enough of a total to be represented.
The total was $14,636

Fig. 6.7. Georgetown and Scott County: Payroll tax and net profit tax, 1986–1997.

GROWTH AND CHANGE: 1985–1999

The rate of growth of Georgetown-Scott County was not rapid in the first five years after Toyota's announcement; it gradually accelerated in the next five and is now growing at a significant pace. With a 28 percent population increase between 1990 and 1997, Scott County is the sixth-fastest-growing county in the commonwealth. The population of 21,813 in 1980 grew to 23,943 in 1990 and was estimated at 29,446 in 1998. Projections by the Kentucky Data Center estimate that Scott County will grow to 39,658 by 2010 and to 45,853 by 2020. This growth in absolute numbers is more than that projected for Lexington-Fayette County, despite the fact that Lexington has a base ten times larger than Scott County (table 6.1).

Georgetown has grown by a series of annexations tied directly to planning policies. No rezoning for urban land use is granted without the applicant agreeing to annexation. The property must be contiguous to existing city boundaries, consistent with the comprehensive plan, and served by the city's water and sewer system. These policies were tightly bound together within two years of Toyota's arrival. During the planning review of 1991, it was discovered that the water and sewer district was developing a plan that ignored the comprehensive plan, following the single criterion that water runs downhill. Mayor Prather forced reconsideration by the district, and the pro-

Table 6.1. Georgetown and Scott County: Patterns of growth and change, 1985–1998

	1985	1998
Population		
Scott County	21,813	29,446[a]
Georgetown	11,000[a]	15,714[a]
Unemployment rate	8.7%	2.4%
Per capita income	$10,407[a]	$21,887
Budget		
Scott County	$2,027,948	$13,418,737
Georgetown	$1,840,000	$11,068,761
Payroll tax		
Scott County	$1,126,592	$7,222,058
Georgetown	$531,079	$6,797,501
Assessed value of property	$440,701,570	$3,978,104,552
Number of building permits	178	914
Value of building permits	$7.6 million	$86.2 million
Number of pupils		
Scott County schools	4,098	5,359

Notes: a = estimated.

jected new sewage plant was relocated to a site best serving the comprehensive plan. From that time forward, urban water and sewer extensions have been entirely consistent with other related planning and development policies.

The pattern of urban growth since 1985 is best reflected in the comparative maps of Georgetown's annexations and in 1989 and 1998 aerial photographs. Urban development has reflected a contained, systematic evolution. The majority of new growth has been urban, bringing Georgetown to a population exceeding Scott County's rural population for the first time in history.

Patterns of rural development, however, reflect the legal and policy-making problems of preserving prime agricultural land, supporting current and alternative agriculture, defining suitable rural residential development, implementing transfers of development rights, defining cluster development to sustain agriculture, and maintaining green belts. About 48 percent of new development has occurred in rural areas, with the minimum-five-acre-lot requirement causing the loss of more than five thousand acres of agricultural land. A rural cluster development option designed to preserve agricultural land has been difficult to perfect. Finding that these issues are more difficult to resolve than urban policies, the planning commission continues to seek suitable answers. Historically, Scott County has had a five-acre-minimum-lot-size requirement for residential development. Landowners and speculators have taken advantage of that to get approvals for as many five-acre tracts as possible before the opportunity might be foreclosed. A twenty-five-acre minimum has been under discussion and might be adopted in the future.

The pace and pattern of rural land development, and the ability to control it for public purposes, has been exacerbated by two unrelated events during the past five years. Scott County Fiscal Court implemented a program to provide safe water to all rural residents, inadvertently making rural development easier at public cost. Lexington-Fayette County further tightened land availability for development, causing increased pressure for development on Scott County agricultural and rural land.

Few of Kentucky's 120 counties have planning, and fewer have joint city-county planning commissions. Agrarian and mining traditions dominate land-use practice. A mobile home park located on the Scott County-Fayette County line in the 1960s fueled controversial debate about the need for planning. Following his reelection in 1965 in which planning and zoning had been the main issue, County Judge Charles Brooking moved to enact a joint city-county commission as a watch guard on land use and change in Scott County. A tradition of open public deliberation on land use was established more than fifteen years prior to Toyota's arrival. The city and the county made separate appointments of commissioners, and each bore half of the cost, but there was a tradition of support of commission decisions by both political bodies. Even when appointments to the commission were contested, personal faction more often than policy drove the contest. The agenda was not affected.

Kentucky planning law requires the update of comprehensive plans every five years. In response to the Toyota location, the 1985 comprehensive plan revision was quickly accomplished in January 1986 to accommodate the newly designated site. Few other changes were made. By 1990, it was time to reconsider the comprehensive plan in light of the fundamental changes that were in process and to take a considered view of the future.

The issue of land use and growth is at the heart of traditional local planning consideration and action. It received the most attention during the planning review. Due to the long tradition of planning, an urban service district and strict annexation policy were already in place. Consequently, most discussion focused on marginal changes to the existing boundary to accommodate new growth and innovations to deal with special rural development districts (i.e., transfers of development rights, new cluster policies for the preservation of farmland, development around the two other small communities, and rural crossroads neighborhoods). The community and the commission have refined what was set forth in the plan and decided about their common "preferred future." The commission has tended to deal mostly in specific land-use decisions, while the city and county have moved to implement other elements of the plan when the timing was right. The fundamental continuity and consensus has been extraordinary.

During the mid-1970s, the local Soil Conservation Committee worked to educate the community on the preservation of prime agricultural land, a belt of land in the southern portion of the county from the Lexington-Fayette County border to five miles north of Georgetown. When Toyota announced the plant site in late 1985, a citizen commissioned a report from a natural resources planner on how to begin a trail system and take actions to preserve and enhance Elkhorn Creek, which drains the Bluegrass, and its north fork which flows through Georgetown. Water resources had been highlighted a few years earlier in a successful citizen protest against an experimental coal gasification plant on the edge of town. The commissioned study on Elkhorn Creek was presented to the January 1986 meeting of the planning commission, and its principles were soon incorporated in all planning reviews. The effort to preserve Elkhorn Creek led to the creation of the Elkhorn Land and Historic Trust, reinforcing awareness and public-private cooperation without strident conflict.

Because of a pattern of conflict between the city and county governments, many people believed local government was not capable of dealing effectively with the challenges posed by Toyota, and they called for extensive restructuring of local government. Discussion of governmental reorganization in Georgetown had been ongoing for several years. Efforts by the Chamber of Commerce and Scott County United to promote city/county merger were stimulated by the Toyota plant and the expectation of rapid growth and change. A petition drive to form a merger commission was completed by mid-1987, and in December, the city and county made appointments to the forty-member merger commission. The commission met for six months to draft a charter for merged city-county government. The issue was placed on the November 1988 ballot and was defeated.

Coordinated services have become the norm. In June 1993, the city and county implemented an inter-local government agreement on police services and, in 1994, an agreement on ambulance service. These combined with already existing joint efforts in parks and recreation, planning, international programs, and so on. The list of joint agreements and funding arrangements has grown routinely and is now considered the first option for any new program or function. Some expect another referendum on merger in the foreseeable future.

The dynamics of community change and challenge were greatly facilitated by Georgetown College President Dr. H. William Crouch. Georgetown College had been an important presence in the community since the 1840s, when it became a Southern Baptist college, reflecting the dominant local and regional religion. Many local residents and its principle leadership had attended the college; they remained loyal, continued in the faith, and otherwise connected with traditions and old associations. In the years just before Toyota's arrival and through the late 1980s, the institution kept a low profile in the community. With the appointment of its new president, the college began to

Toyota has supported programs and activities at Georgetown College. For years the Baptist college has played an integral role in the community. (Photograph by P.P. Karan)

reach beyond campus borders. It quickly became apparent that the futures of Georgetown-Scott County and Georgetown College were intertwined.

Georgetown College participates in a joint agreement among city, county, college, school system, and community and business leaders to enhance learning technologies and communications. Georgetown College built a $15 million learning resources center; Scott County Library has broken ground for a contemporary new library; Scott County schools continue their leadership in classroom technology in Kentucky; and local governments have moved forward with the Geographic Information System (GIS) and communications. The college built its first new building in twenty-five years when it opened an art building and gallery to clear the site for its new learning resources building, and it provides a pre-season training facility for the National Football League's Cincinnati Bengals.

PROGRESS AND TRADITION IN GEORGETOWN-SCOTT COUNTY

Looking back, the worst fears about growth and change destroying the way of life in a small town have not materialized. While the business community embraced Toyota, local elected leadership were apprehensive. While shock gave way to fear of being overrun, several key individuals and activities began to shape a process by which the community would respond to the new challenges and seek to shape change to achieve local community goals. Local government was able to implement several decisive actions, such as adoption of a county payroll and net profits tax, annexation of the plant by Georgetown, and adoption of the innovative Georgetown-Scott County Comprehensive Plan of 1991, which enhanced the community's ability to promote its own interests.

While the plant was enthusiastically welcomed by many, it brought an array of stresses and strains, from traffic to housing to wastewater treatment. The rate of growth was less than initially projected, but the past few years have brought substantial increases in population, employment, and housing. Through its comprehensive plan and other policy actions, the community has been able to significantly influence the patterns of growth and its impact on the community, seeking to define the community's preferred future of economic achievement and enhancement of quality of life. The Georgetown-Scott County Comprehensive Plan of 1991 won a regional American Planning Association award for best plan shortly after it was completed. Other authors have praised its far-reaching scope and innovative solutions. While refinements will be continually made, it is unlikely that the fundamental philosophy will be altered. It truly reflects Georgetown-Scott County's preferred future.

During the past thirteen years, Georgetown-Scott County has used two public slogans: "Scott County Pride" and "Where Progress and Tradition Meet." Both are apt, and each played its part in the comprehensive plan that is officially adopted policy.

New public wealth from the local tax system established in the early years after the decision to locate the new plant in Scott County has resulted in fulfilling long-established goals for additional public services and facilities. Among the dramatic changes to the community are

- emergence of new political leadership and cooperation among city and county governments;
- a fivefold increase in funding;
- a professionalization of governmental services;
- improved transportation networks;
- a vibrant housing industry;
- growing commercial businesses;
- expanding global contacts;
- implementation of Elkhorn Creek trail system and riparian reforestation;
- construction of a modern general aviation airport;
- upgrade of education, technology, and library facilities; and
- expanded recreational and leisure activities,

Globalization of the community has produced the most noticeable change. It is not that a substantial number of Japanese have moved to the community. The plant manager has lived in town close to the plant since its beginning. Informal estimates suggest that Scott County may be home to as many as one hundred Japanese, nearly all of whom are trainers on three- to five-year rotations. Three-quarters of the one hundred are Toyota employees, and the remainder work for subsidiary companies. Consequently, their housing pattern is scattered throughout the community, the result of available long-term contract rentals through their companies. Few Japanese living in Scott County are permanent residents. Existence of a Japanese school in Lexington and the dry status and reputation of Scott County are often cited as factors that lead to Japanese families living in Lexington rather than Georgetown. The subtle nuances of American drinking behaviors, laws, and history are lost on most foreign visitors. With Toyota's headquarters located in Boone County near the Cincinnati Airport, it is unlikely that there will be substantial increase in the Japanese population in Scott County.

International and sister-city exchanges with Tahara-cho are commonplace. Tahara (population 34,450), a town built on reclaimed land in what was formerly Tahara Bay, has cement factories and a Toyota factory. The Toyota plant was built in Tahara about five years before the Georgetown plant was built. Mayor Shibata and other officials formalized the relationship in Georgetown in 1990. Soon afterward, Seisho High School and Scott County High School established a sister-school relationship. In 1992 Tahara sent a municipal employee, Toshi Suzuki, to live in Georgetown for a year to learn about governance and community dynamics and to get acquainted with local people. Georgetown-Scott County was ill-equipped for such a relationship and the international dynamic that was implied in such a connection. However, its sister, Tahara-cho, had been a leader of the "opening to the West" from the late Edo Period. The link of the two small communities through the sister-city program relationship has led to new advances and opportunities for Georgetown and Scott County. A special relationship was established to send Georgetown College graduates as assistant English teachers to Tahara under the more general Japan Exchange and Teaching (JET) program in Japan.

Fundamentally, Georgetown-Scott County is an openly democratic community in the traditional definition—both before and after the arrival of Toyota. Elections are contested, but agendas rarely change significantly as a result. Decisions are made with full discussion and consideration, often in settings similar to a New England town meeting. That fact has been critical in the dynamic and positive results that followed Toyota's arrival. With full discussion, consensus could be formed and agreed upon values and goals were reached. As time went on, the shaping of consensus for a common future became easier, moving discussion to agreements for implementation.

The arrival of a powerful global corporation only temporarily caught the community off balance. But the new resources have provided the opportunity for achieving the community's preferred future. A leap from the nineteenth century to the twenty-first century has taken place in the social, economic, and political environments of Georgetown-Scott County.

REFERENCES

Gelsanliter, David. 1990. *Jump Start: Japan Comes to the Heartland.* New York: Farrar, Straus, Giroux.
Georgetown Scott County Planning Commission, *Comprehensive Plan, 1991.* Annual report, 1997–1998.
Hoyman, Michele M. 1997. *Power steering: Global Automakers and the Transformation of Rural Communities.* Lawrence: Univ. Press of Kansas.
Kentucky Cabinet for Economic Development. 1996. Kentucky Resources for Economic Development: Georgetown.
Kentucky Society of Architects and the Kentucky Chapter, American Society of Landscape Architects. 1987. Georgetown Scott County Kentucky Design Assistance Team." 11–14 June. Scott County United Printing.
Kentucky State Data Center. 1998–1999. News, Vol. 16, No. 2, (winter).
Scott County United. 1985–1997 statistics.

Scott Education Foundation. 1993. Greater Scott County Learning Resources System: Creating a Learning Community Through Cooperation, Libraries and Technology. December.

Urban Studies Center, The University of Louisville. 1987. Impacts of the Toyota Plant on Scott County, Kentucky.

Yanarella, Ernest. 1986. Class-Based Environmentalism in a Small Town: ERDA's Gasifiers in Industry Program and Georgetown, Kentucky, Controversy. Kentucky Political Science Conference, February.

Part III

Economic, Social, and Environmental Impacts of Japan in Kentucky

7

Toyota Motor Manufacturing, Kentucky, and the Kentucky Economy

CHARLES F. HAYWOOD

IN DECEMBER 1985 TOYOTA MOTOR CORPORATION and the Commonwealth of Kentucky announced plans to build a plant to assemble passenger motor vehicles at a site in Scott County near the city of Georgetown and fifteen miles north of Lexington. With the prior approval of the Kentucky General Assembly, Kentucky Governor Martha Layne Collins and Toyota President Shoichiro Toyoda signed on February 25, 1986, an "Agreement" confirming the commitments between the Commonwealth of Kentucky and Toyota Motor Corporation.

State government's participation took the form of an incentives package covering the costs of certain construction activities and the training of workers. Its components were as follows:

Land purchase	$10,273,524
Site preparation	20,000,000
Water and gas lines	10,286,743
Training center	7,200,000
Wastewater facility	12,239,733
Highway improvements	32,000,000
Training and education	55,000,000
Total	$147,000,000

Toyota's commitment was to invest $800 million to build and equip an assembly plant to produce two hundred thousand passenger motor vehicles with a workforce of three thousand and an annual payroll of $90 million.

Ground was broken for the assembly plant in May 1986, and construction was completed in May 1988. Pilot production of Toyota's new Camry was initiated at that time, and volume production was achieved in July 1988.

Norfolk-Southern Toyota Support Yard at the Scott County, Kentucky, plant. The state paid for the infrastructure development at the plant site. The $305 million spent on incentives is projected to produce $1.5 billion in tax revenues over a twenty-year period attributed to Toyota's expenditures in Kentucky. (Photograph by P.P. Karan)

During the calendar year 1992, the annual production rate of Camry automobiles reached approximately 230,000; employment was forty-three hundred; and the annual payroll was approximately $185 million, excluding benefits costs estimated at 37 percent of payroll. That is, by 1992 actual performance by Toyota Motor Manufacturing, Kentucky (TMMK) exceeded the level of operations projected when the "Agreement" was consummated in 1986.

TMMK EXPANSIONS

Even before the completion of the assembly plant, TMMK announced (November 1987) that a facility to produce engines and axles would be added to the initial plan. Construction of the power train plant began in mid-1988. Plant capacity was projected at three hundred thousand engines, with two hundred thousand targeted as the normal production level. Production of axles began in October 1988, four-cylinder engines in November 1989.

In November 1990 TMMK announced that the capacity of the

Georgetown plant would be doubled by adding a second assembly line. Targeted capacity would be increased from two hundred thousand to four hundred thousand motor vehicles per year. Construction began in June 1991 and was completed in early 1994, with pilot production beginning in March 1994. In September 1994 TMMK initiated production of Toyota's new Avalon on the second assembly line.

Further expansion of the power train plant was announced in January 1992. TMMK indicated that the capacity of the power train plant would be increased to five hundred thousand engines, including V-6 cylinder engines as well as four-cylinder engines. The expansion was completed in the summer of 1994, and production of V-6 engines began in August.

Major additional investments, largely in equipment, were made at TMMK in 1996 and 1997 in support of a redesign of the Camry and the initiation of assembly of the new Sienna minivan. By the end of 1997 the cumulative original-cost investments in TMMK's Georgetown facility reached approximately $4.6 billion, or almost six times the $800 million expected when the Commonwealth's incentives package of $147 million was proposed in late 1985.

As noted above, the expectation in late 1985 was that the Georgetown facility would be only an assembly plant, capable of turning out two hundred thousand vehicles. In 1997 the Georgetown facility assembled 325,123 Camry sedans, 80,277 Avalon sedans, and 26,746 Sienna minivans, for a total of 432,146 vehicles. Manufacturing output included 435,709 four-cylinder and V-6 engines and, in support of the assembly of vehicles and manufacture of engines, the necessary numbers of axles, steering components, machined blocks, cylinder heads, crankshafts, camshafts, and rods and axles assemblies.

ECONOMIC IMPACTS IN KENTUCKY, 1986–1997

Table 7.1 shows the economic multiplier effects of TMMK's outlays in Kentucky during the period 1986–1997. The column captioned "TMMK Outlays" includes TMMK's Kentucky payroll (excluding employee benefits), purchases of parts and supplies from Kentucky vendors, and local construction expenditures. The next three columns—the "Effects" columns—were calculated using multipliers from input-output analyses by the Regional Economic Analysis Division, Bureau of Economic Analysis, and U.S. Department of Commerce and are usually referred to as "RIMS (Regional Input-Output Modeling System) II multipliers." Three economic impacts can be calculated using the RIMS II multipliers: total output effects—the total volume of transactions generated by the indicated "initial" outlays, earnings effects—the amount of household income resulting from the indicated "initial" outlays, and employment effects—the number of jobs that can be attributed to the

Table 7.1. TMMK's economic impacts in Kentucky, 1986–1997

Year	TMMK outlays ($ mil.)	Total output effects ($ mil.)	Earnings effects ($ mil.)	Employment effects (number)	State tax revenues Annual ($ mil.)	Cumulative ($ mil.)
1986	10.6	26.6	10.0	259	0.8	0.8
1987	226.6	569.4	216.4	5,464	14.3	15.1
1988	270.1	681.7	262.6	7,770	18.3	33.3
1989	157.7	426.9	191.2	6,987	14.2	47.5
1990	302.0	802.5	327.3	10,840	22.7	70.2
1991	523.5	1,368.6	541.8	16,415	43.4	113.6
1992	574.5	1,503.0	563.4	17,883	47.7	161.3
1993	1,053.3	2,712.4	845.6	25,968	62.6	223.4
1994	1,107.5	2,864.9	912.9	26,513	67.3	290.7
1995	1,435.1	3,689.8	1,104.4	30,577	82.5	373.2
1996	1,610.0	4,147.4	1,273.5	33,419	94.6	467.8
1997	1,702.7	4,408.1	1,406.6	34,544	103.7	571.4

Source: 1986–1992—Charles F. Haywood, *Review & Perspective: The Economic Significance of Toyota Motor Manufacturing, U.S.A., Inc., in Kentucky,* Center for Business and Economic Research, College of Business and Economics, University of Kentucky, December 1992, pp. 3, 6. 1993–1997—"TMMK Outlays" from Toyota Motor Manufacturing, North America, Inc.; other columns calculated by Charles F. Haywood using updated multipliers from 1992 study.

indicated "initial" outlays. The last two columns of table 7.1—State Tax Revenues—will be discussed in a later section of this paper.

The multiplier effects shown in table 7.1 include direct and indirect effects. In 1997 the total output effects were $4,408.1 million. Included were $1,702.7 million of direct effects, consisting of purchases of parts and materials of $1,141.7 million, payroll of $470.4 million, and equipment purchases and related activities of $90.6 million. Indirect effects totaled $2,637.2 million, including the household expenditures of TMMK workers, spending by TMMK's suppliers and their workers, and subsequent rounds of expenditures by businesses and workers as the dollars moved from one transaction level to the next. The total output effects are the sum of the successive rounds of spending, starting with TMMK's expenditures as the first round, direct output effects and the further rounds of spending as the indirect output effects.

TMMK's earnings effects of $1,406.6 million in 1997 included direct effects in the form of TMMK's payroll of $470.4 million plus estimated contractors' payrolls of $45.3 million. Indirect effects of $890.9 million were the income payments to households associated with the successive rounds of total spending described above.

The employment effects in 1997 totaled 34,544 jobs, of which 8,170 jobs (7,689 TMMK jobs; 481 estimated contractor jobs) were direct effects

A worker at Y H America plant in Versailles, Kentucky. Y H America, owned by Yokohama Rubber Company and Yokohama Hydex Company, makes air conditioning and power steering hose, fittings, and hose assemblies. Toyota is one of its major customers. A large number of Japanese parts suppliers have established production facilities in Kentucky and contribute to the region's economic development. (Photograph courtesy of Y H America)

and 26,374 jobs were indirect effects at supplier and other business locations throughout the commonwealth where the successive rounds of spending called forth increases in the production of goods and services.

PROJECTION OF ECONOMIC IMPACTS IN KENTUCKY, 1998–2005

Table 7.2 projects TMMK's outlays and related multiplier effects through the year 2005. The main reason for making such projections is to provide the basis for a cash flow analysis evaluating the return on the state's investment in the construction and training activities noted at the beginning of this paper.

Underlying the projections to 2005 is an assumption that employment at TMMK will be constant at a level of 7,850 full-time-equivalent employees between 1998 and 2005. At present, there do not appear to be any plans to expand further the capacity of the Georgetown facility. Increases in TMMK outlays, total output effects, earnings effects, and state tax revenues from

Table 7.2. Projection of TMMK's economic impacts in Kentucky, 1998–2005

Year	TMMK outlays ($ mil.)	Total output effects ($ mil.)	Earnings effects ($ mil.)	Employment effects (number)	State tax revenues Annual ($ mil.)	Cumulative ($ mil.)
1998	1,740.3	4,505.4	1,437.7	34,614	105.9	667.3[a]
1999	1,762.8	4,563.6	1,456.3	34,628	107.3	784.6
2000	1,815.7	4,700.5	1,500.0	34,797	110.5	895.1
2001	1,861.0	4,818.1	1,537.5	34,797	113.3	1,008.4
2002	1,907.6	4,938.5	1,575.9	34,797	116.1	1,124.5
2003	1,955.3	5,062.0	1,615.3	34,797	119.0	1,243.4
2004	2,004.1	5,188.5	1,655.7	34,797	122.0	1,365.4
2005	2,054.2	5,318.2	1,697.1	34,797	125.0	1,491.2

a = Includes $571.4 million from period 1986–1997 shown in Table 7.1.
Source: "TMMK Outlays" projected by Charles F. Haywood; multipliers updated to reflect expected increases in wage rates.

1998 through 2005 reflect an assumption that prices and wage rates generally will increase by an average of 2.5 percent per annum. The result of such assumption is that the projection of direct and indirect employment effects in Kentucky rises to 34,797 jobs in the year 2000 and remains at that level.

Cash Flow Analysis, 1986–2005

Table 7.1 shows that between 1986 and 1997 the Commonwealth of Kentucky collected an estimated $571.2 million of tax revenues attributable to the direct and indirect effects of TMMK's outlays in Kentucky. The projections in table 7.2 indicate that the state's tax collections attributable to TMMK's effects will total an estimated $1,490.4 million by the end of 2005.

The $147 million cost of the incentives package provided to Toyota Motor Corporation by the Commonwealth of Kentucky was a "present value" figure. An alternative estimate projected that the Commonwealth would need to borrow funds to cover some portions of the incentives package and would therefore incur interest costs. The total outlay was projected to be $305.2 million spread over a twenty-year period. Those projected costs are shown in table 7.3 in the first column, denoted as "Incentives Costs with Interest." The annual state tax collections shown in tables 7.1 and 7.2 of this report are set forth in the second column, headed "Attributable State Tax Revenues." Subtracting the first column from the second column results in the third column "Net Cash Flow."

Over the twenty-year period 1986–2005, the total of Attributable State Tax Revenues in table 7.3 is estimated, as shown, to be $1,491.2 million.

Table 7.3. Rate of return analysis of incentives' costs and state tax revenues, 1986–2005 ($ millions)

Year	Incentives costs with interest	Attributable state tax revenues	Net cash flow
1986	24.7	0.8	-23.9
1987	25.8	14.3	-11.5
1988	25.8	18.3	-7.5
1989	24.1	14.2	-9.9
1990	24.1	22.7	-1.4
1991	12.8	43.4	+30.6
1992	12.0	47.7	+35.7
1993	12.0	62.6	+50.6
1994	12.0	67.3	+55.3
1995	12.0	82.5	+70.5
1996	12.0	94.6	+82.6
1997	12.0	103.7	+91.7
1998	12.0	105.9	+93.9
1999	12.0	107.3	+95.3
2000	12.0	110.5	+98.5
2001	12.0	113.3	+101.3
2002	12.0	116.1	+104.1
2003	12.0	119.0	+107.0
2004	12.0	122.0	+110.0
2005	12.0	125.0	+113.0
Totals	305.3	1,491.2	+1,185.9

Note: IRR = 36.79%

Source: "Incentives Costs with Interest," from Charles F. Haywood, *Review & Perspective: The Economic Significance of Toyota Motor Manufacturing, U.S.A., Inc., in Kentucky,* Center for Business and Economic Research, College of Business and Economics, University of Kentucky, December 1992, p. 7; "Attributable State Tax Revenues" from Tables 7.1 and 7.2; "Net Cash Flow" and "IRR" calculated by Charles F. Haywood.

Subtracting the $305.3 million of Incentives Costs with Interest results in a Net Cash Flow totaling $1,185.90 million. That is, as a result of its investment in the Toyota incentives package, the Commonwealth of Kentucky will receive almost $1.2 billion in tax revenues over and above the costs of the incentives package. On an annual basis, the discounted cash flow rate of return on the Commonwealth's incentives package, as now projected through 2005, is 36.79 percent.

ATTRACTION OF OTHER AUTOMOTIVE FIRMS TO KENTUCKY

Toyota suppliers are located in several states, mostly in the eastern United States (fig. 7.1). By the end of 1997 there were approximately 175 manufacturing facilities in Kentucky producing automobile parts and materials. Only 55 of these plants were in operation prior to the December 1985 announcement that Toyota Motor Corporation would build an assembly plant in Scott County. That is, approximately 120 plants were opened in Kentucky from 1986 through 1997. Total capital investment in the 120 plants is estimated to have been $2,752 million. The 175 parts plants are located in fifty-six of the state's 120 counties. Prior to December 1985 the 55 supplier plants were located in twenty-seven counties. Only two of those twenty-seven counties did not get at least one "new" plant after 1985. The 120 "new" plants located in twenty-five of the counties which had at least one parts plant in 1985 and in twenty-nine counties which did not have any such plants in 1985. Total employment in the 175 parts plants in 1997 was estimated to be in excess of 40,000 jobs. The 120 new plants accounted for approximately 23,500 of that total. Total manufacturing employment in Kentucky increased from 255,300 in 1985 to 316,100 in 1997.

TMMK does not purchase parts and materials from all of the 175 automotive parts plants in Kentucky. The majority of them sell to other motor vehicle assembly plants in Kentucky and other states. In 1997 TMMK purchased parts and materials from fifty-five manufacturers in Kentucky. TMMK's purchases from its fifty-five Kentucky suppliers are estimated to make up about one-half of the total sales of the 175 plants, and it is further estimated that TMMK's purchases account for between nineteen thousand and twenty thousand of the forty thousand jobs in the motor vehicles parts and materials companies.

The economic impacts attributed to TMMK in tables 7.1 through 7.3 include only those Kentucky plants from which TMMK purchases parts and materials. Those parts plants that located in Kentucky after 1985 but which are not TMMK suppliers have not been considered in calculating the economic impacts of TMMK in Kentucky.

It might be argued that many of the 120 new plants followed Toyota's lead in locating in Kentucky even though there was no expectation of becoming suppliers to TMMK. Therefore, the further argument might be that perhaps an additional impact should be calculated for the nonsupplier plants and some part of it attributed to TMMK. However, there is no need to undertake the difficult task of selecting and defending what weight should be attached to the economic impact of the nonsupplier plants. Tables 7.1 through 7.3 demonstrate that the economic impacts readily attributable to TMMK have made the Commonwealth's incentives package a prosperous investment, indeed. The 1985 decision by the Commonwealth and Toyota Motor Corpo-

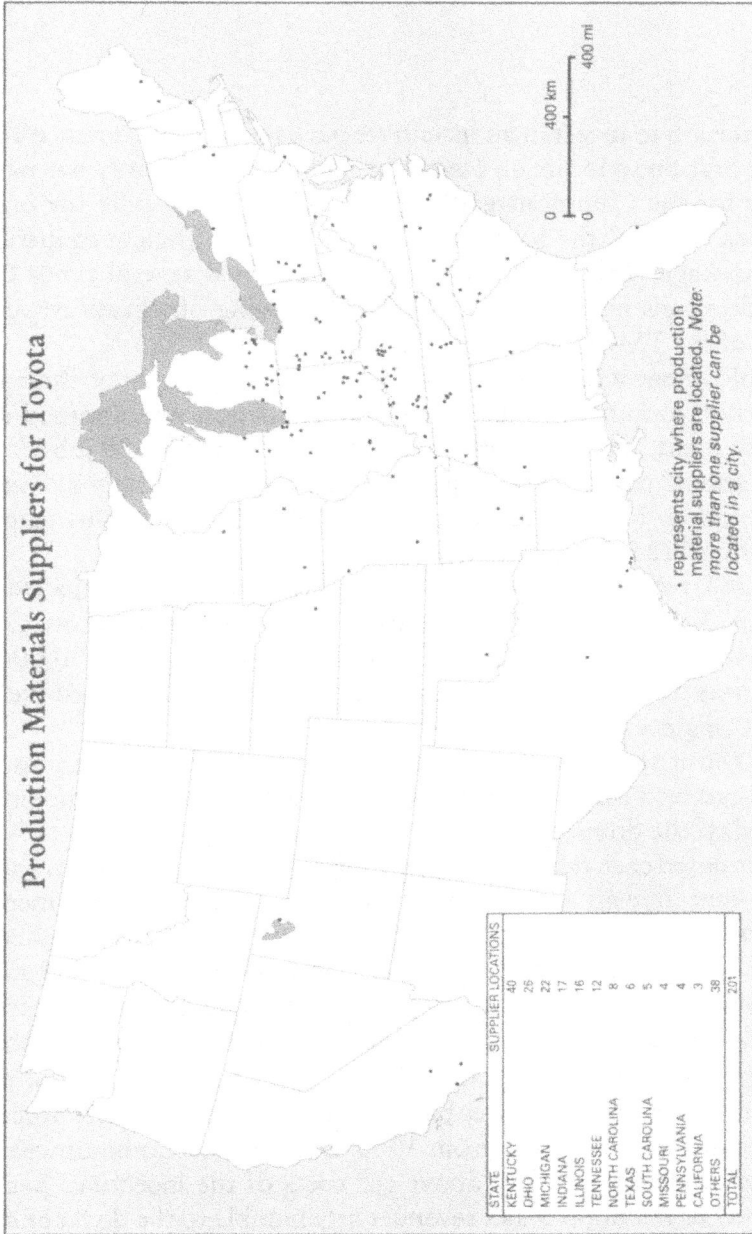

Fig. 7.1. Toyota's suppliers in the United States.

ration has been a significant part of the restructuring and relocation of the motor vehicle and parts manufacturing industry in the United States during the 1980s and 1990s.

Summary

The 1985 decision to invest in an incentives package to help convince Toyota Motor Corporation to locate an assembly plant in Scott County has paid off handsomely for the Commonwealth of Kentucky. Even if only the original plan had been realized, the benefits would have been sufficient to justify the incentives package. The benefits have been multiplied several times by the expansion decisions made since 1985. The following observations sum up key aspects of the TMMK success story.

1. Employment was projected in 1986 to reach a range of three thousand to thirty-two hundred jobs when full production was attained at the Scott County plant. Employment at the end of 1997 was 7,689 jobs.

2. The annual payroll was projected to reach approximately $90 million at full production. In 1997 the payroll was $470.4 million plus employee benefits costing $125.6 million.

3. In 1985 Toyota Motor Corporation's investment was projected to be $800 million. At the end of 1997 the total investment at the Scott County plant was $4,524.4 million. Whereas a production capacity of 200,000 motor vehicles was planned in 1985, today's capacity is 435,000 motor vehicles and 500,000 engines

4. In 1985 it was expected that the domestic content of the motor vehicles produced by TMMK would be 60 percent of the value of the finished product. Today, the domestic content is in excess of 75 percent.

5. Discounted cash flow analysis of Kentucky's 1985 incentives package indicated at that time an annual rate of return of 8.5 percent from increased state revenue collections attributable to the direct and indirect effects of TMMK's projected level of operation. By 1992, adjustment of the 1985 analysis to take account of increases in state tax rates in 1990 and inflation increased the originally projected rate of return from 8.5 percent per annum to 16.8 percent per annum. As shown in table 7.3 the updated annual rate of return on the Commonwealth's incentives package is now approximately 36.86 percent. In the twenty-year period from 1986 to 2005, the Commonwealth of Kentucky will collect, over and above the costs of the incentives package, approximately $1.2 billion of tax revenues attributable to the direct and indirect effects of TMMK's operations in Kentucky.

6. TMMK's 1997 outlays of $1,702.7 million in Kentucky for parts and materials, payroll, and plant and equipment gave rise to $4,408.1 million in total spending, $1,406.6 million in household earnings, and 34,544 jobs in

the state. Outlays for the period 1998–2005 are projected to rise by only the amount of expected increases in wage rates and costs of parts and materials; after increasing to 34,797 in 2000 the employment effect is expected to remain stable at about 35,000 through 2005.

CONCLUDING COMMENTS

The use of an incentives package to help convince Toyota Motor Corporation to locate an assembly plant in Scott County has turned out to be a success beyond anything that was or could have been creditably projected in December 1985. Some of the circumstances that have contributed to that success can be identified as follows.

1. Both sides—the Commonwealth of Kentucky and Toyota Motor Corporation—willingly and graciously lived up to their respective commitments.

2. Approximately 42 percent of the incentives package was for an onsite training facility and for training programs, which have contributed to the high quality of TMMK's output.

3. Evident in the local area and region was a great deal of goodwill to help facilitate the successful development and operation of the plant. There were numerous voluntary initiatives by private as well as government organizations to that end.

4. TMMK and Toyota Motor Corporation evidenced similar goodwill, and neither has made any kind of move that could be regarded as intrusive or as "throwing its weight around." Indeed, the opposite has been true, as TMMK and Toyota Motor Corporation have been assiduous in seeking to blend in with and be a part of central Kentucky.

5. Excellent choices were made in the selection of managers from the onset of the building and operation of TMMK.

6. TMMK's output is a high quality product, in which the workforce (95 percent Kentuckians) can and do take great pride.

7. Once the early success of the venture became apparent, success bred success.

APPENDIX

The multipliers used in this report were derived from multipliers acquired in 1991 by the Center for Business and Economic Research, Gatton College of Business and Economics, University of Kentucky, from the U.S. Department of Commerce, Regional Input-Output Modeling System II (RIMS II). Detailed sets of multipliers were obtained for the state of Kentucky, major areas within the state, and certain metropolitan areas.

The multipliers provide a means of estimating the effects that a change in a specific type of spending in a region (state or other defined area) will have on the region's total output (= total spending), earnings (= household income), and employment (= number of jobs).

The following multipliers for Kentucky were used in this paper.

	Total Output	Earnings
TMMK payroll	2.8670	1.5251
TMMK purchases	2.4724	0.5165
TMMK contractors' payroll	2.8670	1.5251
TMMK contractors' purchases	2.3593	0.7077

Jobs, per $1 million of initial spending	1993	1994	1995	1996	1997
TMMK workers' spending	21.84	20.75	19.71	18.72	17.79
TMMK purchases	17.31	16.45	15.62	14.84	14.10
TMMK contractors' payroll	13.04	12.39	11.77	11.18	10.62
TMMK contractors' purchases	29.84	28.35	26.93	25.58	24.30

The job multipliers were reduced year by year, as shown above, to reflect estimated increases in wages and salaries. The reductions were intentionally on the high side as a way of adding some conservatism to the estimates and projections of job numbers.

The RIMS II multipliers use a "spending" approach rather than a "jobs on jobs" approach to estimate employment impacts. As shown above, the multipliers are expressed in terms of the number of jobs created per $1 million of initial spending, not in terms of some number of total jobs attributable to some specific increase in employment.

The coefficients used to obtain the estimates of state tax revenues for the period 1993–2005 are as follows:

State individual income taxes attributable to TMMK = 0.034 x Earnings
State sales taxes = 0.024 x Earnings
All other state taxes = 0.005 x Total Output

8

Social Impacts of Japanese Businesses in Small Communities of Kentucky

Yukio Yotsumoto

Introduction

Japanese direct investment since the mid-1980s is partly responsible for a strong manufacturing expansion in Kentucky. In 1999 more than one hundred Japanese companies were operating in Kentucky. These companies are located mostly in small rural communities, and most are related to automobile production. Nonautomotive-related companies manufacture a variety of products such as vacuum cleaners, plastic bottles, and animal feed additives. The Japanese companies, located in thirty-nine Kentucky communities, employ about thirty-five thousand Kentuckians and a small number of Japanese expatriates.

In this chapter the social impacts of Japanese companies on small Kentucky communities are examined. As Japanese direct investment in Kentucky is expected to continue, it is important to know what kinds of changes are observed in affected communities. Specifically, the focus is on four issues: (a) interactions between local people and Japanese companies; (b) adjustment of Japanese companies and Japanese employees into communities; (c) assessment of Japanese companies' contributions to communities; and (d) determination of the impact of Japanese companies on the local environment.

For this research, five small Kentucky communities were selected: Bardstown, Berea, Danville, Harrodsburg, and Versailles. The selection is based on an assumption that the smaller the community and the larger the employment by Japanese companies in the community, the more noticeable will be

Table 8.1. Population, income, and labor force in five communities

	Population (1990)	Median household income (1989)	Labor force (1990)
Bardstown	6,801	$21,737	2,849
Berea	9,126	$21,622	4,582
Danville	12,420	$21,119	5,356
Harrodsburg	7,335	$17,363	3,105
Versailles	7,269	$27,220	3,809

Source: Kentucky Population Research, 1996.

the impact of a Japanese investment. The selected communities have a high ratio of employment in Japanese companies.

The data from the U.S. Census and publications by the state government and universities were supplemented by field research. Open-ended interviews were conducted with public officials. Also, at least one company from each community was selected for an in-depth interview. Letters requesting an interview were mailed to all Japanese companies in these communities (nineteen companies). Interviews were scheduled with companies that responded to our request first. We visited seven companies and interviewed several company executives. The interviews, conducted using a tape recorder, as well as a notebook, were open ended. At the meeting with executives, we asked them to distribute an open-ended questionnaire to Japanese employees and American employees. In total, 60 percent of Japanese employees and 80 percent of American employees completed and returned the questionnaire.

First, a brief socioeconomic profile of each community that includes historic, demographic, employment, and educational characteristics is provided. Then, we discuss the social impacts of the Japanese businesses in each community. We conclude this chapter by noting some implications for Kentucky's future.

SOCIOECONOMIC PROFILES OF FIVE KENTUCKY COMMUNITIES

Bardstown

Bardstown, thirty-two miles southeast of Louisville, is the county seat of Nelson County and the county's largest city. In 1990 Nelson County had a population of 29,710. The county's topography includes flat land to rolling hills.

The settlement in Bardstown started in 1780. People from Maryland, Pennsylvania, and Virginia came to the area developed by the Bard family.

Table 8.2. Bardstown: Population change, education, unemployment, and poverty

Population change between 1980 and 1996	+18.64%
High school completion rate for the persons 25 years and older (1990)	51.80%
Percent of people who hold associate's, bachelor's, or graduate/professional degrees (1990)	18.50%
Unemployment rate (1990)	7.05%
Poverty rate (1989)	18.00%

Source: Kentucky Cabinet for Economic Development, 1996.

Initially, the area was granted to David Bard by Governor Patrick Henry of Virginia. Bardstown became the county seat in 1784. In the early days, the city prospered by the presence of craftsmen, lawyers, educators, and political leaders. Their presence brought intellectuals and investment to the city. After the Civil War, the city's economy was based on agriculture and whiskey distilling (Kleber 1992). Bardstown is internationally known for its Bourbon whiskey production. The city capitalizes on the romance of its past and its eighteenth-century buildings to attract tourists. In Bardstown, people can shop in stores that predate the Civil War, eat lunch in a restaurant that's older than most cities, and take care of business on a courthouse square that others drive for miles to see. In Bardstown, the local people's hospitality and gentility has translated into a savvy way of courting Japanese businesses.

Estimated at 7,594 in 1996, the population of Bardstown has increased steadily. The populations for 1970, 1980, and 1990 were 5,816, 6,401, and 6,801 respectively. Between 1980 and 1996 population growth was 18.64 percent (table 8.2). Among the population in 1990, 5,493 were white and 1,235 were African Americans. Other minority groups include 23 Filipinos, 27 Japanese and 8 Koreans. In 1990 educational attainment in Bardstown was higher than the state's figures. Among persons twenty-five years and older, 29.7 percent had less than a high school education. Among persons twenty-five years and older in Kentucky, in contrast, 35.4 percent had less than a high school education. In Bardstown, 51.8 percent of persons twenty-five years and older completed high school. The state's figure was 46.9 percent. Also, 18.5 percent of persons twenty-five years and older in Bardstown had associate, bachelor's, and graduate/professional degrees. In the state, 17.7 percent of the age group had those degrees.

People of Bardstown work in various industries. The total labor force in Bardstown was 2,849 in 1990. There were 216 unemployed persons and a 7.05 percent unemployment rate. Manufacturing industry was the largest employer, with 870 persons. The second major industry was the wholesale and retail trade industry, which employed 581 persons. Professional and re-

Table 8.3. Bardstown: Number of employment in major industries, 1990

Total labor force	2,849
Manufacturing	870
Wholesale and retail trade	581
Health, education, and other professional services	560

Source: Kentucky Cabinet for Economic Development, 1996.

lated service industries, which include health, educational, and other services, employed 560 persons. Median household income in Bardstown in 1989 was $21,737, slightly lower than the state's median household income of $22,534. In 1989, 18 percent of Bardstown's population was under poverty level; this is similar to the state's figure of 19 percent. Bardstown's transportation system includes the Bluegrass Parkway, U.S. Highway 62, U.S. Highway 31 East, U.S. Highway 150, Kentucky 49, and Kentucky 245. Using the Bluegrass Parkway, Interstate 65 is twenty-three miles from Bardstown. The Louisville International Airport is thirty-seven miles from Bardstown.

Berea

Berea is the second largest city in Madison County. The county had a population of 57,508 in 1990; its county seat, Richmond, had a population of 21,183. Berea is located thirty-nine miles south of Lexington in the foothills of the Cumberland Mountains near the edge of the Bluegrass region.

Berea's history began with the establishment of Berea College. Rev. John Gregg Fee, an abolitionist, organized a church for nonslaveholders and established a school. The school became Berea College in 1858. Fee thought that the founding purpose of the college was to educate former slaves and children of poor Appalachians. As a symbol of the city, Berea College influenced the city's characteristics. At first, the proposal by Fee and his followers to establish an integrated school was postponed by an armed mob led by Richmond's anti-abolitionists. It was not until the end of the Civil War that Fee started to pursue his ideal. With his effort, interracial neighborhoods were created around the church and the school. Building houses and constructing facilities at Berea College boosted the city's economy. Berea College was an integrated school of blacks and whites, women and men. However, in 1904, the Kentucky legislature enacted the Day Law that prohibited the integrated school. Because of this law, administrators at Berea College shifted their focus to poor white Appalachians. At last, Berea College implemented reintegration in 1950. Currently, Berea College is a center of tourist attraction in the city where

Table 8.4. Berea: Population change, education, unemployment, and poverty

Population change between 1980 and 1996	+16.36%
High school completion rate for the persons 25 years and older (1990)	37.30%
Percent of people who hold associate's, bachelor's, or graduate/professional degrees (1990)	29.30%
Unemployment rate (1990)	5.93%
Poverty rate (1989)	17.35%

Source: Kentucky Cabinet for Economic Development, 1996.

crafts of Appalachian heritage are famous. Tolerance of different cultures, lack of concern for status symbols, and an earthy, environmental outlook characterize Berea. Beyond the college, craft industries, and tourism, hidden among the rolling hills on the town's edge, is a fast-growing manufacturing sector. One manufacturer after another has flocked to Berea's industrial park.

In 1996 Berea's population was estimated at 10,007. The population of this city is increasing. The populations for 1970, 1980, and 1990 were 6,956, 8,600, and 9,126 respectively. There was a 16.36 percent increase between 1980 and 1996 (table 8.4). In 1990 there were 8,640 whites, 338 African Americans, 124 Asians, and 24 persons of other races. Among the Asians, 29 were Japanese. Educational attainment in Berea was slightly higher than the state's figures. In 1990 among persons twenty-five years and older in Kentucky, 35.4 percent had less than a high school education. In Berea, 37.3 percent had completed high school. Also, 29.3 percent of persons twenty-five years and older in Berea had associate, bachelor's, or graduate/professional degrees, compared to 17.7 percent in the state.

Berea's total labor force was 4,582 in 1990, with 289 unemployed persons and a 5.93 percent unemployment rate. Service industries employed a large number of people; 1,847 persons were employed in health, education, and other areas of professional service. Manufacturing industry was the second largest employer, with 829 persons. Wholesale and retail sale trade in-

Table 8.5. Berea: Employment in major industries, 1990

Total labor force	4,582
Health, education, and other professional services	1,847
Manufacturing	829
Wholesale and retail trade	779

Source: Kentucky Cabinet for Economic Development, 1995.

dustries were the third major employer, with 779 persons. Median household income was $21,622 in 1989, lower than the median household income ($22,534) in the state. In 1989, 17.35 percent of the population was under poverty level, slightly better than the state's figure of 19 percent. Berea's transportation system is excellent. Berea includes Interstate 75 and U.S. Highway 25. Also, the Blue Grass Airport in Lexington is forty-three miles northwest of Berea.

Danville

Danville, located thirty-five miles south of Lexington, is the county seat of Boyle County. The city was founded by Walker Daniel, the first district attorney of Kentucky in 1783–84. It was incorporated in 1836. In the late eighteenth century, the legislature of Virginia decided to have a supreme court of the District of Kentucky. It was housed in the town square of Danville. In 1782, the first convention produced the first constitution of the Commonwealth of Kentucky. Danville's Centre College, a private four-year liberal arts college, offers excellent academic programs. Railroads made Danville a transportation and commercial hub. In addition, the city had steady industrial development throughout the nineteenth and twentieth centuries. During the 1960s, new industrial development occurred in the western and southern parts of the city.

Danville has an exceptional quality of life, and visitors are quick to recognize the amenities. It has assets found in few, if any, Kentucky cities its size. Local government and politics appear to be scandal free. The schools are good, and the cultural environment exceeds anything found outside Louisville or Lexington. The streets are clean and well-maintained. Growth remains moderate and orderly. Few vacant storefronts face each other across Main Street. Renovated old homes border Danville's tree-lined streets, and the town might have more porches per capita than any other city in the state.

In 1996, Danville's population was estimated at 16,059. Between 1970

Table 8.6. Danville: Population change, education, unemployment, and poverty

Population change between 1980 and 1996	+24.08%
High school completion rate for the persons 25 years and older (1990)	47.40%
Percent of people who hold associate's, bachelor's, or graduate/professional degrees (1990)	19.50%
Unemployment rate (1990)	8.60%
Poverty rate (1989)	20.00%

Source: Kentucky Cabinet for Economic Development, 1996.

Table 8.7. Danville: Employment in major industries, 1990

Total labor force	5,356
Health, education, and other professional services	1,460
Wholesale and retail trade	1,142
Manufacturing	1,139

Source: Kentucky Cabinet for Economic Development, 1995.

and 1980 the population increased, but it decreased slightly from 1980 to 1990. The populations for 1970, 1980, and 1990 were 11,542, 12,942, and 12,420 respectively. The growth rate from 1980 to 1996 was 24.08 percent. In 1990, 10,384 residents were whites and 1,939 were African Americans. Other races include 37 American Indians, 24 Japanese, 15 Samoans, 7 Koreans, and 14 persons of other minority groups. Educational attainment in Danville was slightly higher than educational attainment in the state. Among persons twenty-five years and older in Danville, 33.1 percent had less than a high school education, compared to 35.4 percent in the state. In Danville, 47.4 percent of person twenty-five years and older completed high school. The state's figure was 46.9 percent. Also, 19.5 percent of persons twenty-five years and older in Danville had associate, bachelor's, and graduate/professional degrees, compared to 17.7 percent in the state.

Danville's labor force was 5,356 in 1990, with an 8.6 percent unemployment rate. Professional and related services industry was the largest employer in Danville, followed by wholesale and retail trade, and the manufacturing industry (table 8.7). Median household income in Danville in 1989 was $21,119, lower than the state's median family income of $22,534. In 1989, 20 percent of the population was under poverty level; this is similar to the state's figure of 19 percent. Danville is served by U.S. Highways 127 and 150. The Norfolk Southern railway serves the city. The Blue Grass Airport in Lexington is thirty-eight miles north of Danville.

Harrodsburg

Harrodsburg, thirty-three miles southwest of Lexington, was Kentucky's first settlement, and "the sense of history here is almost haunting," according to the city's Mayor Walters. It was founded by James Harrod in 1774. During the early settlement of the city, settlers fought against raids by American Indians. The city had thrived as an agricultural market center since the late eighteenth century, but during the Civil War, Harrodsburg sided with Confederate forces. This position was detrimental to the city's prosperity. After 1862, when

Table 8.8. Harrodsburg: Population change, education, unemployment, and poverty

Population change between 1980 and 1996	+6.92%
High school completion rate for the persons 25 years and older (1990)	48.40%
Percent of people who hold associate's, bachelor's, or graduate/professional degrees (1990)	9.20%
Unemployment rate (1990)	9.37%
Poverty rate (1989)	23.00%

Source: Kentucky Cabinet for Economic Development, 1996.

Harrodsburg was raided by a Union force, the city was placed under federal martial law until the end of the war. After the war, it thrived again as a market center for agricultural products. During the twentieth century, Harrodsburg's economy was based more on manufacturing and tourism. Manufacturing products include glass, clothing, electrical products, and bathroom accessories. Old Fort Harrod State Park, opened in 1927, is a main attraction for tourists.

Despite its history and the townspeople's proud heritage, Harrodsburg never has and does not now exist in a vacuum. An industrial park is located on the north end of town, and more than two thousand people work in factories of one kind or another. Some of the industrial newcomers are Japanese engineers and managers at Hitachi Automotive, one of the town's largest employers. At first there was concern that the plant might cause resentment in a town that does not forget the past. Sixty-six Harrodsburg men were killed or captured by Japanese forces in the Philippines during World War II, and survivors were forced on the infamous Bataan death march. The huge Army tank that sits on a hill at the edge of town as a memorial to those men now overlooks the Hitachi factory. Japanese in Harrodsburg say that they are well accepted in the community.

In 1996 Harrodsburg's population was estimated at 7,768. The population has increased slowly. The populations for 1970, 1980, and 1990 were 6,741, 7,265, and 7,335 respectively. Between 1980 and 1996, the increase was 6.92 percent. In 1990 there were 6,618 whites and 673 African Americans. Also, there were 30 Japanese, 6 American Indians, and 8 persons of other minority groups. In 1990, among persons twenty-five years and older in Harrodsburg, 42.4 percent had less than a high school education (compared to 35.4 percent in Kentucky). Harrodsburg's rate for higher education was very low compared to the state. In fact, only 9.2 percent of persons twenty-five years and older in Harrodsburg had associate, bachelor's, and graduate/professional degrees. This was in contrast to the state's figure of 17.7 percent.

This Army tank, a memorial to the sixty-six local men who were killed or captured by Japanese forces in the Philippines during World War II, sits on a hill at the edge of Harrodsburg, Kentucky, and overlooks the town's Hitachi plant. Japanese employees say that they have been accepted into the community and that there is no resentment toward Japan in the town. (Photograph by P.P. Karan)

Harrodsburg's labor force was 3,105 in 1990 with an unemployment rate of 9.37 percent. Manufacturing industry was the largest employment sector with 857 people. The second major industry, employing 724 people, was wholesale and retail trade. The third major industry was professional and related services. Median household income in Harrodsburg was $17,363 in 1989, much lower than the state's median household income of $22,534. The poverty level in Harrodsburg was 23 percent, compared to 19 percent at the state level. Harrodsburg's transportation system includes U.S. Highways 68 and 127 and Kentucky 152. The Bluegrass Parkway is sixteen miles from the city. The nearest commercial airport is the Blue Grass Airport in Lexington, thirty-two miles northeast of Harrodsburg.

Table 8.9. Harrodsburg: Employment in major industries, 1990

Total labor force	3,105
Manufacturing	857
Wholesale and retail trade	724
Health, education, and other professional services	518

Source: Kentucky Cabinet for Economic Development, 1996.

Residents of Harrodsburg, including Mayor Carol Walters, told us they have accepted the fact that their town is changing but agree that change does not necessarily mean that nostalgia and historic preservation must disappear. Amid two-hundred-year-old buildings and farmlands lined with black fences, alongside people whose local lineage pre-dates the Civil War, Japanese engineers and workers go about their daily business—tradition and modernity coexisting amicably.

Versailles

Versailles, located thirteen miles west of Lexington, is a typical small town. People are polite and congenial. At the corner drug store fountain, residents drink coffee and solve the problems of the world. A civility in Versailles overshadows even the bickering between residents who want to protect the small-town, rural atmosphere and those who favor further residential and industrial growth.

The city was established in 1792 by Hezekiah Briscoe and his guardian, Marguis Calmes. In the early days, the city became an agricultural trading center due to surrounding rich farmlands. During the twentieth century, industrial development brought factories producing such items as electrical transformers, thermostats, and fluorescent lights.

In 1996 the estimated population was 6,882. The population increased steadily between 1970 and 1990, from 5,679 to 7,269. Among the population in 1990, 6,507 were whites, 754 were African Americans, and 8 were other minority groups. Educational attainment in Versailles was higher than the state's average. In 1990 among persons twenty-five years and older in Versailles, only 30.5 percent had less than high school education. In Versailles, 50.1 percent of the persons twenty-five years and older completed high school. Also, 19.5 percent of the persons twenty-five years and older in Versailles had

Table 8.10. Versailles: Population change, education, unemployment, and poverty

Population change between 1980 and 1996	+7.08%
High school completion rate for the persons 25 years and older (1990)	50.10%
Percent of people who hold associate's, bachelor's, or graduate/professional degrees (1990)	19.50%
Unemployment rate (1990)	3.59%
Poverty rate (1989)	9.80%

Source: Kentucky Cabinet for Economic Development, 1997.

Table 8.11.Versailles: Employment in major industries, 1990

Total labor force	3,809
Manufacturing	1,147
Wholesale and retail trade	691
Health, education, and other professional services	658

Source: Kentucky Cabinet for Economic Development, 1997.

associate, bachelor's, and graduate/professional degrees (compared to 17.7 percent in the state).

Total labor force in Versailles was 3,809 in 1990 with a 3.59 percent unemployment rate. Manufacturing industry was the biggest employer in the city. The second major industry was wholesale and retail trade industry. The third major industry was professional and related service industry. Also, there were 208 people working in agriculture. Median household income in Versailles was $27,220 in 1989. This was much higher than the state's median household income of $22,534. In 1989, in Versailles, 9.8 percent of the population was under poverty level. This was much lower than the state's level of 19 percent. Versailles transportation system includes U.S. Highways 60 and 62. The Bluegrass Parkway is accessible at three miles south of Versailles. The Blue Grass Airport is eight miles east of the city.

SOCIAL IMPACTS OF JAPANESE BUSINESSES IN THE FIVE COMMUNITIES

Bardstown

The city of Bardstown has eight Japanese manufacturing companies. Five companies came to the city in the late 1980s, and three companies arrived in the 1990s. Most of the companies are automotive-related manufacturers. In total, they employ more than fourteen hundred people. Japanese companies have made an important contribution to the growth of the manufacturing sector in the 1990s. The industrial park in the north part of the town is a mix of old and new: bourbon whiskey distilleries and Japanese automotive-related industry. The park accommodates all the town's Japanese companies except one (fig.8.1). They built the factories close together, making the park look more crowded than industrial parks in other communities we studied. The industrial park is along Kentucky 245 which connects to Interstate 65. Access to the Bluegrass Parkway is also easy from the location.

The industrial park is the site of Trim Masters, a Japanese company that makes auto seats and door trims. The plant in Bardstown produces door

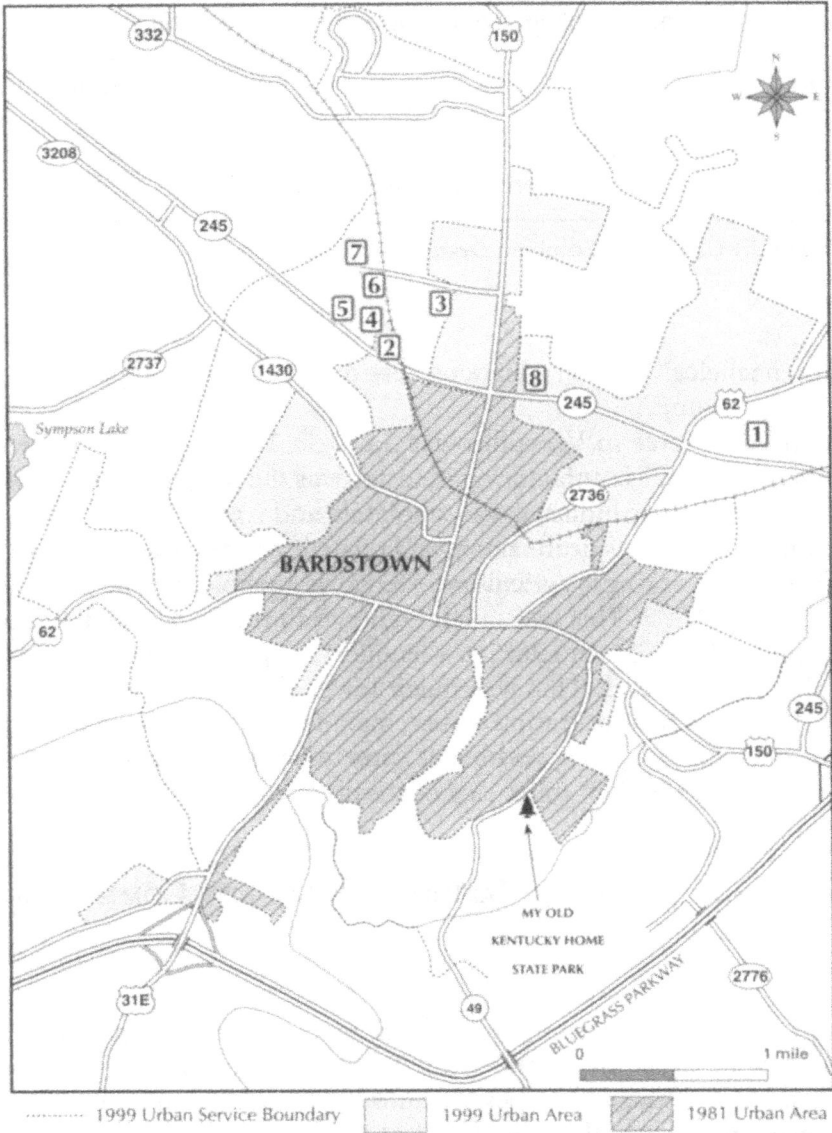

Japanese Automotive Parts Plants

1 Mabex Universal Corp.   5 Intertec Systems LLC

2 FET Engineering   6 AMB, Inc.

3 JIDECO of Bardstown, Inc.   7 Trim Masters, Inc.

4 Inoac Packaging Group   8 Sumitok Magnetics Co.

Fig. 8.1. Bardstown: Growth, 1981–1999. (*Source:* Field survey, 1999).

Trim Masters has plants in Bardstown, Nicholasville, Harrodsburg, and Leitchfield, Kentucky. The facility in Bardstown began producing automotive interior components (door trim assemblies) in 1991. The Nicholasville facility started producing complete seating along with forming and welding metal components in 1994. The Leitchfield plant, established in 1997, produces trim for car seats, and the Harrodsburg facility has been operating since 1988 and specializes in the intricate cutting and sewing of auto seat and door trim covers. Utilization of an efficient *kanban* system (just-in-time manufacturing environment) guarantees delivery of products in time to automakers. Trim Masters employs a workforce of nearly sixteen hundred at its facilities in Kentucky. (Photograph by P.P. Karan)

trims for Toyota Camry and Toyota Avalon. Trim Masters employs 283 persons including two Japanese. One Japanese is administration coordinator; the other is engineering coordinator. A general manager of the plant thinks Bardstown is a good location for the factory. The area offers a good workforce. The company looks for people who are inexperienced in manufacturing. They do not need highly trained people. They need people who can learn a new style of manufacturing through in-house training. As a parts supplier to Toyota, Trim Masters uses the Toyota style of manufacturing which emphasizes quality and flexibility. The company trains employees; therefore, they do not want experienced workers who obtained a different style of production training (e.g., Fordist production system). The Bardstown area offers workers who are very motivated. It has excellent accessibility to I-65 and the Bluegrass Parkway. The company usually ships its auto parts twenty times a day under the just-in-time production system. Easy access to transportation systems is a critical factor for the factory's location decision.

The relationship between the Japanese factory and the city has been very good. The city has been supportive of Japanese companies and Japanese investment. The city initially prepared for industrial development by creating an industrial development corporation. The industrial development corporation, which was not organized specifically to target Japanese companies, planned for infrastructures such as land, water, sewer, electrical capacity, and roads. As the city made its preparations, an industrial development specialist had contact with Japanese manufacturing companies. Before the specialist came to Bardstown, he had worked for the state government to bring Toyota to Kentucky. Eventually, the Toyota investment spun off to Bardstown by bringing Japanese auto parts companies. The first Japanese company to move into Bardstown was welcomed by the community. During construction of the factory, Japanese personnel needed an office. As the first foreign company in the town, they did not know where to stay. City officials were aware of the situation. So, they offered office space in the city hall to the Japanese personnel for several months until the factory was built. The city officials and the Japanese personnel had barbecue luncheons and other parties during their stay in the city hall. This example shows how much the city government tries to assimilate Japanese into the community.

More than half of Bardstown's employment in the manufacturing sector is from Japanese companies. Some of them are expanding their production as well as employment and facility. A public official estimates that one additional employment of Japanese company has created two or three spin-off jobs. Retail trade and service industries have expanded as a result of the growing manufacturing sector. The city is expecting to have more economic growth. It has started to build two additional industrial parks. New roads and improvement to existing roads are proposed for the further development of the city.

It seems that the growth of the city (fig. 8.1) outweighs the negative impacts of the development. Citizens expressed two concerns. One is traffic congestion. Many citizens complain about the traffic. They have to wait for two or three minutes at a traffic light. This is not an issue for people living in large cities. However, Bardstown was a small rural community. People in Bardstown do not like even this level of traffic congestion. The city needs to have a plan to improve roads and ease traffic flow. Another concern for the community is that too much dependence on automotive-related industry might harm the community in the future. This concern is raised whether they are Japanese, American, or German companies. A public official was concerned that when the automotive industry declines, the community also will decline. Thus, the community's fate will depend on Toyota Motor Manufacturing, Kentucky, in Georgetown. It is a loss of community control (Nash 1987; Hummon 1990). Although the city is supportive of those automotive-related companies in Bardstown, the city wants to have a more diversified economy for sustainable growth.

Environmental problems have not been an issue in this community. The Japanese companies in the community are not generating environmentally hazardous materials in the production processes. This is due to a deliberate planning of Nelson County where Bardstown is located. The county has a strict requirement of what companies can produce in the county. For example, every company has to have a pretreatment program. Before the company discharges wastewater into the sewer, the government needs to know what it is discharging. Anything that the city's sewer plant cannot handle must be shipped outside the county where it can be treated. The same things apply to landfills. The county does not have a site for hazardous landfills. If a company produces a hazardous waste, it has to ship it away. Therefore, a company that produces hazardous wastes is not likely to come to Nelson County. It is costly for the company to transport the hazardous wastes. Although the county is good about preventing environmental problems, the citizens also are conscious about the issue. A company once wanted to build a facility for nickel plates in the county. It involves a toxic process. Because of the danger, the company met much opposition from the citizens and eventually decided to locate in another community. Companies are also working to be environmentally friendly. They try to exceed the requirements of environmental regulations. At Trim Masters, everything that can be recycled is recycled. For example, cardboard used in packing goes to Louisville for recycling. Excess vinyl produced in the manufacturing process goes to Louisville and is then shipped to Germany. Wood mats used in the factory are burned for fuel elsewhere in Kentucky. The facility is also environmentally friendly for employees.

Community is meaningful for these Japanese companies. They want to be community members. Effort to be environmentally friendly is one example. The companies are active in community participation. At Trim Masters, contribution to the United Way is a major community activity. The companies also participate in a Red Cross blood drive and other activities. When employees form a sport team and ask for sponsorship, the company is willing to support it. Executives of the Japanese companies are actively involved in the local Chamber of Commerce. For example, a Japanese executive was instrumental in bringing higher education to Bardstown. As a result, St. Catherine's College set up a branch campus in Bardstown. In order to obtain good workers, Japanese executives are interested in higher education in the area.

The Japanese employees of Trim Masters do not have much time to socialize with Americans outside work. They usually work late. So, they have only a few occasions in which they have parties with American coworkers and their families. Japanese in Bardstown experience interactions with mainstream America through school activities when Japanese employees' children are in school. Japanese children and wives have more interaction with Americans. So, there are two types of interaction between Japanese and Americans. One is the interaction between Japanese workers and American workers. This type is mostly limited to company functions. The other is the interaction at school between American parents and Japanese mothers of children attending schools.

Bardstown has changed from a quiet small town to a dynamic community. The change has been rapid. A housing boom has occurred. There are many employment opportunities that were not previously possible. At one time, when someone wanted to advance or improve his or her life, he or she had to leave the community. Now, he or she has opportunities to advance in Bardstown. Furthermore, people in Bardstown can feel the international community even though it is very small. Before the Japanese investment, many people in Bardstown had no chance to meet people from other countries. They did not have any problems in communication. However, they realized that there are different people. This is a very good educational situation in which people learn diversity. Therefore, Bardstown has become a different community from the community of twenty years ago.

Berea

Berea has four Japanese companies. All the companies are related to the automotive industry. They are located in an industrial park, in the north part of the city (fig. 8.2). The industrial park is very close to Interstate 75. The park is on a rural setting like other communities we studied. It is on an open space.

Matsushita Electric Motor Corporation of America (MEMA) was built in the industrial park in 1995. It employs two hundred Americans and five Japanese. The company started production in 1996. It is an investment of more than $27 million. It produces electric motors for vacuum cleaners, automobile anti-lock braking systems, and power window systems. Since its inception, the company has grown steadily. It reached 72 employees by the end of 1996, 140 by the end of 1997. This company is a part of Matsushita Group. It is a sister company of Matsushita Home Appliance Corporation of America in Danville. MEMA supplies blower motors to Matsushita in Danville for vacuum cleaners. The proximity is convenient for delivery. MEMA also supplies products to auto parts companies. It is a second-tier supplier company. It supplies to Sumitomo in Cincinnati, Ohio, and Ohi America in Frankfort, Kentucky. Then, those companies supply to automakers like Toyota. The locational advantage of transportation is a primary reason for MEMA to choose Berea. Also, the area offers a good stable labor force. The turnover rate of the company is only 2 percent per year. MEMA mainly draws employees from Madison County, which includes Richmond and Berea, and Rockcastle County, south of Madison County. Madison County was instrumental to location of the facility in Berea. The local government has been eager to attract manufacturing companies. It brings more jobs and tax rev-

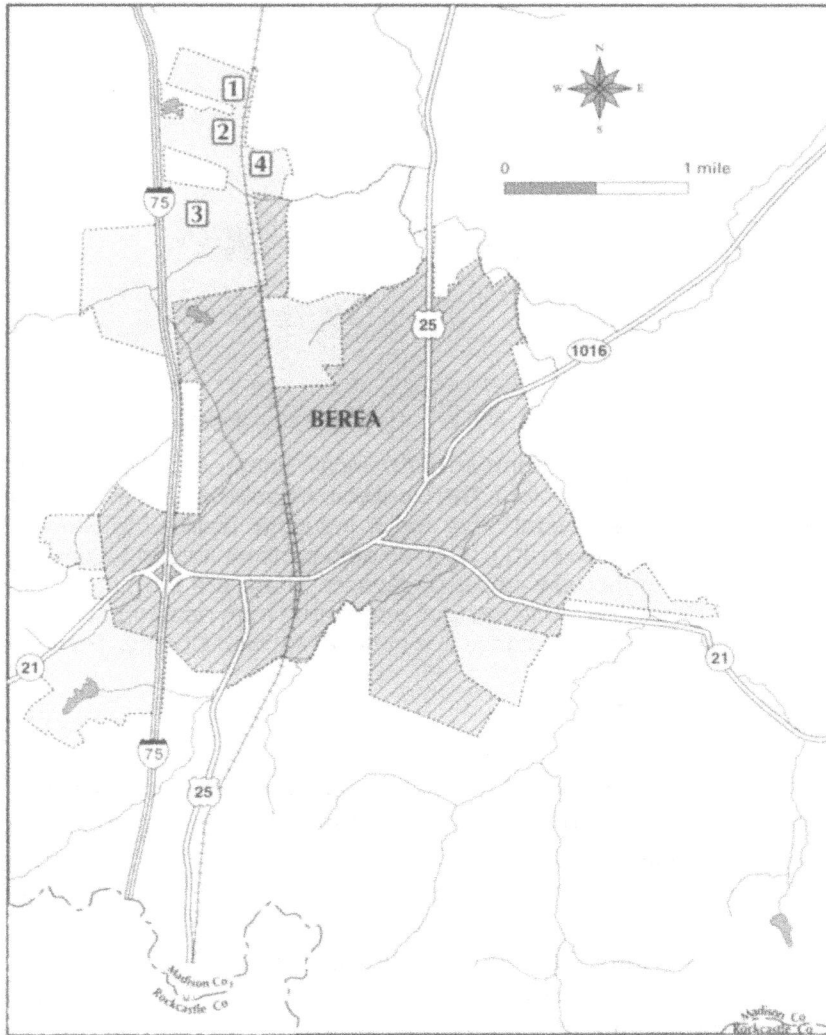

Fig. 8.2. Berea: Growth, 1981–1999. (*Source:* Field survey, 1999).

Matsushita Electric Motor Corporation of America's Panasonic plant in Berea, Kentucky, makes small electric motors. The plant was established in 1995 and employs 160 persons. There are several other major industrial facilities in Berea. Tokico, which makes shock absorbers; KI (USA), an auto parts maker; and Alcan Ingot and Recycling are among the new industrial recruits. There are far more factory jobs than workers in Berea, so the plants pull employees from nearby counties. Nearly half of the workers at Berea factories live outside Madison County. (Photograph by P.P. Karan)

enues. The company has a good relationship with the local government. However, MEMA has more interaction with community agencies in the county. It is actively involved in United Way, a local personnel association, and the Chamber of Commerce. The community is supportive of the business. Thus, MEMA feels comfortable in Berea.

Matsushita group has a worldwide company philosophy that emphasizes the localization of the companies and contribution to communities. Executives in MEMA think the company is the American company and a part of the community. Based on this idea, MEMA has specific goals to contribute to the community. Its goal for United Way in 1999 was to increase a contribution by 11 percent. Last year, MEMA made the fourth largest contribution in Madison County though it is one of the smaller companies in the area. Besides the monetary contribution, MEMA participates in United Way activities. For example, employees participate in a bowling activity and become big brothers and sisters. Another focus of MEMA is fire protection. The company supports and contributes to the local fire department. It includes a support in which schoolchildren are taught fire protection. Many employees are from this area; therefore, contribution to the community means improving employees' well-being.

Although many American employees are from this area, all five Japanese employees live in other cities. One single man lives in Richmond, about fourteen miles north of the city. The other four employees live in Lexington, thirty-nine miles north of the city. A main reason that they do not live in Berea is a lack of educational opportunities. The four employees who live in Lexington came to Kentucky with families. Because they have to go back to Japan several years later, their concern is how they can help their children's education so that the children will not fall behind a Japanese educational standard. They have to prepare for highly competitive university/college entrance exams in Japan. Lexington has a Japanese Saturday school and good junior high and high schools. Commuters to Berea, the Japanese employees do not have much interaction with local Americans except in job-related matters.

MEMA is striving to be a role model in environmental protection. All employees wear a name tag, and a small copy of an environmental policy statement is attached to the tag. So, employees are always reminded of environmental issues. A manual hangs on a wall or is attached to a machine in each section of the work process. The manual is about how to process waste products properly or where to bring them for recycling. Waste metal pieces such as copper, aluminum, and brass, are generated in the processes of production. All of these metals, even tiny pieces, are recycled. They have separate containers for these wastes. Used oil is processed in the factory so that it is used again. MEMA generates waste plastic which is given free to another company which uses it for making other products. Also, the company does not have any drainage to the local sewer. All wastes are recycled or shipped to other places outside the county. Chemical is kept in a special room. The room is designed to be lower than the ground level so that if chemicals spill accidentally, they will not spill over to other areas. The floor consists of special concrete so that spilled chemicals do not penetrate into the soil below. To stock chemicals, they once used a barrel. However, after using the barrel, it became a waste. They thought they can do something about it. So, the company developed a tank in which chemicals are kept and refilled. Also, they do not use paper towels. Instead, they use rugs. They are washed after use. Cardboard is collected and recycled. A truck comes to the factory and picks up the pressed cardboard. These examples show that the company tries to reduce waste as much as possible. In every corner of the factory, there are signs of ideas and efforts to reduce waste materials and increase recycling.

MEMA has three numerical targets for environmental objectives: (1) to reduce solid waste by 6 percent each year, (2) to increase recycling by 5 percent per year, and (3) to reduce hazardous waste by 5 percent annually. A safety/environmental specialist is employed to achieve these targets. In January 1999, the company finished a pre-audit for ISO 14001. ISO 14001 is an international standard concerned with environmental management. The standard asks the company not only to comply with environmental regulations, but also to work on pollution prevention and continual improvement. If a company gets ISO 14001 certification, it means the company has substantial commitment to environmental protection (Ricca 1996). MEMA was expecting to get a final audit for the certification in 1999.

The Japanese companies in Berea try to create a positive image in the community. Tokiko (USA) is the largest Japanese company (employment of 564) in Berea. On the company's signboard, besides the name, ISO 9000 certification is noted. This is another international standard which deals with a quality management system. When a company is certified with ISO 9000, it means that the company produces a quality product. In the United States, more than eight thousand companies have been certified with ISO 9000. Again, this sign is also on the wall of the factory with the company name. By showing the certification, the Japanese company tries to present a positive image in the community.

Danville

Danville has three Japanese companies located in an industrial park close to the downtown (fig. 8.3). Danville has many American companies such as R.R. Donnelley and Sons Company and Phillips Lighting Company. However, the presence of Japanese companies is important in the city. In 1990 there were 1,139 people employed by all manufacturing companies including American and Japanese. Now, Japanese companies employ 2,601 people.

Matsushita Home Appliance Corporation of America employs 1,700 people. This is the biggest employer in Boyle County where Danville is located. It produces vacuum cleaners and microwave ovens under the brand names of Panasonic and OEM. It is the largest producer of vacuum cleaners and microwave ovens in North America. The products are exported to the Middle East, Africa, and Australia. Matsushita initially entered a joint venture with a vacuum cleaner division of Whirlpool Company. In 1990 Matsushita obtained 100 percent share of the company. Thus, locational consideration was not so important for Matsushita being in Danville. However, a Matsushita executive says that Danville has a good labor force. People in this area do not move as easily as people in Los Angeles and New York. Stability is important for operating factories. A relatively safe environment and beautiful landscape are attractive to Japanese people working here. Safety is one primary concern for Japanese. Although Danville is attractive, most Japanese choose to live in Lexington, thirty-eight miles northeast of the city. They commute to Danville every day. For single Japanese, Danville does not offer anything for fun. Also it is a dry county. Usually Japanese workers like to go to bars after work, but the city does not offer this opportunity. Japanese families like to stay in Lexington, which offers better schools and cultural events and Japanese Saturday school. Since they go back to Japan after several years of

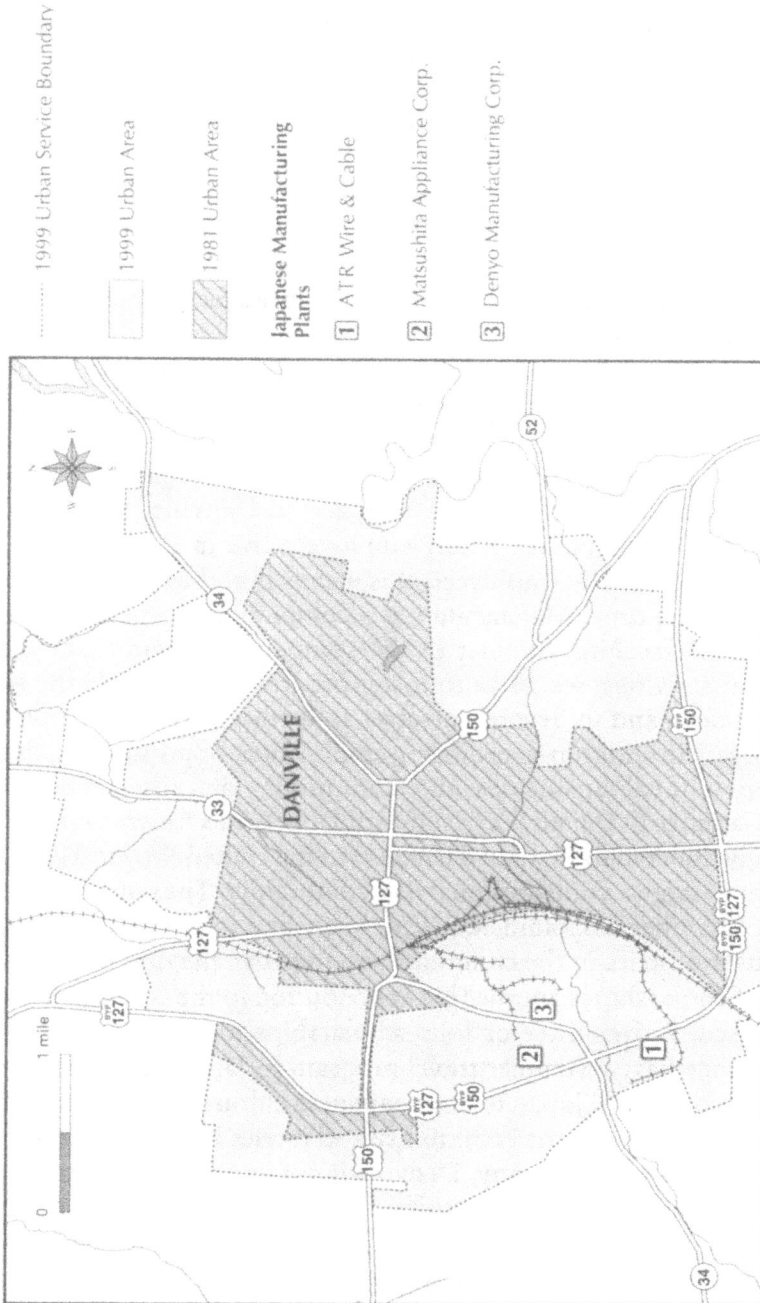

Fig. 8.3. Danville: Growth, 1981–1999. (*Source:* Field survey, 1999).

assignment, their life plan is targeted for how well they can adjust their life in Japan after completing the assignment in the United States (Kanjanapan 1995). The Saturday school is important to keep up with a Japanese educational standard. Also, Lexington is convenient for Japanese wives. There are Japanese grocery stores and Japanese restaurants. Availability of Japanese foods is another important factor to stay in Lexington (Hill, Indegaard, Fujita 1989). For a place to live, Danville does not offer things Japanese need. However, it is a good place to do business. The interaction between local and state governments and Japanese companies is smooth. They cooperate with each other. They have not had any problems that have not been settled. When the companies ask for something, local and state governments are quick to respond. For example, as the economy has grown rapidly in the area, the companies face difficulty in obtaining good workers. The unemployment rate has been too low, and it is difficult to attract workers. When they complained to the state government about this situation, the government was quick to respond. However, what to do to solve the problem of a low unemployment rate is another matter.

Contribution to the community is important for Japanese companies, especially Matsushita. As the largest company in Danville, the company is very visible in the community. Many employees live in Danville. So, if the company thinks about the employees, this means that they think about community at the same time. Matsushita has a company philosophy established by Konosuke Matsushita, founder of the company. He said that "through our industrial activities, we strive to foster progress, to promote the general welfare of society, and to devote ourselves to furthering the development of world cultures." In addition to providing employment opportunities, the company supports local businesses and community activities. Specifically, Matsushita is active in United Way, March of Dimes, and American Red Cross. The company donated more than $100,000 to the United Way in 1999, and it was the second largest contribution in the community. The company is active in the local Chamber of Commerce. They sponsor a job-training consortium with various industries in the community to improve the quality of the local labor force. Scholarship is another big contribution to the community. Annually, the company gives three or four scholarships to local high school students. Also, they have a summer travel program to Japan. They select young people and send them to Japan to learn Japanese culture. Overall, Matsushita wants to be welcomed by the community and it tries hard to achieve this.

Another Japanese company, Denyo Manufacturing Corporation is located across the street from Matsushita. Denyo is a small company employing only 41 people. Among those, 5 are Japanese and 36 are Americans. They make generators, compressors, and welders for industrial use. The plant was established in 1995. The company came to Kentucky for several reasons. The most important reason is an appreciation of the yen. Denyo had exported products to the United States for many years. However, an appreciation of the yen in the late 1980s made export costly. Then, an American company selling Denyo products in the United States asked Denyo to manufacture products in the United States. Also, Kentucky's representative office in Japan was aggressive in attracting Denyo to Kentucky. An incentives package was an additional factor in locating in Kentucky (Yanarella 1990). Other factors often mentioned in interviews were good labor force in the area and good location to do business. So far, the company is content with the location.

As a small manufacturing company, Denyo does not have many community services. When there is a request for donation, they consider participating. However, overall, the company is too small to have a large budget to contribute to the community. The company is in an early stage of establishment and is still focused on building a foundation. The company spends its energy to train employees and to develop middle management. It is essential for the company to satisfy the employees first. They try to avoid over-presence in the community.

Many Japanese in Danville do not have interaction with Americans except in work settings. Japanese meet with Americans at parties organized as company functions. However, since most of the Japanese do not live in Danville, other interactions at schools and neighborhoods are limited.

Both Matsushita and Denyo are concerned about environmental protection. Denyo follows Environmental Protection Agency and Occupational Safety and Health Administration guidelines. The company has hired a special maintenance company to follow the requirements of environmental protection. There has been no incident of environmental problems. Matsushita is also conscious and proactive to tackle the environmental issue. Matsushita wants to be an excellent company in environmental protection. On the walls of the factory floor and office, there are two policy statements. One is a quality policy statement, and the other is an environmental policy statement. The environmental policy statement reads "Our Environment is Our Future." Based on this policy statement, the whole company is working to excel in this area. The company got a certificate for ISO 14001 in 1999. It is a symbol of the company's effort and pride for environmental protection. Japanese companies in Danville are considered friendly to the environment.

Harrodsburg

The city of Harrodsburg has two Japanese manufacturing companies (fig. 8.4). Both companies are suppliers to automobile manufacturers. They employ more than 1,700 people. The employment in the Japanese companies suggests an important contribution of the Japanese investment to the community. Hitachi Automotive Products (USA), established in 1985, was one of the earliest Japanese companies to locate in the small communities of Ken-

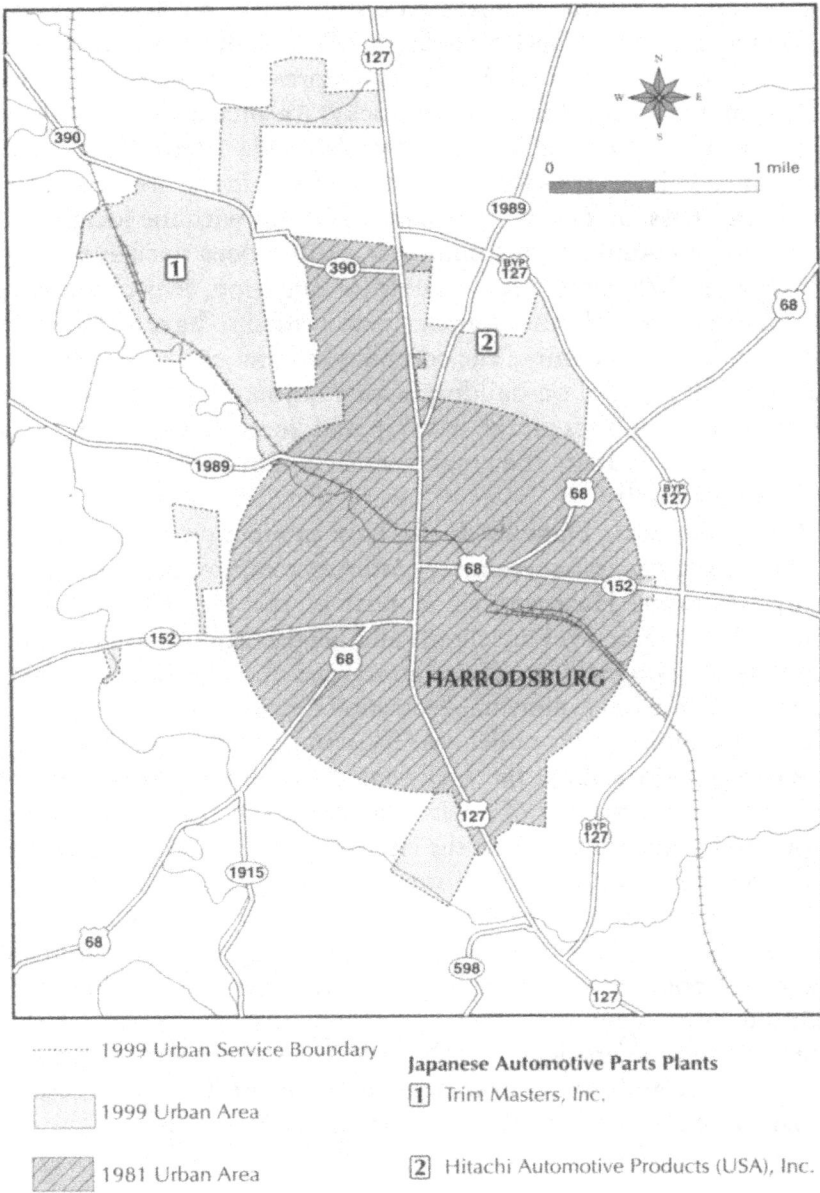

Fig. 8.4. Harrodsburg: Growth, 1981–1999. (*Source:* Field survey, 1999)

tucky. The company is proud of being one of the earliest Japanese manufacturing companies to choose Kentucky, even earlier than Toyota in Georgetown. The company employs 980 people. Among those, 949 are Americans and 31 are Japanese. Electronic devices, alternators, and starter motors for automobiles are its products. Its facility is located in the north end of the city, an annexed industrial zone. In front of the facility is a well-maintained garden. It looks clean and does not create an image of pollutant. Cleanness is one of the company's efforts to show a good corporate citizenship in the city. A public official in Harrodsburg attests that the Japanese companies keep things very clean. The effort is appreciated by local public officials.

Several changes occurred in the community after the arrival of Japanese companies. The most visible change in the community is its economic base. Manufacturing industry became an indispensable economic base for the city. It has created many jobs for the community. A public official perceives this change as positive and as fortunate for being able to bring these Japanese factories. Another visible change in the community is a presence of Japanese. When the Japanese companies came, they brought Japanese families, too. According to a public official, in 1996, ninety-four Japanese families lived in the city—7 percent of the population. Americans have more chance to meet Japanese in the community compared to two decades ago. Americans meet with Japanese at shops, in restaurants, at schools, and in neighborhoods.

The city is eager to accommodate Japanese and their companies as a part of the community. For example, the city asked a grocery store to stock Japanese foods. Also, the city has a language program in which local teachers teach English to Japanese. Sometimes, this program involves one-to-one tutoring. It is a good program to build a personal relationship between Americans and Japanese. Thus, the city tries to assimilate Japanese into the community by finding and meeting the needs of the Japanese family. Cultural diversity is appreciated in the community. The cultural difference is a good thing because the community can learn something from the difference. The ties between Japan and Kentucky are getting stronger as the Japanese direct investment in Kentucky increases.

For Japanese, they are working hard to assimilate themselves into the community. Before the companies sent them to Kentucky, they learned basic English skills and American culture. Also, Hitachi, conscious about a negative image of an enclave, has a philosophy that discourages Japanese employees from living in one place. So, the Japanese employees follow the company philosophy by scattering around several subdivisions in Harrodsburg. In their neighborhoods, they also work hard to be good citizens.

The Japanese companies actively participate in community activities. As a foreign company, being a good corporate citizen is important so that they can be successful in the United States (Besser 1996). Therefore, they make

more effort on being a part of the community than American corporations.
The Japanese company's strenuous effort to be a part of the community has a
positive impact on the city of Harrodsburg. Comparing the Japanese companies to American companies, a public official says that the Japanese companies are more giving and always available for help. They always come forward
before the city asks for help. On the other hand, in the case of some American
corporations in Harrodsburg, when needs arise, the city has to ask them. So,
as for community service, the Japanese corporations are proactive and American corporations are reactive.

Hitachi became a part of the community through public relations efforts. In 1998, 174 Hitachi employees participated in community services. It
was 3,136 hours of community service. The company encourages the employees to participate in community activities. The company contributes to
the community in five areas. They are public education, health and welfare,
charities, environment, and community activities. In the field of public education, employees work on Teacher Exchange Program, Classroom Visits,
Head Start, Junior Achievement and Adult Literacy. The first two are designed to understand different cultures, especially the Japanese culture. In the
field of health and welfare, they participate in Disaster and Emergency Relief,
Red Cross blood drives, Family Resource Centers, and Senior Citizen Projects.
In charities, they donate to American Cancer Society, March of Dimes, and
United Way. As an environmentally conscious corporation, Hitachi is involved
in recycling projects, soil conservation, landscaping projects, and city- beau-
tification projects. This effort on environment is noticed by the community.
In community activities, employees are members of the Chamber of Commerce and Youth Baseball and Soccer Leagues. Their recent pride in community service is a donation of a park shelter in a local park. To avoid conflict,
Hitachi does not participate in political, religious, and labor activities. It also
avoids participation in endowment funds.

A potential negative change of environmental degradation is not an issue in this community. For example, Hitachi is aware of environmental issues
and has a department to deal with environmental issues. The company tries
to surpass the requirements of federal and state regulations. As a result, the
company received an award from the governor of Kentucky. It has received
ISO 14001 certification.

In locating in Harrodsburg, Hitachi is happy with the beautiful rural
landscape, relative safety, climate, and work ethic of the people. Next to the
city of Harrodsburg is Shaker Village of Pleasant Hill. It is a restored Shaker
community with thirty buildings and twenty-seven hundred acres of gently
rolling countryside. Besides the beauty, Harrodsburg is a safe place to live
compared to large cities. This is important for Japanese, who are used to
living in the safe environment of Japan. In 1992 the total crime rate in Mercer
County, where Harrodsburg is located, was 140.0 per 10,000. The violent

crime rate for the county was 45.1 per 10,000. In contrast, the total crime rate in Jefferson County, where Louisville is located, was 523.8 per 10,000. The violent crime rate in the county was 75.4 per 10,000 (Kentucky Cabinet for Economic Development 1995). Thus, Harrodsburg offers a safe place to live. A good climate is also important for Hitachi. Hitachi, as a supplier of automobile parts, practices the just-in-time production system. This system requires suppliers to ship auto parts when auto assemblers need parts. Under this production system, the suppliers have to ship their products several times a day. The auto parts have to arrive just in time for assembly (Kenny and Florida 1993). They can send products to customers in Ohio and Tennessee by truck without delay. A Hitachi executive said that people in this area can come to work early and do not mind working late. This is closer to the Japanese work ethic. The company also knows these people are less likely to form a labor union.

Hitachi perceives two problems with locating in Harrodsburg. The first problem is specific to Harrodsburg. It is a housing problem. Usually a small rural community like Harrodsburg does not have houses available for rent. Instead of renting, most of the residents own houses. However, when Japanese families come to Harrodsburg from Japan, they want to rent a house or an apartment because they will probably go back to Japan after several years. The limited options for choosing rental housing is a big problem for Japanese employees at Hitachi. Another more general problem applies to Kentucky. It is a short supply of engineers and technicians in the area. There are not many college-educated people majored in engineering in the area. Many college-educated people do not stay in rural communities. They want to move to large cities. So, Hitachi is working hard to recruit these workers through advertising in newspapers and on the Internet and using the placement center at the University of Kentucky. The company also participates in job fairs and uses a headhunter. Kentucky's economy is too strong and the unemployment rate is too low to have a pool of good workers. Thus, companies in the area steal employees from each other. A company that pays the highest salary gets the best workers. Both the state government and manufacturing companies in Kentucky perceive this as a problem. For example, the state government has recently emphasized technical schools to create workers that match the state economy. However, solving the problem is not easy and takes time.

Japanese companies in Harrodsburg are adjusting well to the community. It is a collaborative effort by both the city and the companies. Since the city's economy is increasingly dependent on the Japanese companies, the city tries to meet the needs of Japanese through many programs. The Japanese and Japanese companies are also working hard to be part of the community through participation in community activities. The companies make conscious efforts to maintain good reputations within the community.

Versailles

Two Japanese companies are located in Versailles. They are in an industrial park on the north side of the city (fig.8.5). They employ approximately 900 people. In total, Versailles's manufacturing sector employed 1,147 people in 1990. These figures infer that the Japanese companies are important employers in the city. One company, Y H America, produces automotive air conditioning and power steering hoses. The company employs 330 people, including 6 Japanese. The company was established in 1989. Before that time, the company was a joint venture with an American company. Y H America came to Kentucky for two reasons. First, it was a convenient location for the company to supply the products to customers. This area (I-65/I-75) is called an automotive corridor (Perrucci 1994a, 1994b). It consists of Michigan, Indiana, Ohio, Kentucky, and Tennessee. Automotive suppliers like to locate plants along this corridor so that they can take advantage of regional agglomeration (Klier 1998). Second, company officials thought the lower wages of Kentucky would help contain labor costs. Also, people's work ethic is important. A Y H America executive thinks the employees have a work ethic closer to that of the Japanese than do people in other areas. Many employees work hard for the company, and they understand and support the nonunion status of the company.

A Y H America Japanese executive views Versailles as a good community to locate the facility. Vice presidents of Y H America who are Americans usually deal with the local government on issues such as tax and environmental regulations. There has been a cooperative relationship between the company and local government officials. When the company built an additional facility, the local government officials came and gave a speech at a ceremony. The president, who is Japanese, does not deal with the local government directly. It is a job for American executives. The company wants to melt into American society. Although the capital is Japanese, they consider themselves as an American company. They want to be a genuine American company. Therefore, their management style is that Japanese employees do not work in the front stage. They work from behind the scene. This division of labor works for building a good relationship with the local governments.

This company does not have any programs to help Japanese employees settle into the community. They use informal networks to help newcomers from Japan. The old Japanese tell newcomers where to look for Japanese groceries and restaurants. As a rule, the company asks Japanese employees to come to Kentucky alone for the first three months. After the employee settles down, he brings his family to Kentucky. This is one way that the company deals with settlement problems. Also, while in Japan, once they have been selected to come to Kentucky, they have an opportunity to attend an English language school at company's expense. All of the Japanese employees live in Lexington. The city of Lexington has five Japanese restaurants and two Japa-

Y H America plant, Versailles, established in 1989, makes auto air conditioning parts. The plant is located in the industrial park along the bypass which is growing ever more crowded with fast food outlets and stoplights. Many of the factory workers commute from Lexington or Frankfort to Versailles. The city's tranquillity, livability, and accessibility to other areas make it an attractive site for industrial location. (Photograph by P.P. Karan)

nese grocery stores. A Japanese Saturday school is also in Lexington. Since they live in Lexington, there are not many interactions with Americans living in Versailles. The interactions are limited to the company functions.

As a second-tier auto parts manufacturer, Y H America possesses a different characteristic from a large Japanese corporation. It is not active in community activities. Except providing employment and tax, it does not have a major program to contribute to the community. It has only nominal participation in community service. For example, the company once donated small amounts of money to a college. Also, the company has an annual picnic in its facility for employees. Although most of the participants are employees, the picnic is open to the public. The size of the company might have some influence on its passive action on community service. Versailles has several manufacturing companies that are bigger than Y H America. The other Japanese company in Versailles, United L-N Glass, is bigger than Y H America. This position puts Y H America to be a minor actor in the community. Since the company is not so visible in the community, it does not need to spend much time and money on creating a good public image in the community. Therefore, its priority for participation in community is low. Another reason might be that all Japanese employees live in Lexington so that they don't see Versailles as their own community. Also, its profit goes to employees first. Although the company keeps its wages at the prevailing level in the area, the competition to recruit a good worker makes it necessary to consider employees first. Disclosure of company's profit information and profit sharing to the employees are

Fig. 8.5. Versailles: Growth, 1981–1999. (*Source:* Field survey, 1999).

important company policy to build a good relationship between the company and employees. This company's interaction with the community is limited to employees living there.

As for environmental issues, the company meets the environmental regulations. For ten years' operation in Versailles, the company has had no incident of environmental problems. However, it is not pursuing excellence in this field. Currently, it is not interested in obtaining a certification of ISO 14001. Since getting the certification requires a rigorous commitment by a company in terms of time and money, it is hard for a company of this size.

Japanese companies in Versailles try to adapt to American ways of business. Y H America's management focuses on Americanization of the company. Japanese employees work behind the scenes. This management style reflects in the relationship with the community. The company does not show "Japaneseness." The company wants to melt into the American community. Therefore, it is not interested in introducing Japanese culture to the community. It wants to be a genuine American company. Adaptation to American culture is also seen in the United L-N Glass facility. The facility is built on a spacious lawn. A black fence with a brick gate surrounds it. This is a traditional style of horse farms. Horse farms in Woodford County, where Versailles is located, represent a landscape of this area. The company's effort to be a part of the community is seen in the facility. To become the American company is a theme for these Japanese companies.

The Japanese companies contribute to the development of the city. A rapid development has occurred in this area, and unemployment rate has declined. Since the development has decreased the unemployment rate, attracting and keeping good workers is becoming more difficult for the companies. The rapid growth in the community is partly due to the Japanese companies. The population in the community is changing. For example, some American employees came to Woodford County from other places to work for the Japanese company. Now, there are many opportunities in this area. The Japanese companies have affected the growth of economy and population change in Versailles.

CONCLUSION

In Kentucky, there are more than one hundred Japanese companies. Most of them are located in small communities. More than 70 percent of them are automotive-related companies. As a result of Japanese factories, many small communities of Kentucky have grown rapidly. The companies offer employment to local people. They also bring diversity. Although mostly limited to work situations, now, many Americans have a chance to interact with Japanese, whose culture is very different. Many schoolchildren have opportunities to learn Japanese culture. Activities of cultural exchange are held in schools. Before the Japanese companies moved in, when a person wanted to advance, he or she had to leave the community. Now, people can advance in their own communities. The communities even attract people from other states as top and middle management personnel. Japanese companies are embraced by the local communities. The local governments make special efforts to understand and to work with Japanese companies. They help Japanese assimilate to the communities. People also welcome Japanese companies (Fujita and Hill 1995). However, the companies are welcomed not because they are Japanese, but because they can provide good jobs to the communities. So, for the local people, it does not matter whether it is Japanese, American, or German as long as the company can offer a good job.

Executives in Japanese companies think community is important. Therefore, they are concerned with contribution to community and with environmental protection. However, it seems that whether they take action for the issues depends on the size of the company. Although there are exceptions, smaller companies tend not to have many programs to contribute to the communities. On the other hand, bigger companies are active in contributing to the communities. They are proud of how much they can contribute to the communities. Those companies want to be good corporate citizens. In environmental issues, Japanese companies do not have any problems with pollution. However, with some exceptions, smaller companies tend just to abide by the federal and state environmental regulations. Bigger companies tend to be proactive in environmental issues. They challenge themselves to increase recycling and to decrease waste. Many companies pursue a certificate of ISO 14001 so that they can be seen as environmentally friendly. These examples show that projecting an image of excellence for community is important for large Japanese corporations. They want to be visible in the community. In order to project this image, they work hard for community participation and environmental protection. Also, they bring good things from Japanese and American cultures. They do not hesitate to spend money to achieve this. Small Japanese companies do not have resources to project an image of excellence for community. Therefore, they try to be invisible in the community.

From the point of view of Japanese managers and employees, these small communities offer safety (low crime) and provide good workers. However, these communities do not have educational opportunities for Japanese children. They also do not have places to buy authentic Japanese foods. Therefore, it is important that the communities are close to bigger cities like Lexington and Louisville, where employees can enroll their children in Japanese Saturday schools and go to Japanese restaurants and groceries. One major problem the companies face is how to obtain good workers. As a result of rapid growth, now, unemployment rate in the area is too low to get good workers. Specifically, the companies have difficulty getting engineers. There are simply not many engineers in the area. Therefore, this research suggests that if the Commonwealth of Kentucky wants to attract more manufacturing companies to the area, it has to consider producing more engineers and scientists and improve people's education in general through the secondary education so that there will be more skilled workers. Also, maintaining and improving a Japanese Saturday school is critical. For Japanese parents, children's education is more important than American parents might think.

ACKNOWLEDGEMENT

The author is indebted to Dr. P.P. Karan for his tremendous support on this project.

REFERENCES

Besser, Terry L. 1996. *Team Toyota: Transplanting the Toyota Culture to the Camry Plant in Kentucky.* New York: State Univ. of New York Press.

Fujita, Kuniko, and Richard C. Hill. 1995. Global Toyotaism and Local Development. *International Journal of Urban and Regional Research.* 19(1):7–22.

Hill, Richard, Michael Indegaard, and Kuniko Fujita. 1989. Flat Rock, Home of Mazda: The Social Impact of a Japanese Company on an American Community. In *the Auto Industry Ahead: Who's Driving?* Edited by Peter Arnesan. Ann Arbor: University of Michigan Center for Japanese Studies.

Hummon, D.M. 1990. *Commonplaces: Community Ideology and Identity in American Culture.* New York: State Univ. of New York Press.

Kanjanapan, Wilawan. 1995. The Immigration of Asian Professionals to the United States: 1988–1990. *International Migration Review.* v29:7.

Kenny, Martin, and Richard Florida. 1993. *Beyond Mass Production: The Japanese System and Its Transfer to the U.S.* New York: Oxford Univ. Press.

Kentucky Cabinet for Economic Development. 1995. *Economic Resources.* Frankfort, Ky.

———. 1996. *Kentucky: Resources for Economic Development, Bardstown.* Frankfort, Ky.

———. 1995. *Kentucky: Resources for Economic Development, Berea.* Frankfort, Ky.

———. 1995. *Kentucky: Resources for Economic Development, Danville.* Frankfort, Ky.

———. 1996. *Kentucky: Resources for Economic Development, Harrodsburg.* Frankfort, Ky.

———. 1997. *Kentucky: Resources for Economic Development, Versailles.* Frankfort, Ky.

Kentucky Population Research. 1996. *Subcounty Population Estimates 1990–1996.* Louisville, Ky.

Kentucky State Data Center, Urban Research Institute, University of Louisville. 1991. *Kentucky State Data Center Newsletter.* Louisville, Ky.

Kleber, John E. (Ed.) 1992. *The Kentucky Encyclopedia.* Lexington: University Press of Kentucky.

Klier, Thomas H. 1998. Agglomeration in the U.S. Auto Supplier Industry—Recent Evidence from Network Data. Southern Regional Science Association Meetings, Savannah, Ga., April 2–4, 1998.

Nash, June. 1987. Community and Corporations in the Restructuring of Industry. In *The Capitalist City: Global Restructuring and Community Politics.* Edited by Michael P. Smith and Joe R. Feagin. New York: Basil Blackwell.

Perrucci, Robert. 1994a. Embedded Corporatism: Auto Transplants, the Local State and Community Politics in the Midwest Corridor. *The Sociological Quarterly,* 35(3):487.

———. 1994b. *Japanese Auto Transplants in the Heartland: Corporatism and Community.* New York: Aldine De Gruyter.

Ricca, Steven J. *International Adoption of ISO 14001 Environmental Management Standards Expected in 1996.* Downloaded from http://www.jaeckle.com/iso14001.html.

U.S. Department of Commerce, Bureau of the Census. 1990. *U.S. Census Summary Tape File 1A.* Washington, D.C.: Government Printing Office.

Yanarella, Ernest J., and William C. Green (eds). 1990. *The Politics of Industrial Recruitment: Japanese Automobile Investment and Economic Development in the American States.* New York: Greenwood Press.

9

Japanese Corporate Environmental Practices in Kentucky

MIRANDA SCHREURS

WHILE THERE HAS BEEN MUCH RESEARCH about Japanese investment at the aggregate level, there are relatively few in-depth studies of the effects of Japanese investment on specific American communities. Moreover, to the best of my knowledge, there has been no appraisal of the implications of Japanese investment for environmental protection in the United States. The commonwealth of Kentucky provides an interesting laboratory for this kind of study. Japanese investment into the state rapidly took off in the mid-1980s. Thus, it is possible to assess what the sudden influx of Japanese corporations has meant for Kentucky's environment.

This chapter is divided into several parts. First there is a brief discussion of the relationship between investment and the environment. This is followed by a general comparison between U.S. and Japanese corporate and environmental practices. The next sections address the structure of Japanese investment and the general environmental and economic situation of Kentucky. This places Japanese-owned (or –partially owned) corporations in Kentucky into a larger context. A few brief case studies of the environmental practices of Japanese corporations in Kentucky are then presented. Finally, the conclusion suggests that the strong relationships between Japanese parent corporations and their United States-based subsidiaries are leading to a transfer of Japanese strengths in energy efficiency and recycling to their United States–based firms. More problematic for Japanese firms is addressing the complex toxic chemical regulations and reporting requirements that exist in the United States.

CORPORATE INVESTMENT AND THE ENVIRONMENT

Most studies of the environmental impact of investment examine how investments by first world corporations in the developing world affect the developing state's environment. There are two competing perspectives on what this kind of foreign investment means for the environments of developing nations. One is that heavy polluting industries will switch their operations to developing countries, where environmental standards are more lenient. This tendency may be exacerbated by developing nations, which use their weaker environmental standards to attract foreign investment. Corporations will flee their home countries when environmental regulations are strict and the cost of doing business is somewhat higher and move to developing countries where environmental regulations are less stringent and weakly enforced. The other perspective is that first world corporations tend to have better equipment and production processes. Thus, their operations tend to be more energy efficient and are often less polluting than are developing-country firms. They may also require that their suppliers meet certain environmental standards, thereby pulling up the pollution control measures of domestic firms (Leonard 1988). If this is the case, then the environment may actually improve as a result of foreign investment. Foreign investment also can bring jobs. Thus, if the structure of foreign investment in a region is such that it brings jobs but has minimal adverse environmental consequences, it can contribute to achieving sustainable development.

Japanese investment and its environmental implications has been a subject of considerable attention, not all of which has been positive. Most Japanese investment in the developing world has been in Asia. Japanese corporations have been accused for the role they played in tropical deforestation in southeast Asia (Dauvergne 1997), transfer of highly polluting firms to developing regions, and employment of weaker pollution control practices overseas than those applied at home (Karan and Jasparro 2000). On the other hand, Japanese corporations have much more environmental know-how than do firms in many Asian countries where Japanese investment levels are high. Today, as Japanese environmental awareness grows, Japanese investment practices in Asia appear to be slowly changing and becoming somewhat more environmentally sensitive. The hope is that this will have positive implications for the environment in other Asian countries and that their domestic industries will be forced to improve their own energy efficiency levels and environmental standards to meet the expectations of large Japanese multinationals. Large companies may also contribute to the development of basic pollution control infrastructure.

Surprisingly, there has been little research on the implications of Japanese investment for the environment in the United States. For that matter, there has been virtually no research done on the impact of foreign investment on the environment when that investment is between advanced industrialized states. The probable reason for this is an assumption that all advanced industrialized states have relatively similar environmental standards, and therefore, investments by corporations of one nationality or another should not make much difference in terms of environmental performance. Yet, an abundant literature shows that states of similar economic levels often approach environmental protection differently (e.g., Enloe 1975; Lundqvist 1980; Brickman, Jasanoff, Ilgen 1985; Schreurs and Economy 1997). These differences can have important implications for environmental outcomes.

GOVERNMENT-INDUSTRY-NGO RELATIONS IN JAPAN AND THE UNITED STATES

Political cultures and institutions influence the environmental policies and practices adopted by corporations. Relations among government, industries, and nongovernmental organizations (NGOs) influence the policy-making process. In contrast to the United States, where a large and vocal environmental NGO community exists, in Japan, the environmental movement is weak and there are few large NGOs. Government-industry relations also are different in the two countries. In the United States, the Environmental Protection Agency (EPA) regulates industry, but industry often challenges the EPA in court. In Japan, where government-industry relations tend to be closer and more cooperative, there is much less reliance on detailed regulations or on the courts. Instead, greater reliance is placed on broad regulations and administrative guidance to alter corporate behavior (Pharr and Badaracco 1986; Leane 1991). At the local level in Japan, thousands of informal environmental agreements have been reached among industries, municipalities, and citizens' groups. These agreements are a means for introducing the concerns of citizens into environmental protection at the local level. They are also reflective of a general orientation in Japan to rely heavily on voluntary pollution control measures by industry.

On the whole this has meant that in the United States, where the system is more open, environmental issues get onto the political agenda more quickly than they do in Japan. However, the enforcement of environmental regulations is often delayed in the court system for years because of industrial challenges to EPA rulings. It has also meant that in the United States, companies have to contend with large environmental NGOs that may target them if they do not maintain adequate environmental standards.

In Japan there was a period when many small citizens' movements demonstrated against polluting industries and brought companies to court to sue for damages. Once stringent environmental regulations were established in the early 1970s, however, the citizens' movements became much less active. Since the 1970s, administrative guidance has been widely used to bring industries into compliance with regulations. In Japan decision making may be slow because of the need to build societal consensus, but once decisions are reached, implementation is relatively fast and efficient.

Learning how to operate in a different regulatory environment and in a different political culture is a challenge for Japanese corporations that are establishing affiliates in the United States. To the extent that United States–trained employees are hired, however, these difficulties can be overcome.

DEVELOPMENTS IN ENVIRONMENTAL PROTECTION AMONG JAPANESE INDUSTRIES IN JAPAN

Japanese corporate attitudes toward environmental protection have changed substantially during the last three decades. In the 1960s Japanese corporations obtained a notorious reputation as heavy polluters that often ignored citizen complaints of severe pollution problems. So serious was the pollution at this time that Japan's environmental movement was for a time one of the strongest in the world. Outbreaks of mercury poisoning (Minamata disease) from the dumping of untreated effluents directly into water streams and *itai-itai* disease from cadmium poisoning horrified the nation and the world. Japanese corporations and the Japanese government came under strong pressure to introduce pollution control technologies and to prevent pollution.

After a series of new environmental laws was established in Japan in 1970, Japanese corporations began to invest heavily in pollution control technologies. The oil shock of 1973 became an additional strong incentive for Japanese companies to improve energy efficiency. By the end of the 1970s, Japanese companies were among the most energy efficient in the world and had made major strides in reducing emissions levels of many air pollutants.

A third phase in Japanese corporate attitudes toward the environment began in the early 1990s. Because of growing international concern with the global environment and Japan's strong international corporate presence, Japanese companies have begun to take a more proactive stance on environmental preservation. In the past, improvements in energy efficiency and pollution control were the main goals of Japanese companies, but since the 1990s, the establishment of environmental management systems, recycling programs, and green environmental images have gained in importance.

There are many signs of change in Japanese corporate philosophy toward the environment. For example, in April 1991 *Keidanren* (the Japan Federation of Economic Organizations) prepared a much-publicized Global Environment Charter—a list of environmental guidelines for industry to follow in domestic and overseas operations. The charter pronounces that each company must aim at being a good global corporate citizen. The charter states:

The task before us is not merely one of rethinking the problems

Chisso Corporation plant at Minamata, Japan. The organomercury compounds discharged by the plant into Minamata Bay polluted the local fish population; via fish consumption, a disease similar to acute anterior poliomyelitis appeared in the area between 1953 and 1960. By 1979 the number of officially designated patients totaled 1,293 with another 305 dead. In addition 6,000 victims filed application for recognition as Minamata disease patients. The Japanese corporations did not pay much attention to environmental degradation until 1969. Jane Allen Offut, a Scott County resident, showed up at public hearings on Toyota in Georgetown carrying (*Life* magazine) pictures of Japanese disfigured by the Minamata pollution. Her crusade led to tighter enforcement of water quality standards. The state built a pipeline through her land that releases the effluent from TMMK at a point well beyond the sink holes. Offut sensitized the local people to the need for more effective pollution control. (Photograph by P.P. Karan)

caused by the pursuit of affluence in a culture that encourages mass consumption; we must also come to grips with the global problems of poverty and population increase, aiming to hand over to future generations a healthy environment that allows sustainable development on a global scale. . . . Japan must not rest content with its good record in pollution control thus far. The business world, academic circles, and government must pool their resources to create innovative technologies for preserving the environment, conserving energy, and cutting back on resource consumption. While drawing on the Japanese experience in reconciling economic development with environmental protection, we must actively participate in international environmental undertakings. . . .

Following this, in July 1996 Keidanren announced an "Environmental Appeal"—a voluntary action plan aimed toward environmental conservation in the twenty-first century. Four specific fields were mentioned: measures to cope with global warming, establishment of a recycle-based society, restructuring of the environmental management system and environmental auditing, and introduction of environmental considerations into overseas operations. Individual industries were asked by Keidanren to draw up action plans. By December 1996, twenty-nine industries and 131 industrial organizations had drawn up plans with yearly review plans. A June 1997 Keidanren report announced that these numbers had climbed to thirty-seven industries and 137 industrial organizations (Keizaidantairengôkai 1997).

A majority of industries are focusing on improvements in energy conservation and energy efficiency. This focus includes plans for energy conservation in offices and efficiency improvements at the level of laborers, equipment, and processes. Others have announced plans to make improvements through the development of new technologies. Other plans include the efficient use of waste heat, electricity production from waste, the use of co-generation, the introduction of new energies, fuel conversion, and the use of nuclear energy by the electric industry or, as a backup, improvements in the performance of nuclear power generation systems. Some industries have also announced plans to make improvements at the design stage of products, to make contributions to energy conservation through international technological cooperation, and to promote reforestation.

The importance of the automotive industry to Kentucky demands attention to the environmental goals of Japanese automobile manufacturers' headquarters in Japan. Considerable efforts are underway by Japan's automobile manufacturers to develop low-emission vehicles. Because of the substantial contribution of automobile carbon dioxide (CO_2) emissions to the greenhouse effect, low-emission vehicles are seen as a potential solution to transportation-related emissions. At the moment, however, low-emission vehicles are not cost competitive.

Because of commitments to reduce greenhouse gas emissions made by Japan at the Third Conference of the Parties to the Framework Convention on Climate Change (the Kyoto Conference), Japanese automobile companies have been under considerable pressure to develop cleaner and more energy efficient models. This has led to competition to develop alternative automobiles. In 1995 Mitsubishi Motors Corporation announced that it had developed the world's first in-cylinder direct-injection gasoline engine, which will slash nitrogen oxide (NOx) emissions by 90 percent. The new engine technology will also improve fuel consumption by 25 percent (Bureau of National Affairs, Inc. May 31 1995, 422). As of 1997 both Toyota and Mitsubishi were selling vehicles powered by direct-injection engines.

In February 1997 Honda Motor Company announced that it had developed a car that is powered by compressed natural gas. The car discharges "almost zero" emissions.[1] Nissan Motor Company also has developed basic technology for low-emission vehicles that can improve fuel efficiency by 50 percent (Bureau of National Affairs March 5, 1997, 207–08).[2] At the Kyoto Conference, Toyota Motor Corporation debuted the Prius, its eco-car. The Prius gets sixty-six miles to the gallon and uses both a gasoline engine and an electric motor as power sources. In an effort to be at the forefront of an anticipated large eco-car market in the future, Toyota announced that it would initially sell the car at a substantial loss. Toyota is also working on a hydrogen-powered fuel cell (*Washington Post* December 14, 1994, H1).

ISO 14001 ENVIRONMENTAL MANAGEMENT SERIES AND JAPANESE ENVIRONMENTAL MANAGEMENT SYSTEMS

Sustainable development has become an important global policy imperative, but until recently it was largely ignored by the Japanese business community. Japanese corporations lagged behind their business counterparts in the United States and Europe in terms of corporate environmental reporting. The World Business Council for Sustainable Development has brought some multinational companies together and raised awareness of environmental management principles like eco-efficiency. Today, growing numbers of corporations in Japan are moving to incorporate eco-efficiency as a key component of their long-term business plans (Park 1997). Obtaining International Standards Organization's (ISO) 14001 environmental management series certification has become an important goal for many of Japan's large manufacturers and suppliers.

Certification under the ISO 14001 environmental management series involves certification from an environmental auditor that the company is in

KI (USA) Corporation (Berea, Kentucky), which makes components for shock absorbers, displays International Standards Organization's (ISO) 9002 environmental management series certification alongside its name. Certification from an environmental auditor means that the company is in compliance with existing environmental laws, has an environmental management system in place, and takes a proactive stance on environmental issues. ISO certification has become an important goal for many Japanese companies in Kentucky. (Photograph by P.P. Karan)

compliance with existing environmental laws, has an environmental management system in place, and takes a proactive stance on environmental issues. Because the process is cumbersome and expensive, certification can be challenging for smaller firms to obtain.

According to the Agency of Industrial Science and Technology of the Ministry of International Trade and Industry, a total of 248 Japanese applications for the ISO series had been accepted as of April 1997. Consumer electric and electronics makers accounted for 59.7 percent of the applications; machinery makers, 14.1 percent; chemical, 8.5 percent; precision instruments, 5.2 percent; oil products, 3.2 percent; and others, 9.3 percent.

By December 1998, 1,542 firms had acquired ISO 14001 certification in Japan, the highest level of any country in the world (in comparison there were 210 acquisitions in the United States) (Environmental Governance and Electric/Electronic Industries—ISO 14001, pp. 71–73). Reasons for the higher rate of ISO 14001 certification in Japan may be the high degree of dependence on exports for many Japanese industries. This makes Japanese corporations particularly sensitive to conditions and trends in other countries. Most of the major manufacturers in Japan have already achieved ISO 14001 certification and are now expecting their foreign subsidiaries to follow suit. This has implications for many of the subsidiaries in Kentucky. American companies have shown far less interest in the ISO 14001 series, possibly because they do not think the benefits of this certification are worth the cost of obtaining it.

The informal connections that exist among Japanese firms that are part of a *keiretsu* system have been used by parent corporations to push their subsidiaries to obtain ISO 14001 certification. Sony Corporation, for example, expected all of its manufacturing facilities to obtain certification by the end of fiscal 1997 and all of its nonmanufacturing facilities to do so by 2000. Matsushita Electric Industrial Corporation initially targeted the end of fiscal 1998 for all of its manufacturing facilities except those in China. Both Hitachi and Toshiba Corporation targeted the end of fiscal 1999, and Mitsubishi Electric Corporation announced a similar goal for the end of fiscal 2000 (Bureau of National Affairs April 30, 1997, 434). The Japanese oil refining industry announced that it plans to lower benzene and sulfur levels in its oil products to obtain certification under the ISO 14001 series and in expectation of stepped-up benzene regulations that are likely to go into effect in 1999 (Bureau of National Affairs September 18, 1996, 833).

Japanese Corporate Investment in the United States and in Kentucky

Efforts to attract Japanese investment to Kentucky are part of a larger plan by the state to diversify economic activities and stem the economic decline experienced by the state in the early part of the 1980s. Manufacturing and tourism are becoming increasingly important parts of the state's economy. In 1995 farm marketing was worth $3.1 billion to the state and mining was worth $4.4 billion. In comparison, tourism brought the state $7.1 billion and manufacturing brought $30 billion. Small firms represent more than 85 percent of all Kentucky firms and employ 25 percent of the state's workforce. This creates many challenges for environmental policy implementation in the state because of the cost of introducing pollution control equipment and the difficulty in monitoring the implementation of environmental programs in numerous small firms.

Within the manufacturing sector, the automobile industry has rapidly become one of the most important to Kentucky. After the oil crisis of 1973, auto plants in the United States began to cluster along Interstates 75 and 65. This region is considered a desirable location for investment by automobile manufacturers and their suppliers because of its central location in the country. Because manufacturers produce for the national market as opposed to regional markets, this region provides a central location from which to ship cars to customers (Brunger and Kim 1997, 7). Relatively low levels of unionization and incentives provided by states to firms that invest in the region are other reasons this area has become the center of automobile manufacturing. Kentucky, for example, provided a record amount of financial incentives to attract Toyota to the state.

Like their American and European competitors, Japanese automobile companies have congregated along Interstates 75 and 65. Honda built an auto plant in Marysville, Ohio, and Nissan set up an operation in Smyrna, Tennessee, in 1980. Mazda took over the Ford plant at Flat Rock, Michigan, in 1985, the same year that Toyota built its plant in Georgetown, Kentucky. The following year Subaru and Isuzu located plants in Lafayette, Indiana, and the Diamond Star joint venture between Chrysler and Mitsubishi located its plant in Normal, Illinois. Japanese automobile manufacturers in Canada also established operations along the I-65 and I-75 corridors. The only exceptions to this Midwest-centered investment by Japanese automobile manufacturers are the Toyota–General Motors joint venture in Fremont, California, and the Ford-Mazda plant in Mermosillo, Mexico (Brunger and Kim 1997, 7).

Studies of Japanese investment in Asia in the 1970s suggest that one reason Japanese firms may have moved manufacturing operations overseas was to avoid the strict environmental regulations that had been established in Japan early in the decade. While there is no reason to believe this was the case with Japanese automobile manufacturers in the United States, it is worth asking whether or not the automobile industry was attracted to this region because of low energy prices. Kentucky has among the lowest electricity prices in the country.

The heavy concentration of automobile manufacturers in the Midwest has attracted auto parts producers to the region. The just-in-time delivery system used in Japanese manufacturing demands that suppliers be proximal: they must be able to schedule deliveries by the hour. In a study of the automobile industry in the United States, Rubenstein found that 150 new Japanese auto parts companies were set up in the United States between 1985 and 1990 (Brunger and Kim, p. 7). Kentucky now ranks third among auto producing states.

Attracting foreign investment was an important goal for Kentucky's economic development. As of the late 1980s, foreign investment accounted for 3 percent of total manufacturers and an investment of more than $4.3 billion. Japanese firms represented more than one-third of this foreign investment.[3] Of the 140 foreign firms (including joint ventures with American firms) that had been set up in the state by 1989, 57 were Japanese. By the end of the 1980s, Japanese firms in Kentucky represented an investment of more than $2.5 billion and employed more than 16,000 workers. In addition, three Japanese banks and six Japanese trading companies had moved into the commonwealth. A decade later these figures had doubled. The state's 109 Japanese firms provide 35,546 jobs and represent more than $6.9 billion in investments (Kentucky Cabinet for Economic Development March 30, 1999).

Most of these Japanese plants were established after Toyota announced its plans to locate in Georgetown in 1985. At its start, Toyota Motor Manufacturing, Kentucky, was a $1 billion investment that created three thousand jobs. Expansions since the plant's inception include the establishment of engine and steering assembly operations. Toyota Motor Corporation also decided to establish its North American headquarters in the state. As of 1999 the TMMK had 7,800 employees. As a result of Toyota's big investment in the state, more than half of the Japanese plants that invested in Kentucky after 1985 are automobile parts suppliers.

The 109 Japanese companies in Kentucky can be divided into the following three categories, based on workforce size: 500 employees or more (21), 100 to 499 employees (46), and less than 100 employees (42). The environmental externalities caused by production are typically associated with company size and the nature of the product being produced. Most but not all of the largest Japanese companies to invest in the state are related to the automobile industry.[4]

On the whole, Japanese investment in the state has been viewed positively. Perhaps because Japanese investment brought new jobs and a richer cultural environment to the state, it did not received the negative attention that other investments by Japanese corporations—such as the purchase of Columbia Pictures by Sony or the purchase of the Rockefeller Center by Mitsubishi Real Estate—attracted elsewhere in the country in the 1980s.

THE ENVIRONMENTAL IMPLICATIONS OF JAPANESE INVESTMENT IN KENTUCKY

A state's environmental problems are closely linked to the structure of its economy. Because Japanese investment is so heavily concentrated in the automobile industry, its environmental impacts also are restricted to a subset of environmental problems. Before attempting to assess the environmental impacts of Japanese industrial investment and the environmental behavior of Japanese companies in the state, it is important to understand the geographical and environmental context in which that investment is occurring.

Population density in Kentucky is low. With a population of about 3.8 million, Kentucky ranks twenty-fourth nationally in terms of population size. There are no real large urban areas. The largest cities in the state, Louisville and Lexington-Fayette Urban County, have populations of approximately 270,000 and 238,000 respectively. The next ten largest cities have populations that range from 24,000 to 54,000. On a national scale, these rank as small to medium-sized cities. Thus, urban environmental problems are less pressing than they are in some other states. This also means, however, that when a new large employer like Toyota moves into a region, it will inevitably affect transportation patterns, housing development, and resource use.

The two biggest polluting industries in Kentucky are agriculture and coal. Kentucky is a largely rural state. It has the fourth largest number of farms of any state in the country. Tobacco, horses, cattle, corn, dairy products, and soybeans are its largest agricultural industries. Many of the most serious environmental problems facing the state are related to agriculture and include chemical contamination from pesticides and eutrophication of streams and waterways caused by runoff from farms.

Kentucky is blessed with an abundance of coal. Kentucky is the nation's third leading coal producer, producing 158 million tons, or 15 percent of the nation's total, in 1996 (*1996–97 State of Kentucky's Environment*). Abundant reserves of coal keep energy prices low in the state, and 95 percent of Kentucky's electricity is generated by coal-fired power plants. The negative consequences are that much of the coal has been obtained by strip-mining and that coal burning has led to high sulfur dioxide concentrations. Sulfur dioxides are a major contributor to local air pollution as well as acid rain. Approximately 90 percent of sulfur dioxide emissions in the state are emitted by the power plants.

While air pollution from the power plants overwhelms that of other contributors, as Kentucky diversifies its economy, industries and automobile

A part of the Toyota plant in rural Scott County, Kentucky. The environmental impact of Toyota on Scott County engendered the greatest amount of controversy when the company announced its intention to build a plant there in the late 1980s. When the Kentucky plant opened in 1988, Toyota met all standards set by the Environmental Protection Agency. It continues to be responsive and sensitive to the local environment of the Bluegrass region. The company encourages input from all of the plant's team members on ways to improve environmental protection activities. More than two thousand environmentally related suggestions were received in 1998. (Photograph by P.P. Karan)

tailpipe emissions will contribute increasingly large amounts to the environmental problems of the state. The Clean Air Act Amendments of 1990 that essentially required the installation of scrubbers and pollution control devices helped reduce industrial and power plant emissions of sulfur dioxide by more than a third from 1980 to 1995. Because corporations in Japan have had to meet stringent domestic air quality and energy efficiency standards—standards that at times are more stringent than those in the United States—Japanese transplants are likely to have few difficulties in meeting U.S. air quality standards, particularly for sulfur dioxide and NOx emissions.

The biggest area for concern related to Japanese investment in the state may be industrial toxic chemicals. Under the Toxic Release Inventory, large companies are required to self report the amounts of more than six hundred toxic chemicals generated (prior to 1995 reporting requirements were for three hundred chemicals). Toxic releases are on the decrease in Kentucky. According to the *1996–97 State of Kentucky's Environment,* toxic releases had declined by 57 percent since 1988. The requirement that industries disclose to the public their use of toxic chemicals places pressure on them to reduce use of those chemicals. Concerns about meeting regulatory requirements also provide incentives for reducing the use of toxic chemicals.

Ten facilities released 54 percent of toxic emissions in the state in 1994. Among these top ten emitters to the air was one Japanese firm: Toyota. Toyota released about 1 million pounds of toxic chemicals to the air compared with more than 3 million pounds for DuPont and 1.3 million pounds for Ford. In terms of the top ten emitters of toxic chemicals to the water, there was also one Japanese firm: AK Steel. Compared to the top five emitters, AK Steel's emissions were not so large. The largest emitter, ISP Chemicals, released more than 141,000 pounds of toxic chemicals into the water. AK Steel released about 7,400 pounds. The top ten emitters of toxic chemicals to the land also included one Japanese firm: AK Steel. Imco Recycling, the largest polluter, released 670,000 pounds. AK Steel produced about 15,000 pounds, roughly similar to levels produced by Dow Corning and ISP Chemicals ("Toxics" *1996–97 Kentucky State of the Environment,* 5).

For the purposes of this chapter, it also is noteworthy that the Environmental Defense Fund (EDF) recently ranked Toyota's Georgetown plant as one of the worst toxic chemical waste producers among the nation's fifty-four auto assembly plants. The Toyota plant's low ranking was because of the relatively high levels of toxic waste generated in the production of each vehicle. A spokesman for the company said the statistics were misleading because unlike most other assembly plants, Toyota produces its own engines. The spokesman claimed that 43 percent of the total toxic chemical waste for Toyota was scrap steel that had come into contact with a rustproofing chemical or oil making it toxic. But since the chemicals are later removed and the steel is recycled, the actual figures are much lower. The EDF report suggested that the Toyota plant could reduce waste by introducing a "block painting" technique, by which several cars in a row are painted the same color to reduce the amount of solvent needed to clean hoses between paint jobs. Interestingly, the EDF report surprised environmental groups in Kentucky because they tend to have a good relationship with the firm. The Toyota firm anticipates obtaining ISO 14001 certification in the near future.

ENVIRONMENTAL PRACTICES OF JAPANESE CORPORATIONS IN KENTUCKY: CASE STUDIES

In order to get a picture of the environmental practices of Japanese corporations in Kentucky, I requested by letter information from all the Japanese firms in the state. Nine responded. Of these, one responded to say it would not be able to participate and two simply wrote that they were too small to have much of an environmental impact. The small size of many of the Japanese transplants suggests that this may be the case for many of them. It appears that some of the most environmentally progressive firms were the ones that chose to respond. From the responses, several interesting developments can be noted that deserve further exploration. First is the push among several of the companies in Kentucky to obtain ISO 14001 certification. Another is the use of corporate environmental plans and efforts to build a corporate environmental ethos. Recycling efforts are big among the firms surveyed.

Matsushita Appliance Corporation

Matsushita Appliance Corporation (MAC), the largest producer of microwave ovens and canister vacuum cleaners in the United States, is an interesting case study. The company is part of the Matsushita Group of Companies. The parent company of this keiretsu is Matsushita Electric Industrial Company (MEI), which was established in 1918 in Japan. Matsushita Electric Corporation of America was established as a subsidiary in 1959, after which time the Panasonic name brand was introduced in the United States. MEI is the eighth largest manufacturer, based on sales, worldwide, and as of 1987 ranked as the world's eighteenth largest employer. Matsushita has more than twenty thousand employees in North America; twelve thousand of those employees are in the United States, with two thousand in Kentucky.

MAC was established in 1990 in Danville, Kentucky, and is one of the top five manufacturers in Kentucky in sales. It is made of up two distinct division companies: the Matsushita Floor Care Company, which manufactures vacuum cleaners, and the Matsushita Microwave Oven Company, which manufactures microwave ovens. In addition to its Danville operations, MAC has a parts, service, and subassembly building with approximately eighty employees in Winchester, Kentucky, and a Technology Development Department for microwave ovens with about twenty professional staff in Franklin Park, Illinois.

MEI drew up the Matsushita Environmental Charter in 1991. The policy states that "humankind has a special responsibility to respect and preserve the delicate balance of nature, and we at Matsushita acknowledge our obligation to maintain and nurture the ecology of this planet." In 1997 the company established a Corporate Environmental Affairs Division and inaugurated a Corporate Environment Conference. There is a new emphasis in the corporate group on environmental matters. This is consistent with a growing concern among many Japanese multinational corporations about green consumerism. As international environmental awareness grows and consumers, stockholders, and environmental groups place demands on large Japanese corporations to become more environmentally friendly in their operations, a new environmental awareness is taking hold in Japanese firms. Matsushita is one of many large Japanese corporations that are working to improve product recyclability, develop pollutant-free products and processes, and reduce energy consumption.

Matsushita plants in Japan had reduced industrial waste per unit of sales by 57 percent from fiscal 1992 levels by the end of fiscal 1997. By fiscal 2001, the company intends to further reduce this to 25 percent of the fiscal 1992 total. Furthermore, the Matsushita Electric Industry set a goal of reducing CO_2 emissions from its plants in Japan to 1991 levels by the end of the 1999 fiscal year (ending March 1999). By the end of fiscal 2001, the volume of energy consumed per unit of sales is to be reduced by 25 percent from that of fiscal 1991. While these goals are limited to Matsushita plants in Japan, the company has announced that it was part of the Matsushita corporate group's goal for all of its manufacturing companies worldwide to obtain ISO 14001 certification by the end of fiscal 1999.

MAC announced in its daily in-plant newsletter of October 15, 1998, that the company had adopted an Environmental Policy that will help the company pursue ISO 14001 certification. The Environmental Policy of the company pledges the company to "the prudent, sustainable use of the earth's resources and the protection of the natural environment" while contributing to "enhanced prosperity for all." The company lists protection of the ozone layer, reduction of industrial waste, reduction of global warming, and efficient use of resources as top environmental goals. In addition, the company plans to encourage the use of Environmental Management Systems by suppliers and contractors and to design products in such a way as to minimize its environmental impacts in production, use, and disposal.

Matsushita Electric Motor Corporation of America

Another Matsushita affiliate, the Matsushita Electric Motor Corporation of America (MEMA) located in Berea, Kentucky, received ISO 14001 certification from Underwriters Laboratories in May 1999. MEMA is a young company, established in December 1995. Production began in November 1996. MEMA is a $27 million investment on a 64-acre site and employs about two hundred people. The company produces electric motors for vacuum cleaners and for automobile anti-lock braking systems and power windows used by the automotive industry.

The company's strict environmental rules prohibit the dumping of any chemicals or processes water into sinks or drains, and floor drains were plugged to keep any spills from contaminating the environment. The policy allows for the use of new chemicals only if they receive prior approval from the safety/environmental specialist. The company's environmental objectives include reducing solid wastes by 6 percent per year; increasing recycling of aluminum cans, cardboard, and paper products by 5 percent per year; and reducing hazardous wastes by approximately 31 drums (1,705 gallons) in one year. MEMA also advocates the use of recycled packaging.

To obtain ISO 14001 certification, the company had to show it had a proactive environmental policy, was committed to comply with legal environmental requirements, and had a continually improving environmental management system in place. ISO 14001 has many of the same characteristics and requirements as the ISO/QS 9000 quality management system but specifically addresses protection of the environment. (Steve Bratcher, MEMA safety/environmental specialist, e-mail communication October 28, 1999).

According to Steve Bratcher, MEMA safety/environmental specialist (telephone interview March 12, 1999), Japanese corporations tend to be very energy efficient and recycle-oriented. For example, MEMA recycles 99 percent of processed material from scrap motors. Bratcher also suggested, however, that although Japanese companies may be concerned about recycling and environmental protection, they may not thoroughly understand U.S. environmental regulations. Japanese companies prefer to use Japanese products. In some cases, Japanese companies will order chemicals from Japan that contain substances not allowed in the United States. There are examples of Japanese companies incurring heavy penalties under the Toxic Substances Control Act. Therefore, Bratcher stressed the importance of employing individuals who have a thorough understanding of these regulations and concluded that "superior environmental performance can be achieved through environmental education and training."

ATR Wire and Cable Company

ATR Wire and Cable Company is another Japanese firm in the Danville area. The company was established in 1970 by Firestone but then was bought by Tokyo Rope Manufacturing Company, in conjunction with ITOCHU and Mitsubishi, in 1981, at which time it was given its current name. The company produces steel cord, and its major customers are tire producers. In June 1990 the plant underwent a major expansion at which time state-of-the-art equipment and environmental controls were installed. This resulted in the company's receipt of the Outstanding Environmental Leadership Award at the Governor's Conference on the Environment in 1991. Two major areas of focus for the company's environmental cleanup efforts have been reduction in the use of toxic chemicals and reduction of solid waste by implementing programs to remove recyclable materials from the industrial landfill. A new plating process enabled the company to eliminate the use of lead and cyanide compounds entirely by 1990. In this year, the company reduced by one-third all hazardous waste generated. The company's efforts at waste stream reduction won it recognition in 1991 from Kentucky's Cabinet for Natural Resources and Environmental Protection.

The company's progress in solid waste reduction placed the company six years ahead of EPA targets for industrial landfill materials. By isolating recyclable materials leaving the plant, the company was able to reduce by two-thirds the amount of solid waste going to the landfill. As a result in October 1995 the company received the Governor's Environmental Excellence Award for its "Associates for Total Recycling" program at the Governor's Conference on the Environment.

Given this record it is not surprising that the corporation's promotional brochure lists environmental safety as a top concern. In its opening sentence the brochure states: "We at ATR are proud to be at the forefront of the steelcord industry, a position we attribute to our guiding principles of operation: uncompromising quality, customer satisfaction and environmental safety. ATR manufactures and ships only those products which satisfy our exacting standards of quality, while conforming precisely to our customers' needs. We accomplish all this and lead our industry in fulfilling our environmental responsibilities to both local and global communities."

The success of environmental groups in lobbying for new laws regulating toxic chemicals has made the use of toxic chemicals increasingly expensive for companies. This has pushed some companies like ATR to switch production away from these chemicals to environmentally safer ones.

Y K K Corporation

Another example of a subsidiary of a large Japanese keiretsu, is Universal
Fasteners, of the Y K K Corporation. The Y K K Corporation, following the
trend of large corporations in Japan since the early 1990s, established an
Environmental Pledge in 1994: "It is recognized today as being a most important duty for all humankind that we preserve the abundantly endowed global
environment and that we transfer it to the next generation in sound condition. Striving to be an 'earth friendly company,' Y K K Group proclaims that
we will address and promote harmony with the environment as the highest
priority of our business activity." Y K K's Environmental Action Guideline
includes a pledge to address environmental concerns related to its overseas
activities.

The plant employs 325 people and produces metal buttons, rivets, burrs,
and hook-and-eye fasteners for the clothing industry. Waste generated from
the plant includes used oils and machine coolants, scrap metals, and general
plant trash. Hazardous wastes include paints and wastewater from burnish-
ing/electroplating operations.

In January 1996 the Kentucky Pollution Prevention Center (KPCC) of
the University of Louisville prepared a preliminary report containing observations and suggestions for waste reduction. The report included many suggestions for ways in which the company could reduce waste and prevent
pollution. The KPCC's legislative mandate, given at its creation in 1988, is to
provide information and technical assistance to help Kentucky manufacturers to voluntarily reduce hazardous waste by 25 percent. The KPCC works
primarily with small and medium-sized firms like Universal Fasteners. Its
operations are primarily funded by a hazardous waste assessment fee on Kentucky manufacturers and businesses that produce hazardous wastes or use
Title III Section 313 toxic chemicals.

In June 1998 Universal Fasteners established a Corporate Environmental Policy. The main purpose of establishing such a policy is to help management identify waste streams and to advise on waste reduction opportunities.
The environmental guidelines of the company establish environmental protection as a line responsibility and an important measure of employee performance as is the case with safety issues. They also call for the minimization or
elimination of the generation of waste and promotion of the reuse and recycling of process materials. The Environmental Policy notes that incentives for
the company to promote facility-wide waste reduction above and beyond
that of environmental protection and resource conservation include substantial economic returns, reduced liability, ease of regulatory compliance, and
good public image. Also noteworthy was a postclosure permit requirement
that required the facility to submit documentation of the waste minimization
program at the facility.

CONCLUSION

Japanese corporations have been received in Kentucky with open arms. On the environmental front, Japanese firms based in Kentucky appear to be actively pursuing energy and resource efficiency improvements, and several are obtaining ISO 14001 certification. The heavy concentration of Japanese investment in auto-related industries means that Japanese firms contribute to only a subset of the environmental problems facing Kentucky. Moreover, because most of the Japanese firms in Kentucky were established in the mid-1980s, they came after parent firms in Japan had already made major strides in energy efficiency improvements and pollution control practices. Thus, firms often came to Kentucky with already strong environmental standards. The biggest problem area may be different expectations regarding the use of toxic chemicals where the laws in Japan and the United States are somewhat different.

NOTES

1. The new vehicle is called the Civic GX and can drive 248 miles on a full tank. The carbon monoxide (CO) emissions of the vehicle are 98.4 percent less than those of comparable Honda vehicles; hydrocarbon (HC) emissions are 94.6 percent less; and NOx emissions are 98.6 percent less. Honda already has introduced its first low-emission vehicles, the 1.6-liter Civic Ferio and Partner. These cars discharge only one-tenth the CO, HC, and NOx of comparable Honda models. Both models have maximum power output of 105 horsepower at 6,400 rpm (revolutions per minute) and a maximum torque of 14.3 kilograms at 4,600 rpm. Fuel consumption is comparable to similar Honda vehicles.

2. Nissan's technology uses a reciprocal engine and an electricity generator to power an electric motor. The experimental car makes use of a 1-liter gasoline engine, a 55-watt motor, compact lithium ion batteries, and a generator. Emissions of CO, HC, and NOx are about half of comparable gasoline-powered vehicles. The experimental car has a maximum speed of 120 kilometers per hour and fuel consumption of 15–20 kilometers per liter. The company reported that to achieve almost zero emissions, it used a "tumble port design" that enhances stable combustion after the engine starts, an air-fuel ratio controller with fuel adhesion compensation for maintaining a precise air-to-fuel ratio, a thin-walled catalytic converter/integrated exhaust manifold for immediate catalytic converter activation after the engine starts, and a 400-cell catalytic converter to increase the contact area.

3. Brunger and Kim (1997, 9) argue that the concentration of Japanese firms in a region brings other benefits to Japanese firms as well. As the level of experience with Japanese corporations in a community increases, it is easier for subsequent firms to locate there. Translation services, Japanese cultural activities, Japanese food supplies, and the like become embedded in the region. This may also help explain the large increase in Japanese investment in Kentucky since the mid-1980s. At a November 1989 conference on Japanese investment in the United States, the Economic De-

velopment Office of the State of Kentucky noted that its office was especially mindful of the sociological and cultural ramifications associated with foreign investments, "since such changes can have a profound affect on future efforts to attract new foreign investment" (Japanese Investments in the US: American Responses 1989, 41). The successful bid for the Toyota plant has put Japan on the map for Kentuckians. By 1989 five Kentucky high schools were offering Japanese language courses to their students. In 1986 a U.S.-Japan International Management Institute opened, and in 1987 the Japan-America Society of Kentucky was established. The University of Kentucky has steadily increased its Japan expertise during the past decade as well.

4. The largest Japanese companies are: Toyota Motor Manufacturing, Kentucky (7,800 employees), Matsushita Appliance Corporation (2,000), AK Steel Corporation (1,600), Sumitomo Electric Wiring Systems, Morgentown (1,000), Hitachi Automotive Products (USA), Inc. (950), Ambrake Corporation (950), Link-Belt Construction Equipment (900), Trim Masters (700), Sumitomo Electric Wiring Systems, Edmonton (700), Technotrim, Glasgow (690), Technotrim, Maysville (650), AP Technoglass Corporation (600), Obi Automotive of America Corporation (600), TG (USA) Corporation (600), Topy Corporation (590), A T R Wire and Cable Company, Inc. (564), Tokico (USA), Inc. (564), Mazak Corporation (520), Jideco of Bardstown, Inc. (500), and United L-N Glass, Inc. (500).

REFERENCES

Brickman, Ronald, Sheila Jasanoff, and Thomas Ilgen. 1985. *Controlling Chemicals: The Politics of Regulation in Europe and the United States.* Ithaca: Cornell Univ. Press.

Brunger, Scott, and Young-Bae Kim. 1997. *Effects of Japanese Investment in a Small American Community: A Case Study of Autoparts in East Tennessee.* Commack, N.J.: Nova Science Publishers, Inc.

The Bureau of National Affairs, Inc. *International Environmental Reporter,* Washington, D.C., March 5, 1997, pp. 207–8; May 31, 1995, p. 422; April 30, 1997, p. 434; Sept. 18, 1996, p. 833.

Dauvergne, Peter. 1997. *Shadows in the Forest: Japan and the Politics of Timber in Southeast Asia.* Cambridge: MIT Press.

Enloe, Cynthia. 1975. *The Politics of Pollution in Comparative Perspective.* New York and London: Longman.

Environmental Quality Commission, *1996–97 State of Kentucky's Environment.* Frankfort: Kentucky Environmental Quality Commission.

Institute for Global Environmental Strategies, *Business and Environmental Governance* Tokyo: IGES, March 1999.

Japanese Investment in the U.S.: Conference Proceedings, November 15, 1989. Conference held at the Nitze School of Advanced International Studies, Washington, D.C.

Karan, P.P., and Chris Jasparro. 2000. Geographic Patterns of Japanese Foreign Investment in Southeast Asia. *Reitaku International Journal of Economic Studies* 8:13–30.

Keidanren, "Chikyû Kankyô Kenkshô" (Global Environmental Charter), April 23, 1991.

Keizaidantairengôkai, "Keidanren Kankyôjishu Kôdô Keikaku" (saishu happyo), June 17, 1997.

Kentucky Cabinet for Economic Development, Announced/Reported *Japanese Industrial Investment in Kentucky (At Least 10% Foreign Owned)*, March 30, 1999.

Leane, Geoffrey W.G. 1991. Environmental Contracts—A Lesson in Democracy from the Japanese. *University of British Columbia Law Review:* 361–85.

Leonard, H. Jeffrey. 1988. *Pollution and the Struggle for the World Product: Multinational Corporations, Environment, and International Comparative Advantage.* Cambridge: Cambridge Univ. Press.

Lundqvist, Leonard. 1980. *The Hare and the Tortoise: Clean Air Policies in the United States and Sweden.* Ann Arbor: Univ. of Michigan Press.

Park, Jacob. 1997. Companies Try to Reconcile Environmental Protection, Profit. Opinion Section, *Nikkei Weekly,* 14 July.

Pharr, Susan, and Joseph L. Badaracco Jr. 1986. Coping with Crisis: Environmental Regulation. In Thomas McCraw, ed., *America versus Japan* (Boston: Harvard Business School Press, 1986).

Schreurs, Miranda A., and Elizabeth Economy. 1997. *The Internationalization of Environmental Protection.* Cambridge: Cambridge Univ. Press.

10

Assessing Environmental Performance of Japanese Industrial Facilities in Kentucky

GARY A. O'DELL

REPRESENTING MORE THAN $7 BILLION invested in more than a hundred plants, Japanese corporations have been the most important source of foreign direct investment in Kentucky during the past decade. The economic impact of this investment is substantial and benefits the commonwealth through direct employment, increased tax revenues, and multiplier effects. Other aspects of the Japanese presence are less easily quantifiable. Although the proliferation of manufacturing firms serves to diversify and strengthen Kentucky's economy, quality of life in Kentucky is not limited solely to economic considerations but includes the state of the environment.

Economic activity places stresses on the environment in the production and consumption phases, for the environment serves as a source of materials and energy, as an assimilator of waste, as a source of amenities, and as a life-support system. Provision of these services is dependent on preservation of the environment and maintenance of in situ natural resources and stable ecological relationships. The concept of sustainable development attempts to unite the need for current economic output with the need to maintain the continued productivity of environmental and natural resources (Pearson 1985). When the ability of the environment to renew materials and absorb waste is exceeded, the environment deteriorates.

Assessment of environmental impacts of human activity may be made using two different frames of reference: absolute and relative. Evaluation on absolute terms requires long-term collection of baseline data against which to measure departures from ambient norms. Evaluation on relative terms does not seek to measure changes but rather to provide an indication of potential environmental impact, using performance criteria.

A primary cause of environmental degradation is the uncontrolled release of waste residuals, or pollution. Many industrial operations produce waste that is potentially harmful to the environment. The amount and types of waste generated by a facility are important indicators of risk to the environment, but more significant is the manner in which such waste is managed. Through production modifications and proper handling, the amount of potentially hazardous waste released into the environment may be greatly reduced. Comparison of waste generation and waste management practices among industrial facilities provides a means to assess the environmental performance of specific facilities or industry segments. The focus of this chapter is to determine whether Japanese-owned firms operating in Kentucky differ significantly from those of other ownership in their environmental performance. Schreurs, in the previous chapter, focused on the development of environmental policies of Japanese industry; this chapter is concerned with their real-world practices.

Performance evaluation of Japanese firms was undertaken using data on hazardous waste generation reported to the Kentucky Division of Waste Management under the provisions of the federal Resource Conservation and Recovery Act (RCRA) of 1976 and the federal Toxic Release Inventory (TRI) established by the Emergency Planning and Community Right-to-Know Act (EPCRA) of 1986. Each of these programs requires industrial facilities to report on materials that are potentially harmful to human health and the environment, and each of these programs was established prior to a significant Japanese industrial investment in Kentucky.

An additional assessment of environmental performance was conducted by visiting five large-quantity hazardous waste generators in Kentucky. These facilities were Toyota Motor Manufacturing, Kentucky (Georgetown), KI (USA) (Berea), Zeon Chemicals (Louisville), Universal Fasteners (Lawrenceburg), and Hitachi Automotive Products (USA) (Harrodsburg). The firms visited were selected from the list of large-quantity hazardous waste generators to provide a diversity of industrial types and facility sizes. At each facility, the environmental staff was interviewed concerning environmental policies and practices and the plant was toured to inspect waste reduction measures implemented.

ENVIRONMENTAL PERFORMANCE ASSESSMENT

Evaluating environmental performance differs considerably from environmental impact assessment in its approach. Impact assessment generally deals in absolutes; performance evaluation considers relations. Impact assessment is focused on changes that occur in the condition of the environment as a result of human activity. Therivel (1992) describes environmental impact assessment (EIA) as "the process of predicting and evaluating an action's impacts on the environment, the conclusions to be used as a tool in decision making." Since EIA was first formalized following the National Environmental Protection Act of 1969 and the subsequent establishment of the U.S. Environmental Protection Agency, it has been applied primarily to specific proposed actions or projects. The basic steps followed in an EIA are to review the state of the environment and the characteristics of the action and possible alternatives and to then predict the future state of the environment with or without the action (Baker, Kaming, and Morrison 1977).

Ideally this cause-and-effect approach requires that the environment be well enough understood that the effect of various actions can be modeled in some fashion. This requires the accumulation of a substantial volume of data in many categories from which ambient conditions may be determined against which to measure or predict changes. The situation is further complicated because environmental systems—ecosystems—are not static but are constantly evolving in response to both internal and external dynamics. The response to this complexity has been attempts to develop specific indicators that reflect either environmental changes or potential risk to the ecosystem. There is at present no universally adopted set of indicators. In the words of one researcher: "No generally accepted approach is available to measure these local and regional impacts: we do not have an ecological indicator for use on the evening news that is comparable to the GNP" (Karr 1992, 229).

Ecosystems are complex open systems having a constant interaction of material and biological inputs and outputs. For this reason cause-and-effect is not a simple linear association but an intricate set of relationships. Therivel's (1992) discussion of cumulative environmental impacts reflects on this complexity. Environmental impact assessments do not adequately consider cumulative effects of one or more projects or activities. Cumulative impacts include additive, synergistic, threshold/saturation, induced/indirect, or time-crowded and space-crowded effects. An additive effect results in environmental degradation from a sum of activities where any one activity by itself causes little harm. When the total impact of several activities exceeds the sum of their individual impacts, this is a synergistic effect. A threshold or saturation effect occurs when the environment is resilient up to a certain level and then rapidly degraded. Induced and indirect impacts occur where one development project stimulates secondary developments and infrastructure. Time- and space-crowded effects occur when the environment does not have the time and space to recover from one impact before subjected to another.

Indicators for performance evaluation do not attempt to ascertain effects but rather are useful in comparing the potential environmental risk of activities. Tracking environmental performance of specific facilities over time provides a means to ascertain whether potential environmental risks posed by that facility's operations are increasing or decreasing; that is, as a measure of changes in environmental efficiency. Frequently, performance indicators can be used in association with absolute measures to provide an assessment of environmental impact. For example, the most recent edition of the *State of Kentucky's Environment* (Cole, Richards, and Siegel 1999) notes that there has been an overall decline in Kentucky in the average air concentration of sulfur dioxide, a pollutant harmful to human health and other biological systems. The report also notes that industrial emissions of sulfur dioxide have significantly declined since 1980. Thus there is a link between performance evaluation and impact assessment. It is not a direct one-to-one linkage, for there are other sources of contaminants beside industry, but comparison of total annual rates of release of industrial chemicals to ambient air quality implies correspondence.

Environmental impact assessment can be a long and tedious process involving years of monitoring to establish baseline conditions; the larger and more complex is the area of study, the more difficult becomes the task of linking cause to effect. Assessing the environmental impact of Japanese industrial firms in Kentucky, in absolute terms, would be an enormous challenge requiring analysis of many sorts of data. The most troublesome aspect of such an undertaking is the inherent difficulty in isolating effects resulting from Japanese facilities from those produced by the numerous other forms of economic activity in the state. The solution proposed in this study is to use environmental efficiency in terms of waste generation and management as a surrogate for environmental impact. Waste from industrial processes is related to environmental degradation, in that it represents poor resource utilization and places stresses on the assimilative capacity of the local ecosystem. Because waste products also reflect inefficiencies in industrial processes, environmental efficiency is, to a certain extent, a mirror of economic efficiency.

ASSESSING ENVIRONMENTAL PERFORMANCE OF JAPANESE FACILITIES IN KENTUCKY

Two data sources provide the primary information used for performance evaluation in this study: state and federal (under the provisions of RCRA) hazardous waste reporting systems and the federal TRI established by EPCRA.[1] Each of these programs requires facilities to report on materials that are potentially harmful to human health and the environment, and each of these programs was established prior to the Japanese presence in Kentucky. Although there is overlap, the programs differ in the classes of materials with which they are concerned.

TRI reporting is more selective than RCRA, in that TRI is concerned with the management of "toxic" substances at industrial facilities[2] whereas RCRA regulates "hazardous" substances that encompass a broader range of materials and include numerous nonindustrial generators. Substances are regulated under RCRA's more inclusive criteria if they exhibit certain characteristics of toxicity or ignitability, corrosivity, or reactivity (EPA 1997). The legislation regulates and manages hazardous wastes from generation to disposal, taking a "cradle-to-grave" approach "intended to protect human health and the environment through proper management practices, to encourage conservation and recovery of valuable resources, and to alleviate the need for future corrective action cleanups. In contrast to the Superfund[3] program, which is designed primarily to clean up contamination from past waste disposal, RCRA is largely prospective in approach" (Openchowski 1990).

There are, however, certain inherent difficulties in the use of data from these sources. Associated problems arise from overlapping causes that may be categorized as data inconsistencies and compilation delays. Data inconsistencies arise from changes in program requirements and definitions and from incorrect reporting of information by facilities. In the first case, federal and state programs are subject to constant modifications by both legislatures and regulatory authorities. Both RCRA and the TRI have been substantially revised on several occasions. This results in data sets that vary over time as to the number of chemical substances included, the reporting requirements for facilities, and the way in which information is organized. Furthermore, the information reported by facilities is not always accurate, sometimes intentionally but more frequently inadvertently, so that figures may be subject to retrospective adjustment. The net effect is to produce substantial delays in report compilation, so that the most accurate data is usually several years old. For these reasons, 1996 has been chosen as the base year for comparison of facility environmental performance, since data collected for more recent years is generally not yet in usable form.

During 1996 there were ninety-one Japanese-owned industrial facilities operating in Kentucky, representing 1.6 percent of the manufacturers in the state (Manufacturers News 1997). In that year, twenty-five of the Japanese firms were classed as large generators of hazardous waste and regulated under RCRA, and thirty-one firms produced sufficient toxic chemicals to qualify for regulation under TRI. These two overlapping segments of Japanese industry comprise the study group for which environmental performance is evaluated.

RCRA Hazardous Waste

The RCRA program in Kentucky is managed by the state Division of Waste Management under federal mandate. Federal and state hazardous waste laws focus on the regulation and management of RCRA hazardous waste produced by large-quantity generators (LQG) regardless of facility type. LQGs are defined as producing more than 2,200 pounds (1,000 kilos) of hazardous waste per month. Less closely regulated, small quantity generators (SQG, 10–100 kg) and conditionally exempt generators (1–10 kg) report on hazardous waste in less detail than LQG facilities.

Through 1990 all facility hazardous waste generation was classed as a single entity. Beginning in 1991, the U.S. Environmental Protection Agency divided this waste into two categories, managed waste and exempt waste. Exempt hazardous waste, more than 90 percent of the total, is primarily corrosive wastewater that is relatively easy to treat and is exempt from most hazardous waste requirements (Cole, Richards, and Siegel 1999). In addition, cleanup or remediation of existing contamination sites can result in large quantities of managed waste attributed to a corporation that is unrelated to the current-year hazardous waste generation for the facility. Because of this restructuring of waste classification, only the data for the period 1991–1996, excluding remediation waste, are used in this paper to analyze waste quantity trends.

The total number of LQG firms in the state increased steadily from 260 in 1981 to a peak of 482 in 1992, since declining to 409 by 1996. In any given year, about one-fourth of LQG are nonindustrial and often transient on the list, consisting of facilities such as gasoline service stations, hospitals, oil and gas pipelines, and universities that occasionally produce moderate amounts of hazardous waste, in addition to some relatively large generators such as military bases. These nonindustrial sites represent, in most years, less than 5 percent of all large-quantity hazardous waste generation. The number of industrial plants generating hazardous waste remained fairly constant during the period 1991–1996, averaging about 300 facilities. In 1996 industrial LQG constituted about 5 percent of nearly 6,000 manufacturing firms operating in Kentucky. Twenty-five Japanese firms were classed as LQG in 1996, about 8 percent of the 309 LQG in that year. Since the 91 Japanese firms then extant constituted only about 1.6 percent of all Kentucky manufacturers, a fivefold greater proportion of Japanese firms were producing hazardous waste than in the general population of industrial companies. The number of firms generating hazardous waste is not in itself necessarily significant, however; of greater import is the proportion of total waste and the manner in which it is managed.

In 1996 Kentucky industrial firms produced 405,867 tons of managed hazardous waste and nearly 17.4 million tons of exempt waste. Of these state totals, Japanese firms generated 9,203 and 86,030 tons respectively in the two categories. The Japanese contribution represents 2.2 percent of all managed waste and roughly corresponds to the proportion of Japanese facilities in the general industrial population. Historically, the trend line for the Japanese contribution as a percentage of total industrial LQG waste is nearly flat, showing neither significant increases nor decreases since 1991 despite consid-

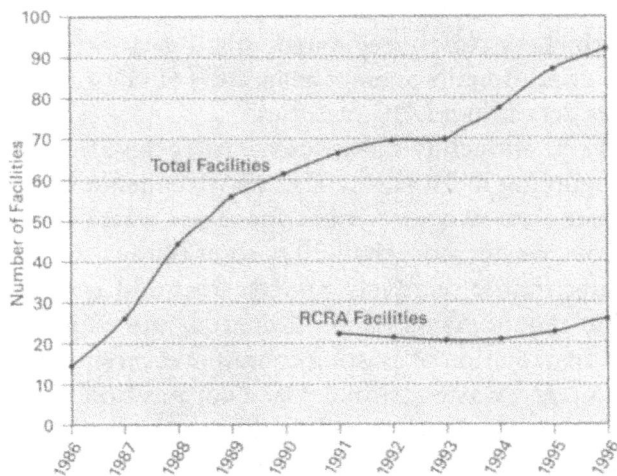

Fig. 10.1. Rate of increase of Japanese RCRA, 1986–1996.

erable increase in both the number and capacity of Japanese plants (figs. 10.1 and 10.2). During the same period, the actual amount of managed waste generated by Japanese firms has increased about 50 percent from 5,830 tons to 9,203 in 1996. This is attributable to growth rather than a decreasing effectiveness in environmental protection.

Another form of analysis may be conducted by "normalizing" the data through removal of extreme cases. About 80 percent of Kentucky's managed waste is generated by only ten firms, none of which are Japanese. Similarly, about 40 percent of the waste generated by Japanese firms in Kentucky is produced by a single facility, Toyota Motor Manufacturing in Georgetown. Discounting the waste production of these top generators allows comparisons that are more representative of general industry. When managed hazardous waste generation by the top ten firms is excluded, waste generation by Japanese firms excluding Toyota is about 6 percent of the total.

The somewhat larger size of Japanese facilities is likely of significance in accounting for the greater proportion of hazardous waste generated by Japanese firms. Excluding firms having more than 3,000 employees, Japanese LQG industrial plants average 450 workers per facility compared to 275 workers per non-Japanese LQG facility. Including the larger plants, in 1996 the 25 Japanese facilities employed a total of 17,400 workers, whereas the 225 non-Japanese facilities, for which information was available, employed a total of 84,000 persons (Manufacturers News 1997). Using 1996 hazardous waste figures, the amount of managed RCRA waste generated per job was substantially less at Japanese facilities than at non-Japanese, 1,060 pounds per worker

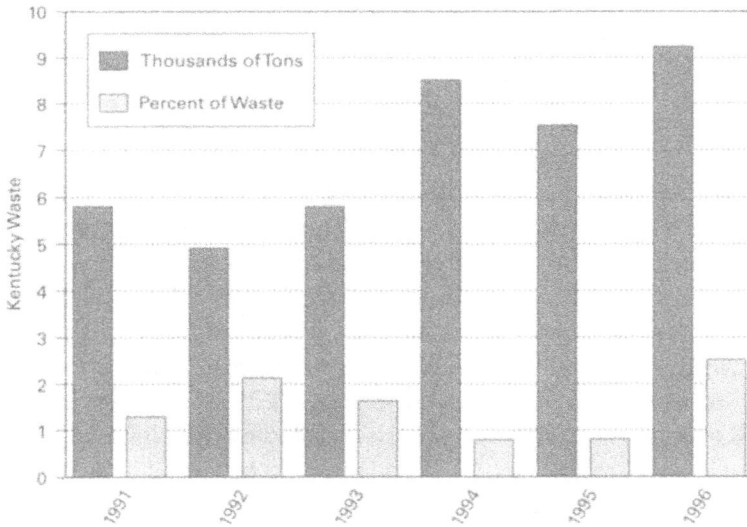

Fig. 10.2. Japanese share of Kentucky's hazardous waste, 1991–1996.

compared to 9,040. Even if the top ten non-Japanese generators are excluded from the calculation, the waste produced per job is still greater for the non-Japanese plants at more than 1,500 pounds per worker. This data appears to indicate a greater efficiency at Japanese plants in terms of waste reduction at the source.

Assessing exempt waste is more problematic because of some serious reporting problems that have recently become evident. The exempt class of hazardous waste, consisting primarily of corrosive wastewater, averaged 4 million to 6 million tons annually between 1991 and 1995. A drastic jump occurred in 1996, to more than 17 million tons. This was not a result of increased waste production but rather from the failure of two of the largest Kentucky generators, Ashland and DuPont, to properly report on this class of hazardous waste in prior years (Cole, Richards, and Siegel 1999), a situation that was corrected in 1996. This implies that the figures for the period 1991–1995 may be substantially underreported by as much as threefold. For this reason analysis of trends in exempt waste must be considered unreliable.

Relatively few of the Japanese facilities produce wastewater as part of the production process. Only five Japanese firms reported exempt class hazardous waste generation in 1996, totaling 86,030 tons or only 0.5 percent of the 1996 Kentucky total. The corrosive wastewater that constitutes most of the exempt hazardous waste is treated and discharged through state water permits to surface waters or to publicly owned wastewater treatment plants.

Toxic Materials

The TRI provides statistical data that may be used to assess the generation of hazardous materials specifically in the manufacturing sector. TRI was established in 1988 as part of the federal Emergency Planning and Community Right-to-Know Act of 1986. The detailed statistics collected under TRI reporting requirements provide a means to assess not only total production toxic waste but also the various ways in which toxics are managed. Generation and management figures, however, are reported by the individual firms and in some cases are best estimates since actual monitoring is not mandated. Furthermore, it is difficult to use the data to indicate trends because the list of regulated substances is constantly evolving. In 1987 there were 300 substances on the TRI list; the number was nearly doubled by the addition of 282 chemicals and chemical categories in 1994. For this reason it is better to consider relative percentages rather than actual volumes of toxics generated.

Companies must report releases and transfers if the facility has the equivalent of ten or more full-time employees and meets established thresholds for manufacturing, processing, or otherwise using listed chemicals. From the program's 1987 implementation through 1990, manufacturers reported annually on the type and amount of chemicals released to the local environment and how much was transferred off the property for treatment or disposal. During 1996, 429 regulated facilities, out of a total production waste of 577 million pounds, released more than 40 million pounds of toxics to the air, water, and land of the commonwealth of Kentucky. Thus a mean 92 percent of production toxics was treated or recycled on or off site and 8 percent was released. During the same year, nearly 76 million pounds were transferred off site for treatment or disposal. Beginning in 1991 facilities also reported on the details of how waste was handled, whether it was treated or recycled on or off site or burned for energy recovery.

About 10 percent of all Kentucky manufacturers produce toxic materials in reportable quantities, compared to one-third of Japanese-owned facilities. Thirty-one of the ninety-one Japanese firms were regulated under TRI in 1996, reporting on just over 11,000 tons of listed TRI chemicals. These facilities represent about 7 percent of the TRI facilities and 3.5 percent of all toxics. Since the percentage of TRI facilities is nearly five times greater than the 1.6 percent Japanese representation in the industrial community yet the proportion of waste generated is equivalent to only twice the overall Japanese component, individual Japanese TRI firms must be producing less toxics than the average manufacturer. This indicates a greater efficiency in source reduction.

The relative size of Toyota's contribution tends to distort the picture. Toyota is among the top ten in the state in the quantity of releases; 1,141 tons of toxics released primarily into the atmosphere is nearly 60 percent of the total for all Japanese TRI. If Toyota is included, the average Japanese release rate of 17.5 percent is significantly higher than the 7 percent average for all. If Toyota is excluded, other Japanese facilities have an average release rate of 10 percent, more nearly par with other industrial facilities in the state.

EPA Priority Toxics

The 33/50 program, established by the EPA in 1991, was named for goals of 33 percent reduction by 1992 and 50 percent reduction by 1995, using base year 1988. Seventeen chemicals were selected from the TRI list as priority chemicals based on relative toxicity, volumes of use, and potential for pollution prevention opportunities. Among the substances Japanese firms have released as wastes into the environment are thirteen of the seventeen on the EPA priority list. These substances are: 1,1,1-trichloroethane, benzene, cadmium and cadmium compounds, chromium, cyanide compounds including hydrogen cyanide, dichloromethane, lead and lead compounds, methyl ethyl ketone, methyl isobutyl ketone, nickel and nickel compounds, toluene, trichloroethylene, and xylene (table 10.1).

Eleven Japanese facilities in Kentucky reported releases of priority toxics in 1996 compared to nine in 1991, despite a 50 percent increase in the number of Japanese firms during the same period. No cadmium has been reported released to the environment from Japanese TRI facilities since 1989, and no dichloroethane since 1990. For each of six of the priority chemicals, three or fewer facilities reported releases during 1996. The primary TRI chemicals released as waste, in descending rank, are xylenes, toluene, lead, nickel, and chromium. Quantities of xylenes and toluene released have doubled since 1991 and now account for 60 percent of all the priority toxics released by Japanese facilities (fig. 10.3).

Comparisons across time can be made for the priority chemicals because all thirteen have been included on the overall TRI list since 1987. Releases of these thirteen chemicals by all Kentucky TRI facilities have shown a steady decrease since 1988, amounting to 30 percent for the period 1991–1996 (fig. 10.4). During the same period, 1991–1996, total releases by Japanese facilities have increased by 30 percent and increased their share of total Kentucky releases from 6.8 percent to 14 percent (fig. 10.5).

The increases in both the quantity and relative proportion of releases of priority toxics from Japanese facilities are primarily attributable to the Toyota facility. Toyota's share of the Japanese priority chemical releases increased from 41 percent in 1991 to 68 percent in 1996, reflecting a doubling of plant capacity in 1994. If Toyota is excluded from consideration, releases from Japanese facilities have remained approximately 4.5 percent of the statewide total for priority toxics since 1991 and thus have not increased their environmental impact despite plant expansions.

Table 10.1. Characteristics of the thirteen EPA priority chemicals released by Japanese facilities in Kentucky.			
Substance	No. of Japanese TRI facilities	Usage	Health effects
1,1,1-trichloroethane	1	Many uses as solvent and cleaner.	Exposure to high levels may cause death from depression of central nervous system. Dermal and mucosal irritant at lower exposures.
benzene	2	Used in the manufacture of many products and to make intermediate chemicals. A component of gasoline.	A known carcinogen. Chronic low-level exposure may result in damage to internal organs; exposure to high concentrations may cause death in minutes.
cadmium and compounds	0	Used for metal plating, in the manufacture of nickel-cadmium batteries, in pigments and plastic stabilizers, numerous other applications.	Probable carcinogen. Chronic low-level exposure may cause lung or kidney damage.
chromium and chromium compounds	4	Used in metal alloys, in plaating, in the manufacture of various compounds, and in many other applications.	A known carcinogen. Has a wide range of possible healrth effects, from minor to severe, depending on compound form.
cyanide compounds	3	Used primarily in electro-plating, metallurgy, and production of organic chem-icals, the making of plastics, and other applications.	Acute and deadly poisons.
dichloromethane	0	Used in metal cleaning and as solvent in the production of other organic chemicals. Also used as a degreaser and in the electroincs industry. Used in a wide range of consumer products.	Known carcinogen. Exposure has irritant dermal and mucosal effects and may cause central nervous system depression.
lead and compounds	5	Used in production of batteries and certain other items and in metal products such as solder and pipes.	Probable carcinogen. High exposure levels may cause brain and kidney damage. Accumulates in tissures; chronic exposure may cause death or damage to internal organs. Exposure impairs development in children.

(continued)

Table 10.1. Characteristics of the thirteen EPA priority chemicals released by Japanese facilities in Kentucky. (continued)

Substance	No. of Japanese TRI facilities	Usage	Health effects
methyl ethyl ketone	3	Used as solvent, catalyst,and in the manufacture of several derived chemical substances, including paint removers, cleaning fluids, and adhesives.	Irritant, wide range of possible health effects, including dizziness, dermatitis, and vomiting. Chronic exposure may cause central nervous system depression.
methyl isobutyl ketone	1	Used primarily as additive to protective surface coatings, also in the manufacture of adhesives, ink, and certain oils. Numerous other uses.	Exposure has irritant dermal and musosal effects and may cause central nervous system depression.
nickel and compounds	4	Used to make steels and alloys, permanent magnet materials, nickel-cadmium batteries, and in electro-plating and ceramics.	Several compound forms are probable carcinogens. Chronic low-level exposure produces dermatitis and mucosal damage.
toluene	5	Primarily used as a component of gasoline; also as a solvent in paints, inks, adhesives, and cleaning agents and in manufacture of organic chemicals.	Primary health effect is dysfunction of central nervous system through inhalation. May produce birth defects.
trichloroethylene	2	Used primarily as solvent and cleaner, particularly in automotive and metals industries.	Known carcinogen. Possible death from exposure at high levels and damage to internal organs from chronic exposure.
xylenes	6	Used as solvent, and in gasoline manufacture, raw material for productino of certain organic chemicals, dyes, and insecticides.	Flammable. Exposure to high levels may cause dizziness, passing out, and death. Chronic exposure may damage bone marrow or developing fetus.

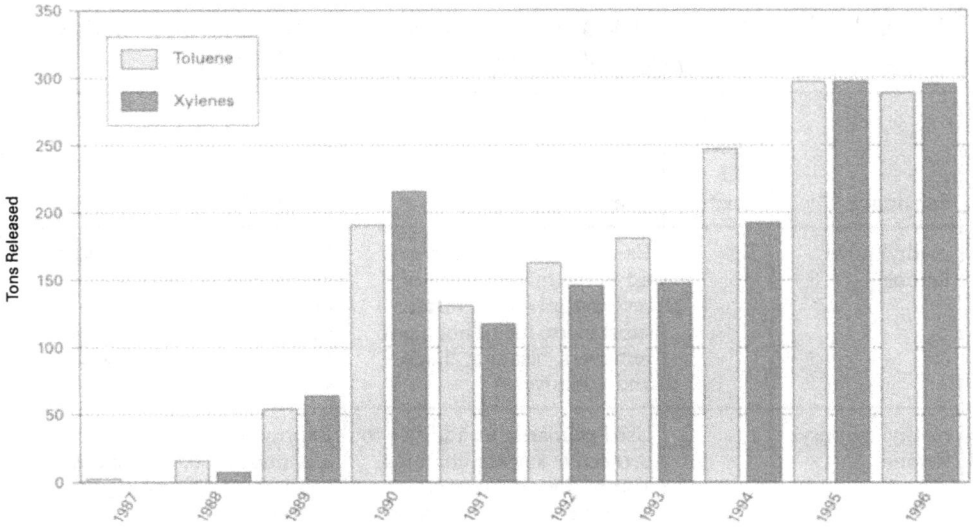

Fig. 10.3. Release of toluene and xylenes by Japanese facilities, 1987–1996.

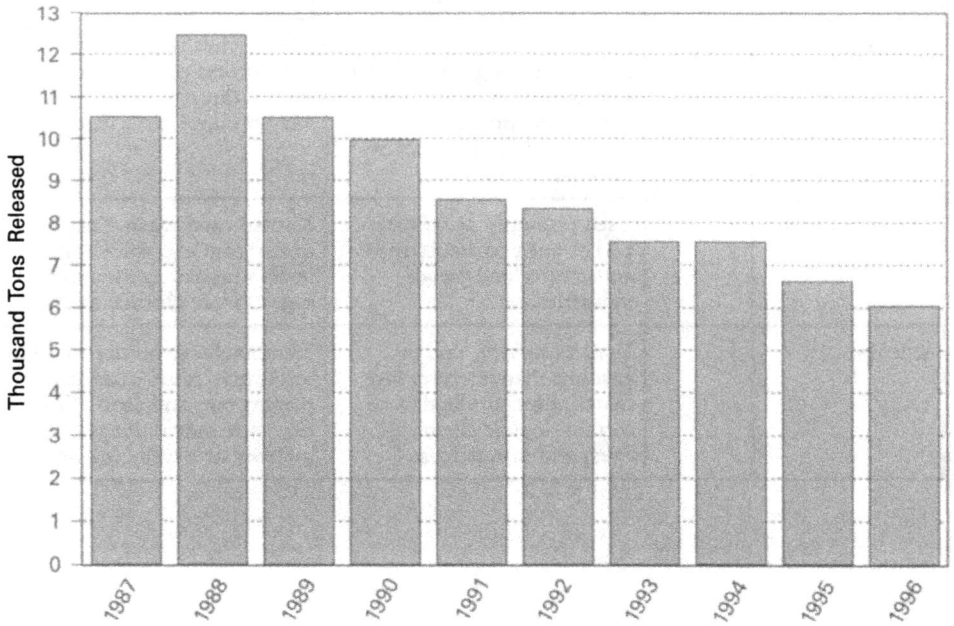

Fig. 10.4. Amount of thirteen priority toxics released by all Kentucky facilities, 1987–1996.

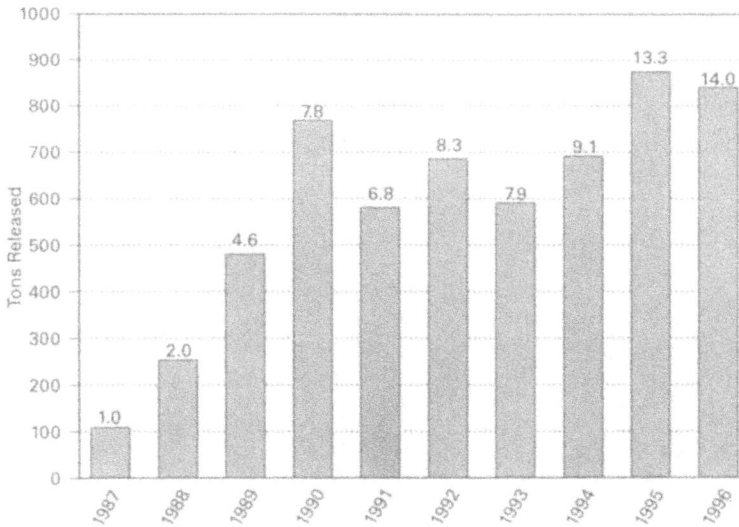

Note: Number at top of bar represents percentage of all KY priority taxes.

Fig. 10.5. Amount of thirteen priority toxics released by Japanese facilities, 1987–1996

Waste Management

While the amount of production waste generated may be considered a measure of the efficiency of resource usage, the quantity in itself is not necessarily harmful to the environment. Not until that waste interacts with the environment, on or off-site, can there be environmental consequences. Thus the waste management policies and practices of a facility do more to determine its actual environmental efficiency than do generation figures. Environmental impact is reduced if practices such as recycling are implemented wherever feasible, following the Japanese model of "continuous improvement," to reduce the amount that is released to the environment or disposed of in landfills.

The role of TRI in identifying the waste management activities of industrial facilities was expanded following the passage of the 1990 Pollution Prevention Act (PPA). Since 1991, TRI companies have been required to report waste management practices in some detail, indicating the quantities of toxics that are recycled or treated on- or off-site or burned for energy recovery, in comparison to that released or disposed of off-site. Source reduction was established as national policy by the PPA as the preferred approach to managing waste. Source reduction is defined by the Act as "any practice that reduces the amount of any hazardous substance, pollutant, or contaminant entering any waste stream or otherwise released into the environment (including fugitive emissions) and, reduces the hazards to public health and the environment associated with the release of such substances, pollutants, or

At the Matsushita Electric Motor Corporation of America plant in Berea, Kentucky, waste products are separated and shipped for recycling. The company is dedicated to proactive environmental protection, prevention of pollution, and continual improvement of environmental programs. (Photograph by P.P. Karan)

contaminants." Practices can include equipment, process, procedure, or technology modifications; reformulation or redesign of products; substitution of raw materials; and improvements in maintenance and inventory controls. Facilities must report any source reduction activities.

Source reduction is considered the most desirable form of waste management, followed in ranked order by recycling, energy recovery, treatment, and as a last, undesirable alternative, disposal. Release to the environment is not considered to be a form of management. "Environmentally sound" recycling, according to the EPA (1997), shares many of the advantages of source reduction: "Like source reduction, recycling reduces the need for treatment or disposal of waste and helps conserve energy and natural resources." On-site recycling is recovery of the toxic chemical for further use. Off-site recycling is transfer of the material to a facility beyond the plant boundaries for recovery or recycling. The same on-site/off-site distinction exists for treatment and energy recovery operations. "Treatment" is the destruction of the toxic material in waste treatment operations. "Energy recovery" is limited to just that, concerned with materials that are combustible and release energy, not those that require energy to be incinerated.

About 80 percent of TRI chemicals produced in 1996 at all Kentucky facilities were managed on site (fig. 10.6) through recycling (46 percent), treatment (21 percent), or burning for energy recovery (12 percent). Of toxics

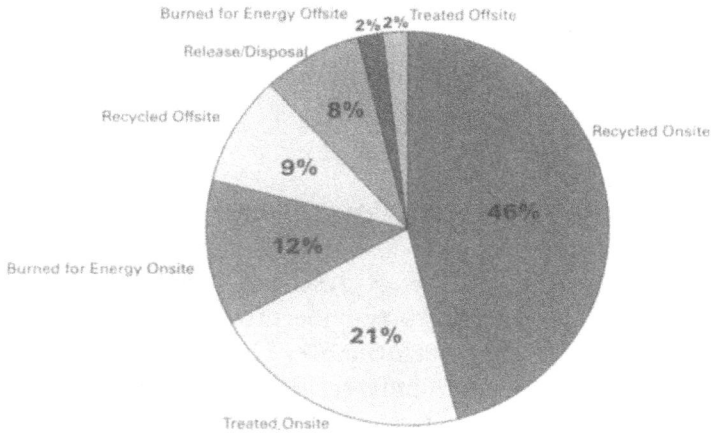

Fig. 10.6. Management of toxic chemical waste in 1996 by all Kentucky TRI.

sent off site, most were handled through recycling. In contrast, Japanese firms depended more on off-site waste management. Toyota sent a little over half of its toxics to off-site facilities for management, most of which was recycled. The average rate of off-site management for all other Japanese plants was one-third of total waste, again mainly handled through recycling. Examination of trend figures for 1991–1996 indicates that there has been very little change in the manner in which waste has been handled by most Japanese facilities (fig. 10.7). The proportions among management categories and whether conducted on or off site has remained relatively stable during the period, although the treatment option did show a slight decrease.

Seventy-six companies with facilities in Kentucky participated in the

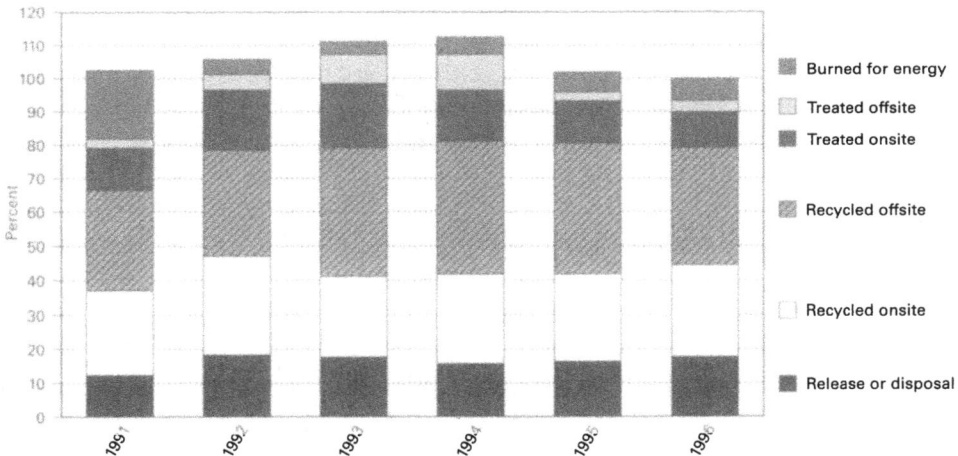

Fig. 10.7. Toxic waste management by Japanese facilities.

33/50 program. The 33 percent reduction goal was met in 1992, but only twenty-four of the companies were able to meet the 50 percent goal by 1995. Among the few companies who achieved the 50 percent reduction goal was A T R Wire and Cable, a Japanese firm.

CASE STUDIES: ENVIRONMENTAL POLICIES AND PRACTICES

Five Japanese manufacturing plants, representing a diversity of industrial types and facility sizes, were selected to provide case studies of current environmental policies, practices, and performance. The accounts are based on plant visitations, interviews with environmental staff, company brochures, and data from RCRA and TRI. The facilities investigated were Toyota Motor Manufacturing, Kentucky, at Georgetown, flagship of Japanese enterprise in Kentucky; KI (USA) at Berea; Zeon Chemicals LP at Louisville; Universal Fasteners at Lawrenceburg; and Hitachi Automotive Products (USA) at Harrodsburg. Figure 10.8 shows the location of these facilities.

Although specific problems vary from facility to facility since different industries have different technologies and generate waste in different ways, the firms are linked by common themes and concerns. Among these are the need to meet regulatory standards and reporting requirements and to maximize production efficiency through waste reduction. Toyota, the largest firm with more than 7,800 employees, manufactures and assembles automobiles. Hitachi, with 950 workers, makes electronic controls for vehicle systems. The 312 KI employees produce metal stampings of certain parts for the automotive industry. Zeon, with 290 workers, makes more than one hundred varieties of synthetic rubber, and about half of the company's production ends up in automotive applications. Only Universal Fasteners has no connection, direct or indirect, with the auto industry, since the buttons and snaps made by the facility's 298 workers supply apparel manufacturers.

Four of the five firms, excepting only KI, are classed as LQGs of hazardous waste. All the firms reported release of TRI toxic chemicals during 1991, but only Toyota and Universal Fasteners indicated release of priority toxics.

Toyota Motor Manufacturing, Kentucky (TMMK), Georgetown

Toyota Motor Manufacturing, Kentucky, is by far the largest Japanese facility in Kentucky and certainly one of the major industrial concerns of the state by any measure. The plant, an integrated facility for assembly of three vehicle models, is located on a 1,300-acre tract just north of Georgetown. Ninety percent of the 8,000,000 square feet under roof is production area. Most of the necessary parts are manufactured on site; only a few are brought in from

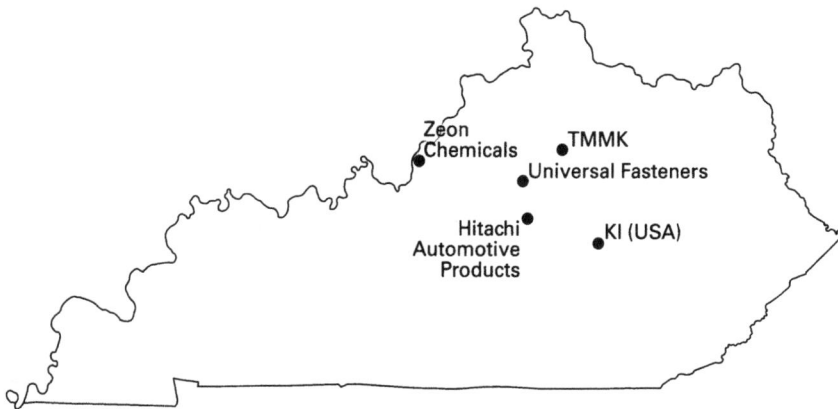

Fig. 10.8. Location of five Japanese Companies selected for case studies of environmental policies and practices.

outside suppliers. The original plant, which began production in 1988, promised to employ three thousand people to assemble two hundred cars annually. After two major expansions, the most recent in 1994, the facility now employs more than seventy-eight hundred workers who turn out nearly a half-million automobiles each year.

Toyota is in the process of obtaining International Standards Organization (ISO) 14001 certification for all of its manufacturing facilities worldwide (Chappell 1998a), and the Georgetown plant is so certified by third-party audit. Staff responsible for primary policy decisions are located at the headquarters in Erlanger, Kentucky, and coordinate among plants in North America. The fourteen-member environmental team at Georgetown is solely concerned with the local operation.

Each of seven specialists on the environmental team has primary responsibility for a certain geographic area of the plant and a specialty focus in a particular program such as water, air, or waste. The specialist in "air" coordinates on matters of that nature with all the geographic area specialists, so that there is a central point of responsibility and a consistency of implementation. On the production floor, each work team has a team leader, who serves to bring ideas and suggestions from the workers. There also are extensively used suggestion boxes, receiving more than eighty thousand submissions each year. Employees receive financial bonuses for ideas that result in savings. Many of the suggestions that come by these routes are concerned with improving the plant's environmental performance.

Each proposed process modification is evaluated for potential environmental impact. Waste management, termed Internal Resource Management, is the primary focus of environmental policy. The environmental team writes a process description and calculates the materials balance, raw materials in

Toyota Motor Manufacturing, Kentucky. Air emissions are the Toyota plant's most serious environmental management problem. Toyota had the best available pollution control technology at the time of its construction in 1987 but has twice the emissions rate of an equal-sized 1994 expansion that incorporated newer technology. Air stack clusters are associated with paint operations for auto bodies and plastic bumpers. (Photograph by P.P. Karan)

versus waste out. The team's operating philosophy is that material that does not become part of the car is a wasted resource. The evaluations are sent back to the shops for ideas and input from the workers. This ensures that more people become involved, that perspectives and ideas derive from more than just the environmental team. To provide incentive, a scoring system was developed to calculate points gained in waste reduction in every aspect of a suggestion, by which means financial rewards to the innovator could be fairly determined. Initially this feedback system was primarily concerned with reducing usage of raw materials, but recently pollution prevention has been added to the evaluation.

The rapid growth of the plant, which doubled in size in 1994, has brought with it some environmental problems. Potential environmental impacts were addressed in the initial design of the plant, and have been dealt with on a continuing basis since production began. Now that the expansion phase at Georgetown has ended, they plan to "take a hard look" at some ways to improve their environmental efficiency. The role of the plant as one of the largest emitters of airborne pollutants in the commonwealth is not an image that the company desires.

The Toyota plant is classed as a LQG of hazardous waste and has increased its generation by nearly 50 percent from the 2,667 tons produced in 1991 to 3,648 tons. Prior to the 1994 expansion that doubled production capacity, hazardous waste generation was stable at about 2,500 tons annually from 1991 through 1994. After the expansion, waste production appears stabilized in the vicinity of 3,500 tons. Production waste in TRI chemicals reported by Toyota for 1996 was 3,440 tons, of which 1,141—one-third—were released into the environment. An additional 11 tons required disposal. Most of the waste was managed by off-site recycling although a substantial portion of the remainder was burned for energy recovery. Releases of priority chemicals during 1996 amounted to half of all TRI releases at the facility, 574 tons of eight different chemicals. More than 90 percent of this was in the form of methyl isobutyl ketone, toluene, and xylenes.

When the plant size was doubled in 1994, next-generation environmental controls were installed, resulting in greater environmental efficiency for the newer facility reflected in the fact that both the quantity of TRI releases and the hazardous waste managed increased by only half. In other words, the newer facility produces half the quantity of toxic releases as the part built seven years before. An example of the difference is in the process modifications made from the older facility to the new. The best control technology available for paint booths in 1986 was installed when the plant was designed, but volatile organic compounds (VOCs) were a major problem. The best technology in 1994 did a better job of handling VOCs, and a materials change in certain production lines replaced solvent-borne paints with water-based coatings.

Paint is one of the most important areas that can be manipulated to reduce environmental impact; for example, air sprays can be replaced with electrostatic painting. This was taken one step further at Toyota when the company found an environmentally friendly solution for the ultimate fate of paint sludge recovered from wastewater. The sludge is shipped to a company in Ohio that processes it into a pulverized building material used by manufacturers to make decorative garden border bricks, roofing material, low-strength concrete, and road-building material (Chappell 1998b).

After pretreatment, about 1.2 million to 1.3 million gallons of wastewater per day are discharged to an adjacent city treatment plant, dedicated solely to serving Toyota, that the company helped build. In 1988, Toyota's wastewater failed an environmental monitoring test and low levels of toxicity—nickel and zinc—were found at the Georgetown treatment plant. Several modifications were made in Toyota's pretreatment system to reduce the metals content of wastewater sent along to the city treatment plant. Success in this endeavor is confirmed by TRI data, which show a trend of decreasing nickel releases.

Planning to improve the Toyota plant's future environmental performance is currently focused on reduction of air emissions, the company's largest vector for releases. Current investigation of materials substitutions may lead to significant source reduction, if solvent-based paints can all be replaced by water-borne or powder coats. One way in which Toyota measures its own environmental progress is through evaluating release of airborne toxics in terms of VOC emissions per car produced. In the past year, largely as a result of focusing on a specific issue—reclaiming solvent sullied by its use in purging or cleaning of paint guns—VOCs released per car dropped from 15.5 pounds per car manufactured to 14 pounds in six months. Additional incentive is provided by a specific regulation addressing automobile manufacturers expected in 2000.

KI (USA) Corporation, Berea

KI (USA) has three manufacturing facilities in Japan and a single international venture, the nearly 200,000-square-foot Berea plant that began production in 1989. The three hundred workers at the facility produce a variety of metal stampings and welded assemblies for the automotive industry. KI products including engine mounts and brake boosters are used by automobile manufacturers such as Toyota, Nissan, Honda, and Ford.

Until recently, environmental management issues at the plant were handled by a specific team, but all such matters are now included among the duties of the engineering manager. The company is dedicated to high standards of product quality, receiving ISO 9000 and QS 9002 certification in October 1997, but has chosen not to seek ISO 14001 certification.

TRI production-related waste from the Berea plant amounted to nearly 4 tons, of which 87 percent was treated on site or recycled off site; most of the remainder was disposed of off site. Less than 1 percent was released to the environment. None of the priority toxics have been released by KI during the period of TRI record-keeping.

About 1,000,000 gallons of wastewater, effluent from surface coating equipment, are annually processed at KI's own treatment center before being released to the Berea treatment facilities. During a recent twelve-month period, the company exceeded the standards for heavy metals in wastewater only once. KI is not classed as a LQG. Hazardous waste resulting from the production process includes a water-based paint containing lead, sulfuric acid used in cleaning, and a petroleum-based oil used in parts stamping. Paint waste is sent to a hazardous materials facility for disposal. Sulfuric acid is recycled or filtered. Most of the oil is constantly reused in the presses; the small amount that temporarily adheres to scrap metal is captured and stored, sent periodically to a recycler for use in making heating oil. Manufactured parts are initially placed in bins equipped with trays to collect oil drips. All nonhazardous materials are sent to local landfills rather than recycled. Cardboard, for example, cannot be recycled because it is frequently oil-saturated.

The facility constantly seeks, in the name of efficiency, to reduce the amount of energy and materials used and waste produced. Installation of metered equipment is currently replacing manual dispensal to reduce the quantity of chemicals used. A reverse-osmosis system was installed in the paint line in September 1998 for the same reason. Parts and supplies are both received and shipped in returnable containers.

Zeon Chemicals, Louisville

The corporate office for Zeon Chemicals LP, a subsidiary of Nippon Zeon Company of Tokyo, Japan, is located at the facility in Louisville. The parent company has four major plants in Japan and a European subsidiary. Additional U.S. plants are located in Texas and Mississippi, while the USA Sales and Product Services Office and a Research and Development/Technical Service Center are located adjacent to the Louisville plant. The 180,000-square-foot Zeon facility, acquired in 1989, employs 290 people to produce a variety of elastomers (synthetic rubber) using an emulsion polymerization process. Zeon's specialized rubber is used in the manufacture of automobile hoses, gaskets, and seals; in many oil field, aerospace, and industrial products; and in a variety of adhesives.

Zeon Chemicals has a full-time environmental team stationed at the Louisville headquarters. The team consists of a corporate environmental manager, whose duties embrace all Zeon's U.S. facilities, and a facility environmental health specialist. The company has ISO 9002 certification but has no immediate plans to seek ISO 14001 certification. Zeon is working with the Kentucky EMS (Environmental Management System) Implementation Alliance and the Kentucky Pollution Prevention Center at the University of Louisville to develop a revised internal EMS that is similar in many respects to the ISO 14001 standards. Because Zeon is part of a much larger industrial complex located in a densely urban region, known locally as "Rubbertown," linkages have been developed with the community to assure coordinated emergency planning and information sharing. A company publicity brochure notes: "We take pride in the fact that in every community in which we are located our own environmental standards place us well ahead of the various regulatory standards."

Zeon is classed as a LQG of hazardous waste, but has shown a steady decline in hazardous waste production during the period 1991–1996, from a peak of 16 tons annually in 1992 to about 3 tons in 1996. Under the TRI program, Zeon reported a total production waste of about 3,100 tons in 1996, of which more than 95 percent were managed without release to the environment. There have been no priority toxics recently released through the production process at Zeon; the use of methylene chloride and 1,1,1-trichloroethane as cleaners was eliminated a few years ago.

Zeon produces somewhat less than one million gallons of wastewater that is treated by a plant shared with three other facilities; Zeon's contribution is about one-third of the total flow through wastewater treatment. Two separate drainage systems serve the Zeon facility. One takes only storm water, and the other collects production wastewater throughout the plant. The storm water access manholes are painted bright yellow with stern warnings not to dump anything into the system. The separate wastewater collection system is continuously supervised through a network of automatic monitors. Hazardous waste is stored in a roofed area with a sump that drains to the wastewater system.

Aboveground bulk storage tanks, transformers, and other stationary objects subject to possible leaks are enclosed by two-tiered spill containment systems. At ground level is a concrete-walled basin with a liner beneath it. The liners vary in their composition according to the type of material stored. Certain air emissions receive treatment in the stacks, going through a catalytic oxidizer. Zeon recognizes both a problem and an opportunity to reduce releases in dealing with airborne styrene and acrilonitrile emissions. Recovery of these two materials is a difficult technological issue. Although a recent process modification attempting to recover a greater percentage was unsuccessful, the plant continues to explore other ways to handle the problem. Zeon's current five-year plan incorporates planning to reduce both hazardous waste and TRI substances.

Environmental management has improved since the facility was acquired by Zeon. Better plant housekeeping and the use of computer controlled flows reduces hazards both to workers and to the environment. Environmental management is enhanced by the company's long-term viewpoint and willingness to accept longer-term payback and benefits from environmental innovations.

Universal Fasteners, Lawrenceburg

Universal Fasteners is the U.S. subsidiary of the privately held Y K K Corporation. Y K K's home offices are in Tokyo, and the corporation conducts operations in more than forty countries. Originally established in 1895, Universal Fasteners was acquired by the Japanese corporation in 1987. The headquarters of its U.S. operation is at the plant in Lawrenceburg. Universal Fasteners has two additional manufacturing facilities in Tennessee and a warehouse location in El Paso, Texas. The Lawrenceburg plant comprises approximately 300,000 square feet in two buildings, of which 160,000 square feet are production space. The facility employs 298 people in production and administration and has a traveling sales force of about 50 people to market its line of buttons, snaps, rivets, and burrs for the apparel industry.

Environmental affairs for the entire U.S. operation are handled by a full-time environmental engineer stationed in Lawrenceburg. Green management principles are set out in the Y K K Environmental Charter of the parent company. The Action Guidelines of the charter promote "conducting business activities friendly to the environment" through technological development, energy efficiency, employee education, and internal review of activities. Universal Fasteners is certified under the ISO and QS quality standards and is pursuing ISO 14001 certification.

The plant recycles nonhazardous material wherever possible. Production of hazardous waste by Universal in 1996 was 57 tons of managed waste and 20,000 tons of wastewater pretreated and released to the local treatment system. Multiyear data indicate an overall trend of waste reduction, although significantly higher figures in certain years have resulted from the voluntary cleanup of contamination sites on the property that date from before the Japanese acquisition. For example, in 1997 more than 20,000 tons of managed hazardous waste resulted from the cleanup of one such site. Universal completed all site remediation during 1999.

According to TRI data, of 410 tons of production waste in 1996 entailing toxics, 1.5 tons, or less than .5 percent, were released to the environment. The primary methods for waste handling were treatment on site and off-site recycling. Priority toxics released by Universal during 1996 included cyanide compounds, methyl ethyl ketone, and xylenes. Priority toxics comprised 57 percent of the plant's TRI releases.

Universal Fasteners has two primary waste streams of hazardous material that result from the paint and lacquer and the electroplating operations. Some relatively simple changes made in the production process in recent years have greatly reduced the amount of waste generated. Paint and lacquer waste has been reduced from a dozen 55-gallon drums generated per month to about three drums monthly by the purchase of a solvent still that distills the solvent back out for reuse.

An even greater reduction was made by dividing a single waste stream into two. Formerly wastewater from the plating and burnishing operations was combined and all the sludge that was separated from this water was treated as hazardous waste. About 40 cubic yards of combined sludge was produced each month. When wastewater treatment was separated into two waste streams, only the sludge resulting from the plating operation qualified as hazardous material. The burnishing sludge was nonhazardous material and could be disposed of in a special waste landfill. Hazardous waste generation from wastewater treatment was reduced from about 40 cubic yards monthly to only about 4 yards per month of plating sludge. The resulting savings in transport and disposal costs allowed the investment to pay for itself in only two years.

Making changes in the production process to implement pollution prevention is not difficult when it can be shown to upper management that proposed changes will pay for themselves in a few years. Administrative staff at Lawrenceburg has authority to approve production modifications.

Hitachi Automotive Products (USA), Harrodsburg

The Hitachi plant in Harrodsburg has grown rapidly from its establishment in 1985 as a facility of only 40,000 square feet to the present structure covering 390,000 square feet and employing more than 650 workers. The plant manufactures a diverse range of automobile electronics including high-technology controls for air, fuel, ignition, and transmission systems. Hitachi products are used in vehicles manufactured by Honda, Ford, Nissan, Isuzu, Subaru, and Toyota. Hitachi facilities are located on every continent except South America and include four plants in the United States. The Harrodsburg plant is the headquarters for U.S. operations.

The Harrodsburg plant maintains a staff of six full-time employees in its Environmental Safety Group. Hitachi has been an industry leader in meeting ISO standards, obtaining ISO 9001 and QS 9000 certification in December 1995 and achieving ISO 14001 status in March 1998. Proposals for new techniques or chemicals to be used in production undergo an approval process to assure consistency with ISO standards. The facility undergoes an assessment every six months by a third-party registrar to assure compliance with the standards and with state and federal regulations.

Hitachi's efforts to improve its environmental performance, particularly in terms of waste generation and management, have been highly successful. Generation of managed hazardous waste was fairly constant during 1991–1996, fluctuating between 15 and 25 total annual tons. TRI records provide data that indicate a progressive reduction of toxics from 1991 to 1996; the 5 tons of toxics reported in 1991 is only 7 percent of the 72 tons generated in 1991. At the same time, releases to the environment were reduced from 90 percent of production waste to less than 1 percent. In terms of actual gain, the 62 pounds released in 1996 is only 0.05 percent of the quantity released in 1991. There have been no priority toxics reported for Hitachi during the period of record.

Near every work station are waste bins. All waste materials, hazardous and nonhazardous, are sorted according to composition. About 90 percent of the nearly 100,000 pounds of hazardous waste (mostly alcohol and lead) annually produced at the plant is recycled, primarily in fuels blending. In addition, each year nearly 2,000,000 pounds of other materials, such as cardboard and aluminum shavings and castings, are recycled. The recycling program earned $138,000 for the company last year. Surprisingly, these earnings are viewed as a failure rather than success, simply because material that needs to be recycled represents inefficiency and waste in the production process.

Hitachi Automotive Products (USA), Harrodsburg, Kentucky. The Hitachi staff continuously seek opportunities to reduce the operation's environmental impact through small, inexpensive process changes. The operation in which alternator windings receive a varnish coating provided an opportunity for hazardous waste reduction by switching from a solvent-based varnish to a water-based coating. Unlike the solvent-based coating, excess water-based varnish could be recycled back into the process. (Photograph courtesy of Hitachi Automotive Products)

The environmental team constantly seeks ways to reduce the environmental impact of Hitachi's operations. For example, alternator windings are coated with a varnish in one stage of the manufacturing process. The varnish cures on exposure to air, so that any excess material becomes quickly unusable. The team is investigating the use of a water-based varnish that requires heat curing, so that the excess can be reused. Another present concern is the necessity to dispose of small containers emptied of nonhazardous materials. The use of large (250-gallon) returnable containers is among alternatives being considered. Many parts obtained from suppliers are received in returnable cartons. In another example, plastic scrap from injection molding is returned to the production process and incorporated, up to 20 percent by weight, into new moldings. In 1995 the company abandoned the use of chlorofluorocarbons (ozone depleter) for cleaning circuit boards and switched to alcohol. One of the highest priorities for the team is to find a way to eliminate lead from the soldering process.

Upper management tends to be receptive to innovations that reduce the environmental impact of the plant when it can be demonstrated that these innovations improve efficiency. Since the reduction of waste in all aspects of manufacturing is a prime concern, such proposals generally receive favorable attention. The Harrodsburg Hitachi facility received the 1998 Kentucky Governor's Award for Environmental Excellence.

ENVIRONMENTAL PERFORMANCE INDICATORS FOR INDUSTRY

Many possible waste management criteria might be used to evaluate the environmental performance of individual industrial firms. Such criteria may represent simple accounting of total quantities of waste generated during the production process or the totals or percentages attributed to various postproduction methods for recovering or disposing of the wastes. More sophisticated approaches may compare multiple variables, such as waste generation per unit of production, per unit of company revenue, or per worker, in an attempt to define an indicator comparable across different facilities.

Any meaningful indicator of industrial environmental performance must take into account three distinct aspects of waste generation and management: magnitude, potential hazard, and efficiency. Magnitude is concerned with the total quantities of the residual substances involved; hazard refers to the risk posed by different substances to human and environmental health; and efficiency concerns the proportion of waste that is not reused or recovered but escapes the production cycle to interact freely with the environment. A further dimension of waste efficiency involves the hierarchy of waste management strategies, in that options such as source reduction or recycling are both more efficient and more ecologically desirable than treatment or disposal.

The interplay among these factors is critical to assessing environmental risk. For example, a firm that generates a large amount of waste might seem to be a greater environmental threat than a firm that generates a small amount. Waste does not, however, become an environmental hazard until it begins to interact with the environment. If the large-quantity waste producer has implemented strategies that recover nearly all the waste and the smaller producer has not, then the smaller producer may be releasing more waste material to the environment. Further, environmental risk is greatly dependent on the relative toxicity or other hazardous attributes of any materials that are not recovered. A small amount of a highly toxic substance is likely to pose a greater environmental risk than a larger amount of material of low hazard. Thus any single facet of industrial waste generation is wholly inadequate for assessing either environmental performance of the firm or the potential risk to the environment.

Table 10.2 illustrates the complexities inherent in environmental performance assessment. The table depicts several different ways of assessing performance, using either or both of the factors of magnitude and efficiency. The

Table 10.2. Environmental statistics for study group (1996 data)

Facility (# workers)	RCRA HazWaste Generation		TRI Toxic waste generation		TRI toxic waste releases		
	Total (tons)	Per jpb (lbs)	Total (tons)	Per jpb (lbs)	Total (Tons)	Per jpb (lbs)	% total waste
Toyota (6,600)	3,648.3	1,105.5	3,440.54	1,042.6	1,141.43	345.9	33.2
Hitachi (650)	16.5	50.8	5.05	15.5	0.03	0.09	0.6
KI (350)	n/a	n/a	3.94	22.5	0.04	0.23	1.0
Universal (250)	57.4	459.2	410.43	3,673.6	1.52	12.2	0.4
Zeon (165)	3.3	40	3,104.36	37,628.6	137.87	1,671.2	4.4

issue of hazard is partly addressed, in that the classes of materials represented by the RCRA and TRI programs are hazardous by definition, yet there is still considerable disparity among the different substances. Acknowledging, then, that any system that does not fully incorporate all three factors imperfectly represents environmental risk, the two factors of magnitude and efficiency appear suitable to assess environmental performance in terms of a facility's ability to reduce or eliminate waste residuals.

Data for the five case studies facilities are used to make comparisons of environmental performance (table 10.3). The table includes RCRA and TRI data, both evaluated on the basis of total waste generation, and, for TRI only, total releases.[4] Total waste generation, as noted, does not address either production efficiency or environmental risk. Environmental risks can only be assessed if waste generation is compared to waste management practices. Nor can examination of practices alone convey a sense of environmental risk. For example, the release rate for Toyota is 33.2 percent of production waste and for Zeon, 4.4 percent, but a simple percentage figure tells us nothing about the magnitude of the problem. Conversely, the total quantity of releases reveals little about the relative efficiency of the production system in terms of waste management. Clearly, neither comprises a meaningful evaluation when used without other contextual information.

To assess environmental performance, measures of magnitude and efficiency need to be combined in terms of some production ratio generalizable across industrial categories. Toyota's use of waste emissions-per-vehicle-built as an indicator of environmental progress might be applied to automobile

250   Gary A. O'Dell

Table 10.3. Environmental performance rating of five Japanese facilities

Zeon	1,655.28
Toyota	345.28
Universal	13.2
KI (USA)	0.20
Hitachi	0.10

assembly plants but cannot be applied to the manufacturers of other products, including automobile parts suppliers, because the units are not comparable. Waste releases per assembled vehicle does not, by any means, correspond to waste releases per auto brake pad, garment zipper, or VCR manufactured. Another method might be to use waste generation per dollar revenue, but accurate information concerning corporate finances at the plant level is often difficult to obtain. This is particularly true for Japanese companies, most of which are privately held. One per-unit measure that may be applied using readily available information is the use of waste releases-per-worker. Whereas releases, when contextualized, are relative to efficiency, the number of workers roughly corresponds to the scale of the operation and is therefore relative to the magnitude of production. The combination of releases-per-worker thus has implications for environmental efficiency.

This is shown in table 10.2, in the column listing TRI toxic waste releases per job. For example, total toxic waste generation for the Georgetown Toyota plant in 1996 was equivalent to 1,042.6 pounds per worker for each of the factory's 6,600 workers. Since the calculated rate of releases for that year is equivalent to 33.2 percent of total waste generation, a rate of 345.9 pounds of waste releases per job can be derived. This provides a measure of environmental efficiency that takes into account both the magnitude of waste generated and of the proportion released and the effectiveness of waste management. Note that, according to this method, Toyota would be credited with a greater efficiency than Zeon even though the automobile maker had nearly eightfold greater releases both in total quantity and as a percentage of total generation. This is a consequence of Toyota's far lower rate of production waste per worker employed.

Although this method provides a measure of environmental efficiency, this should not be confused with environmental impact. The potential impact to the environment from Toyota's airborne emissions is greater than Zeon's simply because Toyota's contribution is much larger. Theoretically, if Zeon operated on the same scale as Toyota, the chemical company's impact on the environment would be greater than the automobile plant because although Zeon's percentage of releases is less, the releases per worker are five times larger. In reality, however, economies of scale would probably invalidate a direct projection of this sort.

The releases-per-worker method, while providing a means to estimate environmental efficiency, is subject to several qualifications. A primary weakness in this system is that it only applies to that select group of facilities who are regulated under RCRA and/or TRI. This group is, however, by definition most likely to have significant environmental impacts. The method does not reflect inherent differences in many classes of industry nor the varying hazard depending on the type of waste produced. Nor does it take account of resource depletion through overconsumption nor of the inefficiency implied by the existence of waste. A low rate, however, is a reflection of the collective environmental effectiveness of the plant's technology, policies, and practices. It means that waste is being managed effectively through various strategies so that there is minimal impact on the environment.

An environmental snapshot consisting of a single year's waste data says little about trends. A more significant evaluation requires the use of multiyear data. Despite the problems with federal waste data previously noted, particularly in regard to data inconsistencies from year to year, performance assessments may often be made over time. This may require examination of a single chemical substance or a group of chemicals that have been in consistent use throughout the period. The case of Hitachi demonstrates a distinct commitment by the firm to reduce or eliminate waste in the production process (fig. 10.9). In 1991 the Harrodsburg plant generated more than 72 tons of TRI toxic waste, of which more than 90 percent was released to the environment. Through process modifications and materials substitutions, by 1996 the company had steadily reduced its total waste production to no more than 5 tons, of which all but 1 percent was recycled. Using the releases-per-worker assessment, Hitachi has achieved a reduction from more than 200 pounds per worker in 1991 to less than one-tenth of a pound in 1996.

The value of environmental performance assessment lies in its ability to permit evaluation of the effectiveness of waste management practices for individual firms, to make comparisons among firms, and to track improvements in environmental efficiency over time.

ECONOMIC EFFICIENCY AS ENVIRONMENTAL EFFICIENCY

Observations from the case studies suggest explanation for the trends evident in the RCRA and TRI data. Waste management is an important concern for industrial firms; efforts are being made to reduce or eliminate residuals from manufacturing by implementing process changes, new technologies, and materials substitutions. Such innovations are not limited to Japanese-owned industrial firms, but Japanese companies appear to be more committed, or at

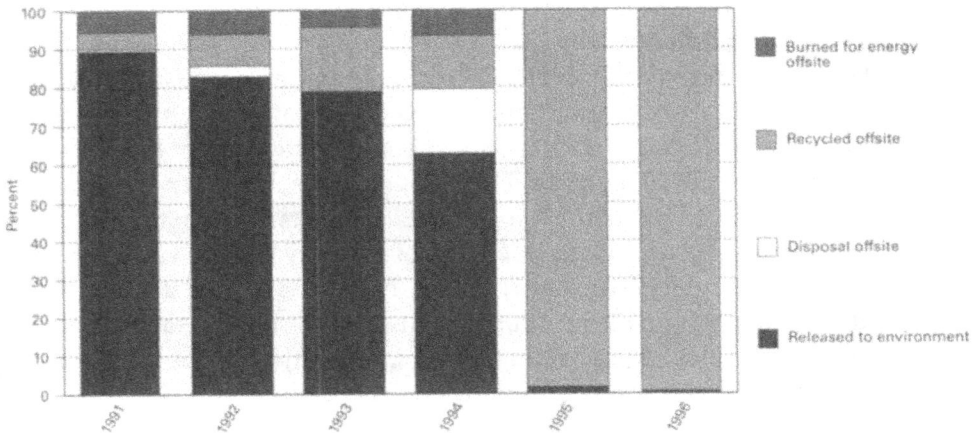

Fig. 10.9. Toxic waste management at Hitachi, 1991–1996.

least more successful, in waste reduction. This is reflected in data trends which indicate that (1) total hazardous waste produced by Japanese firms has remained a stable percentage of the total hazardous waste production for all RCRA firms in Kentucky despite a substantial increase in both number and capacity of Japanese plants, (2) the number of Japanese industrial plants producing toxic waste is proportionately five times greater than for the general industrial population, yet generates only twice as much of this waste category, and (3) releases to the environment of both RCRA and TRI chemicals, when compared on a per-worker basis, are significantly less for Japanese facilities than for those of other ownership.

The evaluations conducted in this essay suggest that improvements in environmental efficiency are carried out by Japanese industrial facilities as part of a process designed to increase their general efficiency and profitably. Every environmental staff member encountered emphasized the concept that economic efficiency and environmental efficiency are tightly linked aspects of industrial facility management. In the words of the environmental staff team leader at Toyota, "environmental protection almost always is the result of an efficiency gain."[5] Policies and practices that reduce waste increase the efficiency of the production process and benefit the environment. Environmental standards and regulations help drive the push toward efficiency.

Toyota's team leader further noted, "Our philosophy is to get as close as possible to the regulatory requirement and to do it better if it results in cost efficiency." This is an indicator of priorities among various incentives for facilities to seek greater environmental efficiency. Cost efficiency remains the primary impetus for facilities to consume fewer resources and produce less waste. This is not surprising, since this is the central premise that underlies a corporation's existence. Cost efficiency and environmental efficiency appear to be converging toward a common goal, that of minimal environmental impact by minimal waste production. Fueling this trend are environmental laws and regulations so numerous and complex that it is often more economical to implement ecologically sound source reduction and waste management practices than it is to cope with mountains of paperwork from myriad agencies and to wield squads of lawyers in litigation.

A further benefit of pollution prevention is that industries that are regulated tend to be classed by certain thresholds, and it benefits the corporate image to be placed in the lower ranks. No corporation wishes to be reviled in the media as a result of belonging to a class considered particularly harmful to the environment. Because of threshold classes such as those in RCRA where a jump in class results in tighter regulation and stricter reporting requirements, there is strong incentive driving facilities to reduce waste generation and thereby sink below the threshold to a less demanding regulatory level, such as from LQG to SQG. Facilities whose numbers are just above or just below a class threshold seek sanctuary by achieving and remaining within a lower ranking.

Evidence from RCRA and TRI data combined with observations and conversations during facility visits suggests a hierarchy of incentives for the improvement of environmental performance. Foremost is economic efficiency, followed by and driven in part by laws and regulations. Following this is corporate image, which affects not only its status in the community but the company's ability to market its products. Interwoven among these concepts are health and safety issues. A facility's workers are not only the plant's direct link to the external community; in many cases they are the community. Degradation of the local environment is likely to affect the health of the population and consequently productivity. For this reason many facilities believe that health and safety issues are of equal or greater import than environmental issues, and sometimes have a separate staff. Environmental issues and health and safety issues are so closely linked that respective staffs tend to work closely together.

Measures taken to improve environmental efficiency are part of an ongoing process in the facilities visited. In the case of Toyota and many other firms, this is part of the company's *kaizen,* or continuous improvement practice. From the examples in the case studies, it is evident that often simple and relatively inexpensive changes made in the production process can result in substantial reduction in the environmental impact of industrial operations. These changes may incorporate new technologies, for as Ayres and Ayres (1996, 24) have observed, ". . . it is not safe to assume (as macroeconomists tend to do) that every technology in place is the optimal choice, as if it had been the winner in a Darwinian competition against all possible candidates." Improvements in environmental efficiency resulting from small technological investments are usually within the means of even aging, less competitive facilities. New plants tend to incorporate newer, more efficient technologies on a larger scale: the dramatic improvement in waste reduction for Toyota's recent expansion is evidence of environmental improvement through newer, "best available" pollution control equipment. For many waste management problems, however, technological solutions have not yet been devised and so the lack of appropriate technology sometimes forms a presently insurmountable barrier to waste reduction. The case studies demonstrated that not all solutions need to be technological. Process modifications as simple as substituting one material for another or dividing a single waste stream into two have paid off both in environmental and economic efficiency.

A facility may be guilty, in both economic and ecological senses, of being inefficient and squandering natural resources by a production process that results in a great deal of wastage. When process modifications are implemented that result in reduced demand for resources and reduced waste production, a significant move has been made toward sustainable industrial production. If process waste is contained or is released to the environment in quantities no greater than the ability of an ecosystem to sustain itself in a healthy condition while absorbing and transforming the byproducts of civilization, then environmental degradation is not occurring. In this way two different but overlapping approaches to environmental assessment can be reconciled.

The economist pursues the goal of efficiency in all phases. This ideal meets the criteria for the ecosystem health paradigm as expressed in Haskell, Norton, and Constanza 1992: "An ecological system is healthy and free from distress syndrome (irreversible process of system breakdown leading to collapse) if it is stable and sustainable, that is maintains its organization and autonomy over time and is resilient to stress"; and in Karr 1992: "A biological system is healthy when its inherent potential is realized, its condition is stable, its capacity for self repair when perturbed is preserved, and minimal external support for management is needed." To both economist and ecologist, the ideal is for zero waste production, and failing that, zero releases to the environment. "Actively seeking zero wastes and pollutants," states Hirschhorn (1992) in an essay aimed at corporation executives, "is still the best path to economic success. This kind of zero-waste vision is key to the economic conversion of costs into profits."

Industrial firms may be proactive within their own terms, promoting environmental efficiency wherever a gain in economic efficiency can be demonstrated, or may be simply reactive, responding only to the extent required by government regulations and public opinion. The data analyzed and the case studies suggest that, while there is still considerable variation in the environmental efficiency among different plants and particularly for different industries, most facilities under Japanese ownership tend to be environmentally proactive insofar as it serves their own interests. The key, perhaps, resides in a greater appreciation by Japanese management that a sustainable environment does, indeed, often serve corporate interests.

IMPLICATIONS FOR AN INDUSTRIAL ECOLOGY

Conventional industrial systems are primarily linear in nature. Raw materials and energy enter one part of the system and are transformed to products and waste residuals; some wastes are recycled or used within the system, and others are dissipated into the environment. Traditional approaches to managing pollution involve attempts to shift wastes from places where they are potentially harmful to places where this potential can be controlled, or to alter the wastes into forms less damaging to the environment. These end-of-the-pipe approaches do not usually reduce the actual volume of waste. The solution is to use materials more efficiently or to find ways to transform wastes so that they are no longer wastes but become useful economic commodities. The closer that industry comes to achieving these twin goals, the more it has maximized both economic and environmental efficiency.

The manner in which particular wastes are managed is a function of the relative costs of methods of waste management. Conventional economic theory defines a waste residual as a nonproduct that has a market value less than the costs of collecting, processing, and transporting it for use. According to Kneese and Bower (1979), "the definition is time dependent, that is, it is a function of (1) the level of technology in the society at a point in time and (2) the relative costs of alternative inputs at that point in time." As evident from the case studies, more efficient use of resources may involve application of technological innovations, process modifications, or product redesign, so that production wastes are reduced or eliminated. Transforming waste residuals into commodities is usually accomplished by recycling back into the production system on site or through off-site recycling by materials processors. It is again evident from the case studies that efforts to reduce waste are implemented when production costs can be reduced by so doing, or if pressure to reduce waste is externally imposed, as in the case of government regulations or a response to public opinion.

In 1998 the Toyota Motor Manufacturing plant in Georgetown adopted an innovative approach to transforming one class of production waste, paint sludge, into a commodity. Paint sludge is now shipped to an out-of-state facility that detoxifies the waste and turns it into a brick-like building material. As plant officials readily admit, this is not the most economically efficient solution to the problem of paint waste, since the handling costs for this strategy are greater than those that would be incurred by simply sending the material to a landfill (Chappell 1998b). This waste commodification represents, however, not only an astute public-relations exploit but also a substantive experiment in seeking both economic and environmental efficiency by further deviating from a traditional linear industrial system.

This precise sort of waste commodification along with efficient use of resources represent the central concepts in a multidisciplinary body of industrial theory that has become known as industrial ecology. The major focus of industrial ecology, according to Ayres and Ayres (1996), is "to identify opportunities for reducing wastes and pollution in the materials-intensive sectors by exploiting opportunities for using the low-value byproducts (i.e., wastes) of certain processes as raw materials for others." Industrial ecology is a biologic metaphor, reflecting on the similarities between industrial and natural systems. Both industrial and natural systems assimilate energy and materials or nutrients and produce waste. Whereas conventional industrial systems exploit materials and energy in linear fashion, natural systems, however, tend to recycle most essential nutrients and are driven by solar energy.

An industrial ecosystem is therefore conceptualized as a symbiotic relationship among a group of firms that closely emulates nature by utilizing the waste products of each component firm as raw material—food—for another. In such a cyclic system, there is no such thing as waste, in the sense of a material without value; all residues are absorbed within the industrial system and do not impact natural systems. The primary goal of industrial ecology, according to Garner and Keoleian (1995), is to promote sustainable development at the global, regional, and local levels through the sustainable use of renewable resources and minimal use of those that are nonrenewable. More precisely, "industrial ecology as applied in manufacturing involves the design of industrial processes and products from the dual perspectives of product competitiveness and environmental interactions" (Graedel and Allenby 1995).

The necessary components for establishment of an industrial ecosystem are described by Ayres and Ayres (1996). A multifirm industrial ecosystem will usually require a large operational scale and both vertical and horizontal integration. "An industrial ecosystem must look like a single economic entity (firm) from the outside. It will have consolidated inputs and outputs (products). It will compete with other such entities (firms) in both raw material and product markets. It will also compete with other firms for capital. From the inside, however, central ownership with hierarchical management is almost certainly not the optimum solution. Too much depends upon very sensitive and continuous adjustments between the different components of the system" (p. 290).

The authors note that a modern conglomerate, where autonomous units are linked to a corporate parent by a purely financial set of controls, each competing for funds on the basis of profits, also does not provide a satisfactory solution. Industrial ecosystems will require close long-term cooperation and planning between waste producers and consumers, since neither can change either processes or production levels without affecting the other. Thus, internal technological choices and financial transactions must be premised on what is good for the industrial system as a whole, rather than any one firm. An industrial ecosystem is likely to consist of a single major waste exporter with numerous satellite waste converters using the residuals of the primary firm to manufacture other products. The low value of residual materials dictates local use, so that a centralized industrial organization is necessary in which all firms involved are in relative proximity to one another.

The Ayreses identify three current industrial organizational strategies that might serve as models on which to build an industrial ecosystem. The first is the common ownership model of vertical integration, exemplified by corporations such as IBM and GM that own all or most of their suppliers and manage the entire collection centrally. A second model may be found in the retail marketing organization, such as those created by Wal-Mart or McDonald's. Both of these potential models have significant flaws. Vertical integration tends to be cumbersome, often losing markets to more agile competitors due to a centralized decision-making process that is slow to react to changing circumstances. The marketing organization provides little incentive for cooperation among suppliers.

The third model for interfirm cooperation might be derived from the Japanese system of *keiretsu,* a family of firms normally controlled by a large bank, with links to a common trading company, and several major first-tier manufacturers spread over a range of industries. Each of the first-tier companies generally has a number of smaller satellite suppliers. As a model for an industrial ecosystem, the keiretsu suffers from some of the disadvantages of the other organizational types, but it has several advantages, including a primarily horizontal integration and a tendency for close geographical association of unit firms.

At present, industrial ecology remains more of a concept than a practical reality, but points the direction for future industrial production in a sustainable manner. Primary problems associated with realization of the concept are likely to be development of technologies to recover a greater percentage of waste that now escapes capture, development of products and markets based on reclaimed materials, and breakdown of barriers in interfirm cooperation. Toyota of Georgetown symbolically closed one production cycle with a structure constructed of bricks manufactured elsewhere from its own waste products. While this represented only a small fraction of waste generation at the plant, it was a first important step in the development of interdependent linkages in a potential industrial ecosystem.

ACKNOWLEDGMENTS

I would like to thank the following industry environmental staff for taking the time to show me around the facilities and discuss environmental issues:

Roy Short and Deanna Helmers, Hitachi Automotive Products (USA); Bruce Freisinger, KI (USA); Tom Herman, Zeon Chemicals; Todd S. Baldwin, Universal Fasteners; and Steve Green, Toyota Motor Manufacturing, Kentucky. Linda Shearer, Hazardous Waste Branch, Kentucky Division of Waste Management, assisted in locating and explaining RCRA documentation. Appreciation is due to Scott Richards and Eric Siegel of the Kentucky Environmental Quality Commission for information and advice.

Notes

1. RCRA information was obtained with the assistance of the Kentucky Division of Waste Management under the Provisions of the Freedom of Information Act. TRI data was obtained on the Internet through the Right-to-Know Network: *http://www.rtk.net*.

2. Federal facilities have also been required to report TRI data, but constitute only about 1 percent of the total. In 1997 the TRI scope was expanded to include additional classes of facilities, including most electric utilities, petroleum bulk stations, and wholesale chemical distributors.

3. Officially, the Comprehensive Environmental Response, Compensation, and Liability Act.

4. Differences between the two federal programs are immediately apparent in terms of total waste generation. The large discrepancies are attributable primarily to the different reporting requirements of the two programs.

5. Interview with Steve Green, Toyota Motor Manufacturing, Kentucky, March 1999.

References

Ayers, R.U., and L.W. Ayres. 1996. *Industrial Ecology: Towards Closing the Materials Cycle.* Cheltenham, UK and Brookfield, Vt., USA: Edward Elgar.

Baker, M.S., J.S. Kaming, and R.E. Morrison. 1977. *Environmental Impact Statements: A Guide to Preparation and Review.* New York: Practising Law Institute.

Barbier, E.B.1989 *Economics, Natural-Resource Scarcity and Development: Conventional and Alternative Views.* London: Earthscan Publications Limited.

Chappell, L.1998a. Toyota Seeks ISO Label by 2001 for All Plants in North America. *Automotive News,* 17 August.

———.1998b. Circle of life: Toyota Is Building Pride and Money by Finding Uses for Paint Sludge. *Automotive News,* 23 February.

Cole, L., S. Richards, and E. Siegel. 1999. *1998–1999 State of Kentucky's Environment: Charting a Path of Progress into the next Century.* Frankfort: Kentucky Environmental Quality Commission.

Garner, A., and G.A. Keoleian. 1995. *Industrial Ecology: An Introduction.* National

Pollution Prevention Center for Higher Education. Ann Arbor, Mich.: University of Michigan.

Graedel, T.E., and B.R. Allenby. 1995. *Industrial Ecology.* Englewood Cliffs, N.J.: Prentice Hall.

Haskell, B.D., B.G. Norton, and R. Constanza. 1992. What Is Ecosystem Health and Why Should We Worry about It? In *Ecosystem Health: New Goals for Environmental Management,* ed. R. Constanza, B.G. Norton, and B.D. Haskell, 3–19. Washington: Island Press.

Hirschhorn, J.S. 1992. Economics of Waste Reduction, Resource Recovery, and Recycling. In *the Greening of American Business: Making Sense of Environmental Responsibility,* ed. T.F.P.

Sullivan, 144–59. Rockville, Md.: Government Institutes, Inc.

Karr, J.R. 1992. Ecological integrity: Protecting Earth's Life Support Systems. In *Ecosystem Health: New Goals for Environmental Management,* ed. R. Constanza, B.G. Norton, and B.D. Haskell, 223–38. Washington: Island Press.

Kneese, A.V., and B.T. Bower. 1979. *Environmental Quality and Residuals Management.* Baltimore: Johns Hopkins Univ. Press.

Manufacturer's News, Inc. 1991–1999. *Kentucky Manufacturer's Register.* Multivolume. Evanston, Ill.: Manufacturer's News, Inc.

Openchowski, C.1990. *A Guide to Environmental Law in Washington, D.C.* Washington, D.C.: Environmental Law Institute.

Pearson, C.S. 1985. *Down to Business: Multinational Corporations, the Environment, and Development.* Washington: World Resources Institute.

Therivel, R., E. Wilson, S. Thompson, D. Heaney, and D. Pritchard. 1992. *Strategic Environmental Assessment.* London: Earthscan Publications Ltd.

U.S. Environmental Protection Agency (EPA). 1997. *1995 Toxics Release Inventory: Public Data Release.* EPA 745–R–97–005. Washington: U.S. Environmental Protection Agency.

Part IV

Attitudes and Public Perception of Japanese Investments in Kentucky

11

Attitudes toward Japanese Investments in Kentucky

Stanley D. Brunn

How can we gauge public reactions to crucial issues facing a population and an economy? This is the central query of this paper. Reactions and perspectives might be obtained through public opinion surveys, advocacy or opposition groups, and official statements and pronouncements of public and civic leaders. However, we also can use the media to help measure sentiments. We can evaluate the amount and content of coverage of particular events and issues, the positioning of stories (on the front page of a newspaper or at the top of the news hour), letters to editors, cartoonists' depictions, and editorials.

In this study I am using editorials in Kentucky newspapers to examine how the public viewed Toyota's decision to construct an auto assembly plant in Georgetown in 1986 and subsequent impacts on the regional and state economies. I want to answer four questions: (1) What newspapers published editorials on the Toyota decision? (2) What were the natures of these editorials, (i.e., What issues were considered to be paramount for readers?) (3) When did the editorials appear? (4) What differences, if any, existed in the content of editorials from various city newspapers? These questions are couched in the context of using editorials to help us to understand how one influential arm of public opinion, in this case newspapers, can be used to assess reaction to the decision to build the Toyota plant in Georgetown and its impacts.

The discussion below is divided into sections that discuss the role of newspapers as gatekeepers of information, the methodology used to examine Kentucky newspaper editorials, and the results of the analysis of the editorials. The focus is on the content of editorials concerning Japanese investment in Kentucky published from 1985 to 1998 in two major metropolitan newspapers, the *Lexington Herald-Leader* and the *Louisville Courier-Journal,* and in the *State Journal,* the newspaper published in the state capital of Frankfort.

Newspaper Editors as Gatekeepers and Their World Views

Two concepts are especially useful in examining newspapers and newspaper editorials: *gatekeeping* and *world views.* Newspaper editors are gatekeepers in the sense that they assimilate information from various sources, filter it, and disseminate it to others. In this case the editorial serves as the dissemination of the "written word." Thus, what one reads in a newspaper, be it in an editorial or in a report on a local or international event, is the product of what the gatekeeper wishes to relay to a large audience. Gatekeepers, whether they are newspaper and magazine editors or radio and television broadcasters, have specific backgrounds that influence how they look at the world. Since newspapers and radio and television stations are the sources of most of our news about contemporary events and interpretations of those events, they reflect the views of the owners of the media outlets. Those owners often have philosophical, ideological, and political views that are reflected in what information is presented to a media audience. The concept of world view, as used by those in the social sciences, describes how institutions and individuals "organize, structure, and look at the world." They may look at the world through the perspective of the editor's or the owner's political views or ideology or philosophy. Those views may be influenced as well by the local and regional culture, or they may be views that are not in concert with the local readership. Thus the gatekeepers' world views may be similar to or at odds with the local or regional culture. Editorials thus serve several purposes: they can reinforce prevailing opinions among the readership; they can be contrary to the vast majority of their readers; or they can educate a readership and may influence changes in attitudes.

Research Methodology

I obtained from the Kentucky Cabinet for Economic Development a publication titled "Announced/Reported Japanese Industrial Investment in Kentucky (at least 10 percent Foreign Owned)." This December 1998 publication listed 107 plants which employed thirty-five thousand workers and had investments of $6.9 billion. From this publication I identified thirty-six counties with Japanese investment. The distribution is concentrated in northern Kentucky, central Kentucky, and south-central Kentucky, west of Interstate 75. The largest number of plants is in Jefferson County (5).

From this list of counties I consulted the *1998 Kentucky Media Guide: Directory of Newspapers and Broadcast Stations* to obtain the newspapers published, and their editors, in the thirty-six counties with Japanese investments. I sent letters—describing the project and asking for copies of their published editorials that related to Japanese investment in the state—to forty-three editors of daily and weekly newspapers in these counties.

The results of this effort were disappointing and surprising. I received letters from only five newspapers, all in central Kentucky. However, one of those letters was from the editor of the *Lexington Herald-Leader*. I contacted the librarian at the *Louisville Courier-Journal* and requested the same information. I visited the Kentucky Department of Libraries and Archives in Frankfort to examine their files of articles and clippings about Toyota developments and especially the editorials from the *State Journal*. That I failed to receive any word from nearly three dozen editors leads me to think they did not publish editorials about Japanese investment. So, not knowing whether there were editorials published in other newspapers in small cities and towns throughout the state, I discuss below only the editorials published in the Lexington, Louisville, and Frankfort newspapers.

RESULTS: EDITORIALS FROM THE FRANKFORT, LOUISVILLE, AND LEXINGTON NEWSPAPERS

Below I examine the twenty-six editorials published in the *Lexington Herald-Leader*, the nine editorials published in the *Louisville Courier-Journal*, and

A worker at Y H America plant in Versailles, Kentucky. Kentucky newspapers have highlighted the employment benefits of Japanese investments in the state. (Photograph courtesy of Y H America)

the seven editorials published in the *State Journal*. Inasmuch as the Lexington and Louisville newspapers enjoy large statewide circulation, the former especially in central and eastern Kentucky and the latter in central and western Kentucky, it seems fitting that they would publish editorials about this important economic development enterprise, especially during the period when it was a major topic of media attention statewide. The Frankfort newspaper, being published in the state capital, may reflect the sentiment of the legislators and the many people employed in various state offices and agencies. Since the capital is in central Kentucky, which is also the site of the Toyota plant, I anticipated that some of the newspaper's editorials would be similar to those appearing in the Lexington newspaper.

The editorials presented views on a number of different subjects, from the impacts on the regional and state economies to incentives provided by the state to problems that affected Scott County (tables 11.1 and 11.2). Some editorials discussed specific issues, such as the legal and constitutional issues raised in the state's incentives package to the corporation, the cost of the gas pipeline Columbia Gas constructed to the Toyota plant, the dollar value of state incentives, and the number of jobs generated by Japanese investments. Others focused on more general subjects, including how the development stimulated an economy that was experiencing problems (downturns in the tobacco and coal economy) and how union activities may deter future outside industrial developments in the commonwealth. Also mentioned were individuals such as former Governor Martha Layne Collins because of her sustained and tireless efforts to bring the Toyota plant to Scott County, former governor Wallace Wilkinson because of his opposition to the investment while he was seeking the office, and union leader Jerry Hammond, who sought to block the investment through legal actions.

Five main themes appeared in these editorials, and several editorials addressed more than one issue. The five themes are: (1) immediate and long-term impacts on the state; (2) the benefits seen to accrue to the Bluegrass; (3) the size, nature, and impacts of state incentives to the corporation; (4) legal and constitutional issues; and (5) problems facing Scott County. Other important issues were raised, but not as frequently.

Immediate and Long-Term Impacts on the State

Editorials in all three newspapers expressed congratulations more than once (usually to former governor Collins and her administration) for encouraging Toyota to select Kentucky as the site for its huge auto assembly plant. There was praise, albeit it sometimes a faint praise, when the decision was announced and also once the plant was opened. The *Courier-Journal* in a November 1987 editorial stated: "There is no question that Kentucky's governor must pursue outside investment. To do otherwise today would be jingoistic and

Table 11. 1. Titles of editorials on Japanese investment in Kentucky, 1985–1998

Date	Newspaper	Editorial title
Dec. 11, 1985	*Lexington Herald-Leader*	"A Noteworthy Performance Brings Toyota to Kentucky"
Dec. 21, 1985	*Lexington Herald-Leader*	"Toyota Incentives Are Worth It"
Jan. 17, 1986	*The State Journal*	"A Little Fiction"
Jan. 27, 1986	*The State Journal*	"Settle Questions Now"
Feb. 8, 1986	*Lexington Herald-Leader*	"Welcome Toyota; Don't Criticize Deal"
Feb. 9, 1986	*Lexington Herald-Leader*	"Base Toyota Discussion on Reason, Not Emotion"
Feb. 17, 1986	*Lexington Herald-Leader*	"Secrecy about Toyota Road Is Silly and Inappropriate"
Mar. 4, 1986	*The State Journal*	"Is It Worth It?"
Mar. 8, 1986	*Lexington Herald-Leader*	"Toyota's Pesky Problems: Knicely's Communications, Coal's Unrealistic"
Mar. 9, 1986	*The State Journal*	"Details, Details, Details"
Mar. 31, 1986	*Lexington Herald-Leader*	"Coal and Toyota: Don't Be a Bully"
May 22, 1986	*The State Journal*	"A Case of Toyota Fever in High Places"
May 27, 1986	*Lexington Herald-Leader*	"Quick: What's 100 Feet Long and Eats Toyotas for Lunch"
June 16, 1986	*Lexington Herald-Leader*	"Cooling Off Toyota Fever"
Aug. 1, 1986	*Lexington Herald-Leader*	"The Hammond Candidacy: Toyota Isn't the Only Issue"
Sept. 1, 1986	*Lexington Herald-Leader*	"Unions in Trouble. Reasons are Evident in Kentucky"
Sept. 12, 1986	*Lexington Herald-Leader*	"Toyota May Still Be Good Deal. But One Such Deal Is Enough"
Sept. 20, 1986	*Lexington Herald-Leader*	"Labor's Pyrrhic Victory in Its Battle with Toyota"
Oct. 27, 1986	*Lexington Herald-Leader*	"The Toyota Deal: Still Looking Good"
Nov. 9, 1986	*Louisville Courier Journal*	"Beyond the Toyota Deal"
Nov. 28, 1986	*Lexington Herald-Leader*	"Unions Win, Kentucky Loses in Settlement at Toyota"
Dec. 4, 1986	*The State Journal*	"Track Record of Success"
Jan. 20, 1987	*Lexington Herald-Leader*	"Is City-County Merger Key to Managing the Change Brought by Toyota Plant"
Jan. 27, 1987	*The State Journal*	"Enough Is Enough for Toyota Motor Corp."
Jan. 27, 1987	*Lexington Herald-Leader*	"Toyota's Gas Deal: Why Is This Incentive Necessary?"

Date	Newspaper	Editorial title
Feb. 9, 1987	*Lexington Herald-Leader*	"Let Toyota Pay for its Own Gas"
Mar. 23, 1987	*Lexington Herald-Leader*	"Wilkinson and Incentive: At Least Toyota Isn't Leaving a Big Hole in Scott County"
Mar. 31, 1987	*Lexington Herald-Leader*	"Toyota Deal: Warts Aplenty, But Still Worth the Effort"
June 13, 1987	*Lexington Herald-Leader*	"Court Ignored Constitution in Toyota Incentives Ruling"
June 21, 1987	*Louisville Courier Journal*	"Constitutional Taffy"
April 6, 1988	*Lexington Herald-Leader*	"Toyota Testing Experience Doesn't Speak Well for State"
June 20, 1988	*Lexington Herald-Leader*	"Results so Far Suggest Deal with Toyota Is Paying Off"
Oct. 9, 1988	*Lexington Herald-Leader*	"Toyota: The Dream Is Open for Tours"
Feb. 2, 1990	*Louisville Courier Journal*	"Kentucky's Loss"
Nov. 11, 1990	*Louisville Courier Journal*	"... We Build Their Cars"
Nov. 28, 1990	*Lexington Herald-Leader*	"Toyota Deal Pays Off: Those Incentives Look Sensible Now, "Don't They?"
July 11, 1992	*Louisville Courier Journal*	"Trading Places"
Dec. 2, 1995	*Louisville Courier Journal*	"Incentives Aside Toyota Choice of Indiana Didn't Hinge on State Bait"
Feb. 21, 1996	*Louisville Courier Journal*	"Headline: Back to the Future?"
May 10, 1996	*Lexington Herald-Leader*	"Top of the Line: Toyota's First 10 Years Worth Every Penny"
July 29, 1996	*Louisville Courier Journal*	"What the Global Economy Means to Kentuckiana"
July 7, 1998	*Louisville Courier Journal*	"Trade War"

Table 11. 2. Topics of editorials related to Japanese investment in Kentucky

Governor Collins mentioned	20
State incentives	16
Benefits reaped by the state and region	14
Legal/constitutional issues	10
Central Kentucky's economy changing	8
Unions and organized labor	6
Governor Wilkinson mentioned	6
Energy: Coal and gas supply	4
Old images and racism	2

Source: The State Journal, Louisville Courier Journal, and *Lexington Herald-Leader.*

irresponsible." It continued: "Toyota's investment also increases Kentucky's credibility with other Asian countries and augers well for the Commerce Cabinet's plan to pursue Korean electronic component manufacturers." The *State Journal* in a December 1986 editorial titled "Track Record of Success," emphasized the importance of the state taking an aggressive posture to be competitive in luring other international companies. It stated: "When word spreads throughout the international marketplace that Toyota—along with Ford and General Motors—are successful with their Kentucky operations, and the ancillary industrial plants that serve them also are successful, that track record may be as attractive to future investors as whatever economic inducements are offered by the state."

Regional Economic Impacts

The Lexington and Louisville newspapers' editorials addressed issues about the impact of Japanese investments, and especially Toyota's, on central Kentucky's economy. The *Herald-Leader* editorials were mostly about the Bluegrass region; whereas, those from the *Courier-Journal* were about benefits the state was reaping from the investments. Only two editorials from the *State Journal* addressed the economic impacts. Editorials in the Lexington and Louisville newspapers expressed support for Toyota decision's to locate in Scott County and the impacts the decision would have on changing central Kentucky's economy from an agricultural base, experiencing the declining role of tobacco, to one in which Kentuckians with good skills and schooling could earn higher incomes. They praised additional Japanese investments in satellite auto parts plants started in Kentucky and southern Indiana in the early and mid-1990s. The *Herald-Leader* noted in an editorial in May 1996 that Toyota was a "model corporate citizen," citing its investments in the Kentucky History Center and investment in state educational and cultural ventures. Six months earlier an editorial praised the corporation for contributing $2 million to the University of Kentucky for its new library and paying local property taxes, even though they were not required, that would be used to construct a new school in Scott County.

State Incentives

A dozen editorials in the *Herald-Leader* commented on the state incentives. While the newspaper was strongly supportive of the corporation coming to central Kentucky, there were also several editorials that noted opposition to this support. The newspaper appeared to take the position of educating the readership on the merits of the state providing incentives for training workers, construction of an interchange, and supplying energy. A major criticism of the incentives package was noted in an editorial on the Kentucky Supreme

Court's decision in June 1987 to uphold the incentives package. While the newspaper applauded the investment, and did not wish for Toyota to depart, it was concerned about the precedent the court set by approving financial packages for firms wishing to do business in the state. The Constitution provides an exemption to the ban on "donations" that are used for "a valid public purpose." This editorial expressed concern for this phrase being used to define reducing employment as a valid public service. In a December 1995 editorial the newspaper commented on the Toyota decision to construct a pickup truck plant in southern Indiana and noted that state incentives were not that crucial in deciding where to locate the plant. Rather the company was more concerned with being located in and around "Automobile Alley" (between Interstates 65 and 75).

Legal and Constitutional Issues

Issues of legality and constitutionality were raised in regard to the incentives package (about $300 million) provided by the state and by union leaders who opposed the tax reform bill. It was suggested in a September 1986 editorial that the state should avoid "financial flirting" with other corporations, which also may want similar incentives from the state. Two editorials in the *Herald-Leader* criticized the unions for taking positions that in the future may deter other industrial investment in the state. The newspaper's position was that Kentuckians would be more interested in the jobs generated by Toyota than victories that might come from organized labor. Four editorials that appeared in the *State Journal* in 1986 raised similar questions of a constitutional nature, including the procedure to award the lucrative engineering contract to the company constructing the roads, the purchase of Scott County land for the factory site, the benefits package the state provided the corporation, and the cost of the Toyota training program. A June 1987 editorial in the *Courier-Journal*, titled "Constitutional Taffy," expressed some of the same concerns and suggested: "If the Constitution no longer serves the state's interests—and much of it doesn't—it needs an overhaul." In a November 1986 editorial, the same newspaper raised questions about the costs (in what it called "murky numbers") of various incentives programs to Kentucky taxpayers, including the Saturday school for Japanese children.

Problems Facing Scott County

Again it was the *Herald-Leader*, more than the other two newspapers that raised questions about problems facing Scott County in a series of editorials in 1987 and 1990. Georgetown and Scott County, more than anywhere else in central Kentucky, were affected by the Toyota plant in the areas of land use, traffic, housing stock, and school system. Real estate speculation was another problem resulting from population growth and land use changes. A March 1987 editorial included comments denoting "warts aplenty" but stating that the development looked "like a real winner for Kentucky" because of providing jobs at a time when tobacco is in trouble. One editorial in January 1987 suggested that a newly forged city-county government, as exists in Lexington-Fayette County, represented the "residents' best chance of managing change and preserving what they like best about their community." It continued by stating that such a merger could be "a trailblazing act of leadership" for other counties. This same message regarding merger was echoed in a November 1990 editorial.

Other Issues

A number of other issues were discussed in editorials, again mostly by the *Lexington Herald-Leader,* which voiced concerns about issues affecting workers, residents, and businesses and political leaders in central Kentucky. On some issues the newspaper responded to positions taken by individuals, such as those seeking political office, who made the Toyota investment a political issue. At other times, it sought to inform the region's residents about issues it considered important to debate as part of the public forum.

I will discuss four topics from the latter category mentioned above. First, the coal industry was taken to task for bemoaning the fact that Toyota corporation decided to use gas rather than coal as an energy source in its produc-

Solid waste at Japanese facility in Berea, Kentucky. Newspapers have generally ignored discussion and reports on the environmental and social impacts of the Japanese investments in the state. (Photograph by P.P. Karan)

tion system and energy source. A second issue, the only single major issue the Lexington newspaper contested regarding the Toyota corporation, was the decision by Columbia Gas to charge eastern Kentucky customers a higher fee to offset the cost of constructing a thirty-two-mile, $3.8 million pipeline. January and February 1987 editorials expressed views that the cost should be incurred by the corporation rather than by eastern Kentucky residents, who would probably only receive marginal benefits from the corporation. A similar editorial in the *State Journal* (January 27, 1987) noted the benefits package the corporation received from a negotiated agreement between Columbia Gas and the Public Service Commission. The newspaper noted that "the real culprit in this ripoff is not Toyota, which is doing nothing but looking out for itself. The blame lies with those who apparently are so mesmerized at the prospect of the Toyota plant that they are prepared to give Toyota whatever it wants and to allow the public, which has no say in any of this, to pay the bill." A third issue was a challenge put to state leaders and legislators to seek ways to improve the quality of education for potential workers at Toyota and future investments. It noted in an April 1988 editorial that in Toyota's screening of job applicants, only 20 percent passed the General Aptitude Test Battery test. The fourth issue was the opportunity for central Kentucky residents to learn about the Japanese people and Japan's important role in the global economy. A February 1986 editorial, only a few months after the decision was made to locate the plant in Scott County, contained this message: "It opened the door for state residents to exorcise some of the misgivings still lingering from World War II and the Japanese economic resurgence." It went on to state that "Toyota executives shouldn't misread the signals coming from Kentucky as being more than isolated opposition towards its plant. Kentuckians are an argumentative lot, and any proposal the size of the Toyota package would be certain to spark some heated debate." It mentioned as well that some of the warning expressed by opponents to the plant "would appear little short of hysterical." Similar strong rhetoric against opponents appeared in a November 1986 editorial; it discussed the victory of organized labor for some construction jobs. It remarked about "always inflammatory and sometimes racist rhetoric used by union leaders" and the threat to hold an anti-Toyota rally on Pearl Harbor Day. It went on to criticize the behavior of construction union leader Jerry Hammond for lawsuits he filed to halt construction of the project and for his "anti-Japanese rhetoric."

Governors Mentioned

Former governor Martha Layne Collins was mentioned in eleven editorials that ran in the *Herald-Leader,* six that appeared in the *State Journal,* and three in the *Courier-Journal*. These credited her for bringing the plant to central Kentucky and supported the incentives package she pushed through the legislature. She, more than any other political leader, is credited for this economic development effort in the region. Her successor, Wallace Wilkinson, was mentioned in six editorials, four of which were in the *Herald-Leader*. He is mentioned in connection with Toyota during his gubernatorial campaign, in connection with a business partner of his Secretary of Commerce who made money on a land speculation, and in connection with being in office when the Toyota plant enjoyed early success.

SUMMARY AND CONCLUSIONS

In this study I used the editorials of three influential major newspapers in the state, the *State Journal*, published in Frankfort, the *Lexington Herald-Leader*, and the *Louisville Courier-Journal* to discern how they looked at Japanese investments in the state during the past fourteen years. This is not to say that other newspapers, perhaps in small counties and small towns in the state, did not also have editorials about Toyota's investment or other Japanese investments in their counties and communities. But the absence of such information, which was requested from editors of newspapers in communities where Japanese plants are located, leads me to conclude that only the newspapers in the two largest cities plus the state capital chose to express on a number of occasions their world views about this significant political and economic decision. The editorials were examined in the context of newspapers being gatekeepers of information and editors using their editorial pages to inform their readers about their own positions on issues. In this process newspapers serve as both filters of information and conveyors of information, in particular about new issues, such as the impact of sizable foreign investment on a state and a region with strong rural economies based on agriculture.

The Louisville newspaper had only nine editorials about Japanese investments, and these were mostly about their magnitude and impacts statewide and globally. A July 1996 editorial noted that Kentucky has "done nicely when it comes to luring foreign investment" to the tune of more than $3.5 billion invested statewide with seven thousand jobs directly and another twenty thousand jobs through suppliers to plants. It concluded by stating that "anyone who says 'global economy' is a synonym for downsizing and impoverishment hasn't been paying attention."

The *Lexington Herald-Leader*, on the other hand, published more than two dozen editorials, most with a focus on where its readers reside. It periodically educated readers about the size of the investment and number of jobs created, praised Toyota's contributions to the local community (Georgetown-Scott County) and to the University of Kentucky, and praised Toyota for helping industrialize the central Kentucky economy. It also took note to comment that Toyota's Georgetown facility is a place that welcomes visitors (an editorial on plant tours ran in October 1988) and that Toyota was serving as a model corporate citizen.

The *State Journal,* as noted above, mostly raised legal and constitutional issues, especially about the awarding of the contract to the Kentucky engineering firm to construct the roads, the costs of the incentives program to "one of the world's wealthiest industrial giants" (May 22, 1986). Six of its seven editorials on Toyota appeared during 1986.

The three newspapers, through editorials that ran during 1986 and later, performed an important public service to their own readers, the residents of Kentucky, and Kentucky politicians at state and local levels about the short- and long-term economic impacts of Toyota's plant on the state and region and about state officials being careful and forthright in explaining incentives to the company and costs to Kentuckians. I believe an October 1988 editorial in the *Herald-Leader* best reflected on the company's impact on Bluegrass area residents and the state: "It's a match made in heaven, come to reality in the rolling fields of Kentucky."

BIBLIOGRAPHY

Kentucky Media Guide: Directory of Newspaper and Broadcast Stations. 1999. Lexington: Clark Publishing.
State of Kentucky, Kentucky Cabinet for Economic Development. 1998. *Announced Reported Japanese Industrial Development.* Frankfort.

12

Public Perception of Toyota Motor Corporation in Kentucky

James G. Hougland Jr.

THE NATIONAL AND WORLD ECONOMIES currently are characterized by a geographic redistribution of industry and employment opportunities. Considerable attention has been devoted to the problems of localities
experiencing deindustrialization (e.g., Bluestone and Harrison 1982). Historically, the impact of new industry on communities also has been a matter
of research interest (Summers et al. 1976). Such attention is appropriate because new industry can represent a significant source of change for a community. As Hallinan (1997) notes, social change is neither linear nor predictable.
At times, it is sufficiently disruptive that one cannot predict whether a system
confronted with change will collapse completely, regenerate in a new form
resembling its former structure, or emerge as a totally new social structure.
Despite its potential for introducing major change in a community or region,
the impact of new industry on communities has received somewhat less attention in recent years. This has occurred in part because of the growing
number of problems associated with plant closings. Recent trends, however,
make new industry—particularly industry that involves Japanese transplant
organizations—increasingly important to study.

It appears that the decreased attention to the social implications of new
industry has occurred despite inconclusive evidence and disagreement about
whether growth (through industrialization or other means) works to the benefit or detriment of local communities and their citizens. Some who have
studied "boomtowns" have stressed the impact of their rapid population
growth on "social disruptions, cultural conflicts, and pathological behaviors,"
but such analyses have been criticized for their implicit antigrowth bias as
well as inadequate statistical controls (Summers and Branch 1984, 154–55).
Albrecht (1982) has noted that such analyses may overlook the *phase* of
change. Early discontinuities associated with growth may dissipate after the

passage of time has allowed primary relationships and community attachments to be re-established.

More positive views of the impact of growth on communities are represented by the work of Eberts (1979), who found from an analysis of rural and urban counties in the northeastern United States that "economic and demographic growth are associated with increases in some of the most commonly used quality-of-life indicators" (1979, 180). He concludes that growth may be important because "economic and demographic structures generate the income and opportunities for individuals and collectivities to invest in the appropriate infrastructure of facilities and activities around which better quality of life can develop" (1979, 180).

Such benefits, however, may not be evenly distributed, and research conducted through the mid-1970s appeared to lead to a firm conclusion that they would not be. Summers and colleagues (1976) found from a review of numerous case studies that, while new industry was associated with increases in median income, the relative economic status of certain segments of the population (e.g., the elderly and minorities) may decrease. In many cases, new industries are found to provide few employment opportunities for the previously unemployed or other relatively deprived segments of the population.

Such findings are consistent with the contention by Molotch (1976) that local growth is of benefit to and supported by only certain segments of a locale's population. As would be predicted from reports by Summers and colleagues (1976) that new industry tends to be associated with increased home construction, real estate valuation, and retail sales volume, Molotch contends that local business interests are most likely to push for continued local growth. As Molotch (1976, 319) notes, survey evidence suggests that "most people's values are . . . more consistent with small places than large." Recent studies also find that agrarianism represents a pervasive orientation shared by urban as well as rural residents (Dalecki and Coughenour 1992). While some may criticize small towns and rural areas for their lack of cultural and recreational opportunities, the overall conclusion suggested by this body of research is that new industry and other aspects of growth are being pushed by a privileged elite whose members will benefit at the expense of the economic interests and preferred lifestyles of most community members.

This analysis may not represent the final word, however. Bartik (1991) has used case study materials, earlier research, and national data sets on the effects of "shocks" to employment in local economies (i.e., increased demand for labor, whether caused by new employers or greater activity on the part of existing employers) on the short-term and long-term economic experiences of local residents. In the short run, increased demand for labor leads to tighter labor markets, resulting in reduced unemployment and increased wages. It is more important, however, to examine long-term effects. Many (e.g., Marston 1985) have argued that local labor demand shocks lack long-term effects because in-migrants will be attracted to localities whose economies are seen to be growing. Bartik, however, contends that mobility is constrained by the financial and psychological costs of moving, and his analysis indicates that labor demand shocks have long-term effects including a small but persistent drop in unemployment and an increase in local labor force participation rates. His analysis suggests that, of one hundred net new jobs for a metropolitan area, six or seven will go to local residents who otherwise would be unemployed, sixteen will go to local residents who otherwise would be out of the labor force, and the remaining seventy-seven or seventy-eight will go to in-migrants (Bartik 1991, 95). Further analysis indicated that a 1 percent increase in a metropolitan area's employment level will lead to a 0.44 percent increase in "real earnings" (i.e., the product of labor force participation, employment rate, weekly hours, and the real wage). Moreover, effects were found to be larger for less educated residents and blacks (Bartik 1991, 157–79). Bartik interprets these results as a reflection of changes in human capital: "In the short run, a shock increasing local growth allows some individuals to obtain jobs who otherwise would be unemployed or out of the labor force. This employment experience alters the 'human capital' of these individuals: they obtain better job skills, or at least they are perceived by employers as having better skills. As a result of improved human capital, they are more likely to be employed in the long run" (1991, 96). In addition, "local growth helps the promotion prospects for blacks and the less-educated significantly more than it helps the promotion prospects for other groups" (1991, 170).

Bartik acknowledges that any progressive effects on the distribution of earnings may be canceled, in whole or in part, by effects on property values. Because of patterns of property ownership, increased property values almost certainly will lead to a regressive distribution of benefits. Bartik's analysis leads him to conclude that individuals in the lowest income quintile will gain more from growth (based on earnings effects alone) than those in the highest quintile will gain from the combination of property value and labor earnings effects of growth (1991, 175). At the same time, he acknowledges that, average differences notwithstanding, "growth will still often have large costs for specific poor individuals and families and large benefits for specific wealthy individuals and families" (1991, 177). These dramatic individual experiences may, of course, affect community members' perceptions to a greater extent than do the average experiences of the overall population. Perceptions may also be affected by changes in non-economic aspects of the community. Bartik acknowledges that community growth may be experienced negatively by local residents because "they are accustomed to the local area as it originally was, and may even have chosen it for its particular qualitative features" (1991, 74). Thus, General Motors' decision to locate its Saturn plant in the small town of Spring Hill, Tennessee, led to concerns about threats to its small-town quality of life and to the viability of farming in the area. Bartik's analysis raises the possibility that classic studies of the impact of new industry may have been overly pessimistic regarding the economic impacts of new industry but on target regarding possible deleterious social impacts.

THE PRESENT STUDY

A 1985 decision by Toyota Motor Corporation to locate an automobile assembly plant in Kentucky created an opportunity to trace changes in public perceptions and evaluations of the plant as it went through its phases of planning, construction, hiring, and early years of manufacturing. The foregoing review suggests that perceptions of the plant's local impact will be of importance. Toyota, in particular, generated opposition on several issues (Yanarella and Reid 1990). Thus, public perceptions of Toyota in central Kentucky may be influenced by early controversies involving the incentives package developed by the state to attract Toyota to Kentucky, the role of unions during the construction phase of the plant, and land and environmental issues.

Perceptions of Toyota's Impact

The announcement of a major new employer often is cause for euphoria, but the euphoria may be short-lived as local residents experience disruptions and become aware of objective limitations in the benefits that the employer will bring to the area. In particular, those who are less likely to benefit from increased property values (Molotch 1976); individuals in the sociodemographic categories less likely to be hired for the workforce of the new plant (Summers et al. 1976), although they may benefit from increased employment in the overall labor market (Bartik 1991); and those who express concern about newcomers in general and the Japanese in particular are likely to have a rather negative view of the impacts of the Toyota plant on the community.

This reasoning suggests the *hypotheses* that perceived impacts of the plant will be more positive for:

H1. residents with more education;
H2. residents with higher incomes;
H3. males;
H4. those who are currently employed;
H5. owners of property or homes in Scott County;
H6. those who expect personal or family benefits from the Toyota plant;
H7. those who have lived in the community for a relatively short time;
H8. those with less attachment to the community as it currently exists;

H9. those who are relatively accepting of newcomers;
H10. those who are relatively accepting of Japanese; and
H11. those who are more knowledgeable about the Toyota plant.

Reactions to the Incentives Package

Incentives packages in general and (as discussed below) the Toyota package in particular have been highly controversial. While individuals may favor or oppose incentives packages on a number of objective and philosophical grounds, it is predicted that attitudes toward the plant will influence evaluations of the incentives package used to attract it to the area. Thus, hypotheses 12 through 22 correspond to hypotheses 1 through 11. In addition, it is predicted that the incentives package will be favored by:

H23. residents who perceive more community benefits associated with the plant and
H24. residents who perceive fewer community problems associated with the plant.

An examination of the foregoing hypotheses will occur in the context of a consideration of the changes that have accompanied Toyota's entry into central Kentucky. While hypothesis testing is only one aspect of this study, it is important from a policy perspective to see what segments of a local population will be more or less receptive to new industry and community change. An identification of those who are less enamored of new industry will provide hints as to the segments of a local population that may need particular assistance or information during a period of change.

STUDY SETTING AND CONTEXT

In December 1985, after considering sites in several states, Toyota announced its choice of Scott County, Kentucky, as the site for its first solely owned manufacturing plant in the United States. (Since 1984, Toyota has been producing cars in a joint venture with General Motors in California. However, the Kentucky plant was to be operated by the wholly owned subsidiary now known as Toyota Motor Manufacturing, Kentucky [TMMK]). Because Kentucky Governor Martha Layne Collins had been disappointed by a recent decision by General Motors to locate its Saturn plant in Tennessee, the recruitment of Toyota received high priority from the governor's office, and a far-reaching incentives package was developed to induce Toyota to choose Kentucky.

The State Incentives Package

The incentives package used to attract Toyota to Kentucky was large in comparison with incentives used to attract comparable manufacturers to nearby states (Milward and Newman 1989). Moreover, examination by the press suggested that the initial public announcements of the size of the package were understated. Original estimates of the incentives package used to attract Toyota to Kentucky were made public in December 1985 and totaled between $120 and $130 million. These estimates were revised in June 1986, with significant increases for some items. While the estimates for land acquisition and the training center remained roughly similar, the cost of site preparation increased by more than 75 percent, from an original estimate of between $20 million and $25 million to nearly $44 million. The increase resulted in part from cost overruns for a sewage treatment plant to serve both Scott County and the Toyota plant. Cost estimates for highway construction were reduced by $10 million, from $47 million to $37 million, but this reduction was based on a decision to use federal highway funds already allocated to Kentucky to finance part of the highway construction in the vicinity of the Toyota facility. Estimates for a state-funded employee training program were revised downward from $33 million to $20.4 million. The 1986 revised estimates for the entire project were put at $122.4 million. Newspaper reporters Miller and Swasy (1986) concluded that estimating all items at their true costs (including federal funding and supplemental state appropriations) led to a total of approximately $155 million, for a total increase of between $25 million and $35 million over the original estimates. Later, the University of Kentucky Center for Business and Economic Research (1992, 2) concluded from an examination of records maintained by Toyota that the best estimate of the cost to the state was $147 million.

Several additional costs were not included in these estimates. These included $224 million in interest on the twenty-year bonds issued by the state, $4 million in additional costs for the sewage treatment plant overruns, $3.7 million for a school for Japanese students, and relatively minor expenditures for legal and surveying fees, impact studies, and the Toyota Planning Center. Taking these additional items into account, Miller and Swasy (1986) estimated the total cost of the incentives package to be about $377 million over a twenty-year period.

The incentives were offered in the belief that Toyota's presence in central Kentucky would strengthen the economy by generating jobs from direct employment at the Toyota facility, support industries associated with the plant, and additional satellite plants. Early calculations suggested that the annual rate of return on the state's investment after a twenty-year period would be approximately 20.1 percent. The plant has been sufficiently successful to lead to announcements of major expansions in its production capacity and workforce. In contrast to its original projections of providing three thousand to thirty-two hundred jobs at full production, TMMK employed seventy-eight hundred people in 1999 (Butters 1999, 11). According to Haywood (1998), TMMK in 1997 purchased parts and materials from fifty-five manufacturers in Kentucky as well as from manufacturers in five other states. His analysis indicates that TMMK accounts for 34,544 jobs in Kentucky (based on its own payroll as well as jobs in its suppliers in 1997) as well as 49,735 jobs in the other five states, for a total of 84,729 jobs (Haywood 1998, 11). Haywood also estimates that Kentucky currently is receiving an annual rate of return of 36.86 percent on its incentives package: "In the 20-year period 1986–2005 the Commonwealth of Kentucky will collect, over and above the costs of the incentives package, approximately $1.2 billion of tax revenues attributable to the direct and indirect effects of TMMK's operations in Kentucky" (Haywood 1998, 16).

While Toyota's success in Kentucky has made its specific incentives package less controversial than it once was, the general wisdom of incentives packages is a matter of ongoing controversy. With debate continuing on a national level, it is unlikely that central Kentucky residents will forget the Toyota incentives package.

Characteristics of the Community and Area

According to the U.S. Bureau of the Census, Scott County had a population of 22,198 in 1985, the year of Toyota's decision. Although this population was larger than that of most contiguous counties, it was appreciably smaller than that of Franklin County, site of the Kentucky state capital (1985 population: 44,137) and Fayette County, which is to Scott County's immediate south and includes the city of Lexington (1985 population: 212,195). Although much of Scott County has a rural or small-town quality, it is part of the Lexington Metropolitan Statistical Area (MSA) and is within reasonable driving distance via interstate highways of two larger metropolitan areas, Louisville and Cincinnati. By the time of the 1990 census, Scott County's population had grown to 23,867, an increase of 7.5 percent since 1985 and 9.4 percent since 1980. County population growth accelerated during the 1990s and was estimated to be 30,685 in 1998. Scott County's percentage increase in population from 1990 to 1998 was 28.6 percent, the highest of the seven counties in the Lexington MSA and the sixth highest of Kentucky's 120 counties. From 1990 to 1998, Georgetown's population increased from 11,414 to 14,365. This increase of 25.9 percent ranked third among Kentucky's thirty-three cities with 1998 populations exceeding 10,000 (Kentucky State Data Center 1999). Although Georgetown and Scott County's growth began accelerating in the 1990s, its slower start in the years immediately following TMMK's announcement may have given the city and county time to adjust and prepare for the coming demand on their infrastructure.

Scott County is not unlike other semirural areas that have been found attractive by incoming industry. It has three incorporated areas (Georgetown and the smaller towns of Stamping Ground and Sadieville). It is the location of a privately funded college and some industrial activities, but agriculture plays an important role in the county's economy. It is linked to major population centers through the interstate highway system. Some research suggests that Japanese firms differ from their American counterparts in their criteria for choosing industrial sites (Doeringer and Terkla 1992). Even so, the characteristics of the Scott County area are consistent with Fulton's (1974, 77–78) identification of the characteristics of communities most likely to attract new industry. The characteristics noted by Fulton (president of the Fantus Company, which acts as a consultant to industries seeking plant sites) are a good highway system, strong community leadership, lack of domination by another single large industry, availability of qualified labor, proximity to a large city, and terrain and industrial sites that can be developed at a reasonably low cost.

Although Scott County has several characteristics conducive to new industry, its residents and government officials were not prepared to deal with some aspects of social and economic change associated with new industry. Local leaders had been allowed little involvement or even information when state officials were attempting to attract Toyota to the area. As a result, they had not been in a position to secure binding promises from either Toyota or the state government. A new mayor of Georgetown had to be appointed when his predecessor suffered a stroke ("brought on, it was said, by now having to work around the clock" [Gelsanliter 1990, 124]) about ten months after Toyota's announcement. City and county officials differed in their tendencies to favor the plant and in their views of the distribution of new tax money.

The city of Georgetown has had zoning regulations since the early 1950s, but the regulations had not had a major revision since 1976 (Stroud 1991a). This set the stage for considerable land speculation that began immediately after the 1985 announcement of Toyota's Scott County location. Property values increased almost immediately by 20 percent or more (Stroud, 1991b), but many developers built houses that were more expensive than those that the typical Toyota employee could afford. As a result, many newly constructed homes did not sell. In the meantime, efforts by the Georgetown-Scott County Planning Office to control growth generated criticism from many developers, who saw the office as taking a "no-growth" approach (Stroud 1991a). The planning office and other county and city officials, however, were caught between the desires of developers to establish new residences and the desire of many county residents to preserve a small-town atmosphere marked by friendliness, quiet, and a rural quality. In addition, they confronted the task of balancing development with the protection of environmental quality.

The inherent contradictions involved in striving simultaneously for development and preservation took a toll but did not completely deter efforts to improve the community. In 1993, the Georgetown mayor who had worked closely with TMMK as it became a member of the community was defeated by a man who had served three terms as mayor during the 1970s and early 1980s. Throughout much of the period, city and county governments had difficulty sustaining cooperation and the planning office experienced turnover in key personnel. These difficulties illustrate Hoyman's (1997, 38) contention that "the road to permanent change in Georgetown was uneven, marked by many bumps, detours, and switchbacks."

However, elsewhere in this volume, Patton and Patton (1999) present considerable evidence that positive development has continued and is gaining momentum. They point, among other things, to new civic organizations, a more representative Scott County Fiscal Court, and the assumption of office in 1999 of a new Georgetown mayor who may be more inclined than his immediate predecessor to support the comprehensive plan and to recognize the ways in which the community is changing.

Corporate Strategies toward Community Relations

Because Georgetown city officials received little information as Toyota was making its site selection, Toyota was viewed initially as a promising but unknown entity that could have disruptive effects on a community whose residents valued its small-town quality. During the months following the announcement, however, Toyota officials began building local ties and making focused monetary and in-kind contributions. Key officials were invited to Toyota Motor Corporation's headquarters in Japan, where they were involved in tours, meetings, and other events intended to symbolize their importance in Toyota's eyes. On a local level, TMMK's top officials became involved in community civic organizations. TMMK made monetary and in-kind contributions that seem to have been designed to respond to local fears about the plant's disruptive impacts. Fears about school overcrowding were offset by monetary contributions to the school system. Fears of increased crime and deterioration of government services were offset by contributions to the police and fire departments and assistance in developing recreational facilities. Meanwhile, TMMK quickly became involved in such institutionalized endeavors as United Way of the Bluegrass, and it symbolized a commitment to higher education through major gifts to the University of Kentucky and cooperative relationships with the Scott County school system. After its assembly line was in production, TMMK tried to satisfy local curiosity with a three-day open house. One of the three days was set aside for residents of Scott County.

In general, Toyota's community and local relations appear to have been designed to build ties with key actors and to speak to the public's major fears about Toyota's impact while making some positive contributions to the community. Comparative research conducted by Hoyman (1997, 147–8) suggests that Toyota's task was not an easy one. Her 1992 surveys of residents of four communities with new automobile plants found that residents of Georgetown and of Spring Hill, Tennessee (home of the Saturn plant), expressed lower levels of satisfaction than did residents of Marysville, Ohio (Honda), or Smyrna, Tennessee (Nissan). However, the survey results presented below show that Toyota's efforts to win community acceptance have been increasingly successful over time. In fact, local residents who are dissatisfied with changes in their community appear to be more inclined to blame state officials than Toyota for their frustrations.

SOURCE OF DATA

The data for this analysis come primarily from telephone interviews conducted by trained and supervised interviewers on the staff of the Survey Research Center of the University of Kentucky. The surveys were conducted over one-month periods in 1986 (approximately eight months after the plant's location was announced), 1987, 1988, 1989, 1990, 1991, 1993, and 1995. In every year except 1991 and 1995, residents of Scott, Bourbon, Clark, Fayette, Franklin, Grant, Harrison, Owen, and Woodford Counties were included in the surveys. Thus, the study includes residents of the county where the plant is located (Scott) as well as eight additional counties that are contiguous to Scott County and/or linked to it by major transportation arteries. Because of limited funds, the 1991 and 1995 surveys were confined to residents of Scott County. Because Toyota's most direct and visible impacts occur in the county in which it is located, much of the analysis will focus on Scott County residents. However, results from other counties are presented for comparison in Appendices A through E.

Different samples were drawn each year to ensure that new residents and young adults would be included in the study. Random-digit dialing was used so that all residential telephone numbers would have an equal chance of being called. Multiple attempts were made to reach all numbers. Once a number was reached, the specific respondent from the household was chosen on the basis of randomized selection of a man or woman aged 18 or older.

Table 12.1 shows the number of respondents and response rates for each survey. The response rate is calculated by dividing the number of completed interviews by the number of eligible households that were called. About two-thirds of the noncompletions for each survey reflect refusals to begin or to complete the interview. The remaining noncompletions reflect such factors as

Table 12.1. Number of respondents and response rates

Year	Number of respondents Scott County	Total	Response rates Scott County	Total
1986	322	1,049	69.7	66.0
1987	397	1,309	70.5	66.0
1988	355	1,269	72.0	66.3
1989	323	716	65.0	63.3
1990	396	979	65.5	66.5
1991	235	235	62.0	62.0
1993	344	977	45.1	42.4
1995	431	431	44.8	44.8

illness, inability to find a convenient time for the interview, and prolonged unavailability because of travel or other commitments.

The potential sampling error for all counties is plus or minus 3 percentage points at the 95 percent confidence interval for questions asked of all respondents in 1986–1988. Because of smaller samples in 1989, 1990, and 1993, the potential sampling error for those years is slightly less than 4 percentage points. For Scott County alone, the margin of error each year is approximately 5 percentage points.

Responses from counties other than Scott were weighted on the basis of 1985 population size. Information about specific questions and scales is provided in Appendix F.

THE TIME PERSPECTIVE OF THE STUDY

Many studies of the impact of new industry focus only on a plant's first few years in a community. The surveys providing the basis for this study have been conducted over a ten-year period, allowing one to observe changes in perceptions of Toyota as it has moved through phases of planning, construction, early production, and expansion. Nevertheless, this may not be long enough to assess TMMK's long-term impacts on the community and region. Freudenberg and Gramling (1992) rather pessimistically note that the most important long-term effects are those that occur after a major industry has pulled out. At that time, community leaders may discover that leadership skills have been lost because key people have left or been transferred and that "the economic flexibility that once characterized predevelopment entrepreneurs may no longer exist" (1992, 944). A community that has tied its fortunes to a single industry may fail both to preserve traditional talents and ways of life and to engage in alternative activities that might represent more promising opportunities.

As noted above, TMMK's brief history in Kentucky has been character-ized by expansion rather than contraction, and Toyota is like most major Japanese manufacturers in that it has a history of avoiding plant closings or layoffs as responses to economic downturns. Nevertheless, the fate of the Volkswagen plant in Pennsylvania, the closings of many plants owned by General Motors and other American manufacturers, and recent problems in Japan's economy (resulting in reduced sales for Japanese automobile manu-facturers) all represent warnings of the risks involved with allowing an area to become dependent on a single industry.

With specific reference to Kentucky's decision (described in somewhat exaggerated terms) "to cast its lot with the auto industry," Falk and Lyson (1988) speculate about the effects of declining car sales: "It takes little imagi-nation to see that layoffs will soon follow. Local people will lose income; the state will lose tax revenues; and the industries involved may have to recon-sider their investment, since they all 'have a business to run' which essentially means a profit to be made. Kentucky has definitely succeeded in attracting a particular industry: but at what price and to be paid by whom and with what guarantees for long-term commitment?" (1988, 163).

Some economic downturns and sales declines have occurred since Falk and Lyson's book was published, but, as of this writing, the layoffs they pre-dicted have not occurred. Vehicles manufactured in Kentucky were exported to Europe beginning in April 1992 and to Japan beginning in July 1992. This may reflect a desire to maintain production during a period of lagging sales in the United States. It also should be noted that neither Kentucky as a state nor the Scott County area is as dependent on the automobile industry as many resource-dependent regions are on the extractive industries that locate there, deplete the resources, and leave. At this time, it does not appear likely that Scott County and central Kentucky will replicate the experiences that some Kentucky counties have had with the coal industry.

FINDINGS

On a broad level, central Kentucky residents have always tended to be opti-mistic that Toyota would benefit their communities. Figure 12.1, which sum-marizes Scott County residents' expectations over time, shows that at least three-fourths of the residents have consistently been optimistic about Toyota's likely community impact. Once the plant moved beyond its somewhat dis-ruptive construction phase and began focusing on actual production, the level of optimism has consistently exceeded 80 percent, and it reached 90 percent in the most recent survey. Appendix A shows specific percentages for Scott

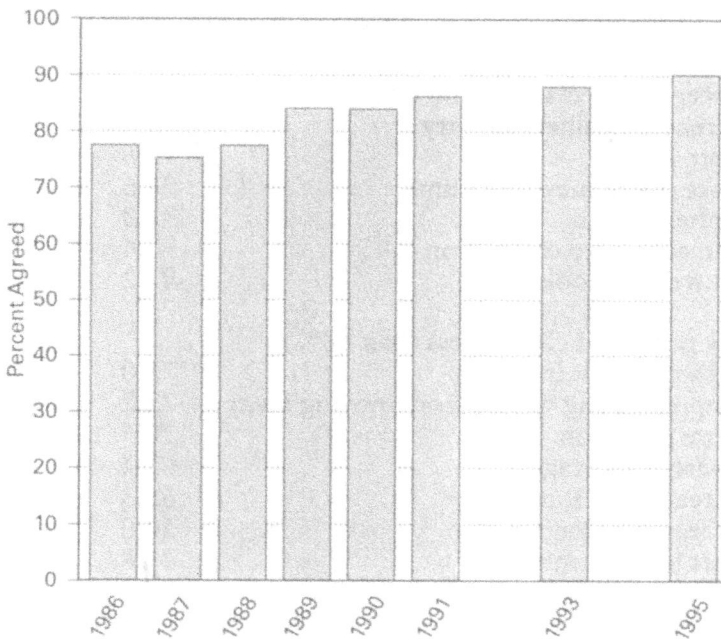

Note: There is no data for 1992 and 1994.

Fig. 12.1. Scott County: Percent saying Toyota is benefiting community, 1986–1995.

County and other central Kentucky counties. In counties other than Scott, optimism about Toyota's community impact dropped somewhat in 1987 and 1988 but then rebounded.

More specific expectations are summarized in tables 12.2 and 12.3. Table 12.2, which summarizes responses from the 1995 survey, shows that the perceived effects generating the most widespread consensus are generally positive. Increased business activity, more jobs, more tax money for the county, and higher wages are all perceived by more than 90 percent of Scott County residents as effects of Toyota's presence. However, substantial proportions also associate the plant with increased congestion on roads (90.4 percent) and in schools (82.2 percent).

Smaller percentages (but well over half) of Scott County's residents associate the plant with a higher cost of living, more pollution, housing shortages, increased personal taxes, and the more positive outcome of keeping young people from moving away. Still smaller percentages associate Toyota with increased union activity, harm to local farming, and increased crime.

A comparison of trends over time (summarized in table 12.3, with more complete information presented in Appendix B) shows that perceptions of several positive outcomes are becoming increasingly prevalent, while concern

Table 12.2. Perceived community effects of Toyota in Scott County, 1995

Widely perceived effects (80% or more)

Increased business activity	95.0
More jobs	93.6
More tax money for county	91.6
Higher wages	91.0
Increased road congestion	90.4
Crowded schools	82.2

Less widely perceived effects (less than 80%)

Higher cost of living	75.0
Keeping young people from moving away	72.2
More pollution	70.5
Housing shortages	65.4
Increased personal taxes	65.3
Increased union activity	50.0
Hurt local farming	47.8
Increased crime	43.0

about some negative outcomes appears to be abating. Thus, respondents to the two most recent surveys were more likely than respondents to the two earliest surveys to perceive Toyota as leading to higher wages and more jobs. By contrast, concern about housing shortages, harm to local farming, and higher cost of living had abated somewhat, and concern about pollution, increased personal taxes, and increased crime had decreased to a considerable extent. Perceptions of increased union activity (which some would view positively and others negatively) also decreased by a considerable margin.

A different set of questions, included for the first time during the survey's third administration in 1988, asked respondents about their views of changes in their community since Toyota's 1985 announcement that it would be locating in Scott County. Results are summarized in table 12.4 and presented more completely in Appendix C. While 1995 respondents did see their community as more congested and more expensive than it had been before Toyota's arrival, most also viewed it as more interesting. Concern about increased congestion, expense, and pollution changed very little between the original and most recent administrations of the survey, but respondents have become more likely to see their community as being more interesting and a more exciting place to live. Such trends suggest that Toyota may have played a role in revitalizing the community and in making residents aware of a broad range of new possibilities.

Figure 12.2 summarizes the results of the analyses reported in tables 12.2–4. As previously discussed, Scott County residents are showing a grow-

Table 12.3. Changes in perceived community impacts of Toyota in Scott County (change from 1986–1987 to 1993–1995)

Increased impacts perceived (5 percentage points or above)

Higher wages	+13.50
More jobs	+5.15

Little change perceived (change less than 5 percentage points)

More tax money for county	+4.85
Keeping young people from moving away	+3.90
Increased business activity	-0.45
Crowded schools	-4.15
Increased road congestion	-4.90

Decreased impacts perceived (-5 percentage points or below)

Housing shortages	-5.00
Hurt local farming	-7.60
Higher cost of living	-8.50
More pollution	-18.55
Increased personal taxes	-20.05
Increased crime	-29.30
Increased union activity	-32.25

ing tendency to be optimistic about their community and its future. Predictions of several positive economic and social outcomes are becoming increasingly prevalent, while concerns about negative outcomes are either remaining stable (e.g., crowded schools, increased road congestion) or becoming less prevalent (e.g., crime, personal taxes, housing shortages).

In counties other than Scott (Appendices B and C), increased business activity and more jobs have consistently been seen as the major effects of Toyota's move into the area. Residents of other counties have shown an in-

Table 12.4. Perceived community change since 1985

	% Responding "Yes" (1995)	Change: 1993–1995 vs. 1988–1989
More congested	91.7	+1.60
More expensive	77.1	-0.05
More interesting	73.2	+9.35
More polluted	58.6	-2.75
A more exciting place to live	56.0	+11.80

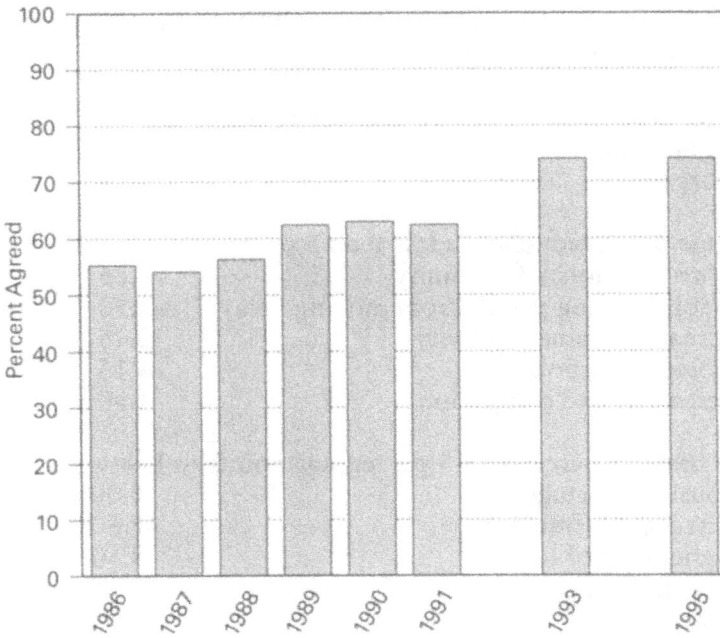

Note: There is no data for 1992 and 1994.

Fig. 12.2. Scott County: Percent considering state funding of Toyota justified, 1986–1995.

creasing tendency to associate Toyota with higher wages. Throughout the survey period, residents of other counties have been less likely than those in Scott County to associate Toyota with negative social or environmental impacts.

Figure 12.3 summarizes another approach to gauging local acceptance of Toyota as a member of the community. Respondents were asked in each survey whether they believed that "a foreign-owned company like Toyota will fulfill its obligations to the community." The phrasing, of course, was designed to call attention to Toyota's national origins and probably had the effect of creating some doubt about the strength of TMMK's long-term commitment to the community. Thus, an expression of "a great deal of confidence" represents a very strong expression of trust in Toyota. It is noteworthy that, even during the somewhat disruptive period of plant construction, tendencies to answer the question affirmatively increased. Since 1991, between 40 percent and 50 percent of respondents have been answering the question with the strongest possible affirmative response. During the 1991, 1993, and 1995 surveys, more than three-fourths of the Scott County respondents (82 percent in 1995) expressed either "a great deal of confidence" or "some confidence," suggesting that TMMK has inspired widespread trust in its commu-

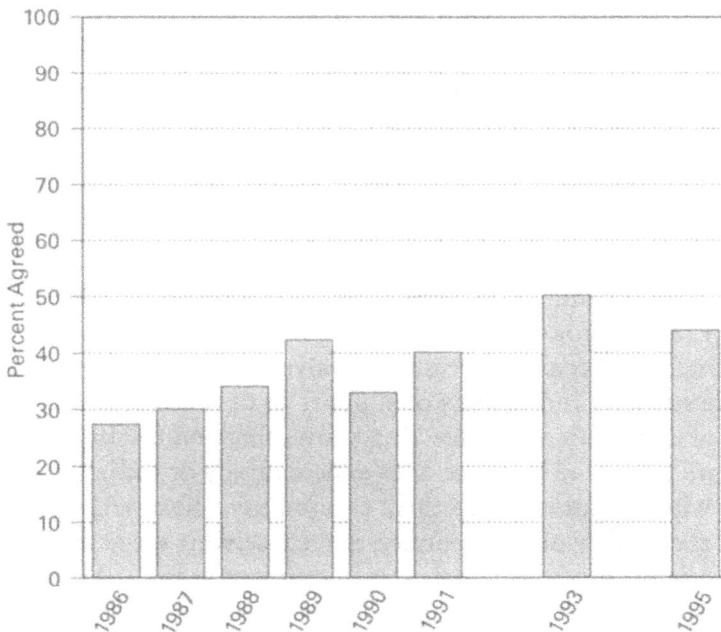

Note: There is no data for 1992 and 1994.

Fig. 12.3. Scott County: Percent with "a great deal of confidence" that a foreign-owned company like Toyota will fulfill its obligations, 1986–1995.

nity. Specific results for Scott and other counties are presented in Appendix D. Outside Scott County, confidence has remained relatively stable.

Figure 12.2 summarizes Scott County residents' responses to a key question regarding the state's incentives package—whether they considered the expense justified. Despite the early disagreements regarding the incentives package, more than half of the respondents to each survey have considered the expense justified. From 1989 on, support has exceeded 60 percent, and about three-fourths of the respondents to the 1993 and 1995 surveys have considered state funding justified. Thus, support for the incentives package is another area in which support has shown consistent increases.

More complete results regarding the incentives package are shown in Appendix E. The appendix shows that trends in other central Kentucky counties largely mirror those in Scott County. Of the three specific questions used to measure support for the incentives package, one produced somewhat lower levels of enthusiasm than the others, but all show clear tendencies for support to increase over time. For all three items, however, support is somewhat reserved. Respondents are more likely to consider the expense "somewhat justified" than "highly justified," and they are more likely to "agree" than to "strongly agree" with current and future incentives.

A follow-up to one of the questions provides additional insights into reactions to the incentives plan. In 1993 and 1995, those who expressed disagreement with state funding for Toyota were asked whether they would support state funding for an American-owned plant. About a third of the Scott County residents and 40 percent of those in other counties indicated that they would. Thus, opposition to incentives funding for Toyota cannot be attributed entirely to philosophical opposition to the idea of state-funded incentives packages.

Tables 12.5–7 summarize correlation and regression analyses regarding predictors of support for or concern about TMMK among respondents to the most recent survey. Because regression analyses control for other variables, they provide stronger indications of support or concern and will be the primary focus of this summary. Table 12.5 shows that community-level benefits of TMMK are perceived by those who expect family or individual-level benefits, those who are attached to their community, those who have positive opinions of the quality of their county, and those who are accepting of newcomers. Two other predictors that were significant at the .10 but not the .05 level were income (with higher income respondents more likely to perceive benefits) and years in county (with relative newcomers more likely to perceive benefits). A positive correlation exists between acceptance of the Japanese and perceived benefits, but this relationship did not survive the regression analysis. Contrary to predictions, knowledge of TMMK, gender, education, property ownership, location in Scott County, age, race, home ownership, and employment status were not significantly related to perceived benefits.

In many ways, relationships in table 12.6, focusing on perceived strains associated with TMMK, are the opposite of those in table 12.5. Perceptions of perceived strains were negatively related to age, property ownership, perception of family or individual-level benefit, acceptance of the Japanese, and acceptance of newcomers. Perceived strains are positively associated with number of years in the county and home ownership. Thus, relatively established residents are particularly likely to be concerned about the potentially disruptive impacts of new industry.

Supporters of the state incentives package (table 12.7) are likely to include those who associate TMMK with community-level benefits, those who perceive themselves or their families as receiving benefits, those with positive views of the quality of the county, and those with higher incomes. Those who associate TMMK with community-level strains and property owners are less likely to support the state incentives package. Although they did not survive as predictors in the regression analysis, the correlation analysis indicated that those who are accepting of newcomers and the Japanese and those with stronger community attachment were likely to support the incentives package, while those who had lived in the county longer and older respondents were likely to oppose it.

Table 12.5. Predictors of perceived benefits associated with TMMK (Scott County, 1995)

	Correlation coefficients (N = 332–376)	Standardized regression coefficients (N = 284)
Perceived knowledge of Toyota	.121[b]	
Family benefit expected	.298[c]	.298[c]
Perceived quality of county	.196[c]	.151[b]
Community attachment	.232[c]	.164[b]
Gender	-.018	
Education	.029	
Income	.189[c]	.098
Years in county	-.097[a]	-.105
Property ownership in Scott County	.040	
Location in Scott County	-.057	
Age	.021	
Race	.027	
Home ownership	.015	
Employment status	.029	
Acceptance of newcomers	.183[c]	.111[a]
Acceptance of Japanese	.135[b]	
Adjusted R^2		.223

Notes
Gender: male=0; female=1
Location in Scott County: outside Georgetown=0; Georgetown=1
Race: nonwhite=0; white=1
Employment status: not employed=0; employed=1
Correlation coefficients are based on all respondents answering both questions. Regression coefficients are based on listwise deletion. Regression coefficients are shown only if p<.10.
[a] p < .05; [b] p < .01; [c] p < .001

While each of the analyses summarized in tables 12.5–7 has some unique results, some common patterns emerged as well. These are summarized in figure 12.5. Relatively consistent support for TMMK can be found among those who expect or perceive benefits for themselves and their families (three significant relationships) and those who have positive views of the quality of the county (two significant relationships). In addition, respondents who express stronger feelings of attachment to the community, those who report higher incomes, those who are younger, those who have been county residents for fewer years, those who are accepting of newcomers, and those who are accepting of the Japanese are shown by some but not all of the analyses to be supportive of TMMK's presence in central Kentucky. The one variable

Table 12.6. Predictors of perceived strains associated with TMMK (Scott County, 1995)

	Correlation coefficients (N = 304–337)	Standardized regression coefficients (N = 264)
Perceived knowledge of Toyota	-.028	
Family benefit expected	-.216[c]	-.166[b]
Perceived quality of county	-.064	
Community attachment	-.037	
Gender	.050	
Education	.000	
Income	-.046	
Years in county	.154	.262[c]
Property ownership in Scott County	.018	-.191[b]
Location in Scott County	-.059	
Age	-.009	-.186[b]
Race	.029	
Home ownership	.060	.229[a]
Employment status	.008	
Acceptance of newcomers	-.155	-.104
Acceptance of Japanese	-.141[b]	-.143[a]
Adjusted R^2		.127

Notes
Gender: male=0; female=1
Location in Scott County: outside Georgetown=0; Georgetown=1
Race: nonwhite=0; white=1
Employment status: not employed=0; employed=1
Correlation coefficients are based on all respondents answering both questions. Regression coefficients are based on listwise deletion. Regression coefficients are shown only if p<.10.
[a] p < .05; [b] p < .01; [c] p < .001

that generated significant but inconsistent relationships was property ownership in Scott County. Property owners were less likely than others to associate Toyota with strains but were also less likely than others to support the state incentives package. The implications of ownership become even more puzzling when it is noted that a particular category of property owners—those who own their homes—are more likely than others to associate Toyota with community strains. It should be noted that none of the zero-order correlations involving property or home ownership in tables 12.5–7 were statistically significant, so the significant but inconsistent regression coefficients could simply be statistical artifacts. However, it is also possible that property owners, on the one hand, could see a potential for appreciating land values based

Table 12.7. Predictors of support for state incentive package (Scott County, 1995)

	Correlation coefficients (N = 319-381)	Standardized regression coefficients (N = 248)
Perceived benefits	.472[c]	.329[c]
Perceived strain	-.274[c]	-.196[c]
Perceived knowledge of Toyota	.074	
Family benefit expected	.419[c]	.236[c]
Perceived quality of county	.195[c]	.149[a]
Community attachment	.083[a]	
Gender	.034	
Education	-.070	
Income	.171[c]	.133[a]
Years in county	-.123[b]	
Property ownership in Scott County	-.001	-.117[a]
Location in Scott County	.024	
Age	-.085[a]	
Race	.005	
Home ownership	-.001	
Employment status	.007	
Acceptance of newcomers	.223[c]	
Acceptance of Japanese	.151[c]	
Adjusted R^2		.381

Notes
Gender: male=0; female=1
Location in Scott County: outside Georgetown=0; Georgetown=1
Race: nonwhite=0; white=1
Employment status: not employed=0; employed=1
Correlation coefficients are based on all respondents answering both questions. Regression coefficients are based on listwise deletion. Regression coefficients are shown only if p<.10.
[a] $p < .05$; [b] $p < .01$; [c] $p < .001$

on TMMK and therefore did not associate it with strain but, on the other hand, tended to hold ideological views leading them to oppose state incentives.

The results summarized in tables 12.5–7 also allow an assessment of the hypotheses that were presented earlier. In general, hypotheses regarding the incentives package fared better than those involving perceptions of the community impact of the Toyota plant. Tables 12.5 and 12.6 are pertinent to hypotheses 1–11. To receive complete support, a hypothesis would need to be supported in both tables. Only hypothesis 6 (personal or family benefits) received consistent support from both tables. Hypotheses 7 (less time as county resident), 9 (acceptance of newcomers), and 10 (acceptance of Japanese) were supported in one of the two tables, and hypothesis 2 (income) was supported in terms of its correlation coefficient with perceived community benefits. Hypothesis 8 was reversed in table 12.5 in that those with higher levels of community attachment were more likely to associate TMMK with benefits.

Regarding support for the state incentives package, results in table 12.7 show that hypotheses 13 (higher income), 17 (perceived individual or family benefits), 23 (perceived community benefits), and 24 (lower perceived community strain) were supported, but hypotheses 16 (property ownership) and 19 (perceived quality of county) were reversed.

DISCUSSION AND CONCLUSIONS

As noted, social change is neither linear nor predictable. At times, it is sufficiently disruptive that one cannot predict whether a system confronted with change will collapse completely, regenerate in a new form resembling its former structure, or emerge as a totally new social structure (Hallinan 1997). As Toyota becomes more established in central Kentucky, it is apparent that it has introduced changes but that these changes have not been so dramatic as to lead to complete system collapse or the emergence of a totally new social structure. Instead, residents of central Kentucky have adapted to change, finding their communities more interesting and exciting than they once were but not so radically changed as to challenge all of their established customs or ways of life.

The increasingly positive responses to Toyota are undoubtedly due in part to the economic benefits and employment opportunities it has brought to Kentucky, but, for every current TMMK employee, there are many who were unsuccessful in obtaining a job there. Besides its direct economic benefits, Toyota's acceptance has been helped by a successful strategy of community philanthropy and involvement and by the fact that some of its critics' worst fears were not realized. Those expecting an influx of Japanese were relieved to learn that most people hired by TMMK were long-time Kentucky residents. Those expecting unmanageable population growth, a destruction of small-town values, and increased crime have been relieved to find that most Toyota employees commute, move to larger cities that can more easily absorb them, or at least delay their decision to move to Scott County. In Hallinan's terms, the change introduced by Toyota has resulted in a community configuration that is new but that resembles its former structure. Because of the resemblance to familiar patterns, the changes created by Toyota have been relatively easy to accept.

Some earlier studies (reviewed above) of the impact of new industry suggest that it will be beneficial primarily to those who already enjoy considerable advantages. However, Bartik's (1991) more recent analysis suggests that new industry may introduce more widespread benefits that will not be confined to the relatively advantaged members of a community. The analysis in this study shows that Toyota is particularly likely to be supported by those who perceive themselves or members of their family as benefitting from it. Interestingly, however, most of the hypotheses based on traditional social capital variables (e.g., gender, education, present employment, property ownership) were not supported in this study. It is likely that TMMK has been more attentive than the more traditional industries from which some hypotheses were generated to principles of affirmative action and aptitude testing in hiring and to carefully developed community relations. Some human capital variables that may have been highly advantageous with traditional employers (e.g., being male or coming from an economically advantaged background) have been less likely to lead to advantages with TMMK. Moreover, TMMK's attention to community relations may have made it less threatening than would otherwise have been the case to those with feelings of attachment to their community and its traditions.

Some disagreements introduced by Toyota's presence may be slow to disappear. The appropriateness of the incentives package that was used to help attract Toyota to Kentucky is something on which complete agreement appears unlikely. Disagreements between the governments of the United States and Japan concerning economic policy are unlikely to disappear completely, and culturally based misunderstandings are an ongoing possibility. For the most part, however, central Kentucky's residents appear to be maintaining a favorable image of their communities and developing a favorable image of Toyota and its management. New industry and the residents of semirural areas and small towns will always be the subject of some tension. Enough examples of corporate disinvestment and layoffs, low wage levels, and environmental damage exist that efforts to attract new industry cannot always be viewed as justified even if a new employer does move into an area. However, Toyota's experience suggests that a combination of new employment opportunities, carefully focused programs of community relations, and a commitment by corporate officials to continue investing in an area can increase the local acceptance of a new manufacturer.

ACKNOWLEDGEMENT

The surveys providing the basis of this study were conducted by the Survey Research Center of the University of Kentucky. Funding was provided by the Toyota Foundation (1987–1995), the Kentucky Governor's Office for Policy and Management (1986–1989), and the Vice Chancellor for Research and

Graduate Studies of the University of Kentucky (1986). I am grateful to Dr. Thomas R. Ford for his indispensable role in initiating this project.

REFERENCES

Albrecht, S.L. 1982. Commentary. *Pacific Sociological Review* 25:297–306.
Bartik, Timothy J. 1991. *Who Benefits from State and Local Economic Development Policies?* Kalamazoo, Mich.: W.E. Upjohn Institute for Employment Research.
Bluestone, Barry, and Bennett Harrison. 1982. *The Deindustrialization of America: Plant Closings, Community Abandonment, and the Dismantling of Basic Industry.* New York: Basic Books.
Butters, Jamie. 1999. Japanese Take Kentucky Personally. *Lexington Herald-Leader,* 3 May.
Center for Business and Economic Research. 1992. The Economic Significance of Toyota Motor Manufacturing, U.S.A., Inc., in Kentucky. *Review & Perspective.* Lexington, Ky.: College of Business and Economics, University of Kentucky.
Dalecki, Michael G., and C. Milton Coughenour. 1992. Agrarianism in American Society. *Rural Sociology* 57:48–64.
Doeringer, Peter B., and David G. Terkla. 1992. Japanese Direct Investment and Economic Development Policy. *Economic Development Quarterly* 6:255–72.
Eberts, Paul R. 1979. Growth and the Quality of Life: Some Logical and Methodological Issues. Pp. 159–84 in *Nonmetropolitan Industrial Growth and Community Change,* edited by Gene F. Summers and Arne Selvik. Lexington, Mass.: Lexington Books.
Falk, William W., and Thomas A. Lyson. 1988. *High Tech, Low Tech, No Tech: Recent Industrial and Occupational Change in the South.* Albany, N.Y.: State Univ. of New York Press.
Freudenberg, William R., and Robert Gramling. 1992. Community Impacts of Technological Change: Toward a Longitudinal Perspective. *Social Forces* 70:937–955.
Fulton, Maurice. 1974. Industry's Viewpoint of Rural Areas. Pp. 68–78 in *Rural industrialization: Problems and potentials,* edited by Larry R. Whiting. Ames: Iowa State Univ. Press.
Gelsanliter, David. 1990. *Jump Start: Japan comes to the Heartland.* New York: Farrar, Straus, Giroux.
Hallinan, Maureen T. 1997. The Sociological Study of Social Change. *American Sociological Review* 62:1–11.
Haywood, Charles F. 1998. A Report on the Significance of Toyota Motor Manufacturing Kentucky, Inc. to the Kentucky Economy. Presented at the Annual Meeting of the Kentucky Economic Association, Lexington.
Hoyman, Michele M. 1997. *Power Steering: Global Automakers and the Transformation of Rural Communities.* Lawrence: Univ. Press of Kansas.
Kentucky State Data Center. 1999. Kentucky Demographic Information. (http://cbpa.louisville.edu/ksdc).

Marston, Stephen T. 1985. Two Views of the Geographic Distribution of Unemployment. *Quarterly Journal of Economics:* 57–79.

Miller, John Winn, and Alecia Swasy. 1986. The Wooing of Toyota: Kentucky Adds Up the Cost. *Lexington Herald-Leader,* 28 September.

Milward, H. Brinton, and Heidi Hosbach Newman. 1989. State Incentive Packages and the Industrial Location Decision. *Economic Development Quarterly* 3:203–22.

Molotch, Harvey. 1976. The city as a growth machine: Toward a Political Economy of Place. *American Journal of Sociology* 82:309–32.

Patton, Janet W., and H. Milton Patton. 1999. Georgetown, Kentucky: The Dynamics of Growth and Change, 1985–1999. Paper Prepared for Presentation at Japan in the Bluegrass Conference, University of Kentucky, April 2.

Stroud, Joseph S. 1991a. Georgetown Losing Fear of Growth. *Lexington Herald-Leader,* 17 March.

———. 1991b. Speculation Sent Scott Land Prices Soaring. *Lexington Herald-Leader.* 17 March.

Summers, Gene F., and Kristi Branch. 1984. Economic Development and Community Social Change. *Annual Review of Sociology* 10:141–66.

Summers, Gene F., Sharon D. Evans, Frank Clemente, E.M. Beck, and Jon Minkoff. 1976. *Industrial Invasion of Nonmetropolitan America: A Quarter Century of Experience.* New York: Praeger.

Yanarella, Ernest J., and Herbert G. Reid. 1990. Problems of Coalition Building in Japanese Auto Alley: Public Opposition to the Georgetown/Toyota Plant. Pp. 153–73 in *The Politics of Industrial Recruitment: Japanese Automobile Investment and Economic Development in the American States,* edited by Ernest J. Yanarella and William C. Green. New York: Greenwood Press.

Appendix A. Percentages saying Toyota plant is benefiting community and its residents

	1986	1987	1988	1989	1990	1991	1993	1995
Scott County	76.9	75.1	77.3	84.0	83.7	86.1	88.3	90.1
Other counties	77.9	71.9	69.6	78.3	75.2		88.4	

Note: Respondents answering "don't know" were excluded. In Scott County, "don't know" responses steadily declined from 12.5% in 1986 to 2.3% in 1995. In other counties, "don't know" responses fluctuated between 11.1% (1989) and 5.3% (1993). Responses from counties other than Scott have been weighted.

Appendix B. Specific perceived community effects of Toyota

	Percentage agreeing							
	1986	1987	1988	1989	1990	1991	1993	1995
Toyota plant has led to:								
Increased business activity								
Scott County	95.8	94.1	94.1	95.9	91.9	92.0	94.0	95.0
Other counties	93.3	93.6	91.8	90.4	92.9		90.8	
More jobs								
Scott County	89.9	84.6	81.0	89.5	86.9	87.7	91.2	93.6
Other counties	87.2	82.4	80.8	88.3	90.0		92.8	
More tax money for county								
Scott County	86.8	88.0	91.4	92.6	90.7	90.0	92.9	91.6
Other counties	70.6	73.5	73.2	76.8	74.5		81.0	
Higher wages								
Scott County	78.6	75.3	81.9	89.0	82.5	85.1	89.9	91.0
Other counties	58.3	64.0	67.6	76.6	76.0		87.4	
Increased road congestion								
Scott County	93.4	96.8	96.2	94.1	92.2	92.7	90.0	90.4
Other counties	84.8	82.4	82.3	78.8	77.6		77.6	
Crowded schools								
Scott County	84.9	88.0	86.7	76.9	73.7	65.4	82.4	82.2
Other counties	48.3	57.3	66.2	59.7	54.2		47.0	
Higher cost of living								
Scott County	82.4	85.3	83.8	76.4	80.2	77.1	75.7	75.0
Other counties	55.7	58.1	63.9	53.8	59.1		51.5	
Keeping young people from moving away								
Scott County	70.0	65.5	59.6	64.5	64.4	61.3	71.1	72.2
Other counties	69.4	59.0	56.0	67.5	62.9		74.0	
More pollution								
Scott County	85.2	84.8	80.8	71.6	70.8	68.9	62.4	70.5
Other counties	67.9	70.1	69.1	64.8	66.4		53.9	
Housing shortages								
Scott County	73.5	65.3	61.1	62.8	52.0	46.8	63.4	65.4
Other counties	40.1	49.5	52.0	42.8	39.7		35.5	
Increased personal taxes								
Scott County	84.3	82.9	76.5	67.9	73.4	69.8	61.8	65.3
Other counties	52.4	63.9	53.4	45.1	53.7		45.1	
Increased union activity								
Scott County	72.9	80.2	64.5	54.1	49.0	51.4	38.6	50.0
Other counties	73.0	68.7	69.4	59.8	57.2		51.6	
Damage to local farming								
Scott County	51.8	52.2	50.3	48.3	45.3	41.3	41.0	47.8
Other counties	33.3	42.2	45.1	42.2	45.2		32.4	
Increased crime								
Scott County	69.7	69.5	58.8	42.9	37.0	32.3	37.6	43.0
Other counties	32.1	33.9	29.4	27.0	26.7		18.0	

Note: Responses are ranked according to the 1995 results for Scott County. Percentages are based on the proportion of those expressing an opinion who agree or strongly agree that TMMK is having the specified effect. Results from counties other than Scott have been weighted.

Appendix C. Perceived community change

	1986	1987	Percentage responding "Yes" 1988	1989	1990	1991	1993	1995
Since 1985, community has become:								
More congested								
Scott County			90.5	92.6	93.7	93.5	94.6	91.7
Other counties			56.2	57.3	64.9		65.2	
More expensive								
Scott County			72.3	71.6	77.6	74.2	66.7	77.1
Other counties			57.7	57.9	62.7		52.0	
More interesting								
Scott County			60.8	61.4	60.5	64.0	67.7	73.2
Other counties			37.2	48.1	40.7		48.0	
More polluted								
Scott County			60.1	54.8	63.1	62.9	50.8	58.6
Other counties			43.5	41.1	54.0		35.5	
A more exciting place to live								
Scott County			40.1	44.9	41.7	45.0	52.6	56.0
Other counties			30.6	36.5	34.1		38.5	

Note: Responses are ranked according to the 1995 results for Scott County. Percentages are based on the proportion of those expressing an opinion who answered "yes." Results from counties other than Scott have been weighted.

Appendix D. Confidence in foreign-owned Toyota to fulfill obligations

	1986	1987	1988	Percentages 1989	1990	1991	1993	1995
Scott County								
A great deal of confidence	27.4	30.2	33.6	41.7	33.1	39.7	50.5	44.3
Some confidence	40.3	36.5	34.8	34.2	40.0	38.9	36.4	38.4
A little confidence	24.2	22.8	21.3	17.9	18.4	14.3	9.2	12.5
None at all	8.1	10.5	10.3	6.2	8.5	7.1	3.8	4.8
Other counties (weighted)								
A great deal of confidence	26.8	31.3	28.8	29.5	24.3		32.4	
Some confidence	41.6	38.3	36.1	43.1	45.6		46.6	
A little confidence	22.8	21.3	24.7	21.8	20.5		14.8	
None at all	8.8	9.2	10.6	5.6	9.6		6.1	

Note: Exact question wording was, "In general, how much confidence do you have that a foreign-owned company like Toyota will fulfill its obligations to the community?" Respondents answering "don't know" (no more than 5% for any one year) were excluded.

Appendix E. Views of Toyota incentive package

	1986	1987	1988	Percentages 1989	1990	1991	1993	1995
EXPENSE JUSTIFIED								
Scott County								
Highly justified								
	11.3	12.8	12.3	19.7	17.3	14.1	23.9	21.3
Somewhat justified								
	44.1	40.9	43.8	42.4	45.6	48.1	50.3	52.9
Somewhat unjustified								
	20.4	19.5	22.1	20.6	17.0	22.2	15.4	13.5
Highly unjustified								
	24.1	26.8	21.7	17.3	20.1	15.6	10.4	12.2
Other counties (weighted)								
Highly justified								
	12.4	11.5	13.0	11.0	8.9		15.1	
Somewhat justified								
	45.9	39.7	44.7	51.3	52.1		57.8	
Somewhat unjustified								
	19.4	27.0	22.4	23.0	20.0		17.2	
Highly unjustified								
	22.3	21.9	19.9	14.8	18.9		9.9	
SUPPORT STATE FUNDING								
Scott County								
Strongly agree								
	3.5	6.3	8.9	7.4	5.5	5.9	10.3	9.5
Agree								
	43.1	34.3	31.8	43.2	34.7	35.8	42.3	44.8
Disagree								
	36.7	37.7	41.8	36.0	45.7	44.1	31.8	33.1
Strongly disagree								
	16.6	21.8	17.4	13.4	14.1	14.2	15.5	12.7
Other counties (weighted)								
Strongly agree								
	4.2	2.6	3.1	3.9	4.1		5.7	
Agree								
	46.3	42.0	32.5	35.4	35.8		47.2	
Disagree								
	30.9	37.9	41.2	45.0	45.6		40.1	
Strongly disagree								
	18.5	17.6	23.3	15.6	14.4		6.9	

If Disagreed or Strongly Disagreed: Would you support state funding for an American-owned plant?

Scott County								
Yes							34.0	30.1
Other counties (weighted)								
Yes							40.4	

	1986	1987	1988	Percentages 1989	1990	1991	1993	1995
SUPPORT FUTURE STATE FUNDING								
Scott County								
Strongly agree								
	6.4	5.2	9.8	7.8	7.1	8.3	14.0	13.6
Agree								
	54.5	51.9	45.8	58.9	54.1	58.2	57.6	56.7
Disagree								
	30.3	32.7	34.9	24.2	31.1	28.7	22.5	23.8
Strongly disagree								
	8.7	10.1	9.4	9.2	7.7	4.8	5.9	5.9
Other counties (weighted)								
Strongly agree								
	9.6	6.2	6.7	7.4	8.0		8.1	
Agree								
	59.7	54.8	50.7	55.0	54.8		62.8	
Disagree								
	20.5	31.9	34.0	31.3	30.5		27.3	
Strongly disagree								
	10.2	7.1	8.6	6.2	6.7		1.8	

Note: See Appendix F for question wording. Respondents answering "don't know" (5.8% to 10.4% for Scott County residents and 4.7% to 8.2% for residents of other counties answering the first question, 2.8% to 7.8% for Scott County residents and 4.3% to 6.4% for residents of other counties answering the second question, and 3.7% to 10.4% for Scott County residents and 3.5% to 8.9% for residents of other counties answering the third question) were excluded.

Appendix F. Measurement of variables

Perceived benefits
Cronbach's alpha = .7516

There are a number of potential effects the Toyota plant may have. For each one I read, please tell me if you would strongly agree, agree, disagree, or strongly disagree that it is having that effect on your community.

More jobs.
Higher wages.
Increased business activity.
More tax money for your county.
Keeping young people from moving away.

Perceived strain
Cronbach's alpha = .7721

There are a number of potential effects the Toyota plant may have. For each one I read, please tell me if you would strongly agree, agree, disagree, or strongly disagree that it is having that effect on your community.

Crowded schools.
Increased crime.
More pollution.
A higher cost of living.
Hurt local farming.
Housing shortages.
Increased personal taxes.
Increased road congestion.

Support for state incentive package
Cronbach's alpha = .7898

Some Kentuckians say that the state funding for the Toyota plant is too much to pay, while others believe the plant will benefit the people of Kentucky enough to justify the expense. Do you think the expense is highly justified, somewhat justified, somewhat unjustified, or highly unjustified?

Now I'd like to read you several statements that people have made about the project and ask if you strongly agree, agree, disagree, or strongly disagree with each.

First, I support the idea of state funding for the Toyota plant in Scott County. Next, the state should provide support for additional industrial development like the Toyota plant in Kentucky.

Perceived knowledge of Toyota
Now I'd like to change the subject just a bit and ask how much, if any, you have heard about the Toyota plant in Scott County. Would you say you have heard a lot, a little, or heard nothing at all?

Family benefit expected
Do you think that you or any member of your immediate family is benefiting (or will benefit) from the Toyota plant? (Yes; No)

Perceived quality of county
Overall, how would you rate your county as a place to live . . . excellent, good, fair, or poor?

Community attachment
Cronbach's alpha = .6898

Now I'd like to read you a few statements about your community. For each one, please tell me if you strongly agree, agree, disagree, or strongly disagree with it.

First, I have very few interests in common with most people in my neighborhood. (-)*
The future success of my community is very important to me.
I share a number of interests with the leaders of my community.
I have more important things to do than getting involved in community affairs. (-)
The quality of my community has little effect on my overall happiness. (-)
When I think of the people in the community where I live, I think of THEY rather than WE. (-)
* (-) indicates item reversed.

Gender (recorded by interviewer)

Education
What was the last grade in school that you completed?

Income
Last year, what was your total family income before taxes? (Under $5,000; $5,000 to $10,000; $10,000 to $15,000; $15,000 to $20,000; $20,000 to $25,000; $25,000 to $30,000; $30,000 to $40,000; or over $40,000.)

Years in county
Let me begin by asking about how many years you have lived in the county you're now in, or have you lived there all of your life?

Property ownership in Scott County
Do you own property in Scott County? (Yes; No)

Location in Scott County
Do you live in Georgetown, Sadieville, Stamping Ground, or another part of Scott County?

Age
In what year were you born?

Race
What is your race? (white, black, Japanese or other Asian, other)

Home ownership
Do you own or rent your home?

Employment status
Are you currently working full-time or part-time outside the home? (Yes—part-time; Yes—full-time; No).

Acceptance of newcomers
If a large number of newcomers happen to move into your community, do you think that, overall, they will be a benefit or a burden to the community, or will they not make any difference?

Acceptance of Japanese
Cronbach's alpha = .8977 (Scott County); .9142 (other counties)

We would like to have your reactions to each of the following groups of people. Please do not give your reactions to the best or the worst members that you know, but think of the picture or impression that you have of the whole group.

I would admit Japanese:
to employment in my occupation (yes; no).
to my street as neighbors.
to my group of close friends.

Note: Cronbach's alpha values are based on 1995 results from Scott County.

Part V

Prospects for the Future

13

Japan and Kentucky in Perspective

P.P. KARAN

JAPANESE INVESTMENT IN THE UNITED STATES is a subject that has elicited considerable attention ranging from the highly journalistic to the scholarly. During Japan's boom years in the 1980s, Japanese investment in the United States soared, leading many to raise questions about what this investment would mean for the U.S. economy as well as for society. The paranoid concern that Japanese investment elicited in the 1980s has given way to more balanced assessments in the 2000s. Perhaps one reason Japan's investment surge became such an issue is because of the different cultural traditions of Japan and the United States. Considerable concern existed about how Japanese management, hiring, recruitment, and promotion practices would affect American workers and communities. Assessments included both positive appraisals of Japan's quality management circles and frustration with Japanese attitudes toward women and minorities in the workplace.

Since the 1980s Kentucky has put out the welcome mat for Japanese companies interested in establishing or expanding operations in the state. Japanese investors have found a haven of resources and motivated business partners (Whitmire 1999). Japanese investments in Kentucky go beyond the production and movement of goods in and out of the United States. The Japanese companies often are significant players in the cultural, social, and educational activities in the communities in which their businesses are located. The Japanese executive takes on a role within the company, a second role within the local Japanese community, and a third role as a member of the community in which the company is located. Communication with the local Japanese community and the community at large are key for executives. Generally, they set the tone for the company's future relationships. The Japanese even simplify their names—Mike for Messamichi, Mark for Mizumoto, Jim for Taiji, Ken for Kenichiro—to blend in better.

Efforts to facilitate cross-cultural relationships are prevalent in Kentucky. These include the Japan/America Society of Kentucky, business associations,

The headquarters of Matsushita Corporation in Minami Semba area of Osaka, Japan. Matsushita operates plants in Danville and Berea, Kentucky. The quality of its engineering and the efficiency of its mass production techniques are second to none. Japanese companies such as Matsushita are going abroad to get away from Japan's high costs. Matsushita, for example, doubled its overseas workforce between 1992 and 1999 to 134,000, but took only 6,000 new people in Japan. Over the same period, Hitachi, which has a plant in Harrodsburg, Kentucky, also nearly doubled its number of overseas employees, but reduced its workforce in Japan by 3 percent to 267,000. (Photograph by P.P. Karan)

Japanese Prime Minister Morihiro Hosokawa addressing the Japanese and American business community and the University of Kentucky faculty and students at the Japan in the Bluegrass conference April 2, 1999. (Photograph by Lee Thomas)

and sister-city connections. Lexington, Berea, Georgetown, Madison County, Elizabethtown, and Morgantown are among the Kentucky communities with sister-city connections to Japan. Many offer home-stay tours for students and adults (Shelby 1999). Japanese firms routinely finance student and group trips to Japan as well as cultural and educational activities in public schools. They are actively involved in facilitating good understanding and cooperation between Japan and Kentucky. The Japanese companies that have been located in Kentucky the longest continue to have major impacts on their local areas. Japanese have a tremendous work ethic, and they get involved in the communities. Kentucky operations of Japanese manufacturers have adjusted to the Bluegrass in ways equally subtle and profound. The Japanese have been largely successful at inspiring their Kentucky employees to adopt Japanese ideals of long-term loyalty and a team-oriented company ethic.

Both Japan and Kentucky are now challenged to find ways to continue forging their economic and cultural relationships in the twenty-first century. Both are trying to expand their economic interests with a more inclusive world view expounded by leaders of Japan and Kentucky. There is belief in Kentucky and Japan that stake in the new international political-economic order rests, more than ever, on being internationalist. Japanese expanding foreign direct investment in Kentucky and elsewhere is one reflection of this historic shift of national purpose. Kentucky's own historical struggle to catch up economically with other affluent American states gives it a strong urge to attract investments from abroad. Kentucky used conditions in the international economy in the 1980s to its advantage in attracting Japanese investment. In both Japan and Kentucky a "new internationalism" began to take shape in the 1980s as exemplified by expanding investment and trade.

For the past twenty years, beginning with the administration of Governor Martha Layne Collins, Kentucky's leadership has been trying to come to grips with the state's new situation, to make a shift in the direction of economic development that reflects the reality of international economy. Collins was a pioneer seeking to chart the future course of state's economic, technological, and social organization. The ferment of ideas that Collins stirred was further stimulated by successive governors (with possible exception of Wallace Wilkinson, Collins's successor, who won the governorship by campaigning against the state's incentives package to Toyota). Many developments gave impetus to the flow of investments and export trade. The essential point was the recognition that Kentucky was on the threshold of a new era in which global trade and investment would be important.

Japan's internationalism is also partly a reflection of its realization that pursuit of the narrow mercantilist policies of the 1970s could leave it isolated in the world community. As Japan racked up record-breaking current account trade surpluses each year, it found itself an outcast in the world economic community. Yayama Taro, a widely read Japanese social critic, described his country in March 1988 as an international outcast because of the pursuit of narrow self-interest (*kokutoku*), and failure to remove impediments to trade, balance of payments adjustments, and opening markets. The new internationalism in Japan is partly a response to the threat of isolation, partly on Japan's conception of its future in the age of globalization. Japan's new internationalism and globalization policies implemented by its multinational corporations are based on a confident belief that Japan is destined by its unique economic, scientific, and cultural skills to project itself as a global leader. An essential part of this role as world economic leader is the stimulation of world economic and technological progress through foreign direct investment.

Japanese foreign direct investment, as discussed earlier in this volume, has grown rapidly in Kentucky since the mid-1980s; it is expected to continue in the 2000s but not at the high rate of the previous two decades. It is a key element of the new internationalism. The obvious arguments in support of investment are made for the benefits to the host state—expanded employment, increased tax revenues, transfer of technology and skills. But the benefits for Japanese are also significant—markets, lowered production costs, easing protectionist pressures, acquiring benefits from the preferential policies of local and state host governments. Among the reasons Japanese auto

Shortage of educated and skilled labor force, particularly engineers and scientists, is a major problem facing future expansion of industries in the state. Kentucky has been noted for its job growth, investment per capita, and location of facilities owned by foreign companies in the "golden triangle" comprising Lexington, Louisville, and greater Cincinnati (Ohio). Future growth will depend on the intellectual capacity of the state to compete in the knowledge-based economy. (Photograph courtesy of Hitachi Automotive Products [USA])

industry came to the United States in the 1980s was the desire of the companies to build their cars in the country where they sold them. The trend will continue because the plants are the best insurance against several political and economic uncertainties. Foreign direct investment is a new critical dimension of Japanese economic development and its success depends on the realization of globalization policies of Japanese multinational corporations, with enhanced sensitivity, tact, and knowledge of cultural conditions in the host areas.

Japan is the United States' third largest export market. The United States is the largest market for Japanese exports. However, in many sectors, U.S. exporters, including Kentucky exporters, continue to have incomplete access to the Japanese market. While Japan has reduced its formal tariff rates on most imports to relatively low levels, it has maintained nontariff barriers—such as nontransparency, discriminatory standards, and exclusionary business practices—and tolerates a business environment that protects established companies and restricts the free flow of competitive foreign goods into the Japanese market. In 1997 the U.S. government cited autos, flat glass, paper products, and variety-by-variety testing of fruits as sectors where Japanese

trade practices give rise to particular concern and noted Japanese port practices as areas warranting continued attention. A rigid and unnecessarily bur-
densome regulatory system, standards, testing, and certification problems
hamper market access in Japan. Foreign direct investment into Japan has
remained extremely small in scale relative to the size of the economy. The low
level reflects the high cost of doing business in Japan, the legacy of former
investment restrictions, and a continuing environment of structural impediments to greater foreign investment. Recently, the Japanese government has
implemented some potentially useful measures from the perspective of increasing foreign direct investment, including easing restrictions on foreign
capital entry. Still, most Japanese government investment promotion measures to date have been dictated by domestic priorities and do not address the
most important concerns of potential investors. In addition, acquisition of
Japanese companies is difficult, due in part to cross holding of shares between allied companies and a resulting small publicly traded percentage of
shares. This practice hinders the efforts of foreign firms wishing to acquire
distribution or service networks through mergers or acquisitions.

TRADITIONAL INDUSTRIES OF KENTUCKY IN JAPAN

Kentucky's exports to Japan were valued at $1,436 million in 1998. This
represented an increase of 87 percent over 1993 (*Lexington Herald-Leader*
2000). Imports have grown too, but state figures are not available. Japan
ranked as the second largest export market, after Canada, for Kentucky. Most
of Kentucky's exports comprised traditional goods such as tobacco and agricultural products, bourbon, and Thoroughbred horses.

Tobacco

The Japanese cigarette market was technically opened to American companies in 1985, under trade pressure from the United States. But the American
companies did not gain a foothold until 1987, when Japan lowered tariffs on
imported cigarettes. Since then, sales of American cigarettes have mushroomed
in Japan. Market leader Philip Morris's share has grown from less than 3
percent in 1986 to more than 12 percent. The U.S. companies now control
more than one-fifth of the Japanese cigarette market. That has forced Japan
Tobacco Company, the government-owned cigarette monopoly, to play defense, selling brands with American names and using Caucasian actors in its
advertising. It also has bought more U.S. leaf for use in its cigarettes, boosting
burley exports to Japan.
    Cigarette advertising is legal in Japan from 11:00 P.M. until 5 A.M. For an
American, watching the ads is like going back in time. For instance, in one

Tobacco field in Kumamoto prefecture in western Kyushu. Although most Japanese cigarettes are made from domestically grown tobacco, imported tobacco from Kentucky and other states is added for improved taste. (Photograph by Cotton Mather)

ad, an attractive Caucasian woman dances around the screen in a short, black chiffon dress. As she performs a graceful flying leap, her legs spread wide. A pack of Salem Lights, about the size of the dancing woman, moves slowly up from the bottom of the screen. A single cigarette rising from the middle of the pack moves closer, then slides back into the pack as it approaches the fading image of the woman. The cigarette, an obvious phallic symbol, is aimed directly between her legs. In another ad, a young blond man on a motorcycle cruises on a highway to the sounds of a wailing rock 'n' roll guitar. A narrator says simply, "American orijinaru" (American original). The ad is for Lucky Strikes.

Perhaps because of the increased advertising, the overall rate of smoking has not slowed. Consumption in Japan, which declined every year from 1984 to 1987, has increased steadily since the American companies entered the picture. An estimated 60 percent of Japanese adult men smoke; among women, 13.3 percent smoke, according to a recent survey. Although smoking is prohibited by any one younger than twenty, vending machines make cigarettes readily available to minors. Japan has become a growth market for American cigarettes.

Bourbon

Along with cigarettes, one of the most successful Kentucky exports to Japan is bourbon whiskey. Bourbon, in fact, has taken such a hold that a Japanese company thought it made good sense to buy a Kentucky distillery in 1992. Takara Shuzo Company of Kyoto, which makes *sake,* or rice wine, bought Age International, of Frankfort, after another company tried to buy it. Age International, which makes Blanton's premium, a popular brand in Japan, and other Ancient Age products, became the first Kentucky distillery wholly owned by a Japanese company. While sales of bourbon in the United States have declined steadily, sales in Japan have continued to rise since 1986. Primarily younger people in Japan started the drinking of bourbon. Now bourbon is becoming popular with many Japanese of all ages and has become a fashion trend (Daily Yomiuri 1993).

In 1969, virtually all restrictions on import of liquor were lifted in Ja-

Vending machines along a street in Matsumoto, Nagano prefecture. These machines sell beer, wine, whiskey, soft drinks, coffee, and cigarettes as well as other personal items. Sapporo (second from left) commands a large share of the domestic market for liquor along with Suntory, Kirin, and Asahi. Sapporo Breweries, founded in 1876, has annual sales of nearly $4 billion. Japan has about 5.4 million of these vending machines. More than $45 billion in goods are sold through the vending machines annually. Because of convenience, many Japanese prefer to drop coins into a machine for cigarettes and drinks rather than to go to a store. (Photograph by Cotton Mather)

pan. Until then, annual quotas based on sales in previous years limited imports. Since the rate of consumption of bourbon in Japan was low, its quota was next to nothing. The market for bourbon grew slowly at first. The Japanese loved their *sake*. When they tried other alcohol, they generally chose Scotch whiskey over bourbon. The companies aimed their sales at college and postcollege consumers, and they set up special "bourbon bars" in Tokyo and other major cities. At the same time, two of Kentucky's three main bourbon producers—Brown-Foreman International, makers of Jack Daniels, Early Times, and Old Forester, and Schenley Industries, which owned I.W. Harper, J.W. Deny, and Ancient Age before it was acquired by United Distillers in 1987—entered a distribution deal with Suntory, a conglomerate that controlled 70 percent of Japan's whiskey market. Sales of bourbon whiskey in Japan have virtually doubled every year since then. The industry got an additional boost in 1989 when Japan lowered tariffs on several goods, including liquor. The rise in the number of Japanese businessmen working in Kentucky probably helped boost the popularity of bourbon whiskey in Japan. These Japanese businessmen discovered the taste of bourbon while they were stationed in Kentucky and introduced bourbon to friends and acquaintances when they returned to Japan. The young, urbanites, and urbane of Japan have embraced bourbon as a liquor for those with savoir faire, causing its popularity to skyrocket over the past decade. Jardine Wines and Spirits K.K. Japan, which distributes I.W. Harper (one of the best selling brands), is trying to further enhance bourbon whiskey's new upmarket image with ads tailored to ultracool, sophisticated, and outgoing drinkers. Though focused on youth, Jardine Japan has not forgotten the older drinkers who now make up an important segment of the bourbon market.

Maker's Mark, the best seller in Kentucky, was a latecomer in Japan. Unlike the bigger bourbon distilleries, Maker's Mark of Loretto could not spend much on plugging its product. But Toyota's arrival in Kentucky was a marketing opportunity which Maker's Mark seized. As Japanese executives arrived, they were presented with Maker's Mark, which made the brand popular among the business community. Maker's Mark sales in Japan have increased since the late 1980s.

Bourbon's popularity is growing among Japanese consumers in their thirties and forties, who have already established their drinking style. Many Japanese who discovered bourbon during the late 1980s are now buying premium quality bourbons. Also, the taste for bourbon is spreading quickly outside of major city centers into more suburban and rural areas, opening up whole new markets. Bourbon whiskey comprises nearly 73 percent of liquor imports into Japan from the United States.

The increased cultural tolerance of drinking and rapid economic expansion in the 1980s also contributed to the surge in bourbon sales in Japan. Japan had never shied away from alcohol consumption. Drunken people are often seen on trains, in the streets, and in other public places. Not only is drunkenness tolerated, but social drinking, often to excess, is common in after-hours business activities. Economic expansion in the 1980s, coupled with rapid currency appreciation, provided many Japanese with disposable income and a desire to discover new fashions and acquire new tastes.

By 2000, the bourbon boom was slowing significantly. Despite its popularity as the drink of choice among young professionals, bourbon has not been able to escape the economic recession. In recent years there has been a drop in import of bourbon into Japan.

Thoroughbred Industry

During the last twenty-five years Japanese Thoroughbred breeders have improved their horses through breeding with superior stock from Kentucky. Nearly all of Japan's breeding farms are in the Iburi and Hidaka regions of Hokkaido. The area lies between the Hidaka Mountains and the Pacific Ocean. Here the landscape is beautiful but rugged, and the climate is cold. The farms, much smaller and less manicured than those in the Bluegrass, rarely include training facilities. Although many of the breeding operations are modeled after Kentucky horse farms, they do not look like Bluegrass horse farms. Most are small (thirty to forty acres) family-run operations. Shadai Farm, Japan's biggest with more than sixteen hundred acres, is divided into four locations. Its facilities are superior to most others in Japan, but they are small as compared with most Kentucky operations. Lack of available grazing and the long winter present difficulties. Lack of training facilities because of space shortage is another problem. Japanese have bought many good stallions and mares; it is the training not the breeding of Japanese horses that is inferior.

Japan Racing Association, the sport's main governing body, has built a massive new training facility for yearlings in the Hidaka region. Within view of the snow-capped Hidaka Mountains, the thirty-five-hundred-acre center includes a huge grass training course, a five-furlong straight indoor track, and a three-furlong oval indoor track.

Although the Japanese have learned some of the basics of Thoroughbred racing at Western tracks, they have developed their own style. Racing in Japan occurs only on weekends and is very popular. Japanese bettors wager more than those of the United States. They do it on track, off track, and by telephone. Jockeys and horses are much bigger heroes in Japan than they are in the United States.

In the late 1980s, as Japan's economy expanded, the surging value of the yen made foreign investment much easier for Japanese horsemen. The effect was felt at horse sales at Keeneland in Lexington, Kentucky. The owner of Shadai Farm and other Japanese buyers established an important presence at the sales. Because foreign-bred horses are allowed to compete in only a hand-

One of Japan's large horse farms between the Hidaka Mountains and the Pacific Ocean near Shizunai, Hokkaido. While the facilities at this farm are superior to most others in Japan, they are small compared to those of most Kentucky horse farms. Foreign-bred horses are allowed to compete in only a handful of Japanese races. If the strict limits on foreign-bred horses are lifted, Japanese may be buying lots of yearlings at Keeneland summer sales, which could make a huge impact on Kentucky's economy. (Photograph by Cotton Mather)

ful of Japanese races, Japanese buyers spent most of their money on stallions and broodmares rather than yearlings. Except for the Japan Cup and a couple of other events, horses with racing experience in other countries cannot compete on Japanese tracks. A Kentucky horse cannot run in the Japan Derby, but a Japanese horse can run in the Kentucky Derby. The Japan Racing Association contends that restrictions on foreign-bred horses are necessary to keep Japanese breeders in business. If Kentucky-bred horses had access to more races in Japan, the Japanese market would be much more substantial for American breeders.

GLOBALIZATION, JAPANESE PRODUCTION SYSTEM, AND KENTUCKY COMMUNITIES

As discussed earlier, Toyota's decision to locate a manufacturing plant in Georgetown, Kentucky, was part of the corporate globalization strategy. The decision had several major advantages. First, by locating the plant in Kentucky, Toyota was able to avoid a quota on exports to the United States. Foreign direct investment was a corporate decision in response to protectionist measures and the trade dispute with the United States. Second, the appreciation of the yen made it profitable to make automobiles in the United States. The third advantage was Toyota's ability to obtain substantial subsidies from the state and local governments for site preparation, land purchase, road improvements, worker training, and education (Milward and Newman 1990). Proximity to market and reduction in transport costs represent additional advantages. Finally, there is a symbolic benefit of a positive corporate image. By locating production in other countries, the automaker can project a global image. It serves to counter the national sentiment, which favors domestic products over imports.

In transplanting, Toyota brought a production system which differs from American firms such as Ford and General Motors. Organizational structures, work process at the point of production, and the company's relationship with suppliers show a unique production system specific to Japanese industries. The Japanese production system in the auto industry is often called lean production (Besser 1996). This system was developed by Toyota Motor Company in Japan. It is different from the production system used by the U.S. auto industry. In the United States, automakers use the Fordist production system. The Fordist production system has several distinct characteristics: (1) a capital-intensive, large scale plant; (2) an inflexible production process; (3) a rigid, hierarchical, and bureaucratic managerial structure; (4) the use of semiskilled labor performing repetitive and routine tasks, often subject to the discipline of scientific management; (5) a tendency toward strong unionization and vulnerability of production by industrial action; and (6) protection of national market (Jary and Jary 1991). It has been a useful production system for mass production with reasonable cost.

The Japanese lean production system is more efficient and cost effective than the Fordist system. The lean production system has five characteristics: (1) efficient use of resources, (2) low inventories, (3) just-in-time production and delivery, (4) rapid product development, and (5) efficient staffing (Kenny and Florida 1993). These characteristics are strengthened by human resources management that differs from Fordist human resources management. Capacity building of workers for the system and for workers themselves are the main objectives of human resources management in the Japanese management model. In a sense, the Japanese production system is designed to avoid the negative characteristics of the Fordist model. That is, the system tries to achieve a flexible production process, a less hierarchical management structure, avoidance of repetitive and routine work, and nonunionization or unionization that is not conflict oriented. Since this system is more efficient, many U.S. automakers are trying to adopt some of the features.

The Japanese production system has developed many organizational features that differ from those of U.S. automakers. Three organizational features—job classification, quality circle, and hiring process—are noted here. Job classification at Japanese auto transplants involves usually three or four classifications. In contrast, the average number of job classifications for General Motors, Ford, and Chrysler is ninety. This difference is manifestation of the Japanese system that avoids a rigid hierarchical management structure. The flat management structure allows suggestions and grievances to go to top management quickly. Also, managers and workers interact more. This environment creates a satisfaction of work situation among the plant workers. In many of the Japanese transplants, managers eat with workers and do not have reserved parking. In addition, managers wear the same uniform as workers. More egalitarian organizational structure is implemented in the Japanese auto transplants.

Quality circle is another feature implemented by the Japanese auto transplants. A team-based activity improves product quality at the shop floor level. Unlike the Fordist production system that controls quality separately from a shop floor, the quality circle is designed to control production quality at each production point by shop floor workers. For this function to work, shop floor workers need to be knowledgeable about products and production processes. Workers' problem-solving skills and knowledge about the products and production process are harnessed through training sessions and on-the-job training. Workers as a team on the shop floor work together to solve quality problems at hand. Quality circle reduces costs by not having inspectors and by more detailed and quick response to quality problems.

The hiring process in Japanese auto transplants differs from the hiring process at many American automakers. It takes a longer time, and applicants are required to have different qualifications. In the Toyota transplant in Georgetown, the hiring process takes at least six months. This is an unusual situation for American applicants who are not familiar with the Japanese hiring procedure. The careful screening involved in this hiring process assures having the best workers for Toyota. Besser describes an example of the hiring procedure: "For the first groups, the process was to fill out an application form and take a half-day aptitude test administered by the state employment service. If an applicant made it through this screening, he or she next completed two days of hands-on and situational tests designed to assess physical dexterity, ability to work with a group, problem-solving skills, motivation, and creativity. An interview with a potential supervisor and a human resources representative followed for applicants successful in the second phase of screening. A physical exam proceeds or follows the interview" (Besser 1996, 56). Japanese automakers hire persons who have initiative, commitment to the company, group orientation, and high level of attendance. The lean production system requires these traits in workers for efficient operation.

In addition to the organizational features discussed above, the Japanese production system also requires a special interorganizational feature for its success. The system requires close relationships with suppliers. As noted before, lean production involves a flexible production system. Flexible production is achieved through the just-in-time supplier system. In the just-in-time system, a core company has suppliers of first tier, second tier, third tier, and so on, and product quality is ensured at each level. A first-tier supplier ensures quality of its product, which is composed of quality-ensured parts made by second-tier suppliers, and so on. Information, technology, and even personnel also are exchanged from tier to tier.

This is very different from the Fordist supplier system. In the Fordist supplier system, production of parts is dispersed, and relationships between the core company and suppliers are tenuous. The relationships are based on price. A supplier that offers the cheapest price can be picked up by the core company. In the just-in-time suppliers system, the relationships between the core company and its suppliers are long-term; they commit to each other. They also are often geographically close to each other. The just-in-time supplier system is designed for productive efficiency.

There are several implications for Kentucky communities where transplants are located. First, the Japanese company's emphasis on group orientation has an impact on the community. In Georgetown the school system has a close relationship with Toyota. Eighth- and tenth-grade students tour the plant and learn Toyota's production system and corporate philosophy. Also, political leaders and school officials have been sent to Japan to learn the Japanese system. Now, as the school officials are convinced about the effectiveness of the Japanese system, the school system implements teaching that emphasizes group skills. Second, the community can expect employment that is more stable than with American companies. Although no explicit agreement exists between company and employees, Japanese automakers are committed to keep employees as long as possible, even when they face slumps. The long-term relationship is an essential component of the lean production system. Third, the surrounding communities can expect more employment opportunities. The just-in-time supplier system requires suppliers to be close to the core company. Therefore, supplier companies are more likely to locate near the host community. Also, if local companies are chosen as suppliers, they may be able to anticipate technology and information transfers that are critical for their own viability. The viable company is beneficial for the community because it generates employment and tax revenue. Fourth, in the communities, Americans have more interaction with Japanese. Many Japanese companies have an official company policy that encourages their employees and their family members to be ambassadors of Japan and the company. They are expected to create a positive image of Japan and the company. For example, Toyota discourages its employees from all living in one area. The company is concerned about a negative image of a Japanese enclave. There-fore, Japanese employees and their families are scattered throughout Georgetown and Lexington. Also, some Japanese wives are involved in local community activities. They teach Japanese language, cooking, and music to Americans in several communities.

Among other things, Japan's presence in Kentucky is enabling local work-ers to recapture core American values that many believed to be lost: the work ethic, a sense of community, and respect for craftsmanship. In the towns where Japanese have built plants, we found little mistrust of Japanese.

Toyota's decision to locate its auto transplant in Kentucky is instructive in understanding the implications of globalization for Kentucky communi-ties. Using Reinicke's argument on globalization as a tool, the auto transplant can be understood better. Although there are many definitions of globaliza-tion, Reinicke says that "globalization appears to be understood as a con-tinuous process of increasing cross-border economic flows, both financial and real, leading to greater economic interdependence among formally dis-tinct national economies" (Reinicke 1998). Also, globalization is a corpo-rate-level phenomenon. Capital flows across the borders, and organizational structures are created in such a way that companies can respond quickly to changing environment. Although it is mainly a corporate-level phenomenon, governments also respond to globalization.

Reinicke notes three policy options: defensive intervention, offensive intervention, and global public policy. Global public policy option is Reinicke's recommendation for governments to adjust to globalization. To understand the impacts of globalization on corporations and governments, defensive in-tervention and offensive intervention are used. Briefly, defensive intervention is government's action to buffer the impact of globalization. Offensive inter-vention is government's action to involve aggressively in globalization.

The Toyota transplant in Georgetown informs us how globalization af-fected Toyota, the U.S. government, and the state of Kentucky. The U.S. government's action to restrict import from Japan can be considered defen-sive intervention. Defensive intervention is a state's strategy that "relies on such economic measures as tariff and nontariff barriers or capital controls that force companies to reorganize along national lines" (Reinicke 1998, 9). It is protection of the U.S. industry specifically and of sovereignty of the coun-try generally. This was the reaction of the U.S. government and automakers to the globalization process. Japanese automakers responded to this political change by foreign direct investment. They established joint ventures, such as New United Motor Manufacturing, Inc. (NUMMI) (a joint venture between General Mo-tors and Toyota in Fremont, California), or they established production plants of their own, such as the Toyota plant in Georgetown. This was a corporate strategy in response to quota imposition and the appreciation of the yen.

The action by the Kentucky state government can be viewed as offensive intervention. In the offensive intervention strategy, "states themselves become global competitors by vying to provide within their respective territories the most attractive economic geography for competition" (Reinicke 1998, 8). It is a zero-sum game among states. As the federal government's devolution proceeds, states have more public responsibilities with smaller budget. In this political environment, offensive intervention was the strategy many states pursued. The strategy worked for states that received Japanese factories. In contrast to the federal government, states actively sought to attract the Japanese auto transplants. In this process many Japanese automakers have benefited.

In sum, automobile companies, the U.S. government, and states are actors in the globalization process. At the same time, all the actors are influenced by globalization. The actors are motivated to act for different reasons. The federal government concerns sovereignty. The state government seeks economic vitality (jobs and tax revenue). Foreign companies seek to survive in competition (profit generation). Japanese investments in Kentucky reflect all these facets of globalization.

The research presented in this book has examined the impact of Toyota and other Japanese employers on Kentucky—and the impact of Kentucky on Japanese managers and their families. It is a useful reminder that relatively free trade—along with a relatively free flow of capital—has brought benefits to Kentucky as well as to Japan. Both Kentucky and Japan have a big stake in globalization. Kentucky needs to press ahead with education so it can attract the good jobs of the twenty-first century, and Japan needs to further open access to its markets to bring benefits of globalization to a long list of government-protected industries, in which anticompetitive behavior locks too much capital and labor with gross economic inefficiency.

REFERENCES

Besser, Terry L. 1996. *Team Toyota: Transplanting Toyota Culture to Camry Plant in Kentucky.* Albany, N.Y.: State Univ. of New York Press.
Bourbon: Old Taste as a New Treat. 1993. *Daily Yomiuri* (Tokyo), 5 August, 10–11.
Jary, David, and Julia Jary. 1991. *The Harper Collins Dictionary of Sociology.* New York: Harper Collins Publishers.
Kenny, Martin, and Richard Florida. 1993. *Beyond Mass Production: The Japanese System and Its Transfer to the U.S.* New York: Oxford Univ. Press.
Kentucky Business Snapshot: Exports to Top Markets Have More than Doubled. 2000. *Lexington Herald-Leader,* 28 February, 10.
Milward, H. Brinton, and Heidi Hosbach Newman. 1990. State Incentive Packages and the Industrial Location Decision. In *The Politics of Industrial Recruitment: Japanese Automobile Investment and Economic Development in the American*

States. Edited by Ernest J. Yanarella and William C. Green. New York: Greenwood Press.

Reinicke, Wolfgang H. 1998. *Global Public Policy: Governing Without Government?* Washington, D.C.: Brookings Institution Press.

Shelby, Graham. 1999. Japanese Sister City Is Like a Slice of the Bluegrass. *Lexington Herald-Leader,* 7 February, 1, 10.

Whitmire, Tim. 1999. Kentucky Meet Focuses on Japanese Impact. *Mainichi Daily News* (Tokyo), 4 April, 6.

Contributors

Wilford A. Bladen is professor emeritus of geography at the University of Kentucky. He has written on contemporary Kentucky's economy and geography and has lived in Japan for several years. His knowledge of Japan dates from 1945, when he served as an officer with the U.S. Occupation Forces. In addition to numerous book chapters, his articles have appeared in many journals such as the *Geographical Review, Environment and Behavior,* and *Journal of Air Pollution Control Association.* He is currently educational affairs director of the Chandler Foundation.

Stanley D. Brunn is professor of geography at the University of Kentucky. His major interests are in political and social geographies, electronic human geographies, scholarly networking and disciplinary histories, and the geographies of the future. During the past three decades he has published articles, chapters, and books in the above areas; presented papers at many national and international conferences; and taught in universities in Europe and central Asia. His chapter reflects his interest in the world views of corporations and states and in the geographies of information and communication.

Charles F. Haywood is National City Bank professor of finance in the Gatton College of Business and Economics at the University of Kentucky. A native of Ludlow, Haywood earned a bachelor's degree at Berea College, a master's degree at Duke University, and a doctorate in economics from the University of California-Berkeley. After working as director of research for the Bank of America, Haywood came to the University of Kentucky in 1965. He was dean of the College of Business and Economics until 1975.

James G. Hougland Jr. is professor of sociology at the University of Kentucky, where he focuses research on the role of organizations in their communities and regions, attitudes on public policy issues, and evaluations of innovative projects in education. In addition to his research on perceptions of the Toyota plant in Georgetown-Scott County, Kentucky, he has examined public attitudes in Kentucky on a variety of issues. His publications have appeared in such journals as *American Communication Journal, International Journal of Education Reform, Sociological Focus,* and *Journal of Applied Sociology.* Hougland has served as chair of the Department of Sociology (1990–

1998) and director of the University of Kentucky Survey Research Center (1986–1991).

   P.P. Karan is a professor, former chair of the Department of Geography, and a co-director of the Japan Studies Program at the University of Kentucky. His research focus is environmental management in development and geography of the multinational corporation. Professor Karan has lectured at many places in Europe, Russia, North America, China, India, and Japan. He is the author of sixteen books, including *Japanese Cities* and *Japanese Landscapes*. Working from his base in Lexington, Professor Karan has led the investigation of the American operations of Japanese companies in Kentucky and their stunning effectiveness in winning over the American workforce and the general public.

   Yuichiro Nishimura is a graduate student in the Department of Geography at Nagoya University. His major research is on relations between social and economic changes and workers' lives in Toyota City. His research includes female labor force participation and changes in the production system at Toyota Motor Corporation.

   Gary A. O'Dell is a doctoral candidate in the Department of Geography at the University of Kentucky. A resident of Frankfort, Kentucky, he has been employed by the Kentucky Department for Environmental Protection since 1991 as manager of the groundwater database. Mr. O'Dell has been involved in the study of human-environment interactions on the karst landscapes of the state. He has examined various natural resource and environmental issues, particularly in regard to water supply and water quality. His research includes environmental implications of the Japanese "lean production" system.

   Kohei Okamoto, a professor of geography at Nagoya University, is Japan's leading scholar of urban-behavioral geography. He has published extensively on urban geography of Japan. His recent books are *Cognition and Behavior in Urban Space* (2000) and *Space and Time in the City* (1996), published by Tokyo Kokon Shoin in Japanese.

   The late **Janet W. Patton** was professor of government at Eastern Kentucky University. **H. Milton Patton** is president of Kimberley Whitney Corporation, developer of the Colony, Scott County's first planned unit development. Authors of many publications on a variety of public policy issues, they have participated in and observed growth and change in Georgetown since the arrival of Toyota in 1985. Mr. Patton, a Democratic candidate for Congress in 1988, has been active in various community organizations. He is currently president of the Scott Education Foundation and the Elkhorn Land and Historic Trust. Mr. Patton has worked closely with officials of Tahara-cho, Georgetown's sister city in Japan, studying comparative community development issues.

David M. Potter, associate professor of policy science at Northern Kentucky University, is now on the faculty of Nanzan University, Nagoya, Japan. He is the author of *Japan's Foreign Aid to Thailand and the Philippines,* published by St. Martin's Press in 1996, and of articles on foreign aid and on political corruption in Japan. In 1990 Dr. Potter received a scholarship from the Japanese Ministry of Education to conduct research at the Tohoku University Faculty of Law. In 1995 he was a visiting scholar at Gifu University in central Japan.

Miranda Schreurs, who received her doctorate from the University of Michigan in 1996, is an assistant professor in the Department of Government, University of Maryland at College Park. Her research focuses on comparative environmental and energy politics in northeast Asia and in Europe. She is completing a book manuscript examining environmental policy formulation in Japan and Germany from the 1960s to the 1990s. It compares Japanese and German policy making regarding air pollution issues, acid rain, stratospheric ozone depletion, and global climate change. She coedited a book that explores environmental, ecological, and energy security and cooperation in northeast Asia (*Ecological Security in Northeast Asia,* Seoul: Yonsei University Press, 1998). She also coedited *The Internationalization of Environmental Protection* (Cambridge: Cambridge Univ. Press, 1997).

Unryu Suganuma is on the Faculty of Law, Hokuriku University, Kanazawa, Japan. Born in China and educated in Japan (Reitaku University), he received master's degrees in Chinese Studies from St. John's University and International Relations from Syracuse University and a doctoral degree in geography from the Maxwell School at Syracuse University. His articles have appeared in *Journal of Asian History, American Journal of Chinese Studies,* and *Geographical Review of Japan,* among others. Dr. Suganuma, who lectures widely in the United States, India, and China, is a visiting research fellow at the Institute of Moralogy (Chiba, Japan), a visiting research associate at the Institute of Social Science of Chuo University (Tokyo, Japan), and director of the Hou Renzhi Foundation in China.

Yukio Yotsumoto is a graduate of Soka University in Japan, where he received a bachelor's degree in Economics in 1989. He received a master's degree in Agricultural Extension Education from the University of Georgia in 1994. He is currently a doctoral candidate in Sociology at the University of Kentucky. His research interests include rural community development, migration, and social impacts of Japanese investment.

Index

www.ingramcontent.com/pod-product-compliance
Lightning Source LLC
Chambersburg PA
CBHW080759300326
41914CB00055B/952